GOVERNING FROM THE CENTI
THE CONCENTRATION OF POW
CANADIAN POLITICS
BY DONALD J. SAVOIE

Redefined during the past thirty years, the centre of government currently extends itself further than ever before. Central governmental agencies are 'where the rubber meets the road,' where public service meets politics, and policy becomes reality. So who's driving this car? Agencies such as the Privy Council Office, the Finance Department, and the Treasury Board exert their influence horizontally, deciding how policy is made and how money gets spent. According to Donald Savoie, these organizations, instituted to streamline Ottawa's planning processes, instead telescope power to the Prime Minister and weaken the influence of ministers, the traditional line departments, and even parliament, without contributing to more rational and coherent policy-making.

This is scholarship at its best: rigorous and riveting. The government operates as a combination of known procedures and the more elusive subtleties of human relationships and unspoken codes of behaviour. Donald Savoie's long-time involvement in government affairs allows him to read through the surface of the results of his extensive research – which included interviews with elites – in order to expose all the levels of power at play. Indispensable reading for students of politics, public policy, and public administration, Ottawa watchers, journalists, lobbyists, and civil servants who want to know what is really going on.

DONALD J. SAVOIE holds the Clément-Cormier Chair in Economic Development at the Université de Moncton.

DONALD J. SAVOIE

Governing from the Centre: The Concentration of Power in Canadian Politics

UNIVERSITY OF TORONTO PRESS
Toronto Buffalo London

Toronto Buffalo London
Printed in the U.S.A.

Reprinted 1999, 2000, 2001, 2004, 2007, 2013

ISBN 0-8020-4476-X (cloth)
ISBN 0-8020-8252-1 (paper)

Printed on acid-free paper

Canadian Cataloguing in Publication Data

Savoie, Donald J., 1947–
Governing from the centre : the concentration of power in Canadian politics

Includes bibliographical references and index.
ISBN 0-8020-4476-X (cloth) ISBN 0-8020-8252-1 (pbk.)

1. Power (Social sciences) – Canada. 2. Canada – Politics and government.
3. Decentralization in government – Canada. I. Title.

JL75.S386 1999 352.3'0971 C98-932933-X

University of Toronto Press acknowledges the financial assistance to its publishing program of the Canada Council for the Arts and the Ontario Arts Council.

University of Toronto Press acknowledges the financial support for its publishing activities of the Government of Canada through the Book Publishing Industry Development Program (BPIDP).

Canadä

To my biggest fan, my dear friend,
my brother, Claude F. Savoie

Contents

Preface

The book is about political power: where it lies and how it is exercised at the centre of government in Ottawa. It is also about how the centre of government is organized and how it supports the head of government – the prime minister. Accordingly, the book deals mainly with issues surrounding the machinery of government. I freely admit that these are not matters likely to make it to the top of Canada's hit parade of public policy issues. Few people are likely to get very passionate about them.

However, what the centre of government does actually matters a great deal to Canadians. It matters because it speaks directly to how our national political and administrative institutions work. The centre of government in Ottawa is at the apex of political power at the national level and it shapes policy, government decisions, government operations, and federal-provincial relations to a far greater extent than has been generally assumed. Understanding how it works and why it works the way it does goes a long way towards explaining how policy and decisions are made in Ottawa.

This book had a few starts and stops and met more than a few sharp turns on the road to completion. I began work in late 1992 and carried out a number of interviews between January and June 1993. However, shortly after the change in government in Ottawa in June 1993, I called a temporary halt to my work. Kim Campbell had announced a massive restructuring of government departments when she became prime minister, and I suspected that the fallout would have important implications for my work. If nothing else, I needed to gain a proper understanding of the role of the centre in designing the reorganization. Jean Chrétien not only left the restructuring largely intact when he assumed office a few months later, his government pushed ahead with its implementation. In addition, within months of Chrétien coming to office, his government launched an ambitious program review exercise designed to review spending in virtually every area of direct federal government activity. It also introduced significant changes to the policy process and to its expenditure management system. The program review itself revealed a different way of doing things and pointed to significant implications for relations between the centre and line departments. I decided to wait, let the dust settle, and see how the changes would affect my study. I undertook a second set of interviews between September 1997 and March 1998.

I started out wanting to write a book about the impact of New Public Management on central agencies. I decided to reorient my research after holding only a few interviews. These early interviews, and subsequent ones as well, revealed that there have been notable developments in recent years in how power is exercised within the federal government. It is important not only to gain an understanding of these developments, but also of the various forces that have shaped them. In brief, though I did not set out to write a book about the exercise of political power in Canada, I ended up doing so.

I want to state with more than the usual emphasis that without the cooperation of Cabinet ministers and senior public servants, both current and former, this book would not have been possible. They all made time available to endure my questions and all were generous with their recollections and insights. Many went further and offered me documents and answered questions that I had not thought of asking, thus widening the horizon of my inquiry. No student of government could have been better served.

I was profoundly impressed by their willingness to meet with me, despite great pressure on their time. I asked ninety present and former officials for an interview and I met with eighty-eight. Only one failed to reply to my request, and a former Cabinet minister did agree to meet, but we were never able to set a time. I telephoned or wrote to all respondents, asking for forty-five minutes of their time. The great majority spent an hour answering my questions – many spent anywhere between one and three hours. In some instances, I met with the same respondent on more than one occasion.

No doubt it would have been entertaining to attribute particular quotes directly. It would also have been inappropriate. Many of my respondents specifically requested anonymity. They, however, know who they are and to what extent I am in their debt.

Readers may well be tempted to speculate on who said what. In some instances, they may well be successful. For example, a knowledgeable reader will immediately recognize comments made by Mitchell Sharp, given what he had to say on how government operated in the 1950s and 1960s. I explained the dilemma to Mr Sharp, and he said: 'You are free to quote me. But I would ask that you not quote me in respect of the present prime minister. I am one of his advisers and it would not be right.' I, of course, have respected his wish.

I cannot possibly thank everyone who assisted me in my research, but I do wish to single out a few. Jocelyne Bourgon, clerk of the Privy Council and secretary to the Cabinet, met with me for three hours to answer questions. Paul Martin, minister of Finance, spent over an hour answering questions in January 1998, at a time when he and his senior officials were busy planning his 1998 budget. Peter Harder, secretary to the Treasury Board, met with me on several occasions. His insights and his knowledge of government operations were extremely helpful. Jim Mitchell, a former senior official with the Privy Council Office, was extremely helpful in many ways. I met with him on four different occasions, each time with a new set of questions. I will always be in his debt for his candid answers, his insights, and his profound understanding of the workings of the machinery of government. The list goes on, and includes other Cabinet ministers, twenty present or former deputy ministers, as well as present and senior advisers to Prime Ministers Chrétien, Mulroney, and Trudeau, and many other senior public servants.

Two colleagues and close friends, Professors Peter Aucoin and B. Guy Peters, have read this manuscript. Both have made important suggestions to improve the study. I owe special thanks to Peter Aucoin, who read several drafts of some chapters and made numerous suggestions for improving them.

Cynthia Williams, a senior official with the Department of Indian Affairs and Northern Development and formally with the Privy Council Office, also a keen student of government in her own right, and Senator Lowell Murray, a former senior minister in the Mulroney government, also have read the manuscript. Given the nature of the book and the fact that I relied a great deal on interviews and on government documents for my research, I felt it important to have the manuscript read by two practitioners, one from the public service and another from the political level, before publication. Hindsight tells me that it was a wise decision. This is not to suggest for a moment that either agreed completely with my conclusions. Still, I greatly benefitted from their comments and suggestions. I also owe a special debt to the reviewers of the University of Toronto Press, for their constructive criticism on an earlier draft of this study. But all the defects of the book are mine.

I was fortunate to be a senior visiting fellow at the Canadian Centre for Management Development in Ottawa while carrying out research for this book. I participated in a number of seminars and meetings on a variety of issues at CCMD attended by many senior level officials. I took notes at these sessions and I make use of some of the material in this study. It is important to mention, however, that CCMD did not provide any financial support for this study either directly or indirectly, and the views expressed in this study are mine and do not reflect the views of CCMD or its officials. I received an SSHRCC subvention in 1997 to undertake research in public administration, and would like to take this opportunity to express my thanks for the support.

I also owe a special thank you to Ginette Benoit for typing and retyping the manuscript. Joan Harcourt made numerous editorial suggestions, and the book is greatly improved as a result.

As always, my family accepted with good cheer my decision to write this book. I can hardly overstate what their encouragement has meant to me and I thank Linda and our children, Julien and Margaux, for their continued support.

I dedicate this book to my brother, Claude. He has always been my biggest fan and a source of great pride for me. I am in his debt for many things, not the least for his very close friendship, his wise counsel, his inspiration, and his encouragement. No brother could possibly be better served.

DONALD J. SAVOIE

GOVERNING FROM THE CENTRE

1

Introduction

This book argues that the Canadian centre of government has evolved a great deal during the past thirty years. By centre of government, I mean the prime minister, his office, the Cabinet, and central agencies. The book also argues that the centre of government is considerably more powerful than it was thirty years ago in a number of key areas. This is true notwithstanding the fact that over this period six prime ministers have held office (albeit three only briefly) and all had different personalities, styles, and approaches to governing.

The centre of the federal government has also been largely redefined in thirty years – it is now considerably larger and extends its influence over more activities than ever before. Yet power has also shifted within the centre itself. This study makes clear, for example, that the prime minister, with the support of advisers in his own office and senior public servants in central agencies, has gained a great deal of power while Cabinet has lost influence. One senior public servant put it succinctly when he observed that 'Cabinet has evolved from a decision-making body under Pearson to a university-type seminar under Trudeau, to a focus group under Trudeau in his later years in office and also under both Mulroney and Chrétien.'[1]

It is hardly possible to understand the centre of government in Ottawa without first gaining an understanding of the roles and responsibilities of the central agencies. There are several central agencies, and they all have different mandates and pursue different goals. The Privy Council Office is concerned with the policy-making and decision-making processes; the Department of Finance with economic and fiscal issues; the Treasury Board secretariat with management issues and the expenditure budget; the Intergovernmental Affairs secretariat with federal-provincial relations and national unity; and the Public Service Commission with the application of the merit principle. Still, they all play on one another's turf and all need the full support of the prime minister to be effective. Indeed, all central agencies, with the possible exception of the Public Service Commission, have a direct link to the prime minister. A recently retired senior federal deputy minister writes that 'central agencies are sometimes described as extensions of the office of the Prime Minister.'[2]

Central agencies occupy that grey zone in government that links politicians to the bureaucracy. To people at the centre of government and in senior positions in line departments, this is 'where the rubber meets the road, where the public service meets politics, and all ... that means.'[3] Central agencies usually have a hand directly in all key policy decisions and play a crucial role in budget making. Indeed, it is to them the head of government should turn for help in articulating broad policy direction or an overarching strategy for government. Central agencies are also involved in many administrative issues – in formulating personnel and procurement policies, and in establishing financial management practices.

They are, as well, invariably at the forefront of all government-wide reform efforts. There have been an unprecedented number of these in most Western democracies during the past fifteen years or so, all designed to reshape government operations dramatically. In Canada, as elsewhere, central agencies have played a lead role in their implementation.[4]

Not surprisingly, then, central agencies are reputed to employ the best and the brightest.[5] They permit the young fast-trackers and the superbureaucrats to look at all policy areas from one central vantage point, to obtain a government-wide perspective on how the machinery of government works, and to become visible to key decision makers in government.[6] Those who serve in central agencies believe that they occupy a privileged position. And they do. They are not only able to view the work of government departments from the very centre of government, they also work closely with the ministry. One central agency official explained, 'I consider myself extremely fortunate to sit where I am sitting. In many ways, you know that you have earned your stripes when you are asked to serve in this office.'[7]

Yet with all their influence and the pre-eminent position they hold in government, we know very little about central agencies, about what they do, why they do it, and how they do it. One is struck by the paucity of studies on the work of central agencies and on the role of the prime minister and Cabinet. Yet the literature is rich in material on public service reforms, the policy process, the budgeting and management of public spending, and on a host of public management issues and specific policy questions. Several years ago, two British scholars observed that 'the roles played by cabinet structures in the decision-making of political executives is an oddly neglected subject in the comparative study of politics.'[8] This is also true of Canada. What studies we do have tend to have an institutional focus rather than a functional one. While one study, now twenty years old, looked at the 'structure and behaviour in central agencies' in Canada,[9] there are few such recent studies, and none at all that look at the work of central agencies, despite its underpinning the work of the head of government.

To be sure, the work of central agencies is not nearly as obvious to those outside government as it is to those inside. Their staff tend to look up to their political masters and down to government departments and agencies, but rarely outside to the public. Their world is one of government processes, of generating and packaging policy advice, and of developing and fine-tuning government policy and practices, all in relative obscurity. Indeed, central agency officials readily admit that they perform away from the limelight and that they much prefer it that way. In any event, few outsiders understand or care about something as tedious as the mechanics of government. Peter Hennessy, a keen student of government with easy access to government officials in Britain, writes about the 'insider-outsider divide' and the 'danger of outsider-scholars in particular ... writing about people and institutions as if they were closed societies in foreign countries.'[10] He made this observation about the British Cabinet and reported on 'the secrecy' of the institution and the Cabinet Office, not just in terms of decisions being made, but also in terms of the process and the work of permanent officials. The same can be said about the government of Canada. In fact, there is evidence to suggest that elected politicians themselves do not fully understand how the machinery of government or bureaucracy actually works even after several years in office.[11] Of course, the work of central agencies is hardly likely to dominate the agenda of political leaders or to rank very high in the list of things that preoccupy the general population. Interest groups can be roused by a government decision to close down a program or alter a given policy. But the machinery of government? One can hardly imagine the cry, 'Give me competent central agencies, or give me another government.'

Still, central agencies stand at the apex of the machinery of government. Though they rarely have line or program responsibilities, their fields of responsibility are extremely broad, highly flexible, and very often ill-defined.[12] In short, they have a licence to roam wherever they wish and to raise whatever issue they may choose. If a political crisis flares up, central agency staff are on hand in no time to oversee its development and its solution, much more often than not on behalf of the prime minister. Central agency staff invariably define their responsibility in lofty terms – as the 'keeper of the public purse,' 'the overseer of probity in government operations,' and 'the crucial link between democracy and where the work of government is actually carried out.'[13] Peter

Aucoin writes that 'central agencies are regarded, among other things (some not fit to print), as gatekeepers of the cabinet decision-making process [and] countervailing centres of policy advice.'[14] The influence and ubiquitous presence of central agencies are such that it is not possible to understand the work of line departments and agencies without first understanding that of central agencies. This and the fact that so little exists in the literature on the centre of government are sufficient reasons to study central agencies.

That begs a number of questions, including where does power lie in Ottawa? How has the role of the prime minister changed in recent years? What do central agencies actually do? Are they able to provide broad policy direction to government? Can they provide a 'cross-cutting' perspective to policy issues? What role have central agencies played in promoting and implementing the New Public Management concept within government?

Robert B. Denhardt is correct in writing that 'many practitioners today are experiencing discouragement, frustration, and exhaustion, part of which is due to the lack of theoretical development.'[15] I also believe that public administration, as a field of study and practice, suffers from theoretical malnutrition. Indeed, I suggest that public administration lacks a coherent intellectual identity. We have abandoned the field to pollsters, consultants, and hired guns for think-tanks. From time to time, we have jumped in to point out the obvious flaws and the superficial nature – if not the severe limitations – of new developments in our field and, for example, criticized many of the ideas found in the New Public Management.[16] However, one has only to take stock of the never-ending succession of government reforms introduced since the mid-1980s everywhere to see that decision makers in government have paid scant attention to our warnings.[17]

The future of our field of study lies in pursuing theoretical development and in turning out quality academic work, not in emulating the pollsters, the consultants, and the think-tanks. Accordingly, while not pretending to offer a new theory of public administration, I hope that this study will prove useful to students of Canadian public administration and public policy and encourage them to explore new theoretical avenues. In brief, its central purpose is to make a contribution, however modest, to the search for theoretical development in public administration. Answers to the questions outlined above hold important consequences on both the theoretical and practical fronts.

This book seeks to make clear that theoretical development in public administration is not possible without being linked directly to theoretical development in the field of politics. It also makes the case that an important place to begin the search for theoretical development in public administration is by studying the incentives and constraints that shape how public servants go about their work and the incentives that motivate them. In turn, there is no better place to gain an understanding of these forces than by looking at the work of central agencies.

What central agencies do and how they do it differs from other government departments. Central agencies operate in a world of their own under circumstances that can never be duplicated elsewhere. Yet at the risk of repetition, what they do and how they do it in many ways shape what line departments and agencies do. As one former central agency official observed, 'Central agencies instinctively think first of the prime minister, second, again of the prime minister, and third, of the Cabinet process, as their "clients."'[18] Departments and agencies and even Cabinet ministers are viewed as agents requiring direction and control. One central agency official put it succinctly when he observed that 'much of what we do is related to the need to keep corralling bouncing politicians and bouncing departments.'[19] Meanwhile, ministers and senior departmental or agency officials must look to more than one group or client at any one time including – with or without enthusiasm – central agencies.

Thus, the main hypothesis of this book is that power in the federal government has shifted away from line ministers and their departments towards the centre, and also, within the centre itself, power has shifted to the prime minister and his senior advisers at both the political and public service levels and away from Cabinet and Cabinet committees. The book also maintains that central agencies are more powerful in some areas and considerably weaker in others than is generally assumed. Their strengths and their weaknesses explain a great deal about how government works.

This book challenges conventional wisdom and a great deal of the recent literature on public policy and public 'management.' For example, bureaucratic bashing has been in vogue for some time, and not just in partisan political speeches – though there has never been any shortage of that – but also in the popular press and even in some of the learned journals. The public choice school, for instance, argues that career public servants are masters at protecting their turf and in seeking opportunities to maximize their budgets. There is also a tendency on the part of many politicians, notably former Cabinet ministers (but, interestingly, rarely if ever former prime ministers), on leaving office to look back at their time in government and claim that they were let down by the permanent civil service.[20]

I argue that career officials in central agencies or, for that matter, in line departments, respond whenever *clear* and *consistent* political direction is given, that when political authority decides to focus its energy on selected issues and clearly lays down the direction it wishes to pursue, career officials will give their best effort to make it work. However, those working in central agencies, whatever influence they may have, can never do what only politicians can do: that is, to make the political decision.

The prime minister, much more often than not, now embodies political authority within the federal government rather than Cabinet or individual Cabinet ministers. But the prime minister, more than anyone else in Ottawa, suffers from an 'overload problem' so that he can only focus on a handful of major policy issues in any given mandate. When the prime minister does focus on an issue and provides clear political direction, the system responds and decisions are made and things do happen. As for the rest, the system will manage the process and the issues, but bold action will hardly be forthcoming.

The failure of our politicians to see or admit that the prime minister has become the key actor who can make government change course has led them to search for solutions where none exist, to spend public funds when it is not necessary, and to ignore areas where solutions may exist. In fact, some of the solutions embraced have not only been expensive, they have been counterproductive. They have slowed down decision making, unnecessarily complicated matters, and made it more difficult to chart a new course.

At the risk of being repetitive, when political action is not forthcoming on key issues from the prime minister, many career officials, including those in central agencies, will invariably tread water, hence the charge that they always favour the status quo. Indeed, when a vacuum exists at the top, it is axiomatic that central agencies will be loath to step in and take action on any given issue. They will get involved in questions of details when they are prompted to do so. But beyond setting central prescriptions and rules, they can only get involved at most in a tiny fraction of administrative issues and government decisions. Yet their very purpose is to assist in shaping the broad policy agenda and to ensure a degree of coordination between programs, to eliminate duplication and overlap, and to ensure probity in government operations and a degree of uniformity in its running.

The influence central agencies have on policy matters is often perceived as negative unless, again, politicians have provided strong leadership and direction. The world of central agencies is one of maintaining the integrity of the government policy and decision-making process, of overseeing the management of the latest political or government crisis, of acting as goalkeepers, preventing silly things from happening, and 'corralling bouncing politicians.' Central agency officials are willing to be held accountable on how well they manage the process. The role of senior public servants is to take political direction, and where it doesn't exist, to tread water until direction is given. In short, the role of public servants is to advise the rulers on complex policy issues, not to make the decisions.

The Approach

The purpose of this study is to test several hypotheses:

- The power and influence of the centre of government has grown in recent years.
- Central agencies fear ministerial and line department independence more than they do line department paralysis. Prime ministers are quite happy to see central agencies hold this bias.
- Despite far-reaching changes to the operation of government recently, change in both style and substance in the work of central agencies has been hesitant.
- The notion that central agency officials 'sit in judgment' of line department activities rather than promoting their own prescriptions about what needs to be done in a particular sector or policy field or even in cross-cutting policy issues needs to be reviewed.
- Though the underlying theme of public service reforms over the past thirty-five years or so has called for central agencies to play a greater strategic, planning, and evaluation role than in the past, they still remain largely incapable of identifying and recommending which line department activities should be cut or expanded, and more generally of providing strategic leadership.
- If there is a phrase that has captured the spirit of the 'new public management movement,' it is that government should concentrate on steering rather than on rowing, on where it is going rather than on how it is to get there. However, officials in central agencies can only respond to clear political direction. Without this, they will more often than not simply tread water. They will not move in to fill a political vacuum. Before they will act, politicians first must point the way, even if it means putting things off until the Greek month of calends. In short, they regard their role as managing the state of affairs rather than providing direction to the affairs of state.

The important question for students of government is what are the central forces that have driven the above development? This study argues that there have been several forces. We know that in the late 1960s and early 1970s then Prime Minister Pierre Trudeau concluded that Cabinet was too large to be a proper forum for decision making on all important issues. Moreover, he felt that some line ministers and their departments had become too powerful. As is well known, Trudeau decided to overhaul the centre of government and the operations of Cabinet.

To be sure, the Trudeau reforms had a major impact on government decision-making. But, arguably, there have been more powerful forces. For one thing, the election of a sovereignist party to power in Quebec in 1976 would have a still more profound impact. National unity concerns and federal-provincial concerns have come to dominate Ottawa's policy and decision-making agenda. Understandably, no Canadian prime minister would wish to see Canada break up under his or her watch. For this reason, if for no other, prime ministers, at least since Trudeau, have all established a capacity at the centre to intervene directly on any national unity or federal-provincial issues. National unity issues in Canada can mean anything and everything. It depends on who holds political power in Quebec, on party standings at the regional level, and on political circumstances. Any issue, however innocent or low profile at first, can quickly blow up in the media and hold important implications for national unity or federal-provincial relations. When this happens, prime ministers will usually turn to the trusted hands of their own advisers or to those of senior officials in the Privy Council Office for advice.

When issues become important because of political developments or federal-provincial concerns, there is no distinction between policy and administration. A purely administrative matter, like replacing windows on a government building, can become an important file. When this happens, the file becomes 'political,' and the prime minister, as head of the party in power, will want to ensure that the file is properly managed. This, in turn, explains why there has been great reluctance in Ottawa to reorganize the centre of government or to cut back the size of central agencies. Yet, this has certainly not been true of line departments, which have all suffered significant cuts resulting from the 1993 reorganization or the recent program review exercise.

This study makes the case that to manage politically sensitive files the centre of government has been redefined even to include line deputy ministers. As we will see, line deputy ministers now spend nearly as much time, if not more, managing sensitive files for the centre, dealing with interdepartmental and intergovernmental issues, and attending meetings at the centre of government as they do overseeing their own departments and operations. Put differently, they now belong as much to the centre as they do to their ministers and departments.

The politicization of important files and, therefore, government operations, also results from increased media attention and scrutiny. The media focus is often on the prime minister. Nowhere is this more evident than during a national election campaign. Powerful regional political figures such as C.D. Howe, J. Gardiner, Ernest Lapointe, and Allan MacEachen are now much less a factor in Canadian politics than in the past. The thirty-second television clip on the nightly news during the election campaign is nearly always about the activities of party leaders.

Globalization is also an important factor. Canadian prime ministers belong to a series of recently created international clubs of heads of government from the G7 to APEC and la francophonie. Deals, even bilateral ones, between heads of governments are struck at these meetings. Canadian prime ministers, unlike many other heads of government, have to deal with precious few built-in restrictions, at least within the federal government, to limit their involvement on specific files. Whatever appears on their radar screens or in their in-basket is fair game.

The globalization of the world economy means that many more issues or files will fall to the prime minister's in-basket. While it may well have been appropriate forty years ago to see sectoral problems in agriculture, transportation, and industry dealt with separately in vertical line departments, it is no longer the case. Everything in a government department now seems to connect to other departments and other governments, whether at the provincial level or abroad.

In addition, and partly related to these developments, the Canadian party system remains competitive. Many local, provincial, and regional issues can, on a moment's notice, become political issues for the federal government. The issues may range from an interprovincial high-profile conflict (e.g., which province gets the contract to service the F-18) or the closure of a local federal government office. If the issue catches the interest of the media, then the prime minister and his advisers will want to minimize the political fallout and will intervene either directly or by calling the shots behind the scenes.

Both practitioners and scholars of late have been speaking and writing about the strain imposed on government officials by 'overloading the engine.'[21] The thinking is that there are only a limited number of individuals in government with effective decision-making authority, that there are only a limited number of hours in the day and only a limited number of processes in place to cope with a never-ending series of demands. This study examines the overload problem as it applies to the federal government.

These, then, are some of the forces that feed into the changes at the centre of government in Ottawa. Understanding these developments is necessary to understanding how our national government works and how policy and decisions are arrived at. This understanding can shed new light on how Parliament works, on federal-provincial relations, on national unity, and ultimately on how Canadians relate to their governments.

Organization of the Study

The first question that will likely jump to the reader's mind is, What is a central agency? The answer is not as straightforward as some might assume. There are core central agencies which have statutory or constitutional obligations to support the ministry. These include the Privy Council Office, the Department of Finance, the Treasury Board, and the Prime Minister's Office. Together, they constitute the exclusive club of central agencies.[22] With the exception of the Department of Finance, these agencies do not have programs of their own to administer. Their influence stems from their direct relationship to the prime minister or the ministry. Finance is also the keeper of the government's fiscal framework and has a strong, if not determining, influence on the size of the government's expenditure budget. The on-again, off-again Federal-Provincial Relations Office or intergovernment affairs group could also be included in the exclusive club. But it depends. It depends on whether the office reports directly to the prime minister or to a minister, if it enjoys independent status, or if it is part of the Privy Council Office. It can be a member of the exclusive club, either as part of the PCO or as a stand-alone central agency so long as it has a reporting relationship to the prime minister. At the moment, the intergovernmental affairs group is part of the Privy Council and reports to both a minister and to the clerk of the Privy Council and secretary to the Cabinet. It thus has a reporting relationship to the prime minister through the clerk.

This study concentrates on the exclusive club; that is, on the work of those central agencies that support the work of the head of government. I pay particular attention to the work of permanent officials. I include the Prime Minister's Office, which is staffed by partisans. I also deal at some length with the budget process and, accordingly, pay particular attention to the role of the Department of Finance and the Treasury Board secretariat. The budget is central to the agenda of any government and administration, and the head of government invariably takes a keen interest in its preparation. As one student of public administration explains, in government 'money steals the stage ... it is the only tool with a natural unit of measure.'[23] Others point out that 'budgeting is the most important annual ritual of government – the World Series of Government.'[24] I also look at the work of central agencies charged with ensuring probity and a degree of uniformity in government operations.

There are, in fact, several types of central or horizontal agencies in the government of Canada. There are departments like Environment and Industry, and regional development agencies with a mandate to coordinate government efforts in a given policy area. There are also departments which have been labelled 'horizontal policy guardian' agencies and include Justice and External Affairs. These departments have a mixture of 'statutory powers and exhortative attributes' to coordinate policy.[25] Some departments, like Public Works and Government Services, not only provide specialized services to line departments, but also formulate policy and administrative guidelines to ensure a degree of uniformity throughout the government. However, not much time is spent on these agencies, given their limited relevance to the central purpose of the book.

The study has three parts. Part I discusses the birth of central agencies and the inevitable tensions that exist for Cabinet ministers between their collective and individual responsibilities. It is not possible to gain a proper understanding of the role of central agencies without first going back to their origins. Several questions come to mind. How were they established? What was their initial purpose? Why have they expanded? Chapter 2 considers these and other issues.

In answering these questions, the book looks briefly to experiences in Britain and, to a lesser extent, the United States. British and American experiences did shape the development of our own centre of government. In addition, a comparative perspective can shed new light on the operation of our own political and administrative institutions. As Woodrow Wilson wrote 100 years ago, 'Our own institutions can be understood and appreciated only by those who know other systems of government ... By the use of a thorough comparative method ... a general clarification of views may be obtained.'[26]

A fundamental issue for Cabinet ministers is how to reconcile their collective and individual responsibilities. How does one strike the right balance between the two? Does the balance change for different issues or does it remain constant? What processes and structures have been introduced over the years to reconcile the collective and individual responsibilities of Cabinet ministers? Chapter 3 explores these issues.

Part II reports on the role of the prime minister and the central agencies. Though the notion of collective responsibility is key to understanding the role of the Cabinet in government, not all members of Cabinet enjoy equal status and power. As well, collective responsibility has come to mean different things to different people. It became clear during the course of the research for this book, for example, that collective responsibility holds a vastly different meaning for the prime minister than it does for ministers. No one, at least in government in Canada, believes any longer that the prime minister is *primus inter pares*. A senior official in the Privy Council Office and long-serving public servant reports that 'one has to go back to Lester B. Pearson [i.e., the 1960s] to see any resemblance to "primus inter pares." Certainly, it has not been the case since 1968, and it seems that every year that goes by we move further and further away from it.'[27] In looking at the status the prime minister enjoys in government and the role of his office, this book argues, as already noted, that his or her hand on government has been considerably strengthened in recent years. The reasons are varied, and they include the role of the media, the requirements of modern government, and the lack of checks within the federal government to define the outer limits of his authority.

In Part II, I also look at the work of core central agencies in some detail. I review the work of the various units in the Privy Council Office with a special emphasis on the role of the clerk of the Privy Council and secretary to the Cabinet. I examine how the office manages the cabinet process, the prime minister's prerogative in shaping the machinery of government, the appointments of senior officials, including deputy ministers, and the work of the intergovernmental affairs group. I look into the traditional areas of interest for Canadian prime ministers, notably federal-provincial relations, foreign affairs, and national security, and report on the support structures at the centre of government he can turn to for assistance.

The minister and Department of Finance occupy a key position at the centre of government. The department establishes the fiscal framework from which the government can operate. It acts as the guardian of the public purse. But it is also the government's chief economic adviser and considers macroeconomic policy its exclusive domain, a turf it jealously guards.

Part II also examines the relationship between the prime minister and the Finance minister, as well as the role the department played in the program review carried out in 1994 and 1995. It explores recent developments in the role of the Finance minister and reviews the impact these have for the cabinet decision-making process.

Part II also looks at the Treasury Board secretariat and the Public Service Commission. The work of the former, in particular, goes to the heart of recent reforms to modernize government operations by introducing the New Public Management. The Public Service Commission, together with the Treasury Board secretariat, plays an important role in human resources management. What both do can have a profound impact on departments and on government operations.

Finally, Part II looks at the centre of government from the perspective of ministers and line departments to establish how they work with the centre of government. It also discusses the role of ministers and assesses changes to this role in recent years. Similarly, the changing role of deputy ministers is examined, and the ensuing consequences for central agency–line department relations.

Part III considers the impact recent reforms have had on central agencies and on government operations. As already noted, I argue that the federal government decides and operates differently from the way it did thirty years ago. The Trudeau reforms, the strengthening of the centre of government, the intrusion of the media, the overload problems, national unity concerns, and federal-provincial relations all have had effects not just on government operations but also on the behaviour of ministers and senior government officials. While I argue that the centre and, in particular, the hand of the prime minister, has been considerably strengthened in recent years, this is not to suggest that the federal government is better able to define new strategic direction or a coherent plan to which all government departments can contribute. It is ironic perhaps that as the hand of the centre has been strengthened, its ability to manage horizontal issues has been weakened.

This book also argues that several cultures or forms of shared values are emerging inside the federal public service. The institution has been hit by several major forces in recent years that have shaken the confidence of public servants. These forces include a consensus among political parties that senior federal public servants had become too powerful and a desire to introduce a business culture to government operations. These and other developments are reshaping the federal public service and how the federal government makes policies and decisions.

Information for this study comes from a number of sources, including published and unpublished government documents. Several senior government officials made available information and material which proved to be extremely valuable in completing the research for this study and in preparing a series of questions for the interviews.

As part of the research for this book, eighty-eight present and former government officials were interviewed, including Cabinet ministers, members of Parliament, deputy ministers, heads of crown corporations, as well as middle- and lower-level government administrators.[28] Off-the-record interviews were done to elicit the most candid comments, although a few respondents specifically asked if they could be quoted. Representative samples, which would have been impractical for the purpose of the study, were not drawn. Lists of potential respondents were developed by consulting several senior government officials in Ottawa. The interviews were largely unstructured, and each was tailored to the position of the respective respondent. Accordingly, a series of common questions were not put to all. All the interviews were with present or former senior government managers, deputy ministers, political assistants (employed either in the Prime Minister's Office or in ministerial officials) and Cabinet ministers.

However, public servants below the executive category were contacted to secure factual information. Twenty-two interviews were carried out between January and June 1993 and sixty-six between September 1997 and March 1998. The first set was designed to secure factual information about central agencies and to gain an appreciation of the workings of central agencies. The aim of the second set was to investigate how decision makers see the system working – in particular, the strengths and weaknesses of the centre of government – from both the centre and line department perspectives. In the second set of interviews, some findings from the earlier interviews were tested on the respondents. It is fitting that my last interview was on 16 March 1998 with the Honourable Marcel Massé, president of the Treasury Board secretariat and a former clerk of the Privy Council Office, secretary to the Cabinet, and head of the Federal-Provincial Relations Office.

PART I

THE SETTING

2

The Centre Is Born

Central direction of government bureaucracy, to the extent it existed at all in the nineteenth century and between the world wars, was largely limited to personnel management. The desire to clean up the spoils system and to strengthen and develop a unified public service had led many governments to introduce legislation to ensure that recruitment would be based on merit. Recruitment also became centralized, and it was assumed, albeit not by everyone, that the new approach was successful.[1] In the United States, for example, the federal government had deeply impressed the business community with its ability to centralize the recruitment of personnel during the First World War.[2]

With the role of government itself limited, the challenge of coordinating policies and programs was easily met. There was also little need to develop a strong central policy and planning capacity. The life of prime ministers and even American presidents was a relatively leisurely one and issues were quickly mastered. We are informed, for example, that Woodrow Wilson 'worked but three or four hours a day and spent much of his time happily and quietly, sitting around with his family,' while Calvin Coolidge is reported to have 'slept on an average eleven hours per day.'[3] Canadian and British prime ministers also had a relatively easy time at work, and the narrow scope of government activity meant that political leaders could easily grasp the issues at hand.[4] If advice was required, they turned to Cabinet or to a few trusted advisers. In brief, the tasks of public servants were largely clerical, and policy decisions, to the extent that they were needed, could still be taken by leisured amateurs operating at the political level.

As this chapter makes clear, Ottawa would look to other countries, in particular Britain and the United States, for inspiration in developing its centre of government. The desire to clean up the spoils system pushed governments, at least initially, to establish a capacity at the centre to deal with recruitment and promotions in their public services. In time, however, governments would move to strengthen their centre to promote greater policy and program coordination, to generate policy advice, and to promote better management practices in government operations. As governments grew and increasingly intervened in the economy, the centre of government took on new responsibilities, particularly on the planning coordination and monitoring fronts.

The Beginning

In Canada's early years, the role of the central agencies consisted essentially of handling financial and administrative matters. Permanent officials in the Department of Finance, for example, were largely preoccupied with bookkeeping, accounting, and auditing issues. At the time of Confederation, new financial arrangements and settlements had to be struck with provincial governments, and some administrative and financial details had to be worked out as new divisions of responsibilities were being established. To be sure, the new arrangements were complex and controversial, but by and large they still mostly involved accounting and bookkeeping issues, and a handful of officials in the Department of Finance in Ottawa managed them.[5]

One of Sir John A. Macdonald's first initiatives as prime minister was to set up by order-in-council on 2 July 1867 'a Board of Treasury with such powers and duties as may from time to time be assigned to it.'[6] The board was made up of four ministers, all with specific financial duties: the ministers of Finance, Customs, Inland Revenue, and the receiver general. Robert Bryce writes that in Canada's early years, Cabinet referred to the Treasury Board 'a variety of financial and administrative matters for its collective advice and ordered that certain proposals requiring approval by the Governor in Council be sent to [the Treasury Board] for consideration.'[7] The government appointed through an order-in-council a 'chief clerk' to the Treasury Board, and the title of his position well describes his duties, given the administrative and clerical nature of government work at that time.

The centre of government was also quite small and officials performed a variety of tasks. The total number of public servants in the Department of Finance in 1867, for example, was twenty-eight. This included officials from the former united province of Canada transferred to the service of the 'Dominion' as prescribed under a provision of the British North America Act.[8] Today, the Department of Finance alone employs about 700 people. The Treasury Board secretariat employs another 800 people. It is revealing to note that the Department of Finance now employs more information and computer systems specialists (thirty) than it had in total staff in the late 1860s.[9]

One can only marvel today at the simplicity of the work of central agencies in their early years, their small size and the ability, not to mention the willingness, to combine several responsibilities into one large, all-encompassing job. John Langton, for example, was appointed on the same day in 1870 deputy minister of Finance, secretary of the Treasury Board, and auditor general.[10] To be sure, the combination of responsibilities was at odds with the doctrine of the independence of the auditor general, and it goes almost without saying that no such combination would be possible today. In fact, it would now be unthinkable. The advantage, however, was that it placed in the hands of a highly capable individual full responsibility for all of the government's financial and accounting practices. Today, the Office of the Auditor General enjoys, of course, full independence from the government. It also employs 535 people.[11]

All of the above is to say that at Confederation, and indeed for a long time after that, the centre of government – like the government itself – was easily understood and highly accessible even to parliamentarians. Indeed, Parliament debated whether extra compensation should be given to John Langton for assuming multiple responsibilities, and the minister had to defend vigorously his government's decision to award an extra $1,000 a year to Mr Langton.[12]

Three forces, however, would change all that. The movement to eliminate the spoils system, the need to plan the war effort, and the development of a new arsenal of economic and social policies would give rise to new machinery at the centre of government. In time, it would grow considerably, and the work of government would become highly complex, far too complex for leisured political amateurs to master without expert advice.

Controlling Personnel Management through Centralization

The most important issue confronting public administration in Western countries in the late 1800s and early 1900s was how to deal with the political spoils systems. Britain had placed the issue on the political agenda as early as the 1850s with the publication of the Northcote-Trevelyan report, which proposed four key reforms: (1) entry into the civil service should be through open competition and examination; (2) promotion should be on merit, based on proper assessments prepared by superiors; (3) a distinction should be established between intellectual and mechanical labour; and (4) measures should be put in place to unify the civil service, including a common basis of recruiting. It took some time for Northcote-Trevelyan to be fully implemented – according to some, not until the end of the First World War.[13] Its publication and implementation, however, signalled a decisive shift towards the centre of government in personnel management and would lead other countries, including Canada, to initiate similar reforms.

In 1917 the British government formally recognized the permanent secretary of the Treasury as head of the civil service, thereby signalling its intention to centralize personnel management still more. It also introduced measures to ensure that promotions to the most senior levels would be decided at the centre, rather than as previously in ministries. The government decreed in 1919 that the prime minister would, on the advice of the head of the civil service, hold full authority to accept or reject all appointments to the top positions in all departments. The prime minister and his or her advisers would, in turn, reserve the prerogative to survey all departments and the whole civil service to identify the most promising candidates for the position of permanent secretary. The Canadian prime minister would also assume the same prerogative.

Although Canadian political institutions have their roots in British tradition, the administrative practices found in the Canadian public service reveal both British and American influences. In the case of the merit system, for instance, the influences have been predominantly American.[14] To be sure, the Canadian battle to rid government of the political spoils system took place at about the same time as the British and American ones. In Canada, however, the early efforts were less successful than in the other two countries. Spurred on by a number of reformers, including a growing number of members of Parliament, the government established a parliamentary committee in 1877, and later, a royal commission, to look into the matter. Although the *Civil Service Act* was passed in 1882, it lacked teeth and little actually changed. R. MacGregor Dawson explains, 'The entrance examination was not competitive and the minister was therefore still free to appoint anyone he chose, subject to the trifling restriction that the candidate was required to pass a very elementary test. Subnormal and illiterate candidates were shut out; but almost anyone else could squeeze through and, if he had the necessary political influence, he could slip into the appointment as before.'[15] Although the pressure for effective reform towards the end of the nineteenth century in Canada was great, the government of the day looked for every opportunity to slip back to the old ways of doing things. It is important to recognize that at the turn of the century the distribution of patronage was still the most important function of the government.[16]

But things began to change in the early 1900s. People with the necessary skills to carry out more complex tasks were increasingly required, and reformers pointed to developments in Great Britain and the United States as the most promising way ahead for introducing change. Moreover, the call for dealing with political patronage in public service appointments began to fall on attentive ears among the general public, which started to comprehend the 'great value' of efficient administration and appreciate the wasteful results of patronage.[17]

Growing public demand for the government to do something, coupled with the need to call a general election, prompted the Laurier government in 1908 to pass a new civil service act. This act established a civil service commission and effectively curtailed the autonomy of departments in the management of personnel matters. Above all, the act sought to ensure that individual ministers could no longer appoint public servants after merely consulting Cabinet colleagues, members of Parliament, defeated candidates, and the local patronage committee.[18]

Canada's Civil Service Commission was to be nonpartisan, and members of the commission given tenure during good behaviour were to be subject to removal only by the governor general on a motion passed by both the Senate and the House of Commons. The commission was charged with setting examinations for entrance to a large number of government jobs. The examinations would be held in open competition and the winning candidate would secure the appointment. Again, however, the old ways of doing things proved difficult to abandon. Although the 1908 changes were far-reaching, the reformers were not at all satisfied. The policies of the Civil Service Commission applied to only parts of the service, the 'In Service.' The 'Outside Service,' which grew considerably after 1908, operated under the old political rules. The Outside Service was so large that, when the Laurier government went down to defeat in 1911, some 11,000 public servants resigned or were fired, mostly for having been guilty of political partisanship.

The reformers, however, finally won the day in 1918 when nearly the entire civil service and virtually all appointments were placed under the Civil Service Commission. The mandate of the commission was strengthened and a new system of classification and pay was introduced. On this front, Canada looked to the American system for inspiration. It did not, for example, recognize a distinct administrative class to which young university graduates would be recruited. It sought to classify positions 'minutely,' according to specific duties and tasks.[19] These developments strengthened considerably the hand of the commission, turning it into a powerful central agency. But it would be a different type of central agency in that it would not fall under direct prime ministerial or ministerial direction. The commission is a parliamentary agency and enjoys an independence from political direction that no other central agency can possibly have.

The reforms, initially at least, proved difficult to implement, and departments began to question the need for a highly centralized personnel-management system. While the business community, at least in the United States, was applauding the government's ability to centralize the recruitment of personnel, some line department officials in Ottawa became nostalgic about the old days when they appeared before parliamentary committees. Two senior deputy ministers went so far as to argue for 'a restoration of the pre-1908 period, claiming that the maligned patronage system was in reality the only democratic way of managing the service.'[20] Some senior officials felt that it was easier to cope with their own ministers and ultimately with political patronage than with all the requirements of an independent central agency and with having to define and classify all positions. But this time, however, there would be no turning back.

The establishment of the Public Service Commission served notice in Canada, as similar central agencies did elsewhere, that a capacity should be established at the centre to oversee an important function, and that it could be made to work. If the objective was to deal with the spoils system and to bring order to personnel management, the solution was to centralize the function. Ministers and government departments, it appears, had to be brought to heel and only then could the objective be met. In short, dealing with the spoils system had to be accomplished through a central agency, and departments and their ministers were not to be trusted to do it on their own.

Supporting the Lloyd George War Cabinet

Britain's prime minister, Lloyd George, has been described as the 'twentieth century's greatest architect of government institutions.'[21] He made a deliberate decision to overhaul the machinery of government, and by the time he left office in 1922, he had refashioned the Treasury, transformed the premiership, and established the Cabinet Office. Planning war efforts would require a new central capacity and wartime political leaders would see to it. It would certainly push governments to redesign their administration and develop a centre to plan, coordinate, and monitor an arsenal of new policies, programs, and activities.

In December 1916, Lloyd George assembled his five-member War Cabinet and then decided to provide it with 'secretarial equipment.'[22] His purpose was straightforward enough – to structure a process to bring matters before Cabinet, to record decisions, and to communicate them to those who needed to know. Thus began the tradition of 'one or two silent men on the right of the Prime Minister at the Cabinet table.'[23] The establishment of the Cabinet Office was no small development – it changed forever how the government made decisions, and, consequently, the process of governing. Indeed, prior to 1916 Cabinet had met without a formal agenda and without a secretary. Ministers simply took action on the basis of their recollection of what had transpired in Cabinet.[24] The prime minister, if he so wished, could later hold them to account if the right decision was not being pursued.

From the very start, the 'silent men on the right of the Prime Minister' knew that they had to perform a delicate balancing act. These permanent officials were reluctant to influence the decisions of ministers and even to offer advice – particularly on nondefence matters. They were well aware of their favoured position with the Cabinet and believed that any attempt on their part to influence decisions could well compromise the confidence of ministers and departments necessary to make the Cabinet Office work.[25] Word that the Cabinet Office favoured a particular position, minister, or department would be certain to get around, and the office's capacity to serve the Cabinet would be compromised. Accordingly, in the office's early years, permanent officials operating at the centre of government were very reluctant to interfere with the work of ministers and departments or second-guess their advice or decisions.

However hard it fought to remain neutral on policy, the Cabinet Office was not without its critics. The opposition Conservative Party, for example, claimed that the secretariat was too costly and a 'dangerous innovation.'[26] Some even saw a constitutional crisis in the making. A new part in the machinery of government had been born, operating at the very centre of the decision-making process without a proper public debate. The fear was that the office could well undermine the concept of ministerial responsibility by interfering with the work of individual ministers and their departments.

Still, at his first Cabinet meeting in 1922, Conservative Prime Minister Bonar Law instructed the secretary to the Cabinet 'to attend meetings of the Cabinet, unless instructed to the contrary, for the purpose of recording the conclusions.'[27] A change of heart, but only up to a point. He still wanted to close down much of the Cabinet Office and to transfer most of its work to the Treasury and to the Foreign Office. In any event, the office's workload declined substantially in peace time. For example, 3,000 memoranda were submitted to Cabinet in 1918. The number had dropped to about 500 by the mid-1920s and remained at about that level until the start of the Second World War.[28] Thus, although it was not abolished, the Cabinet Office staff shrank in size from 120 employees to 39.

The role of government in Britain remained limited up to the late 1930s. Cabinet still dealt with relatively straightforward administrative matters and ministerial workloads remained manageable. There was no obvious need for strong central coordination and planning.[29] A British Cabinet minister serving between 1929 and 1931 summed up the relative unimportance of the Cabinet Office on the policy front at this time, 'There was no Economic Section in existence, no central Statistical Office, no economic planners and but little in the way of information services.'[30]

During the Second World War, Neville Chamberlain and later Winston Churchill would again establish a small War Cabinet, as Lloyd George had done before them. Churchill, like Lloyd George, also established a number of

Cabinet committees to assist the War Cabinet. Though Churchill was critical of the proliferation of these committees, insisting that they were time-wasting and a means of avoiding responsibility, he oversaw the establishment of about 400 War Cabinet committees and subcommittees during the war years. Thus, in turn, the Cabinet Office again expanded substantially to service the new machinery.

The Churchill War Cabinet met about three times a week and the conclusions were circulated the same day. The secretary to the Cabinet, Edward Bridges, attended all meetings, as did two or three other senior officials from the Cabinet Office. In addition, an assistant secretary from the office acted as secretary to a Cabinet committee or, much more often than not, to several Cabinet committees. The office established new units to advise on military affairs and the economy, and by the end of the war it employed 576 people.[31]

It is widely accepted that Britain's wartime effort was a success story.[32] Whitehall threw open its doors to outside experts and never lost sight of its overriding purpose: to defeat Hitler. A totally mobilized society was produced.[33] The Cabinet Office and the Treasury led the efforts at the bureaucratic level to map out new departments (for example, ministries of Food, Shipping, Supply, National Service, Blockade, Information, and Redistribution of Imports), to devise new methods to plan and execute work, and to search for the best people to ensure that the new methods and capacity would function properly. The more important interdepartmental committees were invariably chaired by senior officials from the centre.

Britain's best and brightest also came to government to serve and the centre got more than its fair share of them. The economic section of the Office of the War Cabinet, for example, was able to assemble a veritable who's who of the best economic minds in Britain.[34] Harold Wilson left Oxford, where he had been made a don at age twenty-one, to work in the Office of the Cabinet, joining the likes of Professors Stanley Dennison and John Jewkes. Meanwhile, John Maynard Keynes went to the Treasury and William Beveridge chaired a committee on social insurance. The key strategic planning and coordinating tasks were performed from the centre and no one was critical of its ability to deliver. All in all, the mix of permanent civil servants and highly talented outsiders blended very well during the war years – so much so that this period represented, in the opinion of a keen observer of the British civil service, the 'high point of achievement in the history of the British Civil Service.'[35]

By the end of the Second World War, in Britain, in Canada, and even in the United States, the public's belief in the ability of government was high. Not only had the allies won the war but the governments had planned the war effort and run the economy very well indeed. Unemployment had fallen to zero and yet prices had been held down, at least when the goods were available. It had become clear that national governments were able, in moments of crisis and when moved by an overriding goal, to lead their countries and accomplish great things. The concern now turned to the postwar economy, with many fearing that the end of the war would trigger a recession, if not another depression.

Canada: Looking to Britain

Canada resisted much longer than Britain in establishing a central secretariat to assist Cabinet. It wasn't until 1940 that the Canadian government came to the conclusion that there was a need for a comprehensible record of Cabinet decisions. Before that, Prime Minister Mackenzie King would simply have three boxes in which he would deposit Cabinet memos: some went into a 'No' box, others in a 'Yes' box, and still others in a 'Pending' box. In addition, King often held two Cabinet meetings. At the first meeting, no one was present but himself and his ministers. When the important Cabinet business was concluded, King would push a buzzer to signal the clerk to come in, take notes, and on occasions record specific directions. King would simply declare that Cabinet was resolving itself into council. The clerk of the Privy Council was precisely that, a clerk, and with the help of an assistant clerk, he would keep a register of council minutes. Before 1940 Cabinet operated without a formal agenda, had no secretariat, no permanent official attending the meetings to record the discussions, and no system existed to communicate the decisions to departments.[36]

This system allowed government to function, largely, of course, because of the small number of major policy issues with which it had to deal. As J.R. Mallory explains, 'Until 1939 the major and minor details of government policy were capable of being understood and actively considered by ministers and dealt with by the Cabinet.'[37] Lester B. Pearson provides a first-hand account of what things were like when he joined the federal public service. He writes, 'When I first came to Ottawa in 1928, the Privy Council Office was small in size and clerical in its operations, and presided over certain formal activities. The Prime Minister's Office, including stenographers, file clerks, and messengers, could not have comprised much more than a dozen. If the PM wanted special assistance, he would get it from departments on an ad hoc basis ...'[38]

The Second World War would change this. The government got involved in virtually every sector of the economy and promoted a shift of power away from Parliament to the Cabinet. In addition, King had long complained about the lack of assistance in his own office and at one point claimed that his own staff was not nearly as well organized as that of the Office of the Under-Secretary of External Affairs.[39] He served notice that he was open to suggestions.

King probably got more than he bargained for when in late 1938 he invited Arnold Heeney to become his principal secretary, 'which position would correspond in a way to a Deputy Head of a Government Department.'[40] While at Oxford, Heeney had attended a lecture by Sir Maurice Hanley, the secretary to the British Cabinet, on cabinet procedure, a lecture that had deeply impressed him. As J.L. Granatstein writes, 'The fates must have been at play that evening: fifteen years later Heeney would be the Canadian Hanley.'[41]

Heeney had accepted King's offer on the condition that one day he would be appointed to a position where he would be able to 'develop in Canada the kind of post formerly held in the United Kingdom by Sir Maurice Hanley namely that of Secretary to the Cabinet ... the post will be created and I will be appointed.'[42] The war years provided the impetus, not to mention the workload, to justify appointing Arnold Heeney Secretary to Cabinet and Clerk of the Privy Council. For one thing, Cabinet appeared to sit continuously. Indeed, the War Cabinet Committee, which brought together the most powerful ministers, and which would assume effective control of Canada's war effort and operations of government, held 343 meetings. Heeney attended these meetings and pushed King to impose discipline on their operation. Heeney – and in time King agreed – wanted ministers to give notice of their intention to bring issues before the war committee and Cabinet. He also wanted the Cabinet Office to prepare a formal agenda and a record of decisions. King had been impressed by the way Churchill ran his War Cabinet on his first wartime visit to Britain in 1941 and accordingly was open to Heeney's recommendations to pattern Canadian operations on the British experience. With King's support, Heeney turned to Sir Edward Bridges, the new secretary of the Cabinet in Britain, and Lord Hanley for advice on how to reorganize the work of Cabinet and to establish a Cabinet Office.[43]

This is not to suggest that the change was free of problems or tensions. For one thing, King felt that Heeney all too often attenuated the 'vigour of [his] protests' when drafting the minutes of the war committee and 'soft-pedalled' King's criticism of some of his ministers during the conscription crisis.[44] The prime minister was also uneasy with Heeney's arranging meetings between representatives of competing departments and with his informing ministers that their departmental initiatives were causing problems for other departments. King wanted to be directly involved and to call the shots on all things from major policy issues to relatively minor administrative matters.[45] Heeney, like his British counterpart, felt that his job was to ensure that the government's engine, the Cabinet, would run smoothly, and he would do what he could to ensure that feathers would not be unduly ruffled.

In an article published eighteen years after he left government, Arnold

Heeney wrote about the roles played by the prime minister and himself in the establishment of the Cabinet secretariat. Mackenzie King, he explained, 'visualized ... [the new position of secretary to the Cabinet] as a kind of deputy to the Prime Minister ... his primary, if unacknowledged, objective was to enhance his authority as Prime Minister.' However, things did not work out as planned. 'King,' Heeney wrote, 'must often have regretted the monster he had created ... [and] the role of the Secretary to the Cabinet did not work out the way ... he had hoped and expected.'[46]

Heeney quoted approvingly Harold Wilson's views on the Cabinet Office 'as being [there] to assist ministers in the task of discharging their collective responsibility for the government of the country and the conduct of its affairs both at home and abroad.'[47] Heeney added that though 'the Prime Minister is the *master* [to use the old expression] of Cabinet business ... the Secretary to the Cabinet is one whose chief interest and concern is the formulation, recording and communication of decisions by those who compose the Cabinet of the day [and] the chief function of the Secretary [is] to do everything possible to facilitate and assess the deliberative process onward to informed decisions.' Heeney concluded that 'in his guise of Secretary to the Cabinet, [he] became responsible for the discharge of these duties ... [and] had little or no time to act as the personal staff officer to the Prime Minister.'[48]

Cabinet also learned under Heeney to function even if the prime minister was not in the chair. The Korean dispute was one of the most important international situations for Canada from the end of the Second World War to the first half of the 1950s. With Prime Minister King away in London in November 1947, Louis St Laurent, the minister of External Affairs, and James Ilsley, the minister of Justice, had secured Cabinet approval for their participation to serve on the United Nations Temporary Commission on Korea (UNTCOK) to supervise free elections. When King returned from London, he expressed his strong disagreement and asked St Laurent and Ilsley to resign from the commission. Both, however, stood firm and there was a Cabinet crisis in the making. King avoided a full-blown crisis by coming to an understanding with St Laurent at a private dinner. In the end, however, Canada participated in the work of the UNTCOK Commission.[49]

If King was concerned with his Secretary assuming too much influence, one can only imagine what his ministers felt. A powerful member of the King Cabinet, C.G. Power, outlined the evolution of the role of Parliament and government with deep concern, 'The public began to look to the Prime Minister and the members of the cabinet. They and they alone came to be regarded as responsible for everything concerned with the war. This increased the prestige of the cabinet and Government enormously and correspondingly decreased that of

Parliament.'[50] A look at the number of Cabinet decisions during the Second World War speaks to this point. Between 1939 and 1945, some 60,000 orders-in-council and over 60,000 Treasury minutes were passed. Both figures were well over five times the number taken annually in the late sixties.[51] Parliament could not possibly review all these decisions. The focus of activity and decision during the war years had clearly shifted away from Parliament to Cabinet, and it would never shift back.

Some of the reforms Mackenzie King introduced during the war years have lasted to this day and have had a profound impact in shaping the present-day machinery of government. The most important was the establishment in 1940 of the position of secretary to the Cabinet. The duties of the post were outlined and included preparing for the prime minister's approval an agenda for Cabinet meetings; keeping notes of Cabinet meetings and a record of conclusions as might be required; preparing and submitting to Cabinet members information necessary for their deliberations; communicating to ministers, departments, and others concerned decisions of Cabinet; maintaining liaison between Cabinet and its committees – and any other duties assigned to him by the governor-in-council.[52] Heeney's focus was clearly on the Cabinet and on the Cabinet decision-making process. It was Heeney who coined the term 'Secretary to the Cabinet' and he sought to play the role to the full. A broad mandate to be sure, and some fifteen years later C.G. Power felt that they had created a revolution that had taken on a life of its own. He argued, 'Operating collectively in large affairs the Cabinet's chief advisers became almost a second Cabinet, at times more potent than the first. A managerial revolution was under way and could never be repealed.'[53]

There was also another revolution under way which would have a profound influence on the machinery of government. Canada only had to look to its southern neighbour to see that the era of activist government had arrived.

Roosevelt: Defining a New Economy

President Franklin D. Roosevelt announced in March 1933 that he would ask Congress to grant him broad executive power 'to wage a war against the emergency, as great as the power that would be given to me if we were in fact invaded by a foreign foe.'[54] The enemy was the Great Depression and the battle cry was a New Deal for the American people. Roosevelt unleashed a flurry of activities during his first few hundred days in office. He saw to it that an *Agricultural Adjustment Act* was passed to bring farmers more purchasing power, as well as a *National Industrial Recovery Act* to regulate business activities. He established the Tennessee Valley Authority to assist the destitute Tennessee

Valley, the Home Owners Loan Corporation to help homeowners threatened with foreclosures, an Emergency Relief Administration to make direct grants to states for relief to the unemployed, and a Civilian Conservation Corps to provide work for unemployed youth. He also issued an executive order taking the country off the gold standard.[55] Within two years of coming to office, Roosevelt had established some sixty new agencies and added 100,000 new positions, exempt from regular civil service procedures.[56] In short, the era of limited government and limited presidency was over.

It soon became obvious that Roosevelt's policy ambitions and program measures far outstripped the government's ability to deliver. Boldly stated, the problem was this: Roosevelt wanted twentieth-century solutions to the horrors of the Depression but he was trapped 'with an administrative capacity that properly belonged to the nineteenth century.'[57] Roosevelt needed to infuse the bureaucratic organism with new blood, with officials willing and capable of promoting and implementing New Deal thinking inside government, where he believed resistance was setting in. He concluded that he needed a capacity at the centre of government for creative thinking, for shaping new policies and programs, and for managing the bureaucracy.[58] Roosevelt understood the challenge well and responded with a series of measures. All in all, the scope and intensity of the changes he introduced led two students of American government to label the 1930s a decade of 'extraordinary theoretical ferment and institutional adaptation.'[59]

In 1936 Roosevelt asked a management expert, Louis Brownlow, to chair a president's committee on administrative management. Brownlow tabled his findings within ten months and, to no one's surprise, stressed the need for a strong capacity at the centre of the administration. He explained, 'A weak administration can neither advance nor retreat successfully – it can merely muddle. Those who waver at the sight of needed power are false friends of modern democracy. Strong executive leadership is essential to democratic government.'[60] Few were surprised by Brownlow's recommendations. Indeed, Roosevelt had structured the Brownlow Committee so that it would tell him what he wanted to hear.[61] For example, the opening pages of the committee's report simply stated that there was no need 'to prove once again that the President's administrative equipment is far less developed than his responsibilities.'[62]

Brownlow proposed a number of sweeping changes. He concluded, 'The President needs help. His immediate staff assistance is entirely inadequate.'[63] The short – fifty-page – report started from the premise that the president was constitutionally the head of the executive branch, that he needed 'institutional' assistance to perform his duties, and that the hierarchical principle of organization with its lines of authority and accountability was required for the efficient performance of government. Put differently, there was a hole at the centre of government which needed fixing. The solution was straightforward enough: develop a strong capacity at the centre of the administration. Roosevelt immediately took steps to follow through.

Roosevelt introduced legislation to enable him to appoint six administrative assistants and to prepare reorganization plans to alter executive branch organization. The legislation also enabled him to establish a new Executive Office of the President and to transfer the Budget Bureau to this office. The White House itself became a division of the Executive Office, though it enjoys a special status because it comprises the personal and immediate staff of the president. One can hardly overstate the importance of these developments in terms of their impact on the machinery of government. In brief, Roosevelt laid the groundwork for the modern presidency. He set out to become the chief manager of government, and in the process he substantially enlarged his own office. He established a host of new central agencies that reported to him.

Still, the size of government remained such that Roosevelt could still master issues that came to his attention. He never lost his grasp of the detail of policy and the organization of government. The extent to which he immersed himself in detail is truly remarkable by today's standards. Here is a memorandum he wrote to his budget director, 'I agree with the Secretary of the Interior. Please have it carried out so that fur-bearing animals remain in the Department of the Interior. You might find out if any Alaska bears are still supervised by (a) War Department (b) Department of Agriculture (c) Department of Commerce. They have all had jurisdiction over Alaska bears in the past and many embarrassing situations have been created by the mating of a bear belonging to one Department with a bear belonging to another Department. P.S. I don't think the Navy is involved but it may be. Check the Coast Guard. You never can tell.'[64]

Through it all, whether it was New Deal programs or the war effort, Roosevelt was able to concentrate power in his own office and in his own hands. He was omnipresent and 'he really made his own decisions – most people acting for Roosevelt were messenger boys.'[65] He did establish a number of councils which had decision-making capacity to ensure coordination between departments and agencies, but history now reports that when Roosevelt was not present, the council meetings consisted largely of reading reports already circulated by agency heads. Questions of major importance only came up when Roosevelt attended: 'From that moment, things would begin to happen.'[66]

The Roosevelt reforms were not lost on other political leaders, including Mackenzie King. Roosevelt, it was felt, was modernizing government operations by equipping its centre with a capacity to plan, direct, and monitor government activities. Though forever cautious, King did not need much convincing that the time had arrived for government to become more active on the social policy front. His 1921 election platform spoke to the need for a strong government presence in the economy to ensure that the poor, the aged, and disadvantaged would receive a helping hand from government. The document is remarkably interventionist, even by today's standards. It argues, for example, that 'men and women should receive equal remuneration for work of equal value.' It also calls for an 'adequate system of insurance against unemployment, sickness, dependence in old age, and other disability, which would include old age pensions, widows' pensions, and maternity benefits.'[67] None of these measures were introduced in one Parliament. Indeed, some took twenty or more years to see the light of day. However, it should be remembered that in 1927 the King government was the first in North America to introduce old age pension legislation.

In any event, the Keynesian revolution was about to take root everywhere, and it would serve to strengthen the hand of those who wanted an interventionist role for government in society, including Mackenzie King. It could also serve to strengthen the centre of government.

Keynesian Economics

John Maynard Keynes was a celebrated Cambridge economist who advocated the use of government fiscal policy to adjust demand and maintain full employment without inflation. The Depression and the Second World War were sufficient for the Keynesian revolution to capture the Department of Finance in Canada and the Treasury in the United Kingdom and the United States. Ever since, government has more often than not intervened to attenuate the lows in economic cycles and to soften the sting of economic misfortune. Only since the early 1980s have national governments begun to withdraw from certain program and economic sectors. Keynesian logic provided a solid rationale for government to intervene in the economy. It gave a basis for counter-cyclical budgeting, and hence deficit budgeting. Government programs and measures to stabilize the economy, to promote economic development and full employment, became important. Keynesian economics suggested that with latent demand and no limit to factors of production governments could create the long-sought-after prosperous and rational societies. But Keynesian economics also legitimized government deficits, and in time governments would spend more, tax more, and borrow more – a great deal more.

John Kenneth Galbraith observes that Canada 'was perhaps the first country to commit itself unequivocally to a firmly Keynesian economic policy.'[68] The

Canadian government presented a major policy paper to Parliament towards the end of the Second World War which was clearly Keynesian in outlook. It said that, 'the Government will be prepared, in periods where unemployment threatens, to incur deficits and increases in the national debt resulting from its employment and income policy ... in periods of buoyant employment and income, budget plans will call for surpluses.'[69] When the war ended, everyone was prepared for measures to avoid a return of the Depression years. But the expected severe economic downturn did not materialize and the measures proved unnecessary. Still, the Canadian government was now convinced that it possessed 'a new arsenal of economic policy to achieve high employment and generally manage the economy.'[70]

It only takes a moment's reflection to appreciate the impact of Keynesian economics on government operations. In the pre-Keynesian days, the ideology of balanced budgets prevailed in most political parties, as did a firmly held belief that the role of government should be highly restricted. In Victorian England, for instance, budget deficits were considered 'a great political, and above all, a great moral evil.'[71] British Prime Minister William Gladstone laid down, in simple terms, the budget process of the day, 'New wants are always coming forward, but where ... provision is made for those new wants [it] ought to be counterbalanced by new economies.'[72] Frugality in government spending was a matter of the most basic of principles and 'bubbles' of extravagance were not to be allowed to surface. The way to ensure this, in his view, was to 'estimate expenditures liberally, revenue carefully and make each year pay its own expense.'[73] Gladstone, together with one or perhaps two of his most trusted ministers and a handful of advisers from the Treasury, would sit down year after year and go over proposed spending plans line by line, bursting bubbles of extravagance. This did not change much until the war years and the Keynesian revolution.

The process was not much different in Canada. Line item budgeting enabled politicians and their advisers to review every detail of departmental spending plans and to control input costs. However, the turn to Keynesian economics and the desire to instil balance in national economies saw governments shifting focus away from input costs to planning and implementing a host of measures to manage the economy. In time, the line item budget process would be scrapped altogether and a new program-based budget system would be introduced first in the United States and later in Britain and Canada.

By its very definition, Keynesian economics favours centralization or central planning and direction. Keynes himself urged presidents and prime ministers to take the lead in formulating economic policy. In the 1930s he became convinced that the Depression was exposing all the weaknesses of classical economics, incapable, as it so clearly was, of contending with unsettling economic events. He wrote an open letter to President Roosevelt on 31 December 1933 in the *New York Times* arguing that he placed 'overwhelming emphasis on the increase of national purchasing power resulting from government expenditure, which is financed by loans.'[74] In some ways, however, Roosevelt's New Deal anticipated the publication in 1936 of Keynes's *General Theory of Employment Interest and Money*. Keynes's theory was simply an economic rationale for doing what Roosevelt had concluded needed to be done politically. Indeed, as noted above, Roosevelt had shown through his New Deal measures that to make the concept work in practice the centre of government had to be considerably stronger.

The war years, if anything, only served to solidify Keynesian economics in government treasuries. Keynes and a strong number of his disciples on both sides of the Atlantic served in key positions in government. Classical economists were on the defensive everywhere. They proved unable to come up with solutions for the expected postwar recession or to compete with the new intellectual force increasingly being felt on university campuses. Keynesian economists, meanwhile, did not hesitate to come forward with fresh thinking and take centre stage in government offices.

In Canada, Bob Bryce was promoting the message of Keynes's *General Theory* inside government. He had studied at the feet of Keynes while at Cambridge and had returned to Canada via Harvard, where he introduced Keynesian economics to both faculty and students. Bryce, explains John Kenneth Galbraith, is the reason 'why – the special case of Sweden apart – Canada was the first country to accept and implement Keynesian management of its economy.'[75] Bryce went to work in the Department of Finance in Ottawa in October 1938 on the eve of the Munich crisis. He found the department very small, congenial, and preoccupied with routine tasks and financial and administrative details.[76] He discovered that 'some limited policy work' was being done in the office of the deputy minister and by a handful of senior clerks (six in all) there and in the Treasury Board.

On joining the department, Bryce was immediately asked to work on key policy issues and on the upcoming budget. He marvelled at how a junior economist only a few years out of university could be asked to work directly with the most senior officials in government and on such a key policy document as the budget. He explained, 'The department was so small that, despite my junior status, I participated in the discussions of the budget measures, drafted several portions of the budget speech and did most of the work on the economic portion of the White Paper [a separate paper reviewing economic and financial conditions].'[77] Bryce would, however, soon be working with young economists of like mind on a host of policy issues. The war years and the requirements of postwar economic planning would see the 'upper ranks of the department [Finance] mainly concerned with policy matters.'[78] The result was the recruitment of Keynesian economists such as W.A. Mackintosh and Benjamin Higgins on staff or on contract. Another department, the Department of National Revenue, meanwhile, carried on with the routine or administrative task of collecting taxes.

All in all, the Depression, Roosevelt's New Deal experiment, Keynes and the war years, and the widely held view that the immediate postwar period would be difficult economically made for a potent brew. Keynesian economics represented a sophisticated rationale for politicians to justify government intervention to respond to what they expected to be an agitated working class and returning soldiers expecting a better life. Nothing would be left to chance, and government report after report, all with a strong Keynesian bent, called for a much stronger role for government in the economy. This, in turn, would strengthen the hand of central agencies, in particular the Department of Finance.

The government of Canada produced a White Paper on Employment and Income which committed the government to reduce unemployment. Government would be prepared to produce public works projects to supplement private investment and a comprehensive package of tax concessions, loans, grants, and other forms of assistance to ensure a high level of employment.

The Second World War also bequeathed a creative and smooth-running machinery of government in Ottawa. Certainly, government was the place to be in postwar society if you were fresh out of university, bright, ambitious, and preoccupied with the public interest. In Britain, Archibishop William Temple had promoted, with considerable success, the concept of the welfare state in contrast to Hitler's warfare state. Being a direct participant in the Keynesian revolution could be every bit as exciting for the young university graduates as had been being part of the war effort. Later, during the Thatcher years, when the British civil service would go through a deep period of self-doubt, its most senior officials would contrast their malaise with the 'self-confidence of those golden postwar years.'[79]

All in all, postwar governments in Canada, but also in other Western countries, notably Britain and the United States, proved reluctant to tear down what had been built up at the centre of government. Some retrenching took place, but no government sought to turn back the clock to the 1930s. Indeed, new capacities were established and existing ones considerably strengthened to promote economic planning and to formulate or oversee new government measures.

Attempts at Reform

Though the centre retained its basic form and continued to expand, not everyone was pleased with developments. In Canada, Prime Minister John Diefenbaker's Progressive Conservative government established in 1960 a Royal Commission – commonly known as the Glassco Commission – on government organization. Glassco argued that centrally prescribed rules and regulations were hopelessly out of date and slammed the government's approach to budgeting. Glassco's rallying cry to the government was 'to let the manager manage' – that is, that a central agency should provide the leadership and set the standards, but that the line manager should be left free to manage.[80] A newly elected Liberal government endorsed the findings of the commission in 1963 and immediately began to implement its recommendations.

Even as early as the 1960s, political and public service leaders began to recognize that growth in government spending was creating a new set of problems. New programs and activities were being launched but existing ones were not being dropped or modified. Departments were constantly on the alert to secure new funding from the centre of government, but precious few, if any, were willing to tell the centre where cuts could be made or to identify programs that were not performing well. Not only did line department managers need more authority to manage, the centre of government also needed a new capacity to assess government programs and spending.

The United States Department of Defence argued in the late 1950s that it had actually found the Holy Grail: this was the Planning, Programming Budgeting System (commonly referred to as PPB or PPBS). President Johnson liked what he saw and in 1965 ordered all government agencies to adopt it. He explained that PPBS would 'substantially improve our ability to decide among competing proposals for funds and to evaluate actual performance.'[81] The workings of PPBS have been described in great detail elsewhere and there is no need to go over them here. Suffice to note that PPBS is different from the traditional line item budgeting process in that it concentrates on the objectives to be achieved rather than on the means of achieving them. This, it was felt, would enable politicians to consider larger issues and broader questions. The thinking was that if politicians were given information on administrative details, they would make decisions on details, but if they were given information on policies and programs, they would focus on the broader picture.

A few years after President Johnson announced that PPBS would be introduced throughout the United States government, the Canadian finance minister followed suit. 'PPBS,' he claimed, 'is a major budget breakthrough.'[82] Many in Canada agreed. A leading practitioner in Canada explained that 'PPBS seeks ...

to bring under review all that has been, as well as all that might be, to query the conventional wisdom, and to advance if necessary unconventional alternatives.'[83] The new approach was considered so powerful that permanent officials felt the need to reassure politicians that politics would still weigh heavily in the decision-making process. One deputy minister, for example, wrote 'PPBS must not seek to substitute science for politics in the decision-making process.'[84]

PPBS would also serve to strengthen the role of central agencies. In fact, potentially at least, the biggest winners were officials operating in central agencies, who were thus provided with a window to look into the policies, programs, and operations of line departments and to assess their performance. Central agencies could then alert politicians to what worked, what did not, and what policies and programs were working at cross purposes. It was felt that this knowledge constituted a powerful tool for central agencies and enabled them to marshall effective arguments to support major shifts in policies and programs. It also allowed central agencies to add new positions to oversee the implementation of the new systems.

Disillusionment Sets In

By the mid-1970s, however, it became clear that the various reforms and new budgeting systems were in serious difficulty. Disillusion was rampant. The biggest disappointment was with the shift to a performance-based budgetary process. The attempt collapsed everywhere. By the mid-1970s, PPBS was pronounced dead in both the United States and Canada. It became widely accepted that if 'anyone did a cost-benefit analysis on the introduction of PPBS, he would be forced to conclude that it was not worth the effort.'[85] Certainly PPBS entailed considerable paperwork, countless meetings, and new positions in departments and central agencies, but it led to very few new policies, program terminations, or dramatic shifts in expenditure patterns. Aaron Wildavsky concluded, 'I have not been able to find a single example of successful implementation of PPBS ... PPBS deserved to die because it is an irrational mode of analysis that leads to suppression rather than correction of error.'[86] Evaluations that suggested that policies and programs were performing well were sure to be paraded before central agencies and politicians. Evaluations which pointed the other way did not receive the same treatment.

Central agencies, as already noted, stood the most to gain from the introduction of new performance-based budget systems. In the end, however, they were not able to secure a window on government policies and departments, and in the process they even lost some of their power to nit-pick line departments. In moving away from the line item budget process, the centre loosened its control over costs such as person years, travel, consultant contracts, and the like. Senior central agency officials now report that, as a result, departmental budgets for these items mushroomed in the late 1960s and 1970s. 'It became too easy,' said one, 'for departments to get money for travel, for consultants, for staff, for new equipment, and the like. We lost control over spending and we got little in the way of program reduction. PPBS itself became the problem.'[87] In addition, numerous new positions were established in the areas of planning, evaluation, and policy and program coordination, at considerable cost to the Treasury. In short, the centre of government had championed a new approach to policy and decision making, but everywhere, whether in the United States, Britain, or Canada, it failed to make the approach stick or even to reap much benefit from it, either for departments or itself.

But by 1979 the government of Canada would be back with yet another new approach, a new acronym for the 1980s, to strengthen the capacity of policy makers at the centre of government to take decisions. The Policy and Expenditure Management System (PEMS) was introduced with considerable fanfare inside government as we were being informed that it would serve to 'strengthen the policy-making role of ministers and Cabinet.'[88] Indeed, PEMS was designed as a 'collective top-down decision-making process.'[89] An elaborate Cabinet committee and a supporting cast of central agencies were also established to operate PEMS.

PEMS, it was hoped, would integrate policy and expenditure decision-making more fully than PPB ever did. Under PPB, Cabinet committees approved policy proposals and left the spending issue to Finance or Treasury Board, with the result that new commitments were easily made by the committees. They simply did not have to reconcile their policy decisions with the government's spending plans. A Treasury Board official explained the difference between PPB and PEMS in this fashion, 'You can compare policy and expenditure decisions to a pair of scissors. The two blades must meet for the process to be effective. Under PPB they would never meet. Cabinet committees would make policy decisions and leave it to someone else to make resources available. PEMS ... changed this. Now cabinet committees have to make both policy and spending decisions or see to it that both blades meet at the same time. They have expenditure limits or envelopes consistent with the government's fiscal plan.'[90] In short, the envelope accounting system would face the Cabinet committees with the fiscal consequence of their decision. In the past, the Cabinet committee, if it wanted to approve new spending proposals beyond what was available in the budget, simply reviewed existing policies and programs and their resource levels and then brought about the necessary changes in funding levels to reflect their changing priorities. Now, under PEMS, ministers would have to make tough decisions if they wanted to approve new spending proposals. In short, the intent was to place responsibility for saving squarely on the shoulders of those who spent and turn all ministers into at least part-time guardians. PEMS would also put first things first by establishing priorities and fiscal limits before developing expenditure plans.

The policy areas and the new policy reserves had to be managed. The Cabinet committees managing the policy areas in turn required support in the making of trade-offs necessary to stay within limits of the budget envelopes and in ensuring the integration of policy and spending plans. Given that the bulk of the work was on economic development and social policy, two new central agencies were established in 1979: the Ministry of State for Economic Development (which replaced the Board of Economic Development Ministers and which later became known as the Ministry of State for Economic and Regional Development) and the Ministry of State for Social Development.

These ministries gained their influence by acting as gatekeepers to the policy reserves. Richard Van Loon summed up their role this way, 'Before proposals go to the appropriate Cabinet committee they are normally widely discussed with ministry officials and considered by a committee of deputy ministers (i.e., mirror committees) chaired by the Deputy Minister of State. The Cabinet committee is provided with written advice on the basis of these deliberations and in addition the ministry briefs the chairman of the Cabinet committee and can use that occasion to forward any objections it may have to a proposal.'[91]

A few years after PEMS was introduced, it became obvious that it too would not last for very long. Ministers found the process much too cumbersome. They also argued that instead of gaining influence over decisions, they were actually losing it to permanent officials. Ministers insisted that the decision-making process had become hopelessly bureaucratic and that they could no longer move things forward. Only by successfully organizing end runs around the system or somehow by getting the prime minister onside could a minister secure a decision and get things done.[92]

As early as 1983, a senior official in the Privy Council Office spoke out publicly – in itself a rare event – about the continuing relevance of PEMS by asking a number of questions. Though he did not attempt to answer them, the questions were pointed ones and included, 'Is the system too heavy and burdensome on ministers and officials? Is there too much paper in the system and are there too many rules? Do we have the right balance of the kinds of decisions ministers are being asked to take collectively rather than individually?'[93]

John Turner provided the answers during his brief period in power in 1984. The first thing he did on coming to office was to streamline decision making in government. He explained that the policy process had become 'too elaborate, too complex, too slow, and too expensive.'[94] He disbanded the two central agencies that were playing a key role in PEMS, the ministries of state for Social Development and for Economic and Regional Development. The mirror committees of deputy ministers were also abolished. Departmental strategic overviews, which were part of the PEMS process, were no longer requested by the Cabinet committees, and departments simply stopped preparing them. Prime Minister Mulroney continued with the changes Turner introduced and did not attempt to re-create the ministries of state.

During his second mandate in power, Mulroney formally declared PEMS dead – a fact that had been well known in Ottawa for some time. In reforming the machinery of government in 1989, Mulroney established an Expenditure Review Committee of Cabinet. The prime minister declared his strong commitment to the work of this committee and, as proof, he announced that he would chair it. He attended the first few meetings but soon became preoccupied with other pressing issues, including national unity, and eventually stopped attending altogether. It is now widely recognized that the committee had very limited success. Prime Minister Chrétien did not establish an expenditure review committee of Cabinet. But he did vigorously pursue yet another new approach that Kim Campbell had introduced during her brief tenure as prime minister – the program review exercise – and this approach is reviewed in a subsequent chapter.

Looking Back

Central agencies were established to bring order to personnel management in government, to plan a more interventionist role for government, to assist heads of government to manage government, and to provide a broad policy perspective. In time, central agencies would assume other responsibilities, notably regarding policy development and program coordination. The thinking was that without programs of their own to manage, central agencies could remove themselves from immediate day-to-day operations and provide a detached view to their political masters on what was working, what was not, what needed adjustment, what should be enriched, and what should be reduced or cut. If government departments and agencies are fractious fiefdoms and if the machinery of government moves too slowly to suit the purpose and interests of prime ministers and their Cabinets, then central agencies should be one of the most important instruments available to them to exorcise duplications and overlaps, to push the machinery into action, and to assist in defining and implementing a new policy agenda.

But no sooner were central agencies established than the political leadership began to have second thoughts. For one thing, they at times felt that they had created something that was taking on a life of its own and becoming too powerful. Prime Minister Mackenzie King and at least some of his senior ministers had worried that the new Cabinet secretariat was becoming too powerful, and King on occasion had felt the need to hold back his Cabinet secretary, Arnold Heeney.[95] At other times, the leaders felt that the central agencies were not living up to expectations, at least in assisting them in redefining the public policy agenda. They established new policy processes, especially relating to government spending plans, but these processes never lived up to expectations. Looking back, processes like PPBS and PEMS laid the groundwork for disempowering Cabinet and empowering central agencies. The great majority of ministers are by definition highly practical individuals largely concerned about the well-being of their regions and their political party. By and large, they much prefer making actual decisions involving dollars and cents and see little merit in engaging in elaborate planning exercises trying to establish strategic goals and performance indicators.

It is now clear that the heyday for central agencies was during the war years and the years immediately following the Second World War. Roosevelt was the first to develop a strong central capacity for reasons other than planning and organizing a war effort. But historians now tell us that it was Roosevelt himself and his personality that promoted policy coordination and ensured an inventive government, not central agencies. Arthur Schlesinger writes that 'the proof of his control was the way, once the reins fell from his hands, the horses plunged wildly in all directions.'[96]

One can only conclude that, notwithstanding several major reforms, central agencies themselves and not just new policy processes have been unable to live up to expectations. If they are to political leadership what a steering wheel is to an automobile, then the drivers have been less than satisfied with their ability to steer government in the direction they want it to go. Indeed, Canadian prime ministers, starting with Pierre Trudeau, have time and again overhauled the machinery at the centre of government. New central agencies were established only to be dropped later, and a never-ending procession of Cabinet committees have been established or scrapped in Ottawa during the past thirty years. We have now come full circle, with Chrétien scrapping several Cabinet committees and essentially retaining only four well into his second mandate – Economic Development, Social Development, the Special Committee of Council, and the Treasury Board. The Special Committee of Council was and remains a housekeeping Cabinet committee. It handles all routine issues requiring governor-in-council approval on issues where there is a statutory requirement that the government, rather than an individual minister, makes the decision.[97] Several months into his second mandate, Chrétien added a fifth committee of Cabinet –

Communications – and directed it to promote greater coherence in the government's communications plans. In contrast to Chrétien, Trudeau had thirteen Cabinet committees in his last term in office, while the Mulroney government had ten in its first term and fifteen in its second.[98]

Table I below outlines the evolution of Cabinet structures and central agencies. It is hardly a picture of stability. It makes the case that 'changes in the central machinery of government invariably follow changes' in prime ministers, as newly elected leaders seek to mould structures and processes to meet their political and policy objectives.[99] Prime ministers are completely free to add, delete, and adjust the machinery of government at any time and as they see fit. In contrast, ministers, even the most powerful ones, do not have the authority to adjust their own departmental mandate. Deciding which minister and which department should do what is a prerogative of the prime minister, a prerogative that, as we will see, is jealously guarded at the centre of government.

TABLE 1
Evolution of Cabinet Structures and Central Agencies

Prime Minister	Ministries	Cabinet and Central Agencies
King (1935–48)	16–19	Several committees during war, fewer after Recorded minutes and decisions after 1940 Several Cabinet meetings weekly
St Laurent (1948–57)	20–1	Committees tasked by Cabinet Several Cabinet meetings weekly TB delegated significant powers through FAA (1951)
Diefenbaker (1957–63)	17–23	Infrequent meetings of committees Several Cabinet meetings weekly
Pearson (1963–8)	26–5	9 committees (1968); issues to committee before Cabinet Cabinet meetings weekly Priorities and Planning (1968) TBS split from Finance (1966)
Trudeau (1968–79)	27–33	Fewer committees with more authority FPRO split from PCO (1975) OCG split from TBS (1977) MSED (Ministry of State for Economic Development) established (1979)

TABLE 1 (*continued*)

Prime Minister	Ministries	Cabinet and Central Agencies
Clark (1979–80)	30	Inner Cabinet plus 12 committees PEMS established MSSD (Ministry of State for Social Development) set up (proclamation 1980)
Trudeau (1980–4)	32–7	Priorities and Planning with authority to issue decisions PEMS elaborated Ministry of State function introduced in External Affairs MSERD with Federal Economic Development Coordinators (FEDCs) established in all provinces (1982)
Turner (1984)	29	Communications, Labour Relations and Western Affairs committees wound up MSERD, MSSD and similar function within External wound up and FEDCs to DRIE 'Mirror committees' of deputy ministers wound up Cabinet papers streamlined and Assessment Notes discontinued
Mulroney (1984–8)	40	Foreign and Defence Policy Committee wound up Communications Committee established Envelopes consolidated PEMS rules simplified Cabinet papers further streamlined
Mulroney (1988–93)	39	Priorities and Planning and Treasury Board only committees to authorize expenditure New Expenditure Review Committee Operations Committee reviews weekly agenda 11 Cabinet committees, including several new committees: Expenditure Review, Economic Policy, Environment, Cultural Affairs and National Identity, Human Resources, Income Support, and Health

TABLE 1 (*concluded*)

Prime Minister	Ministries	Cabinet and Central Agencies
Campbell (1993)	25	Member of Cabinet committees reduced to five, including Operations, Economic and Environmental, Social Policy, House Leader's Committee, and Treasury Board All ministries of state abolished
Chrétien (1993–7)	23 8 secretaries of state	Only 4 Cabinet committees, notably Economic and Social Development, Special Committee of Council, and Treasury Board 8 secretaries of state or junior ministers appointed
Chrétien (1997–)	27 8 secretaries of state	Still, only 4 Cabinet committees were sworn into office, with two existing ones renamed the Committee for Economic Union and the Committees for Social Union. Special Committee of Council and Treasury Board continue. Subsequently, Chrétien established a Committee on Communications.

Source: Ian Clark, *Recent Changes in Cabinet Decision-Making System* (Ottawa: Privy Council Office, 3 December 1984), and the Privy Council Office, December 1997

3

Render Unto the Centre

The desire to deal with the spoils system, the war effort, Roosevelt's modernization of government operations, and Keynesian economics, as we have seen, all served to strengthen the role of the centre of government. But the shift towards the centre also raised questions about the fundamental machinery of government, and nowhere was this more evident than in countries working under the Westminster model. Indeed, the questions went to the heart of cabinet government. They include: How are the collective and individual responsibilities of Cabinet secretaries and ministers reconciled? When do line departments and agencies look to central agencies for direction? What would prompt central agencies to get involved in the operation of line departments? What would prompt line departments to contact central agencies? In brief, what belongs to the centre and what belongs to departments?

There are no set answers to these questions. The involvement of central agencies in the operation of line departments and agencies can never be properly defined. It will invariably change to reflect new circumstances, different general personalities, and emerging political crises. There are, however, established policies and practices that point to central agencies for certain issues and to line departments and agencies for others. In addition, prime ministers wishing to ensure a degree of coordination, however limited, in policies and programs will want to turn to central agencies for help. Some basic government exercises and documents, not least the budget, require a capacity at the centre to assist politicians to make policy choices, or if nothing else, simply to add up the numbers. The purpose of this chapter is to sort out the different responsibilities between central agencies and line departments and to explore the nature of the relationships between the two.

Some students of Canadian politics believe that the federal government is shifting towards a presidential system. Indeed, some have been making this case for some time.[1] This chapter also reviews, however briefly, the kind of relationship American presidents have with their cabinets. This will enable subsequent chapters to assess better the role the Canadian prime minister plays in government, in particular with his cabinet colleagues, and to see if, indeed, the federal government is drifting towards a presidential system.

Collective Responsibilities

Cabinet ministers in Canada have to strike a proper balance between their responsibility to the prime minister, to their departments, and to their Cabinet colleagues. To be sure, it is not a straightforward matter. As Richard Rose explains, Cabinet ministers have to perform a 'Janus-like role at the top of departments, facing simultaneously inward as administrators and outward as political leaders, though perhaps giving special attention to one or the other facet of their complex role.'[2]

As is well known, in a parliamentary system the government as a whole is subordinate to Parliament. Ministers are accountable to Parliament and liable to suffer penalties, if any, of parliamentary disapproval. In a British-style system, ministers are drawn from Parliament and the party with the majority of members in the House of Commons becomes the government. Accordingly, if the government loses the confidence of the House of Commons, it must collectively resign. That is, the government has to stand or fall as one administration and it cannot simply jettison an offending minister in the hope of retaining office after the defeat of a substantial bill in the Commons.

Nick D'Ombrain, a former senior official in the Privy Council Office, traces the evolution of collective responsibility in a parliamentary system back to the early eighteenth century. As public expenditures grew, he writes, 'it became more and more important to ensure that it could be defended in the Commons.'[3] The Office of the Lord Treasurer was put into commission early in the eighteenth century to ensure the participation in the debates in the Commons of several ministers competent to explain and defend the estimates. The Treasury Lords would defend government spending and also require their colleagues to justify their proposed spending, for which the Commons would be formally asked to vote supply. The Treasury would in effect reconcile the various demands for funds into a single request for supply. Accordingly, 'the function of reconciling estimates was and remains a crucial element in establishing and maintaining the solidarity of the minister and of ensuring that it retains the confidence of the House of Commons ... Treasury control and Treasury patronage made possible the development of the position of prime minister (and of political parties).'[4] Two leading students of British political institutions, Geoffrey

Marshall and Graeme C. Moodie, write that 'collective responsibility provides a definition of what a government is in our system. The substance of the Government's collective responsibility could be defined as its duty to submit its policy to and defend its policy before the House of Commons, and to resign if defeated on an issue of confidence.'[5]

Still, in Britain collective responsibility enjoys a conventional rather than a legal status. In Canada, however, the written part of the Constitution establishes in law the responsibility government has for presenting spending programs to Parliament. In addition, Parliament in Canada has traditionally delegated power under various legislative acts to the governor-in-council (i.e., Cabinet) rather than to the minister, as is done in the United Kingdom. In addition, in Canada one of Cabinet's important roles is to accommodate provincial or regional interests. The Cabinet, argued R. MacGregor Dawson, is federalized. Tradition dictates that all provinces will be represented and the Cabinet has 'taken over the allotted role of the Senate as the protector of the rights of the provinces and it has done an incomparably better job.'[6] R. Gordon Robertson, a former secretary to the Cabinet, insists that, 'It is behind the closed doors of the Cabinet, and in the frankness of its confidence, that we achieve much of the vital process of accommodation and compromise that are essential to make this country work.'[7]

Thus, within the federal government it is Cabinet which is expected to accommodate powerful and oftentimes clashing regional interests. To be sure, strong regional ministers will take the lead, or at least have in the past, in articulating regional interests. But they do so away from the public limelight, at the Cabinet table, or through special deals struck with the prime minister or with one or several Cabinet colleagues. Regional interests, accordingly, are, in theory at least, either accommodated in Ottawa through the Cabinet process or not at all. Gordon Robertson, a highly respected former clerk of the Privy Council, had little doubt as to who, in his opinion, held power in government. In a widely read article, he wrote, 'Cabinet is where the ultimate decision is taken.'[8]

In Canada, as in Britain, it is the politics of governing that brings home the importance of collective responsibility. John Mackintosh summed up the role of Cabinet in this way: 'It is the place where disputes are settled, where major policies are endorsed and where the balance of forces emerges if there is a disagreement.'[9] The prime minister exercises the power to appoint ministers, which in itself underlines the importance of collective action. The prime minister will also always want to present to Parliament and to the electorate a coherent policy agenda and a coherent government. Ministers openly feuding in the media would be an indication of a weak prime minister, as would major policy initiatives obviously working at cross purposes. If a minister cannot keep his or her own ambitions in check for the good of the government, the prime minister may well want to sacrifice that minister to ensure that the government remains on a solid footing and that Cabinet remains the ultimate director of government policy.[10]

Ministers also know that when they look bad, it reflects on their Cabinet colleagues and the government. One senior Canadian Cabinet minister claims that, 'There is no worse feeling that knowing that you have screwed up and the media is on to you. Walking into the next Cabinet meeting feels like a student being asked to go to the Principal's office for an expected lecture.' He added, however, that 'much more often than not you screw up on little things and not over major policy issues ... Think back to when Marcel Massé took a government jet to go give a speech in Boston shortly after we came to power. It took a long, long time for him and us to get over that one. Everybody could understand that this was naive and a political mistake. You can cut billions of dollars in spending as we did and somehow it isn't quite the same and the damage is not the same.'[11]

Ministers also know that they cannot make government policy or secure funding for their departments without their colleagues' agreement. This is where central agencies come in. Though it has happened, it is a rare occurrence indeed when a minister can bootleg a proposal directly to Cabinet without central agencies having first studied it and put forward their views to the prime minister or to other senior Cabinet ministers acting as chair of Cabinet committees. The Cabinet secretariat in Ottawa has instituted elaborate processes and procedures for ministers to follow in submitting proposals before their colleagues.[12] Ministers who do not respect these guidelines run the risk of being called on the carpet by the prime minister, or perhaps by the clerk of the Privy Council, often on the urging of central agency officials.

The secretariat is also charged with preparing the minutes of Cabinet and, as is well known in government, the economically worded Cabinet minutes very often are the trigger for action for line departments. In addition, central agencies are expected to provide Cabinet with the broader picture whether in terms of defining the challenges and opportunities in pursuing a proposed policy agenda, identifying the constraints involved in a policy option, or in presenting the economic and fiscal outlook. In short, they are responsible for providing ministers with a government-wide perspective of all their activities, a process that ranks priorities to assist in making decisions and defining policy objectives.[13]

Collective responsibility does not mean that all Cabinet ministers exert an equal force in shaping the government's policy agenda or government decisions. More is said about the role of the prime minister in subsequent chapters, but it is important to stress here that ministers have varying degrees of influence with their leader, and often with their Cabinet colleagues. But once a Cabinet decision has been recorded, all ministers, powerful or not, are expected to march to the same beat, or at minimum to refrain from openly challenging it in public. Collective responsibility and the practice of Cabinet solidarity in the parliamentary system have led one student of Canadian government to write approvingly that they 'compel ministers to be discreet and prevent the sort of confusion that sometimes arises in other countries, for instance, the United States, when government spokesmen make pronouncements which reveal differences of view within the administration. It tends to force interdepartmental disputes to the surface at Cabinet meetings, when they are generally resolved one way or another. It identifies government policy in a way that provides a clear focus for public discussion, at least when the facts are generally known.'[14]

To be sure, the notion of collective responsibility does not apply in the United States to the extent that it does in Canada, if at all. Basic differences exist in how politicians, as well as appointed and permanent officials, are held accountable, and, moreover, there are fundamental differences in how the political institutions of the two countries work. The American congressional system is basically one of checks and balances in which the three branches of government – the executive, the legislative, and the judicial – hold certain powers exclusively. In a parliamentary form of government, the judiciary is separate but the executive and legislative branches are joined. Not only does the executive need the confidence of the legislature, but recruitment to the executive is drawn from the legislature. Perhaps the most important point to note for someone who has been reared on the parliamentary form of government is that in the American presidential system no one has the ultimate responsibility for the exercise of all power necessary to take action.

Peter Aucoin reminds students of Canadian politics that 'Congress is not a parliament at all.' He adds that the 'American Congress is not a stronger or more democratic version of the Canadian Parliament.'[15] The point is that the American system of government is vastly different from the Westminster model. Members of Parliament in our system are not elected to govern. Rather, they are elected to hold those who govern accountable for their policies and decisions.

Nevil Johnson summed up the difference well by pointing out that in the congressional system bargains are struck in the legislature, while in the parliamentary system it is almost always the government alone, particularly when it has a majority mandate, that drives public policy and public spending. Johnson could have added that bargains and compromises must also be struck between Congress and the presidency. In addition, to some extent, there is also an implicit set of bargains with the courts as Congress and the president go about their work.

There are, of course, advantages and drawbacks to both systems. A majority government in a parliamentary system can run the risk of embarking on a 'single direction foolishness.' Likewise, the bargaining required of a congressional form can 'become ungovernable and run the risk of falling apart.'[16] It is ironic that reform-minded people in the United States are suggesting that the president should be asked to defend his policies directly in both houses of Congress, that new ways should be found to integrate the work of the administration and Congress more effectively, and that more positions in the bureaucracy should be reserved for career officials rather than for political appointees. In other words, that the congressional should be more like a parliamentary system. At the same time, many reform-minded people in parliamentary systems are looking for ways to strengthen the involvement of backbenchers without limiting the power or responsibility of the government to Parliament.[17] They are also seeking to bring the relations between senior officials and ministers more into the open.

The U.S. Cabinet

The role of the cabinet in the United States has had an ambiguous and difficult history. For one thing, the Founding Fathers had the Senate in mind to perform cabinet-type functions and to provide collective advice to the president.[18] An accident of history would prevent such a development when the concept 'broke down the first time it was put to the test.'[19] President Washington went to the Senate to review an Indian treaty but, the senators reluctant to discuss the matter in his presence, postponed the debate. Washington left the chamber in anger and he subsequently turned to the heads of the executive departments as a source of advice.[20]

That said, Thomas Jefferson, the author, suggested that all important matters should be submitted to Cabinet where the president counts 'himself but one' as a kind of *primus inter pares*.[21] But Jefferson, the president, backed away from this concept, submitting few important issues to Cabinet. He also flatly rejected any suggestion that items be submitted to a vote. Abraham Lincoln and Theodore Roosevelt virtually ignored their Cabinet on all important issues. History also reveals that some members of the FDR Cabinet 'suffered frustration' in Cabinet meetings where, according to one member, only 'the barest routine matters are discussed.' He added, 'I never think of bringing up even a serious departmental issue at Cabinet meetings.'[22] One Cabinet member in the FDR administration, probably like many other Cabinet secretaries since, felt that the most important value in attending Cabinet meetings was that it provided 'a way in which to get into the White House to have a word with the President in private after the meetings were over.'[23] In Canada or Britain, a strong prime minister is one who does not allow 'the fragmentation of the Cabinet into a mere collection of departmental heads.'[24] In the United States for a long time a strong president was one who 'regarded his Cabinet as a body of department heads, to be dealt with individually.'[25] No doubt many observers of American politics and government still hold this view.

It is important to remember that in the United States, the Cabinet is a creature of the president, and presidents 'are at liberty to make considerable use of it as a source of advice, or they are free to neglect it completely.'[26] Though a number of presidents have chosen to neglect it, some have not. President Eisenhower, for example, made use of the Cabinet as an instrument of collective policy making. He insisted on regular Cabinet meetings and on taking all major issues before Cabinet. Other presidents began their days in office intending to use Cabinet as a source of collective policy advice, if not policy making, but subsequently played havoc with their Cabinets. Both Nixon and Carter began their presidencies with a pledge to make full use of their Cabinets as advisory and policy-making bodies. Nixon, for example, declared before assuming the presidency that he did not want 'yes men' in his Cabinet and that he fully intended to involve it in all the great issues of his administration.[27] However, considerable tension developed between the White House and Cabinet.[28] By the end of Nixon's first term in office, it was all too clear that the Cabinet had been made subordinate to the presidential staff.[29] On his part, when Carter confronted a political crisis in 1979, he returned from a special Camp David retreat to dismiss five members of his Cabinet and to strengthen considerably the hand of a few White House staff members.[30] Reagan, meanwhile, established a number of Cabinet councils or committees to deal with specific issues and accordingly relied less on full Cabinet for advice than might have otherwise been the case.[31] Still, Reagan is reported to have enjoyed the 'spectacle of Cabinet meetings, even if he did not always stay awake at them.'[32] Bush assembled a 'friends and neighbours' kind of Cabinet and would turn to it as a major source of advice.[33] Clinton pledged to make full use of his Cabinet as a collective policy-making instrument and as a key source of policy advice, but Cabinet, as opposed to individual Cabinet secretaries, has had limited impact.

At the risk of repetition, the difference then between British- and American-style governments is explained by the fact that in a parliamentary system a statement of policy is in theory not the sole responsibility of the prime minister. The responsibility rests, or at least should rest, with the Cabinet as a collective body. As Gordon Robertson explained, 'Cabinet is where the ultimate decision is taken.' In the American presidential system, the president will want to secure the opinions of members of cabinet on a major policy decision – probably at a cabinet meeting – but he does so to clarify his own mind and to weigh the pros and cons of a proposed policy and not to secure a collective decision.[34] All of this is to say that in theory the Cabinet in a parliamentary system is responsible to Parliament, while in a presidential system Cabinet is responsible to the president.[35]

Individual Ministerial Responsibility

Cabinet ministers are also individually accountable to Parliament. They have the responsibility to explain to the House of Commons whatever subjects prove to be of interest in their jurisdiction to the House. The minister is 'the constitutional mouthpiece through which departmental actions will be defended or repudiated and from whom information is to be sought.'[36] The principle of ministerial responsibility makes the minister 'blamable' for both policy and administration, and the minister in turn can reach into the bureaucracy, organized as it is along clear hierarchical lines, and secure an explanation for why things have gone wrong as well as one for how to make things right.

The public service, meanwhile, has 'no constitutional personality or responsibility separate from the duly elected Government of the day.'[37] The point, as Herman Finer explained in his classic essay, is that the views and advice of civil servants are to be private and their actions anonymous so that 'only the Minister has views and takes actions. If this convention is not obeyed, then civil servants may be publicly attacked by one party and praised by another, and that must lead to a weakening of the principle of impartiality.'[38]

The House of Commons, by design, exerts a negative rather than a positive control, and ministers need to arrange the affairs of their departments so that sensitive issues are brought to their attention. What constitutes a sensitive issue? Virtually anything. It can be a major policy issue or the most trivial administrative matter. It can involve large sums of public funds or none at all. What is sensitive can define what is policy, and what is policy can make what would be a minor issue in other circumstances into something extremely sensitive. The media and the opposition parties also can and very often do define what is sensitive. However a sensitive issue develops, the minister is responsible for explaining it and for correcting flawed policy or faulty administrative action. The important point here, however, is that what is sensitive can come to define the government's agenda.

Accordingly, government officials in Canada operate in a political environment that can become charged on a moment's notice. It would probably be only small comfort to a government manager if he or she were told that they are being called on the carpet by a Cabinet minister rather than by the media or a parliamentary committee. Indeed, recent developments suggest that some ministers prefer to duck ministerial responsibility to let the opposition or the media get at the offending official in full public view.[39]

It is this, perhaps more than anything else, that points to the vast differences between public sector administration and private sector management. It is hardly possible to overstate that control in the public sector is negative and government officials are constantly on the lookout to avoid errors and mistakes, perceived or real. In the private sector, it does not much matter if you get it wrong 30 per cent of the time so long as you can turn a profit at the end of the year and the bottom line remains healthy. In the public sector, it does not much matter if you get it right 95 per cent of the time because the focus will be on the 5 per cent of the time you get it wrong. Individual ministers can publicly take the blame for such errors, as is often expected. But at some point the mistake may become sufficiently visible or the errors so frequent that the matter begins to hurt the political health of the whole government, not just the minister responsible. Hence much as one cannot always predict what politically sensitive issues will emerge, the dividing line between what constitutes collective and individual responsibility is not always evident. It is obviously not possible for prime ministers and Cabinet ministers to predict when and where errors will surface to gain media attention. Delegating authority increases the chance for errors and increasing the chance for errors is 'a problem in a politically accountable system.'[40]

Cabinet ministers also differ in their willingness to work with the centre. Some see issues from a government-wide perspective more easily than others. Prime ministers often prefer their Cabinet ministers to view problems from where they sit at the Cabinet table rather than from below or from the perspective of line departments and agencies. The risk of Cabinet ministers 'going native' is always great. During the Second World War, U.S. General George C. Marshall referred to the danger of 'localities,' when every 'theatre commander' became convinced that the war was being won or lost in his own area of responsibility and that the 'withholding of whatever was necessary for local success was evidence of blindness, if not imbecility, in the high command.'[41] 'Departmentalities' is viewed as a dangerous disease in a parliamentary system. A former British Cabinet minister explains, 'If you contract Departmentalities you will forget that you are part of a Government, that the fortunes of the Government are more important than the fortunes of your own Department, that the fortunes of the Government may well require that your own Department's interests be subordinated to those of another.'[42] Things are no different in Canada.

Where Decisions Are Made

Governments take thousands of decisions every day. The bulk of them are straightforward, predictable, and noncontroversial. Processing applications under national programs where eligibility criteria are clear is one such example. The processing of tax returns usually does not entail a controversial debate, at least in public, though it may hold painful surprises for some taxpayers. These types of decisions are made by what Henry Mintzbergh or James Q. Wilson call 'production organizations.' The work of production or machine-like organizations is predictable and their goals can often be precisely specified and measured.[43] Decisions are usually made in the confines of a single department and very often within a single office.

Central agencies have little interest in these decisions unless, of course, they gain media attention for some reason and become a political problem. Spending estimates of production organizations will be reviewed but even here decisions will likely be straightforward. The workload and program costs can be well documented and measured and agreement between the line department and the central agency on the proposed expenditure budget is often easily reached. Indeed, central agency officials are well aware, for example, that adding one tax auditor to the payroll generates new revenues which are far greater than the salary and associated costs of the incumbent.

Most government decisions can be labelled internal or unilateral and the great majority of them can be made by the responsible front line employee or the program manager without ever consulting the minister. From time to time, however, the program manager may have to move the decision, with a recommendation, up the line to a more senior officer. There are several reasons why this may happen. The manager may well have discretionary authority delegated only to a certain level over which the case has to be considered by a more senior official. Alternatively, a particular case may have become politically sensitive because it potentially has an impact on a group of people or a whole community rather than just one individual, or because a politician of some influence, whether a member of Parliament, a mayor, or a local politician well known for his or her ability to talk to the media, has expressed an interest in the matter. Depending on the nature of the case or the politics of the situation, the more senior official may decide to raise the matter at the political level.

Thus, even in the case of internal administrative decisions, it is not always possible to discern when a public servant's influence wanes or ends and a politician's influence starts and holds sway. It varies depending on the issue, on the newness of the issue perhaps, the level of public funds involved, and the degree of public controversy being generated. Put differently, the level at which a decision is made can shift upward or downward as one senses more or less controversy, or more or less importance.[44] A case in point is the decision made several years ago by the Department of Government Services in Canada to replace all 3,000 windows at the Foreign Affairs building at a cost of $3 million when only a few were defective.[45] Officials calculated that it was cheaper and more efficient to replace all the windows at once rather than doing the work piecemeal as necessary. The administrative decision became a hot political issue when the media gave the story wide coverage in many daily newspapers and television newscasts. The day after the story broke, an official in the department reported that 'the whole place went berserk' after the minister, David Dingwall, declared the decision 'stupid' and 'wanted a full explanation' since he had not been made aware of the file.[46] A week later the minister cancelled the contract, resulting in a 'hefty' cost to taxpayers.[47] When officials made the decision to replace all the windows, no one in the department could have predicted that a purely administrative internal decision would become a hot political issue.

That said, there are important issues, even important policy issues, that can be resolved within a department or an agency. There are also departments that are more self-contained than others. For example, departments or agencies responsible for a country's penal system are relatively self-contained in policy matters while departments responsible for foreign trade or promoting economic development are not.

But even when a Cabinet minister has full authority to make a decision, she or he may wish to consult others – Cabinet colleagues or someone in the Prime Minister's Office. When expecting controversy over a decision, a Cabinet minister may prefer to act in the knowledge that colleagues or the centre have been consulted. At that point, central agency officials, whether at the political or career official level, may well get involved. Accordingly, the Cabinet minister has to weigh which comfort level is preferable – having one's colleagues or a higher political authority onside or delaying the decision because of the involvement of central agency officials. In addition, consulting colleagues or others could well result in a different decision or a modified decision from the one she prefers. A minister should also be careful to 'over-consult' when responsibility for the decision is clearly in his court for fear of irritating colleagues or appearing to be weak. Responsibility shared on questions that can be handled within one's department or office is invariably regarded, at least by the stronger ministers, as responsibility shirked.

Are there firm rules that enable a minister to decide when he should take a matter through the Cabinet decision-making process? The answer is no, as the above makes clear. That said, a deputy minister will advise his minister to submit a proposal to the Cabinet process if it has an impact on the policies or even the operations of other departments. In any event, deputy ministers know full well that the Privy Council Office will expect that any policy or new program proposal having an impact on other departments will be submitted to a Cabinet committee. Given that very few public policy issues fit neatly into the mandate of a single government department, ministers will much more often than not be told that they should submit proposals to the Cabinet process.

This remains true even though the 1993 government reorganization reduced the number of departments from thirty-two to twenty-three. An important objective of the reorganization, as we will see in chapter 5, was to re-create natural decision centres within departments. The large number of departments meant that too many decisions crossed departmental lines so that the Cabinet decision-making process had to be engaged much too often. Officials report that the 1993 government restructuring has helped in 'locating' more decisions in departments but that there are still 'very few important initiatives that do not have interdepartmental considerations.'[48] When a minister decides to engage the cabinet process, it triggers a number of activities outside of her department and outside her immediate control. Central agency officials will immediately begin to monitor all developments and a series of interdepartmental meetings will be held to review the proposal.

There is one individual, however, who can at any time upset the collective versus individual responsibilities and, with no advance notice, take an issue that would properly belong to a minister and her department and bring it to the centre. The prime minister can intervene in any issue – big or small – if he feels that his judgment is required. He may decide to bring an issue to his office if he thinks it is politically important, if it has a national unity dimension, or if he or his advisers become convinced that the minister is not up to the task of managing it.

The prime minister need not ask anyone for permission to take what can be essentially a departmental matter and bring it to the centre. Only his interest and the time he can make available to the issue can limit his ability to intervene. When a prime minister takes an issue away from a minister to manage by remote control, he will likely have a brief chat with the relevant minister to explain the development. The important point here (and more is said about this in the next chapter), is that the prime minister can intervene in a departmental matter when and where he pleases.

Bilateral decisions involve more than one department or agency. If, as can be the case, a Cabinet minister is responsible for two departments or agencies, she or he simply turns to a kind of mini-cabinet committee, group, or council and makes the necessary decision. If the decision entails a transfer of funds from one agency or department to another, then the Cabinet minister will initiate the decision or ratify it. Depending on the circumstances, the involvement of officials from the Treasury Board secretariat or Finance may be necessary.

There are also numerous multi-agency or multidepartmental decisions taken every day. Some are routine and are taken at the desk officer level. Such decisions may result from a requirement that department X (say, Industry) has to consult department Y (say, Transportation) when a decision to provide some form of assistance (say, to the airline industry) is made. Similarly, in a federal system, a federal government department or agency may have agreed to consult one, several, or all provinces before it makes a decision on a given issue. Provided the decision is made within clearly established and well-known perimeters, it will not entail controversy and will be made at the bureaucratic level. A provincial premier, however, will quickly raise a fuss if there are any indications that her region is being shortchanged. If this should happen, career officials will likely lose some control over the file to politically appointed officials in a ministerial office. Hence the recognition that every problem 'no matter how technical it might seem, can assume political significance and its solution can be decisively influenced by political considerations.'[49]

Spending departments and agencies will enter into bilateral negotiations with the Treasury Board secretariat to determine spending ceilings. A central agency or agencies (in Canada, the Department of Finance and the Treasury Board secretariat both have a role in reviewing spending plans) will play the role of guardian in reviewing the spending plans. The negotiations are carried out by bureaucrats and most issues are resolved at this level. Spending ceilings will have already been struck so that departments can get on with sorting out the nuts and bolts of the proposed spending plan. Still, departments can, at least in theory, appeal their ceilings or decisions during the annual review of spending plans with the Finance minister or, in some instances, the prime minister and Cabinet. For such appeals the relevant central agencies prepare extensive briefing material to equip the prime minister or the Finance minister for their meetings with the spending minister.

Some departments within a government will claim that they have, or should have, the mandate to review some proposals being prepared by other departments. For example, the Department of the Environment will quite correctly argue that it can hardly ask private firms to be environmentally sensitive when some government departments are not. This, in turn, will give rise to numerous interdepartmental committee meetings and perhaps new spending plans. Departments and agencies that can lay claim to a horizontal responsibility and a need to review proposed or ongoing activities of other departments play a quasi–central agency role. They will use whatever influence they can muster to block certain initiatives or to amend them to ensure that they are acceptable from their perspective. Such developments, particularly when they call for possible new spending, will trigger the involvement of central agencies.

There are many other examples where departments and agencies claim a coordinating role over other departments or programs. Regional development agencies, for example, will make the case that in order to act as an advocate for slow-growth regions they need the authority to review proposals from other departments to ensure that they square with regional or local economic circumstances and conditions. Without such a mandate, there would be the risk that government programs may work at cross purposes and cancel each other out.[50] These mandates can, however, give rise to a great deal of interdepartmental tension and also slow down the decision-making process considerably. A former British Cabinet minister explains, 'The Department of Economic Affairs was a curious body ... we muscled in on everyone's business. There was to be a debate on Northern Ireland and the First Secretary insisted that, in view of DEA's responsibilities for regional policy, I should wind it up. This was a disaster. Home Office officials were hostile because we were poaching on their ground. My own officials were not happy at offending another department ...'[51]

There are, to be sure, many similar examples in Canada. One, however, has great difficulty identifying instances, at least in Canada, where line departments have successfully muscled in on the turf of other departments. The Department of Regional Economic Expansion had a mandate to coordinate or at least influence the activities of other federal departments.[52] But it failed on this front, which explains in part why it was disbanded in the early 1980s. The Department of the Environment was also given a mandate to influence the policies and programs of other federal departments in the late 1980s, but it too has never lived up to expectations.[53] The list goes on, and includes the Department of Indian Affairs and Northern Development, the former ministry of Urban Affairs, and the Atlantic Canada Opportunities Agency.

Coordinating Cross-Cutting Policy Issues

There are a number of emerging forces currently at play pulling in the direction of still greater interdepartmental coordination. Indeed, there are now cross-cutting policy issues surfacing in virtually every department. The effect of these issues cannot be contained adequately within the single policy sector where they have been usually discussed. For example, it is no longer possible to think about education without also thinking about its impact on competitiveness and labour markets.

Another aspect of the cross-cutting policy issues is that poorly designed and coordinated programs may diminish the impact of one another. For example, programs implemented by the Environmental Protection Agency in the United States to minimize the production of carbon dioxide and other air pollutants from automobiles tend to have a negative impact on other programs (in Energy and in EPA itself) to increase gasoline mileage of automobiles. Likewise, some government agencies in Washington pay farmers to take land out of production, while at least one other (the Bureau of Reclamation in the Department of the Interior) spends large sums of money to make other land arable. In Canada, we have had instances in the past when agricultural programs assisted tobacco farmers while the Department of Health invested public funds in anti-smoking campaigns. In addition to being expensive, these contradictory programs make government look disorganized to the public, if not to itself.

The global economy is also putting pressure on national governments to coordinate better their policies and programs. As we have already seen, regional trade agreements such as the North America Free Trade Agreement push national governments to harmonize a wide variety of laws and policies from one nation state to another. This requires an ability to promote a government-wide capacity to review regulations and programs. In addition, national governments have come to recognize that for their countries to be competitive in the international marketplace they need to be proactive in coordinating key economic and social policies, and in particular their labour market and social programs. In short, no longer can government permit policies and even departments to operate in relative isolation. While it might have been appropriate at the turn of the century to establish vertical sectoral lines to deal with problems in agriculture, transportation, and industry, that is no longer the case.

It is now also clear that the development of the global economy will be leaving in its wake large problems of economic adjustment. National governments will not be able to go to the sidelines and stand idle. They will intervene – as they have already started to do – but the interventions will be coming face to face with serious constraints, not least of which are the difficult fiscal situation confronting most Western industrialized democracies and the multidimensional approach required to have any chance of success. Accordingly, the interventions will have to be creative and draw upon the resources of several departments.[54] This, in turn, will require a capacity at the centre to plan and coordinate the various efforts.

Fiscal issues are also bringing pressure to bear on government operations to adopt a more horizontal perspective. If we have learned anything on the budgeting front over the past thirty years, it is that budgeting is fundamentally a political process. The budget process can never be placed on automatic pilot with the assumption that sophisticated performance indicators will sort out which programs should get what. Choices have to be made among competing demands. This, above all, requires a political judgment about which interests should be indulged and which deprived. To be successful in shaping the major contours of the budget to reflect government priorities, the political leadership needs to structure the budgetary process to assert control over it. It needs to have a knowledge of government policies, departments, and programs that cut across departmental lines and that are both consistent and comparable in quality and content. Deciding on priorities in dealing with fiscal pressures requires the imposition of centralized controls through central agencies or direct intervention by political leaders and their appointed agents.[55]

The political leadership in Canada is also being called upon to deal with real or perceived problems of overlap and duplication in government programs. This issue has been a sore point in federal-provincial relations for the past thirty years or so. The federal government needs a capacity to look at itself and at programs as a whole if it is to attack the problem. Managers and employees on the front line will naturally be preoccupied with the details of the day, and with providing top-flight services to clients (as the new managerialism is asking them to do). It is difficult to imagine that identifying duplication and overlap and then trying to deal with far away Ottawa to sort the problem out will be high on their list of priorities.

Those who operate at the centre of government appreciate all too well the growing need for coordination, a cross-cutting perspective on policy issues. Jocelyne Bourgon, the clerk of the Privy Council Office, and secretary to the Cabinet, established a special task force of senior officials in 1996 on managing horizontal policy issues. The task force, a mix of deputy ministers and assistant deputy ministers from thirteen departments, summed up the task at hand in this fashion: 'Ministers and their departments must fulfill both their individual accountabilities to meet the needs of their clients, stakeholders, and partners – and their collective responsibilities – to serve the broader interest. It is these collective responsibilities, which transcend individual mandates, that challenge ministers and their departments to look beyond their narrow interests and to recognize the interdependence of many policy issues.'[56] In searching for ways to promote a stronger horizontal perspective in government, the task force pointed to organizational culture as key. It held workshops with many senior officials and, based on the findings of these workshops, the task force concluded that 'there is a sense that the federal policy community is becoming less corporate, less collegial, with interdepartmental discussion focusing less on problem solving and more on departmental positioning and turf protection. Further, as departments have become larger, accountability is focused on the internal agenda; with few incentives to help "tackle someone else's issues." There are few rewards in the system – and the current rewards and recognition systems tend to reinforce vertical thinking and competitive behaviour.'[57]

The task force went on to identify another problem with the government's policy-making capacity – that is, that the policy officers in line departments are increasingly preoccupied with managing short-term pressures and issues. Much too often, it argued, they are left trying to spin the latest issue to journalists to make it on the media hit parade rather than focusing on the more important long-term issues. They are also being asked, the task force reported, to manage more and more negative fallout in the media, resulting from a new policy decision or problems with a particular program.

The solution? The task force argued that senior officials, and in particular central agencies, should promote 'a collegial and collaborative culture within the policy community.'[58] This could be done, it suggested, through strong leadership at the centre, new investment in policy research and development, new policy courses for government officials, and promoting informal links between departments.[59]

The clerk of the Privy Council also asked Ivan Fellegi, chief statistician, to chair a task force of senior officials to review the state of the government's policy capacity. This task force submitted its report in April 1995. It concluded that 'the most notable weaknesses at present relate to longer term strategic and horizontal issues. Resources are disproportionately consumed by short term demands. This is true both within departments and across government.'[60] The report was critical of central agencies and argued that they 'do not provide adequate guidance and support' to the management of major horizontal issues.[61] It insisted that central agencies have a vital role to play on this front, but pointed out that 'there is no fully effective central function that helps to define issues of strategic importance, to guide the process for developing longer term and horizontal policies, to promote interdepartmental networks.' The Privy Council Office, the task force concluded, 'is the logical focus for such a function.'[62]

Packaging Proposals

Policy or program proposals, including program adjustments that require new legislation, will also trigger the involvement of a central agency. Although more is said about this later in this study, it is important for now to make a few general observations. In some instances, a central agency will only be playing the role of clearinghouse to ensure that the centre is aware of what is being planned and that the various initiatives are coordinated. In other instances, however, central agencies will be intimately involved in the development of major new policy and program proposals.

An agency or department planning a major policy shift or a new program will set in motion an elaborate interdepartmental consultation exercise. Initially at least, the exercise could be a series of informal meetings involving middle level officials from relevant line departments. More senior level officials may decide to meet, say, over lunch to review in some detail what is being proposed. Meanwhile, interdepartmental committee meetings will be held to which central agency officials will be invited. The timing of the involvement of the political level – the Cabinet minister, Cabinet committees, the prime minister – will depend on the issue. A high-profile proposal will be monitored very closely at the political level even at very early stages and politicians and their partisan advisers will ask for frequent briefings.

In Canada, if the cabinet process is being respected, a Cabinet committee will review the proposal before it is submitted to full Cabinet. At this point, all of the budgetary and administrative implications will have been reviewed and central agency officials will be well versed on the proposal. In fact, the chair of the committee will have been properly briefed by central agency officials, and more often than not, a briefing memorandum may have been sent to the prime minister. The next step is to move the proposal to Cabinet either as a routine matter or as an important item on the Cabinet agenda. Again, this depends on the nature of the issue.

The Cabinet committee structure has evolved greatly over the years. From 1945 to 1964, most operated on an ad hoc basis and were structured to deal with a specific task assigned by Cabinet rather than with properly defined areas. The focus was clearly on the Cabinet itself, which met about three times a week and dealt with a great deal of detailed business (including approving contracts). Issues were submitted to Cabinet first and subsequently referred to a Cabinet committee for consideration. Pearson reorganized the committee system in 1964 to replace the ad hoc committee structure with nine standing committees. He also established a Priorities and Planning Committee of Cabinet in 1968 and gave it a mandate to outline government priorities in line with its overall fiscal position.[63]

Trudeau reorganized the cabinet system and delegated more authority to cabinet committees. Most issues were submitted to a committee before going to Cabinet, a practice that still exists today. Clark, during his brief stay in power, established an inner Cabinet. Turner abolished two central agencies (MSERD and MSSD) and streamlined decision making. Mulroney added new Cabinet committees and had proposals at times going through several committees (e.g., the sectoral committees such as the Economic Development, Operations committee chaired by the deputy prime minister, the Priorities and Planning Cabinet, and then Cabinet).[64] Chrétien, as already noted, scrapped most Cabinet committees so that a proposal only goes through one committee before going to Cabinet. Still, the growth in the number of Cabinet committees had one important effect: starting in the late 1960s, under Trudeau, Cabinet became increasingly structured in a hierarchical fashion and 'full Cabinet met ... seldom as a forum for government decision-making.'[65]

Ensuring Equality

There are core values in government that hold important implications for how its operations are run. One such value is the need for fair treatment for all. Tax auditors, for example, are asked to treat citizens the same. One can only imagine the public outcry if taxpayers were treated differently for whatever reason in the processing of tax returns. Similarly, the great majority of national programs offer the *same* services to different people in different regions of the country. In addition, civil servants themselves will expect their employer to treat them fairly and again to offer equal treatment to all.

Should any of these values be cast aside, politicians will be the first to cry foul. Imagine if a national program to assist farmers only applied in selected areas of the country, if a national energy program applied only in the most populous or least populous regions, if a national child care program for the poor only applied to the poor living in selected regions. Similarly, how long would a member of Parliament agree to civil servants in any given region (other than perhaps his own) consistently having larger offices, better furniture, longer holidays, or being relieved of the merit principle when hiring or promoting staff.

Once one accepts that fair treatment is a basic value for citizens and government employees, one has to accept, the argument goes, that centrally prescribed rules and regulations will need to be put in place, enforced, and audited. It is for this reason, albeit among others, that Canada has a Public Service Commission and also a wide array of centrally defined administrative prescriptions governing the purchase of goods and services. Ministers are not free to bypass these policy and program prescriptions, and if they do, they run the risk of being held to account in question period or, failing that, by the auditor general.

Another core value of public administration is that public funds are to be spent only with due regard for prudence and probity. Unfair advantages ought not to be given to particular individuals or groups – unless a carefully planned affirmative action program has been put in place – in securing employment or winning a government contract. One only needs a brief encounter with front line government officials to hear about the importance of fair treatment for all and the need for integrity in the government financial system. One will also hear about the work of the various oversight bodies regulating the work of government operations.

A review of federal government operations reveals that ministers and their departments are subjected to a number of centrally prescribed rules, regulations, and administrative practices. A central authority lays down how expenditure budgets should be prepared, how positions should be classified, and how functions should be organized. A central authority also prescribes how government managers can hire and promote staff. Guidelines are established for carrying out audits and the evaluation of programs. In addition, some centrally prescribed administrative practices tell managers in some detail how certain purchases should be made. Another central administrative body could also be scrutinizing the purchase or rental of the offices departmental programs managers and their staff occupy and outline the number of sick days employees are allowed annually, how many leave days, and when they can retire on full pension.

Given the above, one may be tempted to conclude that the role of government managers is simply to put their operations on automatic pilot and let centrally prescribed practices take over and run things. There is an element of truth to this view. It is also widely assumed, however, that it is these centrally prescribed rules, perhaps more than anything else, which have made government operations inefficient, bloated, and costly, and have given government bureaucracy a bad reputation.[66] But the desire to modernize government operations has given rise to the New Public Management (NPM) with its emphasis on the application of private sector management techniques to government operations.

The NPM is still very much in vogue. There is evidence to suggest that in Canada some centrally prescribed administrative practices have been scrapped and others have been attenuated or modified all in the interest of empowering front line managers and their employees.[67] There is also, however, plenty of evidence to suggest that there are still numerous centrally prescribed rules and regulations designed to ensure a degree of uniformity in government programs and operations and also prudence, probity, and integrity in the government's personnel and financial management systems. What is not at all clear is whether the shift to public management is having much of an impact on government operations in terms of efficiency and cost.[68]

Looking Back

The very nature of government suggests that one cannot easily lay down clearly and consistently when a minister should look to his collective responsibilities or to his department or decide what is the prerogative of a line department and what belongs to a central agency. The very existence of a central political authority and central agencies to support its work suggests that what belongs at the centre and what belongs in a line department can never be cast in concrete. The challenge for those in government is not to draw a clear dividing line between the two, but rather to manage the tension.

Accordingly, the search for a proper balance between the centre and line department at least in administrative matters is never ending and is always in a state of flux. In brief, the pendulum is rarely stable. In more recent years, managerialism has pushed the pendulum towards decentralization, towards more empowered front line operations, and away from the centre. But the pendulum has been there before, however tentatively in some instances. It was there, for example, in the aftermath of the Glassco report. Long-serving employees are familiar with government scandals or a series of high-profile errors or administrative mistakes unleashing a new set of centrally prescribed regulations and administrative practices.

The above suggests that a great deal of the work in government consists of performing a balancing act between competing demands and forces and adapting some long-standing core values to the requirements of the latest fashion and fad introduced to 'fix' government. The former chairman of the Public Service Commission in Canada, after his retirement, summed up the frustrations he had experienced in government when he observed that the system is 'designed to make eunuchs out of public service managers.'[69] The point is that despite various efforts to decentralize decision making and to empower government managers, the nature of the public sector itself requires a strong capacity at the centre to ensure a government-wide perspective on policies, programs, and activities and a degree of sameness in government operations. What is truly remarkable is that some thirty years or more after the Glassco Commission had called on the federal government to decentralize its operations and to let managers manage, new high-profile initiatives under the managerialism banner are calling for the same changes, as if Glassco had never existed. Yogi Berra, the American grassroots philosopher, would no doubt describe the 'New Public Management' as 'déjà vu all over again.'

If nothing else, this suggests once again that the search for striking the right balance between the centre and line departments and between collective and individual responsibilities for ministers can never be properly defined. When looking at government operations from the centre, there is, by all accounts, an increasingly urgent need to promote a horizontal perspective, to ensure greater cooperation between departments, and to strengthen policy capacity. The task force on horizontal policy issues called for a 'Government of Canada Inc.' approach to policy making. But the task force also made it clear that the tendency in the government in recent years was to go in the opposite direction, with more emphasis being placed on departmental positioning and turf protection rather than on promoting more horizontal thinking. The task force on strengthening the policy capacity, meanwhile, concluded that there was no effective central function to define issues of strategic importance and to promote horizontal policies and that PCO was the logical focus for such a role. The implication, of course, is that PCO is not playing that role. Indeed, the task force also argued that PCO was overly preoccupied with managing short-term issues and political crises.

The chapters that follow seek to bring to life the tension between the centre and departments and between the collective and individual responsibilities of ministers. They report that the federal government has overhauled the machinery of government more than once to get at the problem, but also that it is still anything but happy with the current situation. The federal government task forces on managing horizontal policy issues and on the government's policy capacity brought this point home. But they are not alone.

PART II

THE PLAY

4

Primus: There Is No Longer Any *Inter* or *Pares*

The prime minister occupies the highest peaks of both the political and administrative mountains, from which he can survey all developments in his government.[1] This is not to suggest that he can always shape at will all initiatives and move the machinery of government in the direction and at the speed he wishes. There are some constraints to prime ministerial power, ranging from incessant demands on his time, public opinion, the media – even to inertia, a characteristic found in all large organizations and to which the federal government is certainly not immune. But, no matter the circumstances, the prime minister remains 'the boss.' Prime Minister Chrétien is called the boss, while he, in turn, invariably referred to Pierre Trudeau as 'le boss' when he served in Trudeau's Cabinet.

There is no question that a great deal of power is concentrated in the hands of the prime minister, especially when his party enjoys a majority in Parliament. Abraham Lincoln is reported to have provided an account of Cabinet deliberations by saying 'the Ayes one, the nays seven. The ayes have it.'[2] A Canadian prime minister holding a clear majority in Parliament could easily make a similar claim. Indeed, there have been many instances during the past twenty-five years or so when various prime ministers have chosen to pursue initiatives both large and small without even consulting their Cabinets. Governments are often identified not only in the media, but also in scholarly works by the names of the prime minister, as in the Trudeau, Chrétien, or Mulroney governments, and for very legitimate reasons. Prime ministers have become much more than spokespersons for their Cabinets. They are the focal point of the government and the administration and they clearly dominate inside government. They provide the leadership, the style, and the coherence of the government and the ebb and flow of the fortunes of the government are directly linked to their performance. No single Cabinet minister, regardless of her political base in the party or in the country, can possibly have the same impact as the prime minister. If a minister ever should, it will signal a short-lived government – and no one knows this better than the prime minister.

This chapter looks at the role of the prime minister in government. It examines the levers of power that belong to him or her and the forces that strengthen his hand at almost every turn. The chapter examines the constraints to prime ministerial power but also the tools available to the prime minister to assist him or her in dealing with these constraints. It reviews the role of his own office and considers whether the prime minister's role and power in government have been expanding or receding in recent years.

Primus Rules

Canadian prime ministers, again, particularly when they have a majority government in Parliament, have in their hands all the important levers of power. Indeed, all major national public policy roads lead one way or another to their doorstep. They are elected leader of their party by party members, they chair Cabinet meetings, establish Cabinet processes and procedures, set the Cabinet agenda, establish the consensus for Cabinet decisions; they appoint and fire ministers and deputy ministers, establish Cabinet committees, and decide on their membership; they exercise virtually all the powers of patronage and act as personnel manager for thousands of government and patronage jobs; they articulate the government's strategic direction as outlined in the Speech from the Throne; they dictate the pace of change, and are the main salespersons promoting the achievements of their government; they have a hand in establishing the government's fiscal framework; they represent Canada abroad; they establish the proper mandate of individual ministers and decide all machinery of government issues, and they are the final arbiter in interdepartmental conflicts. The prime minister is the only politician with a national constituency, and unlike members of Parliament and even Cabinet ministers, he does not need to search out publicity or national media attention, since attention is invariably focused on his office and his residence, 24 Sussex. In short, the prime minister is head of government with limited checks on his power inside government or in Parliament. He is not, however, head of state, a role still played by the governor-general as representative of the monarch. This is just as well, since that role is now largely ceremonial.

Each of the above levers of power taken separately is a powerful instrument of public policy and public administration in its own right, but when you add them all up and place them in the hands of one individual, they constitute a veritable juggernaut of power. Other than going down to defeat in a general election, it can only be stopped, or slowed, by the force of public opinion and by a Cabinet or caucus revolt. Even then, public opinion may not be much of a force if the prime minister has already decided not to run again in the next general election. One only has to think back to Trudeau or Mulroney's final years in office to appreciate this. History also tells us that caucus or Cabinet revolts, or even threats of revolts, are extremely rare in Ottawa.

Yet notwithstanding the fact that all these key instruments and so much political power are concentrated in the hands of one individual, one of the main preoccupations of the most senior officials in government is to protect the prime minister. I was reminded of an old political saying on more than one occasion in my interviews with politicians and their advisers: 'If the head goes, the rest of the government is sure to follow.' Partisan political advisers and Cabinet ministers know that, once exposed, any prime ministerial weaknesses, real or imagined, will serve to stimulate the opposition and the media and make it that more difficult to govern. Accordingly, it is important that the prime minister be protected, but also that his or her hand on the Cabinet and the government machinery not be weakened. Some of the officials on the lookout to protect the prime minister are politically partisan, and one can easily appreciate why they would want to protect him. But others are not partisan and they also regard it as their duty to protect the head of government. This is true no matter which political party is in power. Permanent officials in central agencies explain this by pointing out that, though they are not politically partisan, they need to be politically sensitive.

There are plenty of subtle and not so subtle hints suggesting that the prime minister towers above his Cabinet colleagues. At the Cabinet table, the prime minister sits at the middle and decides which ministers sit where. The back of his chair is higher than all the others. Whatever may be the case in theory, everyone knows that in practice the secretary of the Cabinet reports directly to him and not to Cabinet and indeed that it is the prime minister alone and not Cabinet who appoints or dismisses the secretary to the Cabinet. His own personal or political office is well staffed and is headed by a deputy-minister-level official. Some of his senior staff members are allowed to attend Cabinet and committee meetings. Ministers, meanwhile, have, relatively speaking, a modest budget for their own offices. These are headed by junior level officials who are never invited to attend Cabinet meetings.

The prime minister also enjoys a number of special perks not available to his Cabinet colleagues. He is the only government member to occupy an official residence, which is not the case either in Britain or in the United States. If the prime minister wants to contact anyone in Canada, or for that matter in the world, he has at his disposal a highly efficient switchboard capable of tracking down virtually anyone. When Prime Minister Chrétien decided towards the end of a Formula 1 car race that he wanted to talk with Jacques Villeneuve, the PM's switchboard was able to track Villeneuve down in Japan within minutes. No other minister could command this kind of response.

Canadian prime ministers have, since Trudeau, made themselves into television personalities. But the same is not true for Cabinet ministers. A Gallup poll in 1988 revealed that only 31 per cent of respondents could name a *single* Cabinet minister four years after the Mulroney government had come to power. In addition, only 5 per cent of the respondents could identify Don Mazankowski, deputy prime minister and one of the most, if not the most, powerful member of Mulroney's Cabinet.[3]

In Canada, at least since Trudeau, prime ministers rule through good times and bad, with never a hint of serious Cabinet or caucus revolt. British prime ministers can be dumped by their parties even when in office – as Margaret Thatcher can attest – but not, it seems, Canadian prime ministers. Former prime ministers Pierre Trudeau and Brian Mulroney both became extremely unpopular in their latter years in power, all the while without a revolt from either Cabinet or caucus. In both instances, they stayed to the end of their traditional four-year mandate (both Trudeau and Mulroney stayed even beyond their four-year mandates) and their parties went on to suffer humiliating defeats in the next election.

Ministers and members of Parliament can read public opinion polls as well or probably better than anyone else. So why the unwillingness to expel the leader when the party is in deep political hot water? I put the question to a former Trudeau Cabinet minister. He explained:

> It's like you are a deer, frozen there, watching the oncoming lights of a car in the middle of the night. You know that you are going to get hit, but you do nothing. For one thing, the leader is not chosen by Cabinet or caucus. He is chosen by the party. So even though you are in the Cabinet, you are only one voice among many and your opinion is no more legitimate than perhaps a poll captain from Prince Edward Island. In any event, the only way a Cabinet minister would ever get involved in a revolt would be if he had a strong indication that he was being dropped from Cabinet or that he was certain that the revolt would be successful, and success is never a certainty in politics. There is also never any guarantee that a new leader could do better. Turner [i.e., former Liberal leader and for a brief period of time prime minister] made that obvious in 1984.[4]

One could add that Kim Campbell did the same for the Progressive Conservative Party in 1993. I put the same question to a former Mulroney Cabinet minister. His response was brief and to the point, 'It was not for us to decide when the prime minister should leave. It was his decision, pure and simple.'[5]

The Canadian prime minister's power extends beyond the federal government. He deals regularly with provincial premiers and territorial leaders. Premiers are first ministers too, a status they jealously guard, and for good reason. The status enables them to deal directly with the prime minister. Indeed, all first ministers, including those from the smaller provinces, believe that they should have full access to the prime minister without having to go through a federal government minister. They know from first-hand experience that the head of government has the power to make things happen and to give a green light to requests and proposals without consulting anyone, if necessary, while a simple Cabinet minister cannot, no matter how solid his standing in government.

In the summer of 1997, Frank McKenna, former premier of New Brunswick, organized a one-on-one meeting with the prime minister. He put two proposals to Chrétien during a golf game: that the federal government support a conference on the economic future of Atlantic Canada and that it cost share a new highways agreement to continue with the construction of a four-lane Trans Canada highway. The prime minister agreed and instructed his officials to make it happen. One government agency provided some funding to support the conference, and several federal ministers, including Prime Minister Chrétien, attended it. Officials, meanwhile, were instructed to prepare a Treasury Board submission to secure the necessary funding for the highways construction agreement. Within a few weeks, everything had been sorted out and an announcement was made on both an Atlantic Vision conference and a new Canada/Highways agreement. The prime minister did not ask Privy Council and Treasury Board Secretariat officials to prepare a proposal and then to submit it for consideration in the government's decision-making process. His instructions were clear – make these two initiatives happen. This is not to suggest that these two examples represent daily occurrences in Ottawa or that all federal-provincial projects enjoy the same status. But they are revealing in that they are the norm when the prime minister decides to get involved.

In the final planning stages of the post-TAGS initiative for unemployed fishery workers, Premier Brian Tobin expressed his deep disappointment over the slow progress and the proposed level of funding. He called the Cabinet 'derelict' and said that the relevant federal minister, Pierre Pettigrew, was not up to the task. He then appealed to Chrétien to get directly involved.[6] A few days later, the *Globe and Mail* reported that the 'Prime Minister's Office concluded in the final analyses that there was a case to be made that recipients under [TAGS] had previously been promised five years of support to wrap up the program a year early because it was exceeding its $1.9 billion budget. Therefore, the money for the East Coast was bumped up.'[7] In the end, the matter was resolved in a series of bilateral discussions between Tobin and Chrétien, with the federal Cabinet essentially standing on the sideline. As the media reported, Chrétien and his office took full control of the final negotiations even though a seven-member ad hoc committee of Cabinet had been established to review post-TAGS measures and that the Finance minister, Paul Martin, had indicated that only a modest amount of funds (i.e., $150 million) would be made available.

The prime minister's direct involvement in files is not limited to premiers from Atlantic Canada or to premiers from the same political party. In early 1997, the prime minister came back from a visit to British Columbia and instructed the Treasury Board to prepare the necessary documents to spend $50 million to support a variety of projects. He had agreed to this funding at a private meeting with Premier Glen Clark. It was made clear to those preparing the documents that the commitment had been made and that the matter was not for consideration. They were simply told to make it happen. One official who worked on the submission reports said, 'We had been told time and again by central agencies "don't come calling for new money for projects. There is simply no new money." Then all of a sudden we get word that we have to prepare a Treasury Board submission to spend new money in British Columbia.'[8] It will also be recalled that Mulroney, after a late night telephone conversation with Premier Grant Devine, agreed to a $1 billion rescue package for Prairie farmers in 1987. Moreover, it was widely known in Ottawa that Mulroney and John Crosbie were the only ministers in favour of additional federal government investment in the Hibernia project after Gulf decided to walk away from the project.[9]

Contact between first ministers will inevitably draw the prime minister and his advisers into specific files and in government departments in search of information and perhaps resolution of an issue in one way or another. When that happens, ministers and their departments can lose some of their power to make decisions to the prime minister and his advisers.

Premiers also often insist that many of their letters to the federal government be addressed to the prime minister rather than to the relevant federal Cabinet minister. In turn, tradition requires that letters from premiers to the prime minister should be answered by the prime minister, even though the reply may well have been prepared in a line department. Thus, regional or provincial issues, not just national ones, are bought to the attention of the prime minister. This, too, can strengthen the hand of the prime minister and his or her advisers, if they decide to get involved in resolving an issue.

Other countries with both a parliamentary and a federal system have institutional constraints on the power of the prime minister that do not exist in Canada. Like Canada, Australia has a lower house in Parliament where party, discipline is strong and where there is little tolerance for rebels in any party, and in particular in the party in power. Like Canada, Australia is a federal state. But unlike Canada, Australia has a Senate, elected by proportional representation. Since 1980, no government has held a majority in the Senate and its support often has to be negotiated. Patrick Weller explains that in the Australian Senate, 'The balance of power is held by a mélange of minor parties and independents. Since the Senate has in effect equal powers to stop supply and force an election, its support for legislation can never be taken for granted. The government program must be negotiated with minor parties.'[10]

In Britain, and to some extent Australia, political parties tend to debate and stake out policy positions. Election manifestos matter not just during the election campaign but also during the time the party holds power. Though they have lost some of their appeal and influence, political manifestos in Britain remain an important part of the country's political culture and process. *The Economist* reports that the Conservative Party was still able to sell 70,000 copies of their manifesto in 1992 and that political manifestos represent 'the terms of a truce between the factions that are inevitably present in any party.'[11] Peter Aucoin writes that 'in Great Britain, Australia and New Zealand, there are sharper ideological distinctions between the two major parties than in Canada, reflecting a relatively greater capacity to integrate major interest within parties, and there are only two major parties in each of these three systems.'[12]

In Canada, however, federal political parties are not much more than partisan political machines providing the fund-raising capacity and poll workers needed to fight an election campaign. They are hardly effective vehicles for generating public policy debates, for staking out policy positions, or for providing a capacity to ensure their own competence once in office. Robert A. Young argues that 'the Pulp and Paper Association has more capacity to do strategic analytical work than the Liberal and [Progressive] Conservative parties combined.'[13] Sharon Sutherland points to the omnipresent regional factor in Canadian politics as an important reason why national political parties are not good vehicles to debate and formulate policy positions. She writes, 'We do not have party government in the national institutions because of the lack of capacity of parties to reconcile inside themselves regional interests from across the whole country.'[14] Regional cleavages in Canada, as is well known, dominate the national public policy agenda, and national political parties shy away from attacking regional issues head on for fear that it would split the party along regional lines and hurt its chances at election time. The thinking goes, at least in the parties that have held power in Ottawa, that the issue is so sensitive and so politically explosive that it is better left in the hands of party leaders and a handful of advisers. In the two main political parties that have ever held power in Ottawa, the terms of the truce between the various factions are established by the party leader and some of his most trusted advisers.

Some observers may argue that the Liberal 'Red Book' in the 1993 election campaign was an election manifesto in the British political tradition. Though, to be sure, the Red Book was an uncommon phenomenon in Canadian politics, it still does not qualify fully as a national political manifesto. For one thing, the ideas in the Red Book were not born out of the party's rank and file, as happens in Britain. Indeed, there are now several people who claim authorship of the Red Book, but none, either directly or indirectly, are rank and file party members.[15] In brief, the Red Book did not take root in a conference of party members from across the country drawn together to hammer out a political manifesto or an election platform. In the preface to the Red Book, Jean Chrétien writes that before the book was written he convened the Aylmer Conference, which brought together experts from Canada, the United States, Europe, and Japan. He also makes reference to the 1992 National Liberal Party Convention and to the work of the platform committee, cochaired by Paul Martin and Chaviva Hosek.[16] A former political assistant to Chrétien, however, confirmed Paul Martin's view that the Red Book was put together by a 'handful of people in the summer of 1993.'[17]

The purpose of the Red Book was to draw attention away from the negative press coverage over Chrétien's alleged inability to articulate a vision for the country, to present new ideas, and to dispel the charge often heard in the early 1990s that he was yesterday's man.[18] Before the Kim Campbell debacle in the middle of the election campaign, public opinion surveys reported that Chrétien was found lacking on several fronts and that he was being painted in the media as 'idea-less Jean Chrétien.' He and his advisers set out to deal head on with this charge and concluded the Red Book to be the solution. It would draw attention to a series of campaign commitments, and thereby suggest that Chrétien could indeed generate new ideas.[19]

Quite apart from its true purpose, the Red Book had more success before Chrétien came to office than after. Once the party was elected to power, the book lost at least some of its relevance. Finance Minister Paul Martin instructed his departmental officials time and again to ignore it. Martin is quoted as telling his senior Finance officials, 'Don't tell me what's in the Red Book ... I wrote the goddamn thing. And I know that a lot of it is crap ... the goddamn thing [was] thrown together quickly in the last three weeks of July. Things hadn't been properly thought through.'[20] In any event, the government reneged on a number of commitments – both large and small – including the pledge to renegotiate NAFTA, to introduce daycare, to replace the GST, to strengthen the Department of the Environment, and to cut spending on outside consultants by $620 million annually beginning in fiscal year 1995–6.[21]

The Liberal Party produced another Red Book for the 1997 election campaign, but it never gained the kind of visibility and media attention that the first one enjoyed. In any event, the 1997 Red Book was again written by a handful of advisers to the prime minister. The document came under media criticism during the 1997 election campaign for being too general and vague, but it did present a number of specific commitments in a variety of policy fields. After the election, it disappeared from the public policy agenda and precious little reference has been made since in Parliament to its contents or even to its existence.

PMO officials, however, report that they refer to it when reviewing overall government strategy and when considering new initiatives. Still, it would not be an exaggeration to write that the Red Book experience in Canadian politics appears to have been a one-election phenomenon. Canadian members of Parliament running for the party in power have little choice but to adopt the policies of the prime minister as prepared by a handful of his most trusted advisers rather than the policies of the party, to which all members were able to contribute. Thus far, that has been the Canadian way. Harold D. Clarke and his colleagues write that in Canada candidates at general elections have no choice but to 'organize around leaders rather than political principles and ideologies and expect the leader to work out the multitude of compromises required for the party to enjoy electoral success.'[22]

The national electronic media, given the need for the twenty-second video clip and sound bite, will also focus on party leaders at election time rather than on selected party candidates, even those enjoying a high profile in their regions. Journalists buy seats on the chartered aircraft of party leaders and follow them everywhere. In Canada, at least, the media and, by extension, the public, will focus on the clash of party leaders. For one thing, there are the leaders' debates on national television, in both English and French. How well a leader does in the debates can have an important impact, or at least be perceived to have an important impact, on the election campaign, if not the election itself.[23] It is now widely accepted in the literature that 'debates are more about accidents and mistakes than about enlightenment on the capabilities of candidates to govern.'[24] When Mulroney told Turner, 'You had an option, Sir,' referring to Turner's decision to proceed with Trudeau's patronage appointments in the 1984 campaign, or conversely, when Turner told Mulroney that he was standing up for Canada in debating the Free Trade Agreement in the 1988 campaign, the exchanges left party handlers scrambling to minimize political damage. A widely read study of the 1988 election campaign suggests that 'had the debates not happened, there is every indication that the Conservatives would have coasted home.'[25] Chrétien handlers, on the other hand, were relieved after both the 1993 and 1997 debates that he did not fare as badly as some had feared he would.

The election campaign and the leaders' debates have become more of a gladiatorial contest, a clash of personalities, than in-depth policy debates. Similarly, more than anything else, the twenty-second clip on the nightly news defines how well the leader and his party are doing in the campaign. A *faux pas* can take on a life of its own in the media and have a profound impact on the campaign. Prime Minister Kim Campbell's statement that there was little hope that the unemployment rate would drop below 10 per cent before the turn of the century sounded the starting gun of the 1993 campaign, and dogged her party's campaign to the end. Similarly, it was she alone, not other party candidates, who was left to explain and later apologize for her party's television campaign highlighting Jean Chrétien's partial facial paralysis. The incident was replayed on the evening news for several nights during the election, seriously damaging Campbell's campaign.

Increasingly, political leaders appear to be the only substantial candidates in the election race. In the past, Canada had powerful Cabinet ministers with deep roots in the party or strong regional identification and support. One can think of Jimmy Gardiner, Chubby Power, Jack Pickersgill, Ernest Lapointe, Louis St Laurent, Don Jamieson, and Allan MacEachen. We no longer seem to have powerful regional or party figures (Lloyd Axworthy aside) who can carry candidates to victory on their coattails or speak to the prime minister from an independent power base in the party. In Britain and Australia, on the other hand, some Cabinet ministers have deep roots and solid support among rank and file party members, and prime ministers know that they have to give proper weight to their views in Cabinet.

Winning candidates on the government side know full well that their party leader's performance in the election campaign explains in large measure why they themselves were elected. The objective of national political parties at election time is more to sell their leaders to the Canadian electorate than it is to sell their ideas or their policies. Leading students of election campaigns in Canada write that 'Canadian elections, in common with elections in other Westminster-style systems, as well as with presidential elections in the United States, inevitably turn on the question of who – which individual – shall form the government.'[26] They add, for example, that the Liberal surge during the 1988 election campaign 'reflected [then Liberal leader] John Turner's rehabilitation.'[27] A senior PMO official argues that national 'trends,' and to some extent regional ones as well, decide who 'wins a riding and who does not.' The local candidate, he added, 'is not much a factor anymore and he should not feel too badly if he loses.'[28] It should come as no surprise then that if the leader is able to secure a majority mandate it is assumed that the party is in his debt, and not the other way around.

Primus in Cabinet

Prime ministers bring their own style to managing their Cabinets and ministers. Trudeau, for example, was much more tolerant of meanderings and long-winded interventions from his ministers at Cabinet meetings than Chrétien, but unlike Chrétien, he was not particularly adroit at handling one-on-one meetings with his ministers. A student of comparative politics writing in the mid-1980s reported that 'Canadian Prime Ministers, and particularly Trudeau, were usually powerful but patient.'[29] Chrétien, by all accounts, is less patient in Cabinet than Trudeau was, but he is certainly no less powerful. Mulroney made much more use of humour in Cabinet meetings to make his points than Trudeau did, but both Trudeau and Mulroney relied on extensive Cabinet committee systems to manage the flow of Cabinet papers. Mulroney had a particularly large Cabinet, but he had it operate in an asymmetrical manner by concentrating more power in the priorities and planning and the operations committees.[30] Mulroney also spent more time than Chrétien or Trudeau either cajoling or, if necessary, browbeating his ministers to come to his point of view to establish Cabinet consensus. Clark, meanwhile, relied on a formal inner Cabinet and other ministers in managing his Cabinet and ministers.

To be sure, style and personalities are important in understanding how Cabinet government works, and one is constantly reminded of this by politicians, partisan political advisers, and permanent officials in the interviews. But there are things that transcend both style and personalities when it comes to understand the workings of cabinet government in a parliamentary system. Put differently, style and personalities do differ, but there are things that remain constant. First, the prime minister has access to virtually all the necessary levers in Cabinet to ensure that he or she is the 'boss' in Cabinet, and that if he so wishes – and prime ministers usually do – he can dominate Cabinet deliberations and its decision making. Second, prime ministers are convinced that they need to manage their Cabinet, to have a firm hand in shaping its discussions and decisions for their government to function properly.

The first sign that the prime minister has the upper hand is now evident even before they and their party assume power. Transition planning, a relatively new phenomenon in Canada, has become a very important event designed to prepare a new government to assume power. A former associate clerk of the Privy Council writes that 'the first modern effort at transition planning in the public service ... occurred for the June 1968 general election.'[31] He adds that transition planning has grown to become an elaborate planning process and now includes 'the entire deputy minister community.'[32] It is the Privy Council Office (PCO), however, that leads the process and it is clear that the 'transition services [is for] the incoming prime minister.'[33] Indeed, the focal point throughout the PCO transition planning process is on party leaders or would-be prime ministers. In any event, it would be difficult for it to be otherwise, since in the crucial days between the election victory and formally taking power, the only known member of the incoming Cabinet is the prime minister. For other potential Cabinet ministers, it is a 'moment of high anxiety,' waiting to see if they will actually be invited to sit in Cabinet, and if so, in what portfolio.[34]

The central purpose of transition planning is to equip the incoming prime minister to have his hand on the levers of power in the government's first few weeks in office. It is now widely recognized that these early weeks can be critical because they set the tone for how the new government will govern.[35] It is also the period when the prime minister, as recent history shows, will make important decisions on the machinery of government and decide which major policy issues his government will want to tackle during its mandate.

Once the prime minister is in office, it quickly becomes clear that his position in Cabinet gives him far more resources than other ministers, including an ability to shape most of its activities and many of its decisions, at least the ones that matter directly to him or in which he has a strong interest. The prime minister hires and fires Cabinet ministers, sets the agenda, and sums up its deliberations and decisions. In any event, ministers do not usually consider themselves to be guardians of any political theory, including the *primus inter pares* theory. Above all, they are politicians, they are deal makers, and they know full well that they stand a much better chance of striking deals if they are in Cabinet, and if they can count on the support of the prime minister at crucial moments. Ministers are also concerned about their own status in Cabinet, in caucus, and in their own ridings. They know that loyalty to the leader, particularly if he has been able to secure a majority mandate, is much valued in the party. In any event, whatever else may be said about Cabinet deliberations, one thing is clear – most ministers would much rather be on the prime minister's side than against him in Cabinet.

The prime minister appoints Cabinet ministers and parliamentary secretaries, and tradition and, more importantly, political realities require that they are loyal to him and in particular to government policy. Should a minister or a parliamentary secretary disagree with a government policy, he or she has two choices – keep quiet and bear it or resign from the post. History suggests that the overwhelming majority much prefer the first option.

It is true that Canada's prime ministers are not completely free to pick and choose ministers. For one thing, ministers are drawn from the legislative branch and so must come from the talent pool on the government side of the House of Commons, or as a last resort the Senate. In addition, no Canadian prime minister would appoint a Cabinet that lacked a proper regional, linguistic, and gender balance. Some have even turned to the Senate to ensure regional balance if the party failed to win a Commons seat in a province or region.[36]

But prime ministers also never lose sight of the need for strong support in Cabinet. Competence and regional balance are, of course, important, but no less important is the need for the prime minister to make Cabinet and the government his. And to do this, he needs a cadre of loyal soldiers in Cabinet. All Canadian prime ministers are certain to appoint well-known loyal supporters to their Cabinet (Trudeau appointed Roméo LeBlanc, Marc Lalonde, Allan MacEachen, and Lloyd Axworthy; Mulroney had Elmer McKay, Bob Coates, and George Hees; and Chrétien brought in David Dingwall, Ron Irwin, Sergio Marchi, and so on). In Canada at least, who supported whom in the party's leadership race will have an important bearing on who ultimately makes it to Cabinet. The strongest rivals to the prime minister will traditionally make it, but their key caucus supporters are not likely to be as fortunate.[37] They will be bypassed for those who supported the prime minister.

How does one become a Cabinet minister? The first step is to become a member of Parliament with the political party asked by the governor general to form the government. The process begins with a run at the party nomination and culminates with several weeks of intense political campaigning, knocking on doors, speaking to local service clubs, and attending all party meetings. Chances are that an individual who successfully navigates his party's nomination process and then goes on to win the riding for his party will be highly motivated and ambitious. Chances are also that he or she will want a seat at the Cabinet table. There are some members of Parliament who are quite happy not to be in the Cabinet. But they are very much in the minority. One minister suggested that 'at least 90 per cent of the government caucus, if not more, would welcome an opportunity to sit in Cabinet. For the great majority of us, that is why we run for Parliament.'[38]

For those 90 per cent or more, it helps to be from a province with limited representation on the government side (it is unlikely, for example, that Fred Mifflin would have been in the 1997 Chrétien Cabinet if he had been a member of Parliament from Ontario, where the Liberals won all but one seat in the election. He was from Newfoundland and Labrador). It also helps to be noticed. Those with a strong media profile stand a better chance of making it to Cabinet than an unknown backbencher. But one has to be careful in seeking media attention. No prime minister likes to have his Cabinet appointments appear in the press before he makes his choice public. Moreover, as Gerald Kaufman, former British minister, writes, 'Voting against the Government on a confidence motion or personally insulting the Prime Minister is not recommended.'[39] Unless one represents a riding from a province where few government MPs are elected, the best chance for an MP to make it to Cabinet is to establish a track record of loyalty to the prime minister and to have gained the confidence not only of the prime minister himself but also of his close advisers.

The prime minister's power of appointment also extends to the chairs and membership of Cabinet committees. These appointments, especially to the chairs, are significant signals as to who is in the prime minister's favour and who is not.

The prime minister is completely free to decide on the kind of committee structure he needs to support the work of his Cabinet. He can, as we saw in chapter 2, overhaul the Cabinet committee structure at any moment without consulting any of his ministers and add new committees or abolish existing ones at the stroke of a pen. The prime minister also decides not only which issues will come forward to Cabinet but when. In addition, the Cabinet does not take votes, which provides the prime minister considerable latitude in defining the consensus.

To have in your own hands the ability to define the Cabinet agenda and to decide if the time is right to discuss a given issue or a proposal in Cabinet is to have an extremely powerful instrument of public policy. The prime minister, as we will see later, is able to draw on senior staff at the centre of government to keep him informed of developments in departments, to let him know what ministers and their departments are thinking, and to help him decide when a given issue should come before Cabinet.

Pierre Trudeau, as is well known, sought to introduce a much more rational approach to Cabinet deliberations and to see to it that all sides of an issue be fully aired before Cabinet made a decision. He established an elaborate Cabinet committee structure to ensure that this would occur. He wanted, he said, to wrestle policy influence away from departments and to give Cabinet the ability to make policy based on competing advice. Indeed, Trudeau decided to overhaul the Cabinet process precisely to break the stranglehold ministers and long-serving deputy ministers had on departments. He felt that major policy decisions and all administrative issues had become the preserve of line departments and that the centre was left ill-equipped to challenge them. The solution – strengthen the centre considerably. Richard French explains, 'The Prime Minister's often expressed conviction [is] that Cabinet is less easily captured by the bureaucracy than are ministers operating independently.'[40] Peter Aucoin writes that Trudeau launched a major assault on the centre of government to correct 'the abuses and excesses of individual ministerial autonomy [which] had to be replaced by a rigorous system of checks and balances within the Cabinet as a collective executive.' He adds, 'The influence of the bureaucracy had to be countered to ensure that the organizational interests of departments and agencies did not take precedence over required policy innovation and policy coherence.'[41] To sum up, Trudeau wanted policy making to be placed firmly in the hands of Cabinet and removed from those of a few powerful ministers and mandarins running government departments. This, in turn, explains why he decided to strengthen the centre of government by enlarging his own office, expanding the Privy Council Office and establishing new Cabinet committees, effectively giving them the authority to make decisions.

But he saw limits to this approach, notably when he felt that there was a chance the discussions would go in the wrong direction. He explained, 'If I know that I am going to have a confrontation in Cabinet, if a minister is recommending something and I think it's dead wrong, I won't let him put the thing to Cabinet. I'll see him in my office, I'll set up an interdepartmental committee, I'll meet him privately, I'll say, "Look, we're on a collision course, this can't possibly be right." The whole role of the PCO, and the PMO to a certain degree, is to inform me of the genesis of the discussion, how it's going. And if I think it's going in a way that I approve, fine, I'm happy to let the consensus develop. If I think it's not going in the right direction, I ask them to arm me with the arguments and facts and figures.'[42] Ministers, meanwhile, are expected to remain loyal to the Cabinet and accept decisions that go against their wishes after Cabinet has reconciled conflicting positions and the prime minister has defined a consensus. The same, however, is not true for the prime minister, who can easily manipulate the Cabinet agenda to get his way.

Some of the respondents revealed that Chrétien has on occasion been even more direct than Trudeau when seeing proposals that he does not like. One career public servant who worked in the PCO under both prime ministers reports that Chrétien could, before the discussions went too far, simply say to a minister in private or even in front of colleagues, 'I know what you are going to recommend. The answer is no. Forget it.' Mulroney, in contrast, would, from time to time and depending on the minister, take the time to talk a minister out of a proposal or an idea that he did not like. But the consultations also reveal that Mulroney could be very direct in telling a minister to abandon an idea. In addition, Mulroney would rely on his deputy prime minister, much more than Chrétien, to manage 'a stupid idea out of the system.'[43]

The prime minster has yet another advantage in securing the upper hand in managing his Cabinet. In chairing Cabinet or a Cabinet committee, the prime minister has full access to unshared knowledge. For each item coming before Cabinet, the PCO will hand a memorandum to the prime minister outlining the major issues, the positions of some of his ministers, and almost always a recommended position. No other minister can come to the Cabinet table with this knowledge, a view of the total picture, knowing what key ministers are going to argue. Such knowledge, if nothing else, enables the prime minister, if he so wishes, to play one Cabinet minister against another, enabling him to establish the Cabinet consensus according to his own thinking. But here again the prime minister has to be careful in choosing the issues he means to influence. The prime minister's summary and decision or his definition of the Cabinet consensus cannot always go blatantly against the sense of the meeting if he is to retain the confidence of his ministers.

Still, interviews reveal that, at least since Trudeau, prime ministers do not hesitate to make use of their power to define Cabinet consensus to tilt decisions in their favour. One senior PCO official explained, 'When the prime minister sees that 75 per cent of his colleagues are leaning in his direction, there is no problem, and when he sees that 50 per cent are leaning in his direction, there is still no problem. On very rare occasions, when he sees that he is clearly in the minority with, say, only 25 per cent of ministers leaning in his direction, he will often say to Cabinet, "I have to reflect on this and I will get back to you shortly on it." A few days later, he may well direct PCO, through the clerk, to issue a record of decision in his favour or simply hold the matter and have it put on the Cabinet agenda a few months down the road when he thinks that more ministers will speak out in support. My experience with prime ministers is that when they don't have their way the issue is not all that important to them.'[44] Another senior PCO official who attended many Cabinet meetings as a notetaker reports that 'on more than one occasion, I would take the head count, jotting down the names of the ministers I felt were on the yes side and those on the no side. The consensus was clearly on one side, but I would hear the prime minister draw the consensus on the other.'[45]

A minister in the 1993–7 Chrétien government confirms that it is very rare that the prime minister is openly challenged in Cabinet. He reports that 'I can only think of three occasions between 1993 and 1997 when the prime minister was openly challenged in Cabinet, and this is not to suggest for a moment that in the end he did not get his way. If my memory is correct, I believe that the prime minister got his way on two of the three occasions. On the third one, I think that the issue simply died, but I am not sure.'[46] A senior PMO staff member who attends Cabinet meetings remembers things differently. He reports that he does not recall the prime minister being seriously challenged even once in Cabinet in Chrétien's first mandate. He adds, 'That is the problem. Nobody wants to challenge him. In fact, a few of us in PMO do challenge his ideas from time to time, but not so in Cabinet.' He went on to report that 'on a few occasions ministers have come to me to say that the prime minister has it wrong on this or that issue. I say to them, you are a minister, tell him. A few days later, I will raise the matter with the minister to see if he has challenged the prime minister. Invariably, he will say no and that in the end the matter was not all that important.'[47]

The prime minister also has full access to other sources of advice and information that are not open to ministers. These are in the areas of *policy*, *machinery of government*, and *political issues*. On policy, the prime minister can draw on both the Prime Minister's Office, the PCO, and, if he so desires, on individual ministers and their departments. No other minister has this access. On the machinery of government, it is important to stress that the prime minister *alone* has access to the expertise which resides in the PCO. For reasons explained in the next chapter, machinery of government staff operate in relative secrecy even at the centre of government. On political issues, the prime minister has access to full Cabinet caucus and to his own office, which, comparatively speaking, is not only large but also staffed by the most senior partisan assistants in Ottawa.

The Constraints

The prime minister alone thus has access to virtually every lever of power in the federal government, and when he puts his mind to it he can get his way on almost any issue. But there are some constraints which inhibit his always getting his own way.

The first is time. Indeed, prime ministerial time is the rarest of commodities in Ottawa. The prime minister leads an incredibly harassed life, and securing time with the 'boss' is not easy. The flip side to having most key channels of public policy in Canada coming to him is that he can hardly find the time to give each the proper attention and focus it deserves. Unless a prime minister picks policy areas and issues he wants to concentrate on to influence their direction, he may be rendered ineffective by trying to shape too many activities and decisions in too many areas.

There are always telephone calls to return, correspondence to deal with, government and patronage appointments to make, documents to read, meetings to attend, party functions to support, and ministers and members of Parliament to meet. The prime minister will also want to be available to meet foreign heads of government, provincial premiers, and members of the business community. Parliament, Cabinet, and caucus meetings eat into his agenda. The prime minister must also make time available for senior staff in his own office. When in Ottawa, he meets four, and on occasions, five times a week first thing in the morning with his principal secretary and the clerk of the Privy Council Office. Trudeau met with his two senior officials every morning, Monday to Friday, when he was in Ottawa. Mulroney met with them on average two times a week, while Chrétien, like Trudeau, tries to meet with them five times a week when in Ottawa. However, Mulroney made full use of the telephone and the consultations reveal that 'he could be on the phone up to twelve times a day with Tellier [clerk of the Privy Council from 1985 to 1992].'[48] Senior policy advisers and the head of appointments also need to see the prime minister from time to time if they are to do their jobs well. Making patronage appointments often requires consultations with the relevant ministers and other senior party members, including provincial premiers from the same party. The prime minister needs to be briefed on potential appointments, and some of the briefings are better done face to face. Meanwhile, policy advisers need access to the prime minister to gain an understanding of his views and to bounce ideas around to make sure that they can successfully pursue his agenda.

The prime minister is also a member of Parliament and needs to devote time to his constituency, to maintain personal contact with constituents, and to meet with riding association and local opinion leaders. As Marc Lalonde writes, 'The prime minister, like all other MPs, represents a particular electoral riding. The prime minister's responsibility to his constituents is the same as that for any other member of Parliament. Residents of his constituency expect the prime minister to provide them with the same services as are provided by all other MPs.'[49] One president of a federal crown corporation reports that he was 'startled one day to have Prime Minister Chrétien on the phone inquiring about a relatively minor issue involving his riding.'[50]

Prime ministers read or should read about 300-plus pages of briefing material and correspondence every week (it is reported that Trudeau, perhaps because he had such an elaborate Cabinet committee structure, because a great deal of paper was generated for his decision-making process, and because more public funds were available, had about 1,000 pages to read every week).[51] Unless a prime minister reads at least some of the more important briefing documents and correspondence, he will go into meetings unprepared and perhaps not as able to influence the outcome of the discussions as he would like. The 300 pages of material, Cabinet documents, correspondence, press clippings, and briefing notes cover any number of policy issues from international security matters to the government's fiscal health. Some will require a decision from him, others are for information only. But they should all be attended to because a careful prescreening will have already taken place. Officials in his own office and in the PCO are all too aware of the pressure on the prime minister's time and will be careful to weed out less urgent material.

Management literature suggests that current wisdom holds that a manager's proper span of control should have anywhere between three and six people reporting to him. Current wisdom, however, is being challenged by more modern management thinkers, notably the widely read Elliott Jacques. Jacques argues that 'you are likely to be able to get by with up to perhaps ten to twenty immediate subordinates at middle levels, and less at corporate levels.' He adds that one can increase the number of subordinates reporting to a manager 'where the manager has no scheduling or technical problems, does not have to go to any meetings, and can spend his/her time overseeing subordinates.'[52] In line with this argument, the prime minister should be decreasing the number of subordinates reporting directly to him or under his span of control. One can hardly argue that the prime minister does not have to go to meetings or that he can spend most of his time overseeing subordinates like the head of a standardized production line or a typing pool.

The prime minister has twenty-four cabinet ministers and six junior ministers responsible for a variety of policy fields and sponsoring a great diversity of activities ranging from macroeconomic planning (Finance) to relations with foreign countries and development projects for remote aboriginal communities. All of these ministers can ask for a private meeting. Certainly, senior ministers, including the ministers of Finance and External Affairs and the senior political ministers from Ontario and Quebec, can probably see the prime minister on relatively short notice. His chief of staff, senior PMO advisers, and the secretary of the Cabinet also report directly to him. He appoints all deputy ministers and heads of crown corporations, and he will want to be kept informed on how well they are performing. In addition, he appoints all parliamentary secretaries, and here too he will want to be kept abreast of their performance. This is not to suggest that all these individuals report directly to him. But all can claim a link to him and his office and many of them can also make a claim on his agenda.

A great deal of planning goes into putting together the prime minister's agenda. Clearly, there are many more demands on his time than he can possibly accommodate, and his staff will juggle several possibilities for most time slots available. For example, Cabinet and caucus meetings are always blocked off when he is in Ottawa and time is also made available to ensure that he meets a cross-section of people and that he can focus on his priorities.

About twenty-five years ago, Prime Minister Pierre Trudeau's agenda was described as follows:

In an average month, he works about 250 hours. Roughly 90 of them, or 36 percent of his working time, are spent on government business, including Cabinet and its committees, the House of Commons, the governor general and other government officials, foreign visitors and ambassadors, outside groups, and foreign travel. Political activities involving ministers, MPs, senators, or Liberal Party officials account for 50 hours, or

20 percent of his time. He spends 12.5 hours, or 5 percent, in press conferences or other forms of contact with the news media; 30 hours, or 12 percent, with staff in the PMO and PCO; and 67.2 hours, or 27 percent of his time, on paperwork, correspondence, and telephone calls. On a typical day, his activities as prime minister have spanned 11 hours.[53]

I was shown a typical weekly agenda prepared for Prime Minister Chrétien in the fall of 1997. There was not an empty spot anywhere on it. Chrétien's agenda is always subject to last-minute changes to accommodate new political developments that he must attend to. The agenda, however, hardly tells the full story. It does not include more important matters like quick exchanges with key staff members, a private word with a senior minister in between meetings, and more crucially, many important telephone calls.[54] If nothing else, it is clear that the prime minister needs to be able to manage his time very well to influence more than a handful of public policy issues of direct interest to him simply because he cannot influence everything at once.

I put questions to some former staff members of both Prime Minister Chrétien and former Prime Minister Mulroney to see how more recent prime ministerial workloads compare with those of some twenty-five years ago. If anything, I was told, the workload is greater still. More time is now spent on provincial government matters, on trade issues, and with heads of foreign governments than was the case twenty-five years ago. There are now, for example, more international summits (G7, la francophonie, Commonwealth, APEC) requiring the prime minister's direct involvement. Prime Minister Chrétien spent nearly two of his first fourteen months in office outside Canada attending international conferences and promoting trade in Asia, Europe, and Mexico.[55]

There are also constraints on the ability of the prime minister to manipulate the levers of power in managing his Cabinet. To be sure, he can always ask a minister to resign at any time – and without advance warning. But in Canada, prime ministers are loath to do this, and history also tells us that it is rarely done. There are also practical constraints to the prime minister's power to dismiss more than a handful of his ministers in a four-year mandate. The dismissal of even one minister often entails a Cabinet shuffle. This is never a pleasant task: cabinet shuffles are disruptive and the government can suffer, particularly if they occur too frequently.

Dismissing two, three, four, or several ministers on one occasion or over a period of a few months can indicate that the prime minister is losing control of his Cabinet, as was the case during the last years of the Diefenbaker government. The talent pool from some regions can also be severely limited (e.g., Chrétien and Western Canada and Atlantic Canada in his second mandate; Trudeau and Western Canada from 1972 onward; Clark and Quebec; and Mulroney and Northern Ontario in his second mandate). Dismissing a minister from a region which is underrepresented in the party can create new, more serious political problems for the prime minister as he tries to juggle his Cabinet to ensure regional balance.

There is also the risk that a dismissed minister will become a loose cannon, shooting at the government from the outside, but still having intimate inside knowledge. The prime minister has to weigh the advantages and the disadvantages of having a minister in his Cabinet prone to mistakes as opposed to a former minister on the outside acting as a thorn in the government's side.

Notwithstanding the above, the prime minister's power to fire ministers remains a 'potent psychological threat for one reason, uncertainty.'[56] Ministers, particularly in Canada, know full well that they sit in Cabinet only because one person wants them to be there – the prime minister. The prime minister may well be reluctant to swing the axe, but no one knows for certain if or when he will do it. One of the most powerful weapons in a prime minister's arsenal, according to Jim Coutts, a former principal secretary to Prime Minister Trudeau, is surprise.[57] The weapon comes in handy not just in the House of Commons and caucus, but also in Cabinet.

In any event, there are a variety of ways the prime minister can reprimand an offending or accident-prone minister without resorting to ask his resignation. He can take the minister out to the woodshed in full public view, as did Ronald Reagan to David Stockman after Stockman was cited in *Atlantic Monthly* as saying that Reagan's tax legislation was 'a Trojan horse, filled full of all kinds of budget busting measures and secondary agendas.'[58] Less drastic actions include dropping the minister from a key committee, not supporting him in a decision, or even not returning his phone calls promptly.

Caucus also requires time and attention. The prime minister attends weekly caucus meetings while Parliament sits and special caucus meetings when it does not. He also meets with the caucus chair for about half an hour, or longer, if necessary, on a weekly basis to plan caucus strategy and to get feedback on the views of individual caucus members. All prime ministers attach a great deal of importance to caucus support and will invest the necessary time to explain government policies and measures to secure that support. Traditionally, Canadian prime ministers have also insisted that their ministers attend caucus meetings to explain their departmental policies and to answer questions.

Caucus members report that, while at times they have some highly heated debates, caucus is not a very effective policy vehicle. Indeed, they report that they are rarely, if ever, in a position to launch a new initiative, and worse, that they are rarely effective in getting the government to change course. They also do not consider themselves to be an effective check on prime ministerial power.

In fact, present and former government caucus members I consulted told me that they would not want to use caucus to challenge the prime minister openly. Moreover, the interviews reveal that there is a widely held understanding that members should not attack the prime minister directly during caucus meetings. If there is venom or harsh criticism to be dished out, it is directed at the minister responsible for the policy, the program, or the proposed initiative, but never at the prime minister. The prime minister may well decide to come to the defence of the minister under attack, but he is never, or very rarely, the one put on trial at caucus meetings.

One respondent succinctly explained the reluctance to attack the prime minister in caucus: 'To be frank,' she said, 'some of us probably think that we would make excellent ministers, or failing that, judges or senators. We all know who makes these appointments, and why would we want to bite his hand when we can bite the hand of one of his ministers who may need to be replaced at some point or moved out of that department?'[59]

Government caucus members past and present also report that while prime ministers do attend caucus meetings, and while they are quite effective in explaining government policies, caucus nevertheless has limited influence on the government. 'We are not the Cabinet,' one pointed out, 'so that we do not initiate. We simply respond to what Cabinet does, and there are limits to what you can do when you are always reacting.'[60] Another, a former government caucus member between 1993 and 1997, was even more critical of caucus:

> First, there is a regional caucus meeting where we meet every week before national caucus. This meeting I would describe as a regional bitching session. We sat there week after week bitching about this and that. We then went to national caucus. Regional caucus chair would make a presentation. Then very often the bitching would start all over again. Looking back, it is clear to me that we were not very effective. I will give you an example. We in the Atlantic caucus were strongly opposed to changes to the unemployment insurance program. Caucus after caucus meeting, we bitched. We wanted it stopped. But there was no way the changes would or could be stopped. The government simply could not back down. Everyone knew that it had to cut spending and that UI had to be reformed. Instead of trying to come up with some creative ways to cut UI, we stood there against the wind. When we raised the issue, time and again, at national caucus, I could tell that other members were tuning out, reaching for their newspapers or whatever. The prime minister and the Cabinet could then balance some caucus members against others and come out wherever they wanted to, and they did.
>
> Quite apart from that, there is another important problem with the operations of national caucus. When I got up to speak, I had about ninety seconds to say what I wanted to say. Unless you are a Winston Churchill and able to outline in ninety seconds a solu-

tion to complex problems, you do not have much of a chance to influence things, especially proposals that have been worked out and fine tuned over many months by public servants. We also did not have access to the necessary expertise to help us make a case. We were virtually on our own while ministers have all kinds of expertise available. About all we can do then is bitch, and we did that in spades, but it all came to precious little.[61]

Warren Allmand, a former Cabinet minister and a thirty-year veteran of the House of Commons, recently wrote about the limited influence of both Parliament and government caucus. He reports, 'The only time when Parliament has had an impact on policy were periods of minority government or a slim government majority. These relatively rare intervals required governments to consult seriously with the opposition and their own backbenchers.'[62] Regarding the government caucus, he writes that it has actually lost influence over the years. He explains that caucus is not 'as effective as it was in influencing policy. Caucus used to be the place where government policy could be hammered out in private and backbenchers could let the cabinet know what the thinking was at the grassroots. But caucus has become a place where MPs react to government decisions and where ministers try to explain and win support for government policy that has already been decided. Only in one case during this Parliament [i.e., 1993–7] has caucus been successful in turning back a bill. This is reflected even in the way meetings are scheduled; Cabinet used to meet the day after caucus – now it meets the day before.'[63]

Still, the prime minister and his ministers cannot completely ignore caucus. If nothing else, they need to manage the caucus bitching sessions. They have to monitor the criticism to ensure that it does not become too widespread or that it does not take on a life of its own. There are times when a proposed measure, legislation, or government policy will be adjusted to attenuate caucus opposition. The proposed changes may be slowed down to accommodate general caucus concerns or in other instances speeded up if caucus approves them. Only in rare instances will a proposed piece of legislation be turned back and the responsible minister asked to redraft it. To put it differently, the government caucus appears to have, on occasion, the capacity to apply the brakes a bit and slow things down, or push the gas pedal a bit and speed things up. It does not appear, however, to be able to have a go at the steering wheel. Notwithstanding caucus' lack of influence on policy, managing it takes time, and at a minimum the prime minister must devote at least a few hours every week to it.

The prime minister is also leader of his party and must attend to party matters. The party has a full-time executive director and he will want access to the prime minister from time to time. The same can be said about key party officials such as the head of the party in Ontario, Quebec, and so on. Fund-raising and organizational matters often require the prime minister's attention, and in some instances his direct involvement.

As head of the government, the prime minister is accountable to Parliament for everything his government does. He can ask one of his ministers to respond to an opposition question, but opposition members are free to put any question to the prime minister. The role of opposition parties in the House of Commons remains unchanged, notwithstanding the advent of New Public Management. We know that 'a core function of the House of Commons is first to *uncover* and then to *magnify* the complaints of the electorate so that the government hears the signals from the political market and can position itself to respond in such a way as to keep the loyalty of that market. The state of political and administrative readiness – so central to the democratic effectiveness of our system – depends on ministers attending closely to the small and great events.'[64] One thing is certain, no matter is too small, too trivial to raise in question period if it enables an opposition party to score political points and to put the prime minister and the government on the defensive.

In Canada, the prime minister is expected to attend question period whenever he is in Ottawa, and his participation is carefully scrutinized by everyone in the House. In contrast, the British prime minister is only expected to appear twice a week in the House to answer questions. Whether in Britain or in Canada, the prime minister sets the tone for his government in question period and his reputation can be strengthened or weakened depending on how well he is able to field questions. Prime ministers have something to lose in question period. The exercise exposes him to a potentially highly charged political environment where everything simply cannot be scripted in advance. Indeed, question period is not the place for a carefully prepared speech. Accordingly, there is always a risk that the prime minister will end up second-best with the lowliest of backbench MPs.[65] The opposition backbench MP, meanwhile, has little to lose when clashing with the prime minister in question period, and a great deal to gain, including exposure on the evening news and an opportunity to make a name for himself.

Prime ministers will always want to take the time needed to be well briefed for question period. Briefings can come from written material prepared by his own office or the PCO or from oral briefings from one of his assistants. Prime ministers always have on their staff a dedicated legislative assistant whose responsibility is to ensure that the prime minister is properly briefed on anticipated questions in the House and armed with suggested answers. Officials working on this briefing material will look to a variety of sources for information. Ministers, caucus members, partisan political staff members, and briefing material from line departments can all be surveyed for anticipated questions. But the media, above all, will set the tone for the day's question period. As Jim Mitchell, a former senior Privy Council official, and Sharon Sutherland write, 'In our media-driven policy ... the headline in the morning's *Globe and Mail* is the first subject in the afternoon's Question Period.'[66] John Crosbie, a senior minister in the Mulroney Cabinet, writes that 'what television has done is to elevate Question Period from being the focus of the parliamentary day to being, in the public's mind, the entire parliamentary day ... [and] Question Period is a forum for the Opposition.'[67]

The media are likely at the top of the list of natural enemies for staff in the PMO, and it is widely accepted that the prime minister now needs to be protected from them – especially television. A sea change has occurred over the past thirty years between the media and the political leadership in much of the Western world. The new media have many characteristics. One keen observer writes that it is a far cry from the 'credulous coverage of the 1950s and 1960s when the quotes of public figures went unchallenged.'[68] Today, the media, much like society itself, are far less deferential to political leaders and political institutions. Nothing is off limits anymore and political leaders must continually guard against letting their guard down when meeting the press. On this point, former Deputy Prime Minister Erik Nielsen writes that 'the ethical standards of journalists in 1958, when I first came into contact with the parliamentary press gallery, and the standards that prevail today in that same press gallery have, with rare exceptions, altered radically. Perhaps the main reason is the advent of technology, and the increasingly intense competition that the new technology creates between the electronic media and the written media.'[69]

The media now can intrude into the political arena and the operations of government to inform the public quickly, visually, and with considerable impact about what is not working. If things are not working well, or perceived so, solutions to remedy the situation are expected in short order. If these can be secured from the head of government, so much the better. The media are not likely to be impressed by suggestions that the prime minister cannot possibly produce the answer quickly because it lies elsewhere in a government department. Similarly, the media would scorn an answer suggesting that because of the arrival of the New Public Management in government questions should now be directed to managers down the line. In fact, it is very unlikely that a prime ministerial press assistant would ever make such a suggestion for fear of losing control of the media spin.

Yet the breathtaking speed of television news is putting enormous pressure on government to make decisions quickly for fear of appearing indecisive and not in control – one of the worst fears for a head of government. Television can give its viewers a ringside seat to any political crisis in the making. Television news is now widely accessible, even to the illiterate class, and it can zero in on a moment's notice to an issue anywhere in the world and compare virtually any given situation in one country to a similar one in another.[70] The 1997 Kyoto conference to deal with greenhouse gas emissions is a case in point. The media kept a running scorecard before and during the conference to see which national government had unveiled plans to reduce emissions, by how much, and how fast.[71]

A former senior Cabinet minister writes that the media 'have put an almost unbearable pressure on political leaders. Television subjects leaders today to unrelenting scrutiny night and day. How the leader looks and what he or she says is immediately recorded, and is available for use at any time in the future, and in any context whatsoever.' He adds, 'Intense media scrutiny makes it difficult for today's political leaders to make the kind of compromises our leaders have historically had to make to hold their parties together, to implement sweeping national policies, to reconcile the differences of disaffected regions.'[72] The electronic media can hardly follow a government process and they have little interest in describing how it works. They need to focus on political actors and the one that matters the most to their audiences. And the one that can provide an answer to any question in any policy field is the prime minister.

The age of twenty-four-hour television news has also put a great deal of pressure on the print media to provide 'context, perspective, and interpretation, since they infer that many of their audience are already familiar with the basic facts.'[73] In addition, the pressure to produce something new, given TV punditry, Newsworld, RDI, CTV N1, and the like, has seen many journalists 'begin to strain to have something provocative to say.'[74] The need to have something provocative to say has, in turn, given rise to a new subjectivity. A cursory look, for example, at the media in the aftermath of Bill Clinton's victory speaks to the daunting challenge politicians – in particular, heads of government – are now confronting. *Time* magazine declared Clinton Man of the Year for 1992 on 25 January 1993. Three weeks later, *Time* had Clinton on its cover again, this time with the caption 'Stand and Deliver: With tough choices at home and a dangerous world abroad Bill Clinton takes charge.' Only a week later, *Time*'s cover reported on 'Clinton's First Blunder' after the withdrawal of his attorney-general designate. By June, Clinton's honeymoon with the media, or at least with *Time,* was over. Its headline read, 'The Incredible Shrinking President.'

The memoirs of politicians and their key advisers are replete with observations on the influence of the media on government operations. David Stockman, Reagan's head of the Office of Management and Budget, put it succinctly when he wrote, 'Reality happened once a day on the evening news.'[75] Advisers in the PMO also report that developing and implementing strategies to deal with the media and to respond to negative stories take up a great deal of their time and energy.[76] They are not alone.

Political memoirs also reveal that political leaders and their advisers have given up any hope of an objective press. They may well be right. George Bain, one of Canada's most respected postwar journalists, recently wrote a book describing the new breed of journalists who 'grew up in the heady 1960s ... and brought forward certain generational traits [including] ... a distrust of all things institutional, Parliament and notably government and a general anti-everything prejudice founded on fond recollections of press clippings from their time as a generation of idealists.'[77] The news media, in Bain's view, took dead aim at the two Mulroney governments (1984–93) and produced 'the most intense and unrelenting campaign of denigration that any Canadian government has faced at least this side of the Second World War.'[78] Bain is not the only leading journalist to question the work of the media. Elly Alboim, former CBC-TV Ottawa bureau chief, observed on the day he left journalism for a new career, 'I'm tremendously uncomfortable with some of the things journalists are doing. I think we've lost our way a bit. When I joined this business there was an understanding about a certain nobility of purpose and I'm not sure many journalists today understand that or accept it.'[79]

With both the media and the public scrutinizing recent governments as never before, there is a tendency to lay ultimate responsibility for every act at the prime minister's door. Little wonder, then, that the prime minister and his advisers try to keep an eye on everything and to be ready on a moment's notice to fire-fight.

Protecting the Head of Government

In politics, longevity in government is its own reward, and the determining factor of longevity is often how well the prime minister is protected against his natural enemies – the opposition parties and the national media. At his first Cabinet meeting, Canadian Prime Minister Jean Chrétien told his ministers that for the 'good of the government' he expected that they would put in place measures to protect themselves against 'screw-ups' but that *above all* they should always strive to protect the prime minister.[80] On the first point, he bluntly told his ministers, 'The first person who makes a mistake will be out,' and reminded them that there was plenty of talent available on the backbench.[81]

Ministers can falter or even fall, Chrétien explained, but if the prime minister should fall, then the government would likely follow, or at a minimum the party would pay a hefty political price. The point was not lost on his ministers – they were expendable, but the prime minister was not, and he who appoints them ultimately decides who is expendable and who is not. In addition, what matters most is protecting the head of government, and consequently the government itself. Conventional political wisdom is that if the prime minister becomes weak or vulnerable, then the government becomes weak or vulnerable. On the other hand, if a minister becomes weak or vulnerable, the damage can often be contained to that minister alone. What Chrétien said to his ministers could just as easily have been said by another Canadian prime minister at his or her first Cabinet meeting in more recent years, and no doubt it probably was.[82]

How, then, does one protect the prime minister? There is no shortage of ways. Ministers can make a point of praising the work of their leader in their speeches or in media interviews, as they all do from time to time. They can also volunteer, or be asked, to fall on their own sword in order to protect the prime minister. It will be recalled that John Fraser, then minister of Fisheries and Oceans under Mulroney, overruled his department's inspectors and ordered that canned tuna that had been declared unfit for human consumption be released for sale. The day after the story broke in the media, Prime Minister Mulroney rejected opposition demands that Fraser be fired. The day after that, Fraser announced the recall of the tuna but made it clear to the media that he would not resign, and added, 'nor was I asked to.'[83]

Mulroney subsequently applauded Fraser's decision to recall the tuna but also told reporters that it was 'pretty damned obvious that the tuna should never have been on store shelves.'[84] However, later the same day Fraser explained to reporters that the tuna issue had been 'in the Prime Minister's Office in detailed form at least some weeks ago.' The next day in question period, opposition parties took dead aim at the prime minister and his version of events. A few days later, Fraser resigned as minister of Fisheries and Oceans. He later explained that 'Certainly, in view of the contradictions [with the prime minister], I felt that the appropriate thing was to step aside and end the controversy ... I think without the contradictions we could have contained the issue.'[85] Erik Nielsen, deputy prime minister when Fraser resigned, confirms this view. He writes, 'Fraser would now have to go, not because of his original error of judgment but because he had put the prime minister in a bad light by publicly contradicting him.'[86] The message was not lost on his former colleagues – it is one thing for a minister to approve the sale of rancid tuna, but it is quite another to contradict the prime minister and his office in the media.

The Prime Minister's Assistants

The prime minister does not stand alone at the apex of government dealing with an incessant demand on his time, a hostile opposition in Parliament, a media always at the ready with daily doses of criticism, and a large bureaucracy to direct. He has political assistants and others to help him, to protect him from both internal and external threats, and to assist him in 'squeezing forty-eight hours out of the Prime Minister's average day.'[87]

Prime ministers, since Pierre Trudeau, have employed anywhere between 80 to 120 staff members in their own offices. Trudeau, as is well known, is the architect of the modern Prime Minister's Office. He felt that the Pearson years lacked a proper planning capacity at the centre, and as a result were marked by confusion and chaos. He resolved that things would be different in his government. He explained, 'One of the reasons why I wanted this job, when I was told that it might be there, is because I felt it very important to have a strong central government, build up the executive, build up the Prime Minister's Office.'[88] Trudeau, as noted earlier, considerably expanded the size of PMO and identified specific functions and tasks for it to perform. Tom Kent, principal secretary to Prime Minister Pearson, describes the Prime Minister's Office before Trudeau. He writes, 'The PMO was then utterly different from what it became in the Trudeau era and has since remained. There was no bevy of deputies and assistants and principal this-and-that, with crowds of support staff.'[89]

No prime minister since Trudeau has sought to turn back the clock and cut the size of the office back or to limit its functions to what they were before Trudeau. Mulroney, in fact, did the opposite. He increased the staff at PMO by one-third, increased the office's budget by 50 per cent, and added eight professional staff concerned with policy.[90] When Chrétien came to office, one of the first decisions he made was to abolish the chief of staff position in ministerial offices, a position which Mulroney had established. However, Chrétien decided to retain a chief of staff for his own office, who, as already noted, is ranked at the deputy minister level.

Marc Lalonde, former principal secretary to the prime minister, described the functions of PMO in the following fashion: 'The sum total of the role of PMO today – it is a service organization and, as a by-product, it has an advisery capability.'[91] There is no question that a great deal of what the PMO does is to provide administrative services and support for the prime minister. Another former PMO staff member made this clear when he wrote that the office 'regularly helps [the prime minister] answer thousands of letters; makes travel to a number of public meetings in a single day manageable; enables him to deliver a variety of speeches or addresses within hours of one another, or appear on television programs and hotlines across the country. It regularly brings order to a complex schedule of meetings and consultations; reviews thousands of pages of documents and briefs; mobilizes to help him handle problems or crisis.'[92]

PMO service functions have been well described elsewhere, and there is no need to go over them in any detail here.[93] Suffice it to note that the office has a director of communications with a staff of about ten people. They handle all relations with the media, including requests for interviews, and they issue press releases, arrange press conferences, prepare speeches, and monitor press reaction and commentaries for the prime minister. They also promote the prime minister's image by, in the parlance of journalism, spinning stories to his political advantage. A correspondence unit handles the prime minister's mail, and an appointment secretariat reviews names for government or patronage appointments. A legislative assistant, as already noted, is exclusively concerned with the activities of the prime minister as a parliamentarian. Another assistant is concerned with caucus relations. Though they have been given various job titles over the years, there have always been regional assistants in the PMO since Trudeau overhauled the office. Their task is to give the prime minister 'an additional view of social and political developments in each region.'[94] Regional assistants are also responsible for planning and managing the prime minister's visits to their region. However, Chrétien upgraded the position early in his second mandate. In his first mandate, he and his advisers had 'not anticipated how much international travel would have to be done by staffers working regional desks and regional travel advance.' Chrétien's chief of staff, Jean Pelletier, announced in November 1997 that the office would now separate PMO staffers' roles of 'regional assistant and travel advance to free regional assistants to concentrate on regional issues.'[95]

To be sure, prime ministers bring their own style and approach to establishing their own offices and they are completely free to shape it as they see fit. Prime ministers can, at any time, restructure, reorganize, or restaff at will. Still, there is a strong bond of loyalty between the staff and the prime minister. The staff is partisan, of course, and enjoys tenure in office as long as that of their leader. Also most senior staff members were comrades-in-arms with the prime minister in previous political battles. But the office, with an annual budget of over $5 million and a person-year complement of about ninety under Chrétien, represents – at the risk of sounding repetitive – the largest concentration of highly paid partisan political advice found in any one place in Ottawa.

Some prime ministers (e.g., Trudeau) prefer to give a free hand to their principal secretary or chief of staff to let him organize the office as he sees fit and to have all PMO staff report through him, including senior political policy advisers. Others (e.g., Mulroney and Chrétien) prefer a less hierarchical approach, enabling some advisers to bypass the chief of staff and report directly to them.

What goes on inside the PMO? People who work there, or have worked there, report that what goes on is, much more often than not, 'chaotic.' There is never enough time to do well all that needs to be done, to sit back and recharge one's batteries, or to have some time to think. Senior staff members have no choice but to pick and choose the files on which to focus. There is never a shortage of crises, or emerging crises, to manage, and the prime minister's mood always reverberates around the corridors. PMO staff members will determine what the prime minister wants done, the issues he wishes to pursue, and the political problems he wants resolved. In the words of a senior Chrétien adviser, they will 'get to work on them by pushing and pulling whatever needs to be pushed or pulled.'[96]

To be sure, people are busy and the great majority of middle and senior staff members at the PMO put in extremely long hours. They all have specific functions and tasks, but since they know what everyone else is doing, they can come to the assistance of one another. This is not to suggest that the office is free of tension, conflicts, or rivalries. By all accounts, there are plenty of these. But staff members are well aware that, if they are to survive, they need, in the words of one former PMO staff member, to keep their 'eyes on the ball and protect the PM.' He added, 'Our job is quite simple really, make the PM look good.'[97]

The working relationship between the leader and staff and the relative influence of individual staff members can vary a great deal. A staff member not able to deliver the goods or responsible for a screw-up can find himself isolated from important meetings (although usually not for a very long time, given the office's workload). Others will act as the eyes and ears of the prime ministers, and still others will exert a great deal of influence on policy because of their special access to the prime minister. Some will only spend about two or three years in their job, while others will remain for as long as their leader is in politics.

There are also important differences in the way Canadian, British, and Australian prime ministers traditionally have and continue to organize their own staff and offices. British and Australian prime ministers rely on permanent public servants to staff some of the positions in their own immediate offices. Canadian prime ministers generally do not.[98] Staff members in the PMO in Canada are much like staff members in the Office of the President in the United States – they are partisan, temporary, and above all loyal to the prime minister. Accordingly, career officials are not usually welcomed in either Canada's PMO or in the Office of the President in Washington. The difference is important. Career officials are much more likely than politically appointed officials to view issues in terms of the government rather than in the interests of the prime minister. Conversely, political assistants will invariably be more partisan and loyal to the prime minister than to the government and the public service. They have, as noted, fought the leadership or other political battles by his side, or they have a strong personal relationship with him (Trudeau and Marc Lalonde; Mulroney and Bernard Roy; Chrétien and Jean Pelletier), and with only rare exceptions, the same applies down to the senior policy adviser or political assistants levels. They will intuitively seek to protect the prime minister and may well even be suspicious of some senior Cabinet ministers whom they suspect of coveting the prime minister's chair.

No one questions the need for an office to support the prime minister, to attend to his/her administrative needs, and to provide a host of services to assist him to do his job. The more important issue is whether the PMO should play a strong policy advisery role or act as a mini-Cabinet to the prime minister. The argument here is that if the prime minister wants political and policy advice, he should turn to his ministers, and if he should want advice on regional issues, then he should consult the responsible regional minister or the regional caucus rather than appointed officials in his office. When Trudeau decided to enlarge the size and scope of the PMO in the late 1960s, his first principal secretary sought to reassure critics and Cabinet ministers that the office would remain essentially a service-oriented organization. He explained that the office existed to 'serve the prime minister personally, that its purpose is not primarily advisery but functional and the PMO is not a mini-Cabinet; it is not directly or indirectly a decision-making body and it is not, in fact, a body at all.'[99]

It is, of course, not possible to clearly establish what is a service function and what is a policy advisery function. Drafting a letter or preparing a speech for the prime minister can constitute policy making, and many times does. There is also no doubt that several senior officials in the PMO do provide policy advice to the prime minister, and if some in Trudeau's PMO denied this, present-day advisers and assistants certainly do not, nor did those in Mulroney's PMO.

PMO staffers have the prime minister's ear on all issues they wish to raise, be it political, policy, administrative, or the appointment of a minister or deputy minister. They can also work hand in hand with a minister to initiate a proposal, and the minister will feel more secure in bringing the proposal forward, knowing that someone close to the prime minister is supportive. They can also, however, undercut a minister's proposal by raising a series of objections to it when briefing the prime minister. In short, senior PMO staff members do not consider themselves simply a court of second opinion. They are in the thick of it and do not hesitate to offer policy advice or to challenge a Cabinet minister. One official even observed in the interviews that 'if the objective is to challenge the prime minister on a key policy issue, do not ask a Cabinet minister. Ask a senior PMO staffer.' This, he added, after some prompting, 'is as true under Chrétien as it was under Mulroney, but perhaps it was less so under Trudeau.'[100]

If a minister needs to be reigned in for fear that he or she may create problems for the prime minister or the government, PMO staff members will move in and take charge either directly or indirectly. Examples will make this clear.

David Dingwall, the government services minister in the Chrétien government, redirected some highways construction funding to the tune of $26 million from one region of Nova Scotia to his own riding in Cape Breton. The issue was raised in the media, and in question period. Hugh Winsor, a senior Ottawa-based journalist with the *Globe and Mail*, wrote that 'Mr. Dingwall had begun to attract too much bad publicity and the Prime Minister's Office decided it had to act. Indeed, PMO officials had encouraged journalists to keep digging because it would help their case to start tightening the reins.'[101] Within days, the $26 million funding was restored to its original purpose, building a four-lane bypass around a dangerous stretch of the Trans Canada Highway in Nova Scotia's Wentworth Valley.

In the early 1980s, Pierre DeBané, the minister of Regional Economic Expansion in the Trudeau government, became embroiled in a high-profile controversy, at least in the province of Quebec, over the proposed construction of a paper mill in Matane, Quebec, with Yves Bérubé, the provincial Treasury Board minister in the Levesque government. The controversy was essentially over which level of government had committed itself to fund which part of the project and under what conditions. In time, the issue was raised in question period. PMO dispatched two of its officials to sit in DeBané's office to write his speeches and press releases on the issue, and they stayed there until the controversey died down.[102]

Senior PMO staff will get involved in whatever issue they and the prime minister think they should. It can be a major policy issue like NAFTA or the budget, or a minor issue involving a political matter, or a controversy in the media.[103] Again, there are also no established limits to restrict the involvement of the prime minister and his senior staff in whatever issue they decide to take over and manage. The minister can, of course, state his preferences strongly and press for his solution to prevail. But the one who ultimately decides, if he chooses to get involved in the file, is the prime minister. He is the boss. The prime minister, in turn, can seek advice from several sources. The responsible minister will only be one of them.

Certainly the perception among current and past Cabinet ministers in Ottawa is that PMO staff now carries a great deal of influence. When former Fisheries and Oceans minister Brian Tobin heard that one of Chrétien's senior policy advisers was contemplating running for Parliament in a Montreal riding, he applauded the suggestion, observing that 'I'd like to get him in cabinet with me on an equal footing.'[104] Former ministers, even high-profile ones, readily admit that they have been called on 'the carpet for a dressing down' by senior PMO staff members for having committed political mistakes.[105]

Still, the interviews revealed that there are times when the prime minister will decide to leave even his own staff in the dark and take a major decision without consulting anyone. This happened with Trudeau (e.g., with the Bonn spending cuts), Mulroney (e.g., with his support for President Bush in several matters), and Chrétien (e.g., with his decision to invite Stéphane Dion and Pierre Pettigrew to join his Cabinet).

To be sure, there are not enough senior PMO staff members, nor do they have the necessary expertise, to be involved in all policy issues confronting the government. They are also no match for the policy capacity that exists in the Privy Council Office, in other central agencies, or in line departments. But that doesn't matter all that much given that central agencies, notably PCO, are also there to assist the prime minister. In any event, most PMO staffers have little interest in mastering the finer points of the policy process or all policy issues. They regard their stay in government to be relatively short, and they would much sooner spend their energy on promoting the prime minister's priorities, on spinning his success stories, and on fire-fighting crises on his behalf than on becoming policy experts. They will, however, happily haul problems or issues into their own offices even if many of them are not properly within their competence. Most PMO staff members only have a limited knowledge of government. It is important to stress that the central purpose of PMO staff is not to protect the integrity of the policy process in government. Their job is to fix problems or get things done for the boss, to make him, and by extension his government, look good, to score political points, and to manage political errors or embarrassments.

Revisiting *Primus*

Current and former ministers report that something happens to a colleague when he becomes prime minister. Things change, they reveal, and one can never be as relaxed with him as was the case before he became prime minister, no matter how close the relationship was. One Cabinet minister explains, 'When your colleague becomes prime minister, overnight he assumes a different persona, or perhaps it is us who see him differently. We respect the fact that he has an impossible agenda, that now he has to deal with world leaders, and that we can no longer walk in his office for a relaxed chat. We quickly come to terms with the fact that he can no longer be one of us.'[106] A former British Cabinet minister writes that 'only those who have served in government fully realize the gulf between a Prime Minister and even the most senior and eminent of his colleagues. Even in casual conversation with them, he ceases to be addressed as "Anthony" or "Harold" and, except perhaps when there is no one else present, becomes Prime Minister.'[107] Canadian prime ministers are not much different from British prime ministers on this front.

As already noted, students of parliamentary government are writing more and more about a shift towards a presidential form of government. They claim that it is increasingly difficult to write about collective ministerial responsibility or prime ministers as leaders of teams because prime minister are fast becoming – like presidents – individuals at the top of the pile. Patrick Weller, for one, argues: '... their [i.e., prime ministers'] control over government activities is regarded as excessive, and their accountability as far too limited. Observers complain that the system has changed from Cabinet government to prime ministerial government, or that the office of prime minister has been presidentialised.'[108] John Mackintosh was the first to express concern over the growing influence of the prime minister in his study of the British Cabinet in 1962.[109] He was later joined by a number of others expressing the same viewpoint, including a highly regarded Cabinet minister, Richard Crossman.[110] Mackintosh answered his critics in the early and mid-1970s, but by the late 1970s he felt it was no longer necessary.[111] He simply made the point that 'events since [1962] have done so much to confirm the general case argued in this book' that he felt it unnecessary to make the case.[112] The debate is not limited to Britain. A keen student of Canadian politics suggests that Canada 'seems to have created a presidential system without its congressional advantages.'[113]

Few observers in Canada believe that the prime minister is still *primus inter pares*. The only time when the Canadian prime minister is still *primus inter pares* is when he chairs a First Ministers' Conference. Premiers are not his political equals, but they shape the discussions at the conference and advance whatever position they wish, even when it is in sharp opposition to the prime minister's position, as Clyde Wells did during the First Ministers' meetings that led to the renegotiation of the Meech Lake Accord.

First ministers now meet on a regular basis and their meetings cover a wide array of topics. The prime minister will consult with the chair of the Annual Premiers' Conference in preparing the agenda. At one meeting, the first ministers agreed to establish a Federal-Provincial-Territorial Ministerial Council on Social Policy Renewal and subsequently agreed to launch a series of joint initiatives.

At the December 1997 meeting, the prime minister reported on the 'Team Canada' trade initiative and led a discussion on health care, youth employment, persons with disabilities, and on the development of a national children's agenda.[114] All first ministers have a say in shaping the agenda and all can voice opinions without fearing a demotion at the hand of the prime minister. The prime minister is also not free to define the consensus of the meeting according to his own preferences. It is in this sense that the Canadian prime minister is *primus inter pares* when he chairs a first minister's meeting. The same cannot be said about Cabinet ministers. They have become much more the prime minister's subordinates than his *pares*. John Crosbie summed up the situation well when he explained why Brian Tobin left the federal Cabinet to become leader of the Liberal Party in Newfoundland and Labrador. He wrote, 'In politics, never underestimate the importance of being number one. It is inevitably frustrating to work as a member of a government led by someone else. No matter how much power and authority leaders delegate to you or how well they treat you, they are still number one, and, when they choose to exercise their authority, they naturally have their way. If my leader became trapped by some political circumstance and blurted out a policy pronouncement in my area of responsibility – even if he didn't know much about the subject – I had to live with it. Even if he was completely wrong, I couldn't correct what he had done. But if a person is the leader, he can make the final decision.'[115]

This chapter suggests that prime ministers leading a majority government can drive virtually whatever initiative or measure they might favour. Cabinet and Parliament are there, but with a majority of seats a prime minister can manipulate them when it comes to issues that matter a great deal to him. This is more how a United States president operates (without Congress) than what a textbook on British or Canadian politics would suggest is the proper role of the prime minister.

To be sure, prime ministers do not always bypass their Cabinets or only consult them after the fact on the great majority of issues. They will pick and choose issues they will want to direct. Indeed, in some circumstances and on certain issues a prime minister may well decide not to exert his or her authority and let the Cabinet's collective decision-making process run its course. He may also even let government caucus have its day from time to time and accept that a government proposal or legislation should be pulled back and reworked to accommodate the views of caucus members. There are issues on which a prime minister may hold no firm view, and a detached assessment of the costs and benefits of getting involved could suggest that it is best to keep one's political capital in reserve for another day and for another issue.

Prime ministers and their staff, sitting as they do at the apex of power, from where they can survey all developments in the government, come to believe that their political judgment is superior to that of ministers and to value their own opinion over others. After all, they made it to the top of the 'greasy pole' while the senior ministers and their advisers, who also tried, did not.

Public opinion surveys also serve to strengthen the hand of the prime minister and his advisers. They no longer need to rely on the views of even powerful regional ministers to gain an appreciation of political developments. Indeed, the most recent public opinion surveys can enable them to challenge the views of ministers. If, say, the minister responsible for Nova Scotia claims that government spending cuts are hurting the party in that province, PMO staffers can point to a public opinion survey suggesting that the majority of Nova Scotians support the government's efforts to deal with the deficit and debt problem. There are now public opinion surveys documenting the views of Canadians on virtually every public policy issue. It is worth noting that a key speech at the 1998 Liberal Party policy conference was by the party's pollster, Michael Marzolini. Marzolini provided the 'national-mood numbers,' and his speech was as widely reported in the media as the prime minister's own speech.[116]

But there are other forces that serve to strengthen the hand of the prime minister in the machinery of government. We know that globalization has become more than a catchphrase. The emergence of global corporations, and new trade, financial, and communication links are dramatically changing the policy context for national governments in a shrinking world. The nation state, it has been suggested, is being challenged from diametrically opposed directions – from above by international and regional trade agreements and global firms, and from below by the emergence of regionally based nationalism and by linguistic or religious groups challenging the legitimacy of the nation state.

Yet national governments are still the ones being asked to solve many old and new problems. The global economy can set the stage for national and local economies to compete and lay down the rules under which economies and firms must operate. It is hardly possible, however, to imagine a global economy taking shape without conflicts between firms, sectors, regions, and nations or without far-reaching adjustments in some sectors and regions. The designers of the new order in many ways will have to be national politicians and national public services. They alone have the legitimacy.[117] When leaders of national governments come calling in Ottawa, and many do in the course of a year, they always call on the prime minister, and they invariably seek to deal directly with him.[118]

National governments, precisely because of global economic forces, will need to work increasingly with each other and with regional and international trade agreements. They will also need to develop a capacity to move quickly to strike new deals when the time is right, or to change course because of new or emerging political and economic circumstances and opportunities. The focus will be on the heads of national governments because of their ability to unblock files, cut through the decision-making process, and to sign and monitor trade deals.[119] It is the heads of governments that meet at G7, at Commonwealth meetings, at la francophonie, and at the APEC conference. As the national government is being challenged from above and from below, it appears that power is getting even more concentrated at the centre of government.

The Canadian prime minister, unlike the American president, who has to deal with Congress, or the Australian prime minister, who has to deal with a powerful elected and independently minded Senate, has a free hand to negotiate for his government and to make any deal with foreign heads of government adhere. The final hours of negotiations on NAFTA between Prime Minister elect Chrétien and the United States president, through his Canadian ambassador, are telling. At one point, the American ambassador wondered about Chrétien's political authority to agree to a final deal, given that he had yet to appoint his Cabinet. The ambassador put the question to Chrétien, 'What happens if we work all this out and then your new trade minister doesn't agree?' Chrétien replied, 'Then I will have a new trade minister the following morning.'[120]

It is hardly possible to overemphasize the fact that the Canadian prime minister has no outer limits defining his political authority within the government. To be sure, the media, opposition parties, question period, and public opinion can all serve to inhibit prime ministerial power. Similarly, what may appear at first to be a seemingly innocent incident can take on a life of its own and gain a high profile in the media and force the prime minister to reconsider a government strategy or a proposed initiative. But inside government, the prime minister is free to roam wherever he wishes and to deal with any file he chooses. There is ample evidence to suggest that Prime Ministers Trudeau, Mulroney, and Chrétien have all sought to push back the frontiers of their political authority. Events, the requirements of modern government, the role of the media, the role of first ministers in Canada, and the rise of the global economy have all served to strengthen considerably the hand of the prime minister. A strong minister may object, but there is little else he can do, except resign, which, again, Canadian history shows is rarely done. It appears that the most significant limit on the prime minister's political power is time, or a lack of it. There is no question that Canadian prime ministers, like their British counterparts, have for some time been trying to cope with an overload problem.[121]

Still, there is an elaborate machinery of government and policy and decision-making process always at the prime minister's disposal at the centre of government to assist him in defining and managing the issues on which he wants to spend some of his time and to keep the other issues on an even keel. Prime ministers know that they can always turn to a safe pair of hands in the Privy Council Office for help.

5

The Privy Council Office: A Safe Pair of Hands

Never one to overstate a position, Gordon Robertson, former clerk of the Privy Council Office and secretary to the Cabinet, described PCO's role as 'one of information, co-ordination, follow-up and support provided to the Prime Minister and the Cabinet as a whole unit, as a vital aspect, maintaining constant relations with all departments of the government.'[1] The PCO is that, but it is also much more. Indeed, it is hardly possible to overstate the importance of the office to the government's policy and decision-making process. As a former senior PCO official once observed, 'the PCO has a great deal to do with the success or failure of any government.'[2]

The office is, in many ways, the nerve centre of the federal public service. Its purview encompasses the prime minister, the Cabinet, and individual ministers, but also Parliament, other central agencies, line departments, and the media. The clerk of the Privy Council Office and secretary to the Cabinet is also the head of the federal public service, thus occupying the most senior permanent position in government. The office briefs the prime minister on any issue it wishes, controls the flow of papers to Cabinet, reports back to departments on the decisions taken, or not taken, by Cabinet, advises the prime minister on the selection of deputy ministers and briefs chairs of Cabinet committees (with the exception of the Treasury Board), supports the operation of Cabinet and Cabinet committees, advises the prime minister on federal-provincial relations and on all issues of government organization and ministerial mandates, and prepares summaries of strategic memoranda.

Thus, a variety of issues and competing demands come to PCO from all quarters of government, along with the jockeying for position on the part of ministers to promote their pet projects, as well as ambitious public servants trying to gain visibility in order to make it on the list of potential deputy ministers. A senior PCO official explained that 'things are rarely simple or straightforward here. There are many twists and turns, many bumps in the road on the way to getting things done. Sometimes we see things that do not square nicely with what one would assume to be proper public policy making.'[3] To be sure, PCO officials have to develop a strong capacity to secure information from departments about their plans and the views of their ministers. At the same time, they must be very careful with whom they share their information. PCO does not have programs of its own to implement, so here, more than anywhere else, information is power, and one has to become very adroit at using it. For example, it may well be that on occasion information received from a department will need to be employed to keep the department's minister in check. Former British Prime Minister Harold Wilson was asked if he had ever regretted not becoming a permanent public servant in the Cabinet Office, where he served during the Second World War. 'Heavens no!' he replied. 'I couldn't have stood the intrigues.'[4]

In this chapter, I discuss the role of the PCO and its various functions. The PMO, as we have just seen, links the prime minister to the world of politics, Cabinet ministers, caucus members, the party, and the media. The PCO, meanwhile, links the prime minister to the world of administration and to government departments – in brief, to the machinery of government. Accordingly, the prime minister receives two basic streams of paper, one from his own office and one from PCO. The two worlds overlap from time to time and there is close cooperation between the two offices. But both also recognize the line where the world of partisan politics begins, and PCO intuitively tries to avoid it. Still, the two offices occupy the same building, the historic Langevin building on Wellington Street, directly across from the Parliament buildings and where, as one official puts it, they live 'cheek by jowl.' Though there are moments of tension and sharp disagreement between the two offices, it is in their mutual interest to collaborate, and on the great majority of files, there is, indeed, close cooperation.

From time to time, for example, the staff of both offices will organize joint planning sessions or retreats to review a specific issue. In late June 1997, they held a joint retreat in the Gatineau region on citizen engagement. The purpose of the retreat was to clarify the concept of 'citizen engagement and produce principles and models for engagement.'[5] The retreat concluded with a call for more research on the topic and to identify 'change' agents in departments to promote the concept further. It appears that little was actually accomplished through follow-up action, but the point here is that both offices do cooperate and on many occasions work from a joint agenda.

Tension and sharp disagreements will surface, however, because PMO and PCO can have different perspectives on the same issue. But PCO maintains that any such tension can be healthy. In its submission to the 1978 Lambert Royal

Commission, PCO claimed that the different perspective enables 'the Prime Minister to protect himself from the dangers both of narrowly partisan advice and of unrealistically bureaucratic advice. For this process to work, PCO shares its information base with PMO, although the reverse is not the case.' It added that 'the Prime Minister is the focus of the process,' and that 'PCO is the Prime Minister's departmental staff in his capacity as head of government and his functions focus and unite PCO's activities in support of Cabinet.'[6]

To be sure, the prime minister and the clerk of the Privy Council and secretary to the Cabinet enjoy a unique working relationship, one that is not found anywhere else in government. For one thing, the prime minister is completely free to appoint whomever he wishes to the position. No other minister enjoys the same prerogative with respect to his deputy minister. For another, the clerk of the Privy Council is not only head of the public service but is also dean of the community of deputy ministers. The clerk has a direct hand in deciding who should become a deputy minister and who should not. This alone ensures that she will enjoy a great deal of influence inside government. As anyone who has worked in government can attest, no one should underestimate the power of appointment. The one who wields this power decides, at the highest levels in the public service, who wins, who doesn't, who is in the ascendency, and who is not. But that is not the clerk's only source of influence since, by virtue of his/her position at the centre of government, he/she is the prime minister's principal policy adviser. At least from the public service perspective, the clerk represents the final brief for the prime minister on all issues.

Primus in the Public Service

The PCO submission to the Lambert Commission is significant in that the office itself pointed to the prime minister, not Cabinet, as 'the focus of the process,' and stated that it constituted the prime minister's departmental staff. Several years after that submission was tabled, PCO became even more explicit about its role as the prime minister's department. Paul Tellier, clerk of the Privy Council Office from 1985 to 1992, time and again reminded deputy ministers, assistant deputy ministers, and others that he was wearing not one but two hats – one as the prime minister's deputy minister and the other as secretary to the Cabinet. In 1992 he added yet another hat, that of head of the public service.[7] The last position was formally recognized through special legislation enacted to implement the Public Service (PS) 2000 initiative which was introduced to modernize government operations. The legislation in many ways, however, simply stated in statute what had long been established in fact.

Another former clerk argues that there is a fourth hat that the clerk of the

Privy Council should wear since 'he has a *fiduciary* role of custodian of the system as a whole in assuring integrity and continuity in the administration of government.'[8] In *Canadian Public Administration,* Arnold Heeney reports on a seminal event: incoming Prime Minister Diefenbaker met with outgoing Prime Minister Louis St Laurent and argued that 'the British tradition should be followed' in the disposition of Cabinet records. He wrote that Diefenbaker and St Laurent agreed 'that the Secretary to the Cabinet should now be accepted as the custodian of Cabinet papers, responsible for determining what communication should be made thereof to succeeding administration. With that agreement, the Cabinet Secretariat became a permanent institution of Canadian government.'[9]

Within minutes of Canada's being born, the prime minister oversaw the swearing in of the clerk of the Executive Council of the united province of Canada as clerk of the Privy Council of the Dominion of Canada. But for nearly seventy-five years, the incumbent performed largely clerical activities. Arnold Heeney changed all that when, during the Second World War, he assumed a newly created position, secretary to the Cabinet, and added it to the title clerk of the Privy Council. Heeney, like his British counterpart, knew full well that he had to perform a delicate balancing act and again saw his work, above all else, as secretary to the Cabinet. He believed that his principal task was to ensure that Cabinet would ran smoothly. However, he also, it will be recalled, annoyed Mackenzie King from time to time when he attenuated the prime minister's criticism of his ministers. But Heeney, like all his successors up to Gordon Robertson (who held the appointment from 1963 to 1975), saw the focus of his role and functions more properly tied to the Cabinet than to the prime minister. Robertson disagreed fundamentally with Tellier's assertion that the role's main function was as the prime minister's deputy minister. For Robertson, the job of clerk of the Privy Council and secretary to the Cabinet was precisely what it is called – secretary to the Cabinet and not a 'kind of political fixer for the prime minister.'[10]

Some observers believe that Trudeau's appointment of Michael Pitfield as clerk-secretary in 1975 changed the role forever. Trudeau and Pitfield had, for many years, maintained a close friendship. Trudeau appointed Pitfield at the age of thirty-seven and, in so doing, overlooked more senior public servants who had served for many years as deputy ministers both in line departments and in a central agency. Pitfield's experience in government, meanwhile, had largely been acquired in PCO. The argument is that Pitfield turned things upside down, and instead of seeing the clerk of the Privy Council as representing the public service as an institution to the prime minister and Cabinet, he represented the prime minister to the public service. The argument also is that no clerk since Pitfield has been able to revert to the old understanding of the role. If Arnold Heeny successfully resisted Mackenzie King's desire to make the secretary to the Cabinet 'a kind of deputy minister to the Prime Minister,' or 'the personal staff officer to the Prime Minister,' secretaries to the prime minister from Pitfield to today have not been as willing to resist the desire of the prime minister to make the position 'a kind of deputy minister to the Prime Minister.'[11]

When Joe Clark came to power in 1979, he fired Pitfield as being 'too partisan.'[12] Colin Campbell writes that 'when Trudeau restored [Pitfield] to clerk-secretary after his return to power [in 1980], he confirmed definitively the politicization of Canada's top bureaucratic job.' Campbell adds that the fall and rise of Pitfield 'tipped the scales toward the conclusion that the Trudeau–Pitfield friendship had short-circuited the distance that previously existed between the prime minister and a clerk-secretary.'[13] I asked three former Trudeau ministers whether they regarded Pitfield more as secretary to the Cabinet or as deputy minister to Trudeau. All three had no doubt that Pitfield was above all Trudeau's deputy minister and that he was regarded by ministers as such.[14]

Still, no secretary to the Cabinet since Gordon Robertson has sought to describe their main job as secretary to the Cabinet. In 1997, the Privy Council Office produced a document on its role and structure whose very first page makes it clear that the secretary's first responsibility is to the prime minister. It states that the 'Clerk of the Privy Council and Secretary to the Cabinet' has three primary responsibilities:

1 As the Prime Minister's Deputy Minister, provides advice and support to the Prime Minister on a full range of responsibilities as head of government, including management of the federation.
2 As the Secretary to the Cabinet, provides support and advice to the Ministry as a whole and oversees the provision of policy and secretariat support to Cabinet and Cabinet committee.
3 As Head of the Public Service, is responsible for the quality of expert, professional and non-partisan advice and service provided by the Public Service to the Prime Minister, the Ministry and to all Canadians.[15]

The direct link between the prime minister and the secretary to the Cabinet and the Privy Council Office is made clearer still in the office's *mission* and *values* statement. Its *mission* is 'to serve Canada and Canadians by providing the best non-partisan advice and support to the Prime Minister and Cabinet.' Its *values* statement makes absolutely no mention of Cabinet. It reads: 'We recognize the special need of the Prime Minister for timely advice and support. We dedicate ourselves to our work and to the effective functioning of government. We believe that integrity, judgment and discretion are essential to achieving our mission.'[16]

Tellier's decision to add the title of the prime minister's deputy minister to his job and to declare that he was the prime minister's deputy minister simply reflected reality in his day-to-day work. Indeed, the secretary to the Cabinet is accountable to the prime minister, not Cabinet, and the great majority of his daily activities are now designed to support the prime minister, not Cabinet. The prime minister, not Cabinet, appoints the clerk of the Privy Council and secretary to Cabinet; the prime minister, not Cabinet, evaluates his performance; and the prime minister, not Cabinet, will decide if he stays or if he should be replaced. All this is to say that not only does the secretary to Cabinet wear the hat of deputy minister to the prime minister, it is without doubt the hat that fits best and the one he wears nearly all the time. A former senior PCO official observed that 'all clerks since Pitfield have done an excellent job at being deputy minister to the prime minister. As far as secretary to the Cabinet, the performance has been spotty.'[17]

The deputy minister's hat is also the one that gives him most of his influence inside government. His influence begins with the prime minister's power of appointment. A minute of council first issued in 1896 and last reissued in 1935 gives the prime minister the power to appoint deputy ministers.[18] All prime ministers have made it a point to retain this power in their own hands, and for good reason. It is key to controlling government operations and to ensuring that the government goes in the intended direction.

Former Cabinet minister and deputy minister Mitchell Sharp writes that 'the fact that deputy ministers are appointed on the recommendation of the Prime Minister means that, with the exception of the Clerk of the Privy Council, who reports to the Prime Minister himself, they have a degree of independence from their own ministers, which gives them freedom in offering advice and administering the departments. They are in a sense part of the structure by which the Prime Minister controls the operations of the federal government.' He adds that the 'appointment of deputy ministers also enables the Prime Minister to ensure continuity in the administration of a department, notwithstanding his replacement of the minister, the political head of the department.'[19]

The prime minister is, of course, free to turn to several sources for advice on who would make a strong deputy minister. But no one has more influence in this area than the clerk of the Privy Council. The Privy Council Office houses a secretariat, which reports to the prime minister through the clerk and which screens candidates for order-in-council appointments, including deputy ministers, associate deputy ministers, and heads of agencies.

Officials in PCO report that the prime minister will accept the clerk's recommendation on deputy ministers' appointments '*at least* nine times out of ten.' A senior PMO official goes even further and reveals that the clerk's 'batting average on DM appointments' is 1,000 and only in extremely rare circumstances would the prime minister not accept the clerk's formal recommendation.[20] He adds, however, that there are plenty of occasions for the prime minister and the clerk to share views in private on the work of deputy ministers and other senior government officials so that the clerk can gain an understanding of the prime minister's views and preferences. Prime ministers at least since Trudeau (and probably before) will spend time with the clerk to discuss potential deputy ministers so that the clerk knows that the names he formally puts forward for appointment will receive the prime minister's blessing. There are also instances when the prime minister will need to bring the clerk onside in his choice for an appointment. This was the case, for example, when Mulroney appointed Stanley Hartt as deputy minister of Finance. Similarly, there are instances when the clerk will also need to bring the prime minister onside. In all instances, however, there is a tacit understanding that neither one will impose a choice on the other. It appears that neither the prime minister nor the clerk will want to hear from one another 'I told you so' if a deputy minister appointment does not work out.[21]

The prime minister knows full well that his ability to direct the work of his government and to deal with problems and crises as they arise is, to some degree, tied directly to the position and status that the clerk of the Privy Council enjoys with ministers, deputy ministers, government departments, and agencies. If the prime minister has a matter that needs attending to somewhere in government, he knows that no one is likely to be in a better position to help him than the clerk. The clerk knows everybody in government at the senior levels, and indeed, many deputy ministers and associate deputy ministers likely rose to their position on his or her recommendation. If a deputy minister hopes to be assigned to a larger department, then he knows that how the clerk views his abilities will be a key, if not the determining factor. In addition, when the clerk homes in on a given issue, it is rightly assumed that he has the prime minister's full backing. The clerk can very often persuade ministers and deputy ministers to take a certain decision, or even assist a department in difficulty. He can, whenever he decides, also have a private word with the secretary of the Treasury Board or the deputy minister of Finance to move a file forward.

If the prime minister does not accept the great majority of recommendations on senior appointments from the clerk, then word will soon get around Ottawa and the clerk's ability to assist the prime minister on other matters could well be compromised. Indeed, in such instances the prime minister will more than likely decide to replace the clerk and he would be well advised to do so.

What about the role of ministers in the appointment of their deputy ministers? It varies. A few of the more senior ministers in any government have a kind of *droit de regard* and can turn down the clerk's recommendation if they put up a fuss. But precious few ministers enjoy or have enjoyed this privilege. In addition, the *droit de regard* is considered a privilege, not a right, even in the case of the most senior ministers, and it can be revoked at any moment if the prime minister so decides. Marc Lalonde and Allan MacEachen enjoyed a *droit de regard* under Trudeau, as did Don Mazankowski under Mulroney and Paul Martin under Chrétien. But the clerk, better than most, knows which ministers have the *droit de regard* on the appointment of their deputy ministers and will have the good sense to have a private chat with them on a possible appointment or even recommend the individual favoured by the minister. The minister, having in turn gained the confidence of the prime minister, will also be wise to the ways of government and will promote someone who is well known and respected by the clerk. In other words, both a senior minister and the clerk know that confrontation on the appointment of a deputy minister is in neither of their interests and they will usually do what is necessary to avoid it.

Other ministers will be informed on possible choices, and still others (the great majority) will simply be told a day or two in advance who will be appointed as their deputy minister. There have been occasions when even that courtesy was not observed. One former minister reveals that he first learned of the identity of his deputy minister on the radio in the morning while shaving.[22] PCO officials explain that deputy ministers are often appointed in a 'DM shuffle,' which can involve several appointments at a time, and that it would not be realistic to shop around names to see which minister is interested in whom. In addition, the prime minister's prerogative to appoint deputy ministers must always be protected for both the practical reasons of managing the process, and also, as Mitchell Sharp explained, because it is one of the most important levers available to the prime minister to 'control the operations of the federal government.'

The appointment of associate deputy ministers, the final development position before becoming a full deputy minister, meanwhile, is regarded essentially as the preserve of the clerk with the advice of the Committee on Senior Officials (COSO), a committee of deputy ministers. Only rarely will the prime minister or the most senior minister question the clerk's recommendation. This is a relatively new position, about twenty-five years old, and ambitious public servants covet these appointments, knowing that if they perform well at this level, it is only a matter of time before they become full deputy ministers. The last two clerks, Glen Shortliffe and Jocelyne Bourgon, both served as associate deputy ministers before becoming deputy ministers and, later, clerk. Aspiring public servants know that the one person they need to impress to make it to associate level is the clerk.

Selecting deputy and associate deputy ministers remains a highly subjective process. In the world of business, there are clear measures of success, ranging from sales volume to cost of production and market penetration. To establish if a salesperson is successful is a fairly straightforward matter. In the sports world, it is easy to tell if one hockey player is better at scoring goals than another, if one baseball pitcher wins more games than another, or if a golfer is better than others. Even in the world of academe, it is possible to identify the leading scholars in any field of research by consulting the most reputable learned journals.

But things are never that straightforward in government. I continue to marvel at how reputations are made, or at times lost, in the federal public service and at how senior officials become deputy ministers. For any deputy minister there will be six senior officials who will insist that he or she should never have been appointed. Another six will applaud the appointment. There are simply no clear-cut criteria that can apply to every case and at all times to determine the competence of a senior government official. In fact, I doubt very much if such criteria could ever be identified. There are simply too many variables, too many factors at play. In addition, the work of the public service is by nature collective, which makes it difficult for individuals to shine (on a strictly objective basis) over others.

How, then, does one become a deputy minister? A senior government official carried out a review of deputy ministerial appointments and concluded that:

> First, experience in a central agency, most notably the PCO, is now a virtual prerequisite for deputy-level appointment. Second, notwithstanding the increasing recognition of the importance of managerial performance and service to the public, almost two out of three deputies have no experience in program management; experience in line departments is most typically in policy and process management. Previous experience in the department is not usual for deputy appointees except in the case of central agencies and appointments at the associate deputy minister level. Furthermore, most deputies have no federal experience outside the National Capital Region. Overall, deputies are primarily generalists, not specialists.[23]

It is rare indeed for someone to be appointed deputy minister in Ottawa without having worked directly with the current clerk at one point in his career or having caught the clerk's eye for one reason or another. The subjective nature of the appointment process strengthens the hand of the clerk and the centre of government because it gives the centre a relatively free hand in deciding who makes it and who does not.

Jacques Bourgault and Stéphane Dion describe how the performance of deputy ministers is assessed. They report that 'the performance appraisal system of federal DMs is hierarchical in that the final decisions on ratings and bonuses are made by the Prime Minister on the recommendation of the Clerk of the Privy Council. Peers participate in the system at an earlier stage, through a committee whose function is to provide the Clerk with opinions on the performance of each colleague.'[24] Peers participate through the Committee on Senior Officials, which is chaired by the clerk. COSO also includes the heads of other central agencies and several deputy ministers from line departments selected by the clerk. The committee provides the clerk with opinions on the performance of deputy ministers.[25] In addition, the committee will review the performance of senior officials (at the assistant deputy minister level) and offer advice to the clerk on future deputy minister or associate deputy minister level appointments. The clerk will review carefully the advice COSO has to offer, but he/she will always reserve the right to seek his/her own counsel or to turn to the advice of subordinates at PCO on senior appointments. A member of COSO explains: 'We review individual cases and we voice our opinions, but ultimately it is the clerk, and the clerk alone, who holds the short list on possible senior appointments. She can listen to us or completely ignore us. I have seen her do both.' He added, 'We never see the names which she actually sends to the prime minister. She keeps the list very close to herself and perhaps to a handful of her senior advisers in PCO. But she is not alone. As far as I can tell, previous clerks all did the same thing.'[26]

In addition to COSO, the clerk will also consult relevant ministers to get their views of the performance of their deputy ministers and other senior departmental officials. This system applies to all deputy ministers, including members of COSO who are asked to withdraw from the meeting when their own performance is being discussed. The system applies to all that is, except the clerk, 'who has a "different status" appraisal ... this person's performance is done by the Prime Minister alone.'[27] Bourgault and Dion concluded their study with a series of recommendations, including one which read 'that a list of roles, qualities and special considerations be prepared and distributed to COSO members, to serve as a checklist during performance appraisals.'[28]

The above is to make the case that the competence of senior government officials, including deputy ministers, is often in the eye of the beholder – or more precisely in the eye of the clerk of the Privy Council Office. The problem, simply stated, is how can one determine if a government department has had a particularly successful year? It depends on how one defines 'successful' – to some, a substantial downsizing of both programs and staff is a sign of success, while to others it may be how well the department was able to protect itself from further spending cuts. The list of pros and cons goes on. But even if one is able to state that a department has had a particularly successful year, who is to tell who or what was largely responsible? Was it the minister, the deputy minister, lack of media attention, lots of media attention, political circumstances outside the control of the department, pressure from interest groups? And so on.

Though there is no objective and widely recognized measure to determine the performance of senior officials, there is one development that can quickly jolt the career of a deputy minister or an assistant deputy minister who aspires to greater things. A 'screw-up' which reaches the media and which makes the minister look bad or not in control or which makes the department look incompetent can have grave consequences for the deputy minister. Indeed, current and former deputy ministers I consulted put the ability to keep 'their ministers and the department out of political trouble' as the single most important criterion of success.[29]

Given all the above, the clerk has considerable flexibility in determining who should get promoted to the ranks of deputy and associate deputy minister and who should not. This power of appointment constitutes an awesome tool for the clerk of Privy Council to set the policy advisery capacity and management direction and style in the public service. But that is not his or her only point of influence.

The Privy Council Office, through the clerk, will also offer advice to the prime minister on Cabinet appointments. The office can single out departments that face strong challenges, that have had problems in the recent past, or that need some fresh thinking, and then recommend the appointment of a Cabinet minister whom it considers to be particularly well suited to meet these challenges. The office can also provide a kind of report card to the prime minister on who has performed well in Cabinet committee and who works well with his deputy minister and who does not. PCO is, of course, only one out of several sources of advice the prime minister can turn to in appointing his Cabinet or when considering a Cabinet shuffle. I do not mean to suggest that PCO is always the most important source of advice on this front, but PCO's advice does matter, a fact that is not lost on either aspiring ministers or ministers hoping for a more senior Cabinet appointment.

The clerk also chairs the Coordinating Committees of Deputy Ministers (CCDM). The CCDM policy committee meets most Wednesdays over lunch and brings together senior deputy ministers from central agencies (e.g., secretary of the Treasury Board) and several line departments. The committee reviews major policy issues facing the government and debates the main issues of the day, thus constituting a source of advice and information for the clerk of the Privy Council. It is also designed to keep 'the heads of central agencies informed of the collective concerns of the Government.'[30]

But CCDM also has another purpose. The clerk can turn to CCDM to generate advice to the prime minister and, as one former senior PCO official wrote, to 'provide an early warning system for emerging contentious issues that will likely require the attention of the Prime Minister.'[31] Members of CCDM are very well positioned to survey all new potential developments in government departments and to advise the prime minister on any likely bumps in the road ahead.

CCDM has been described as the 'executive committee of the public service and the Secretary [i.e., the clerk] meeting with Associate Secretaries of Cabinet.'[32] This last point is made because deputy ministers of the other central agencies sit on CCDM and, according to some insiders, they are, in effect, 'associate secretaries' to the Cabinet, given the nature of the work of central agencies. Officials in PCO do not deny that this perception exists, but they are quick to point out that CCDM is only an advisery committee and that it has no decision-making authority in its own right. While this is true, its deliberations do influence decisions and its existence enables the centre to request and get a great deal of information about what goes on in departments. In addition, there is a CCDM management committee, which the clerk also chairs and which brings together the heads of all central agencies. But this committee now meets infrequently and, if necessary, management issues are dealt with at CCDM policy meetings.

The clerk also chairs a weekly breakfast meeting of deputy ministers and heads of agencies, monthly luncheon meetings of deputy ministers, and two retreats of deputy ministers every year. At these sessions, the clerk will brief deputy ministers on Cabinet deliberations and discuss new government initiatives, the policy environment, and measures to strengthen the public service. Some deputy ministers can be asked to make presentations on special issues of interest (e.g., the deputy minister of Finance might address the government's fiscal position), particularly so at the retreats which are often held outside of Ottawa.[33] The meetings also provide 'an opportunity for Deputy Ministers to conduct informal business and discuss issues of general interest.'[34]

The clerk attends all Cabinet meetings. She, together with two senior PCO officials, sits away from the Cabinet table along the back wall with one or two note-takers also from PCO, usually assistant secretaries. The clerk does not speak at Cabinet meetings, unless the prime minister specifically asks that she clarify a matter, and this rarely happens. Much more often the clerk or one of the prime minister's own senior officials from PMO will slip him a handwritten note to clarify a point or to provide added information on an item being discussed.

Still, the only permanent officials who know precisely what is said at Cabinet meetings are from PCO. From time to time, a minister who is asked to provide a briefing to Cabinet will bring his deputy minister to the meeting. But these occasions are infrequent and their purpose is largely to provide background information and briefing material to Cabinet. Accordingly, in most cases, departments can only look to their own ministers or to senior PCO officials to get an understanding of how their proposals were received, how their department is regarded, and what the prime minister's major concerns are. What ministers report back is important, but only PCO officials can debrief with authority on Cabinet deliberations. In any event, it is PCO officials, not individual ministers, who write Cabinet decisions on behalf of the prime minister.

The clerk also has direct access to the prime minister as needed. In addition, as already noted in an earlier chapter, the clerk on average meets with the prime minister four or even five mornings a week when he is in Ottawa. These meetings with the prime minister are now restricted to two individuals – the prime minister's chief of staff and the clerk of the Privy Council Office. The clerk of the Privy Council will chair a meeting of several senior PCO officials most mornings to identify issues to raise with the prime minister. They will look to the media, to their own files, and through their own contacts in line departments to identify the issues.

Not only do the meetings provide guaranteed access to the prime minister, they also offer an opportunity to raise whatever matter or to make a recommendation on any issue of interest to PCO or the prime minister. The prime minister, in turn, is also able to raise any issue and to direct the clerk to pursue any matter anywhere in government. The prime minister will very often ask the clerk to handle delicate or sensitive issues rather than asking his political advisers or senior minister. The clerk knows all the key policy actors in government well, including ministers and deputy ministers, and she is a seasoned veteran of interdepartmental battles. The clerk also knows which lever to pull or button to push without setting off alarm bells or giving rise to a series of events that could have political consequences. Outside of purely partisan matters, the clerk is for the prime minister the safest pair of hands available to him to deal with delicate issues or, for that matter, even not so delicate issues.

The clerk is also responsible to ensure that the government's decision making operates as smoothly as possible and that the integrity of due process is respected.[35] To this end, she directs the work of all the secretariats in PCO, and in turn these secretariats have a hand in every policy area. PCO, employing about 500 full-time equivalents, is a relatively large organization, given that it does not deliver any programs, and so it has the resources to keep a running brief for the prime minister on the key issues confronting the government.

Managing the Process

When asked to sum up the work of the Privy Council Office from the perspective of a line department, a former senior line deputy minister observed, 'If PCO, or for that matter other central agencies, were ever asked to ice a hockey team, they would put six goaltenders on the ice.'[36] There is an element of truth in this observation. But it does not tell the whole story. To be sure, the Privy Council Office has a well-honed capacity to stop the great majority of proposals from line departments dead in their tracks, if it has to. But the office also has the capacity to make things happen and to take the lead in certain areas. Indeed, in one area – machinery of government – only PCO has the mandate and the ability to promote and initiate change.

What goes on inside PCO? People who work there, or have worked there, report that there is never a shortage of things to do. The office is organized by functions and, at least until recently, in parallel with the Cabinet committee system. The staff is expected to have an overview of government policies and programs and to be fully aware of cutting-edge issues and problems which are likely to require the attention of the prime minister and Cabinet in the foreseeable future.[37] At all times, PCO staff know that they are responsible for managing the complex system of decision making 'on behalf of the prime minister' and it is this that 'gives them considerable responsibility and influence.'[38]

It is important to review here in some detail the nature of the work carried out by senior PCO staff. As noted above, two senior PCO officials accompany the clerk to Cabinet meetings – the deputy secretary to the Cabinet (plans) and the deputy secretary to the Cabinet (operations). Both these officials are at the deputy minister level, direct the bulk of day-to-day activities at PCO, and oversee relations with line departments (see Chart 1). It is also important to note that the PCO organization has changed a great deal during the past twenty-five years, but only at the margins. The basic structure first established under Trudeau – Planning, Operations, and Machinery of Government branches – has remained stable.

The deputy secretary (plans) oversees the work of the Priorities and Planning Secretariat, the secretariat for Macroeconomic Policy, the Communications and Consultant Secretariat and the Strategic Projects Unit. She is called upon to provide advice on strategic policy issues, and to pay particular attention to the budget, the Speech from the Throne, and other priority issues as identified by the prime minister, the clerk, or by events.

Several specialized units report directly to the deputy secretary (plans). The Policies and Planning Unit provides staff support for meetings of full Cabinet, deputy minister's breakfast meetings, and the coordinating committee of deputy ministers on policy. Another unit, the Secretariat for Macroeconomic Policy,

Chart 1
Privy Council Office

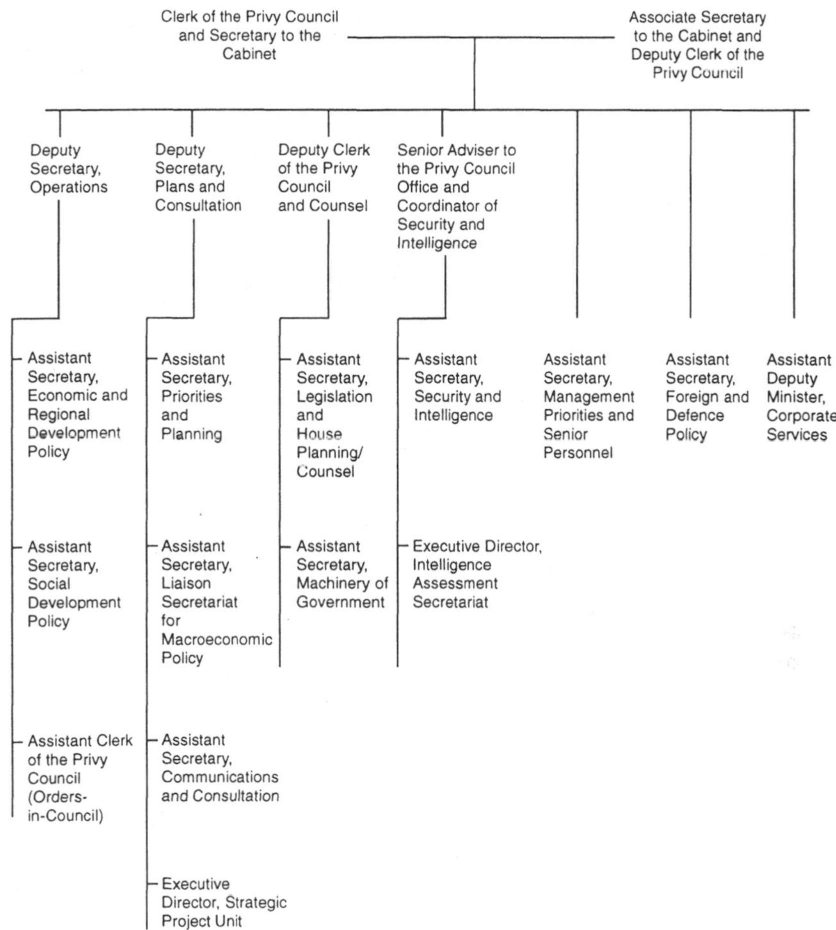

Source: Privy Council Office, December 1997

provides analysis and advice on economic and fiscal matters and on major economic issues, including the budget. The communications and consultation secretariat is responsible for coordinating government-wide communications and consultations efforts.[39] Departments coming to Cabinet with a proposal must include a section that outlines how they propose to deal with the media and with the visibility issue, and the secretariat reviews all communication plans. The Strategic Projects Unit, meanwhile, is responsible for undertaking research in 'various horizontal policy areas identified as priorities by senior management, or on matters of special interest to the Clerk of the Privy Council.'[40]

The deputy secretary (operations) has overall responsibility for the operation of the Cabinet committees for the Social Union, the Economic Union, and for the Special Committee of Council. She directs the work of two policy secretariats (economic and social development) and both are directly responsible for the functioning of the two Cabinet committees. She is also responsible for the approval of orders-in-council, regulations, and other statutory instruments, for planning swearing-in ceremonies at Rideau Hall of new ministers, and all Cabinet shuffles. Another unit provides administrative support services to Cabinet and Cabinet committees. It is responsible for the format, distribution, and control of Cabinet papers, Cabinet committee meeting agendas, memoranda to Cabinet and other documentation, and for preparing the schedule for Cabinet and Cabinet committee meetings.[41]

The Privy Council Office has on staff an assistant secretary responsible for foreign and defence policy. The incumbent has two major functions: 'The first derives from the Prime Minister's responsibility as head of government to be actively involved in the formulation and execution of foreign and defence policy. The Assistant Secretary to the Cabinet provides advice to the Prime Minister on major foreign policy issues, and supports him or her in dealings with other heads of government and heads of state (e.g., correspondence, visits to Canada, and foreign travel). In addition, the Assistant Secretary to the Cabinet deals directly, on behalf of the Prime Minister, with foreign government representatives in Canada and with senior officials of foreign leaders's offices.'[42]

Another assistant secretary is responsible for coordinating the government's legislative program for each session of Parliament and 'advises on tactical matters.'[43] Yet another provides support on all matters relating to the prime minister's prerogative and responsibilities as architect and umpire of our system of Cabinet government. The business of the secretariat includes providing advice and support on the structure, organization, and functioning of government; ministerial mandates and responsibilities; and transition from government to government, including organizing Cabinet and its committees.[44] And still another assistant secretary provides advice and support on the selection, appointment, career planning, compensation, performance review, and termination of governor-in-council appointees, 'with particular emphasis on Deputy Ministers, Associate Deputy Ministers, and Heads of Agencies.'[45] All the assistant secretaries are supported by at least several senior level officials.

PCO also houses secretariats responsible for security and intelligence. These secretariats assist the prime minister by providing information and advice on security and intelligence policy matters and by overseeing the intelligence assessment function, a service designed to produce intelligence assessments on a wide range of subjects for the prime minister and other senior government officials.[46] There are also other units responsible for providing administrative, financial, and personnel support services to the office, including one that is responsible for processing mail addressed to or from the prime minister as head of government.[47]

It is also important to note that the relationship between the commissioner of the RCMP and the head of Canadian Security Intelligence Service (CSIS) on one side, and the prime minister through the PCO on the other, has become so close over the past twenty years or so that the minister responsible – the Solicitor General – for the two agencies is now effectively cut out of some of the most important discussions and decisions. It was not always the case. In the early 1960s, for example, the commissioner of the RCMP regularly met the minister responsible on a one-on-one basis to brief him on sensitive security matters. In turn, the minister would inform and advise the prime minister on specific cases, as required.[48]

Formal job descriptions, by all accounts, do reflect fairly accurately what goes on in PCO and the kind of work the office performs. But, again, it does not tell the whole story. The rest of the story lies not only in what they actually do in their day-to-day activities, but for whom they actually do it. I asked all former and current PCO officials I consulted whether they felt that they were accountable to the prime minister or to Cabinet. Some said the prime minister, but the majority said both. I then asked if they were ever put in a situation which involved a conflict between supporting the prime minister and Cabinet who they would support? Everyone answered that they would support the prime minister. In fact, one expressed surprise that I would even want to ask this question, thinking that the answer should be obvious to all students of government.[49] Only one insisted that he would not pick sides because he could never imagine a scenario when he would be asked to do so. 'The point,' he explained, 'is that the prime minister always has a right of veto in Cabinet, and he will exercise it if he has to. So we will never be asked to pick sides because the prime minister can always have his way if he wants it. He can ask that an item not appear on the Cabinet agenda even though it has successfully gone through Cabinet committee. I have seen prime ministers do precisely that on more than one occasion. He can also establish the Cabinet decision he wants rather than what the majority of ministers want, and I have seen prime ministers do that too.'[50]

None of the current or former PCO officials I consulted could remember a single instance when they were ever asked to take sides between the prime minister and Cabinet. One former official argued that 'such a scenario might have been possible forty years ago, and I do not know this for certain. What I do know is that it would not happen now.'[51]

I put another question to several present and former PCO officials – do you spend most of your time working for the prime minister, for Cabinet, or in managing the Cabinet process? By and large, they responded that it is not possible to divide the three responsibilities into three different and watertight components. The three responsibilities, one PCO official claimed, 'actually come in one package, not three.'[52] However, it became clear in the discussions that the focus of PCO officials in their day-to-day work is first the 'prime minister,' and second, maintaining 'the integrity of the Cabinet process for the prime minister.'

PCO, in its submission to the Lambert Royal Commission, argued that 'the Prime Minister is responsible for the process of Cabinet operations.'[53] PCO officials certainly view their role as being helping hands to the prime minister in managing the integrity of the Cabinet process. Indeed, they are now being asked to focus more on the prime minister and his requirements than at any time in the past. In fact, in many cases, their only client now is the prime minister and his office. It will be recalled that Prime Minister Chrétien abolished several Cabinet committees when he assumed office in 1993, including, among others, Priorities and Planning, Communications, Operations, and Foreign Affairs and Defence. The secretariats in PCO supporting these committees were not, however, abolished, and they continue to be fully staffed and operating.

The Priorities and Planning Secretariat, with the disappearance of the committee, is now focusing more and more of its energy on the budget process and, together with the other secretariats, on managing the prime minister's early warning system – that is, to alert the clerk and the prime minister to emerging issues, potential interdepartmental conflicts, and any matter that might be of interest to either or both.

The PCO secretariats carry out a number of functions for the prime minister, Cabinet, and the two remaining sectoral Cabinet committees. They are responsible for Cabinet papers and for preparing records of decisions for Cabinet and Cabinet committees. They monitor all developments in their sectors and maintain close contact with departments falling in their areas of responsibility. They provide advice to the prime minister and to the chairs of the Cabinet committees. They also frequently act as a kind of broker in mediating jurisdictional or interdepartmental disputes. They can be called upon by the prime minister to search for or 'arrange for a compromise' and to provide the forum for different departments and agencies to get together to sort out differences.[54]

How does the Cabinet decision-making process work and what is PCO's role? In early 1995, the prime minister decided that in future he would hold three Cabinet retreats a year – one on the budget, one on strategic orientation, and one on implementing the government's work plan or agenda. Discussions at these retreats are wide-ranging and very rarely focus on resolving specific issues. Briefing material is presented, for example, on the government's fiscal position, and Cabinet members can voice their concerns and even question some of the points made in it. But they are not asked to approve or reject anything specific. What can emerge from these Cabinet retreats is at best a very broad sense of where the government is at on important issues like the budget. They can also provide a sense of direction for Cabinet ministers as they go about their work.

However, even regular Cabinet meetings tend to focus more on broad policy agenda items than on specific issues. Indeed, Cabinet deliberations today are vastly different than was the case under Prime Ministers St Laurent and Pearson. Cabinet then was expected to make decisions even on questions of detail, such as awarding relatively minor government contracts. Trudeau's decision to establish an elaborate Cabinet committee system pushed many issues away from the Cabinet table down to committees such as Priorities and Planning, which he also chaired. Mulroney did much the same as Trudeau, and when he wanted a consensus on specific issues he decided not to manage himself, he, like Trudeau, turned them over to the Priorities and Planning Committee rather than to full Cabinet.

Chrétien, as already noted, abolished many Cabinet committees, including Priorities and Planning. It appears, however, that Cabinet has continued to function much as it did under Trudeau and Mulroney, and it has not, as envisaged when Chrétien came to power, become 'the senior forum for collective decision-making.'[55] Current and former Chrétien ministers reveal that Cabinet is not where decisions are made. Rather, it is where briefings are presented, information is shared, and where the prime minister and certain ministers provide a general *tour d'horizon*. The issues that keep surfacing at regular Cabinet meetings include the government's fiscal position, national unity, the government's political standing, and foreign affairs. These issues do not lend themselves to Cabinet decisions.

Every Cabinet in Ottawa since the introduction of standing committees of Cabinet in the 1960s, and this includes the Chrétien Cabinet, has had at least two Cabinet committees to coordinate and take decisions in the two broad sectors of economic and social policy.[56] PCO officials provide policy advisery and administrative support to these committees and a strong relationship invariably develops between the relevant assistant secretary and the chair of the committee.

Prime ministers since Trudeau, and again Chrétien is no exception, are quite prepared to let Cabinet committees make decisions. Full Cabinet can always act as a court of appeal for these decisions, and Cabinet documents include an appendix which lists all Cabinet committee decisions for formal Cabinet approval. But very few ministers will want to appeal a Cabinet committee decision before full Cabinet, and it is in fact very rarely done. Still, if for no other reason, the right of appeal serves at least one purpose. It 'is important in maintaining the constitutional myth of collective Cabinet decision-making and responsibility.'[57] Myth, it appears, is the apposite word. Consultations for this book reveal that in Chrétien's first mandate (1993–7) ministers challenged or asked for a review of only *three* Cabinet committee decisions. In all three cases, the prime minister took on the ministers. Current and former PCO officials reveal that prime ministers from Trudeau to Chrétien do not like ministers asking Cabinet to review a committee decision. This is because a request to review a Cabinet committee decision is a clear signal that the committee did not do its job properly. In addition, if they were a 'real problem with the decision,' one former senior PCO official explains, 'the prime minister would have been fully briefed beforehand, and he would have taken steps to resolve the matter or taken the item off the Cabinet agenda.'[58] Another former PCO official who regularly attended Cabinet meetings observed, 'It takes real guts for a minister to question in full Cabinet a Cabinet committee recommendation. Certainly, Chrétien and Mulroney had little tolerance for this, and so did Trudeau, though I am told that he could be a bit more tolerant.'[59]

Prime Ministers Trudeau and Mulroney chaired the Priorities and Planning Committee, where important issues were resolved. Chrétien does not chair any Cabinet committee, but this is not to suggest that the centre of government has less control over its policy agenda or the operation of the remaining Cabinet committees. The prime minister's early warning system operates as well, if not better, than at any time in the past. Indeed, PCO officials now have more time to spend operating and refining it since they do not have to service the elaborate committee systems of the Trudeau and Mulroney years.

How does PCO secure information from departments to feed its early warning system? PCO officials report that they employ 'any number of means,' but that in any event the great majority of departments will happily share information with them. One former PCO official reports that he 'made it a point of regularly having lunch with departmental assistant deputy ministers responsible for policy' and that he had little difficulty in securing all the information he needed to do his job.[60] Assistant deputy ministers know full well that PCO will have a strong, if not determining say, in any future promotion.

Another former PCO official reports that he always insisted that his 'staff attend all departmental retreat meetings, and all major policy meetings in the departments for which they were responsible.'[61] Yet another reveals that most deputy ministers will happily share whatever information they have with PCO because it is very much in their interests to do so. He explains, 'A deputy minister knows that it is not in his or even in his department's interest to shortcircuit the system, to do an end run, or to surprise me or anybody else in PCO. He may get away with it once, but even then the clerk will have a private word with him. If he tried to do it often, he will get clobbered and he simply will not survive. Deputy ministers are all very well aware of this.'[62] I then asked, what if a minister should direct his deputy minister not to inform PCO? His response: 'This happens from time to time. But a competent deputy minister knows better, and he will ignore his minister's instructions in such a situation, or at least in most instances. He will have a private word with someone at PCO, perhaps even the clerk, to explain what his minister wants and what were his instructions.'[63]

It does sometimes happen that a deputy minister is told by his minister to favour a particular position while central agency officials are making it clear to him that they favour another, even contradictory, position. In most cases, the latter know the prime minister's position, and if he agrees with theirs, then everyone knows that the minister will not secure approval for his initiative. And the prime minister usually does agree with the views of his central agency officials, if only because PCO and Intergovernmental Affairs officials have developed a keen sense of where the prime minister would stand on any given issue.

But there are exceptions to the above. There are instances, however infrequent, when a minister is able to get his way by getting to the prime minister before the matter goes to Cabinet. A former deputy minister of Indian Affairs and Northern Development reports, for example, that at one point he was caught between the views of his minister and those of PCO and what was then the Federal-Provincial Relations Office. In response to the Penner report in the early 1980s, the minister wanted to reduce substantially administrative controls attached to the funding of aboriginal programs. Central agency officials made it 'very clear' to him, 'time and again,' that they disagreed 'fundamentally' with his minister on that point. He reports that he accompanied his minister to Cabinet committee (Priorities and Planning) and it 'became clear that my minister had done his homework with the prime minister. The prime minister put me in a difficult position when he specifically asked where I stood on the matter. I had to respond that I was supporting my minister. The prime minister also indicated his support for my minister and in the end my minister won the day. There were a few difficult moments for me with senior central agency staff for a week or two after that, but they understood very well that I was put in a difficult situation. I would add, however, that this kind of situation did not happen very often. In all my years in government, I do not recall PCO officials losing too many battles.'[64]

PCO officials will prepare a brief two- or three-page memorandum for the clerk and the prime minister at the first sign that something is developing in a government department which could be of interest to them. The note usually concludes with a recommendation so that PCO knows where the clerk and the prime minister, or even senior PMO officials, will stand on the matter if it ever goes forward. PCO officials report that at times the note will come back from the prime minister with instructions, but that often, perhaps more so under Chrétien than his predecessors, there will be no feedback. Trudeau, they add, would respond in the great majority of cases, Mulroney not always, but more often than Chrétien. In all cases, however, whenever something caught the prime minister's interest, he would respond with fairly clear instructions and would often continue to follow the issue and ask for briefings from that moment on.

PCO officials will communicate to departments how well their proposal or their issue is progressing in the system, especially if they sense problems. They will, however, usually not say, 'The prime minister thinks, or the prime minister does not like the idea.' A much more popular approach is to tell a department 'this will not fly' or 'you need to adjust your proposal' or 'there are some concerns from several quarters.'[65] Departments will usually respond by adjusting their proposals, but sometimes they do not, and the minister may press ahead and bring a proposal to Cabinet committee.

The chairs of Cabinet committees are also kept in the loop, and PCO officials will inform them of the prime minister's views. Senior PMO officials communicate frequently with chairs of Cabinet committees and will sort out any potential political or policy problems directly with them. Central agency officials report that the chairs are usually on 'the same wave length' as the prime minister and 'they do talk.'[66] As mentioned in chapter 4, one senior PMO official showed me a copy of the prime minister's weekly agenda. He was quick to add, however, that the agenda 'does not even reveal all that much about how things work. The telephone and how often the prime minister uses it is in many ways much more important than what the weekly agenda reveals.'[67] A former senior policy adviser to Prime Minister Mulroney made precisely the same point, and added that the prime minister and Cabinet committee chairs had a strong working partnership. 'The prime minister,' he said, 'trusted their judgment to make the kind of decisions that he would make. That is why he appointed them over others. When committee chairs were not certain where the prime minister stood, or would stand, on a particular issue, they would raise it with him, or with me, or with someone in PMO. The lines of communications were always pretty strong.'[68]

It is important to stress, however, that not all issues raised in memoranda sent to the clerk and the prime minister by PCO staff involve a proposal, a Cabinet memorandum, a potential interdepartmental conflict, or an initiative involving new money. It is also important to bear in mind that not all memoranda to Cabinet require a decision – some are for information purposes only. Short briefing notes are also designed to brief the prime minister before a meeting with a Cabinet minister, or premiers, or a foreign head of government, and so on. PCO officials will secure a full understanding of the issues from the relevant departments and gain an appreciation for what their minister wishes to raise with the prime minister, and brief the prime minister accordingly.

Present and former PCO officials report that a great deal of time is spent managing what they label as visible and invisible errors. Visible errors are those that are brought up in question period or appear in the media. They nearly always involve ministers. Examples include Marcel Massé's decision to use a government jet to deliver a speech in Boston, David Dingwall's decision to use his influence to reallocate federal funding for highways construction from one region of Nova Scotia to his own in Cape Breton, and John Fraser's decision to release rancid tuna for public consumption. Or it may be a minister fumbling the answer to an anticipated question from the media or mishandling a government report. The list goes on.

How does one handle such a problem? PCO officials clearly cannot bring an offending minister back on track and call him on the carpet. The prime minister, one of his senior staff members, or the clerk of the Privy Council can have a private chat with a minister to go over where and how he created problems for the government. PCO officials, meanwhile, will provide a thorough briefing on the issue and certainly communicate concerns from the centre to the minister's senior departmental officials.

What about invisible errors? These are far more common than visible ones and come in 'all shape and sizes.'[69] They are only invisible because people outside government have not uncovered them, or if they have, they have not made an issue of them. In describing an invisible error, a senior central agency official observed, 'Take, for example, the case of Senator Andy Thompson. He spent only twelve days in the Senate since 1990 when it first started taking attendance. Senators knew there was a problem with Senator Thompson, but nothing was done. The *Ottawa Citizen* broke the story and made it front page news. Only then did the problem become visible outside of the Senate. At that point the Senate had to respond because the invisible had suddenly become very visible.'[70] The same applies to government, he adds, insisting that 'there are many, many errors or problems that never become a full-blown political crisis or even a crisis at all. Sometimes we are able to manage them, but more often we simply get lucky.'[71]

I asked for specific instances. Officials mentioned as an example a minister announcing a project or even a policy proposal without having first submitted it to the Cabinet committee and Cabinet process. As I was conducting some of the interviews for this book in the fall of 1997, a minister had made a public statement regarding tobacco advertisement without having gone through the Cabinet process. That was an invisible problem to everyone outside of Cabinet and PCO. If that minister could do it once, he could do it again, and worse, it could encourage others to do the same. There is, after all, no quicker way to introduce a new policy than by simply announcing it. But it also goes to the heart of the integrity of the Cabinet decision-making process. Again, the prime minister, or one of his senior staff members, or the clerk of the Privy Council will have a word with the offending minister to make clear that it should not happen again.

Invisible errors can also include a minister making a statement at a public meeting which is in direct contradiction to government policy. Again, at the time I was carrying out the interviews in PCO in November 1997, word got around that a senior minister had contradicted government policy in a media scrum in Fredericton, New Brunswick. PCO communications officials were quickly in contact with departmental and PMO officials to ensure that everyone knew the facts and that a game plan was ready to deal with the situation in case the media made a story of it. The media, however, never did, and the problem remained invisible. Former PMO and PCO officials also report that it is not uncommon for a minister to be at complete loggerheads with his deputy minister. Indeed, they claim that there have been situations when the two were not even on speaking terms. The problem often has to wait for a minister or deputy minister shuffle for resolution, and the hope is always that in the meantime this situation will not become visible, and that, in addition, it will not give rise to a new political crisis because a file has been mismanaged or left unattended.

A serious conflict between two ministers also constitutes an invisible problem. It may be, for example, that the minister of Industry favours protection for drug manufacturers to promote research and development in Canada while the minister of Health will oppose such protection, insisting that it leads to higher costs for drugs. PCO officials will have an excellent grasp of the conflict even before it surfaces at Cabinet committee or Cabinet. They will work with departmental officials to find common ground and identify a position which both departments and their ministers will support.

A measure of success for officials working at the centre is whether they are able to manage such situations so that they remain invisible. A story on the evening news or in the *Globe and Mail* on a serious disagreement between two ministers is never a welcome development in the Langevin building corridors. One senior PCO official, explaining his role in managing invisible problems, described his job in this way: 'What I do here is to fall on hand grenades. Our role here is to manage problems so that they do not become unmanageable political crises.'[72]

A number of present and former central agency officials also expressed concerns over the use of decks – a series of slides presenting ideas and recommendations in bullet form – to make presentations to Cabinet and Cabinet committee meetings. The deck first surfaced in 1983 in the later months of the Trudeau government. It has now become an instrument of choice for ministers and their senior officials.

Decks, it is argued, fall short of the traditional Cabinet memoranda in a number of ways. For one thing, they are largely empty of analysis. The traditional Cabinet memorandum has numerous headings which must be respected, including the identification of the *issue*, the *recommendations*, *rationale* for the recommendations, identification of *problems and strategies*, *political considerations*, *intergovernmental relations*, and the *position* of relevant departments. It also contains an *analysis* heading under which options to deal with the situation at hand are outlined. Decks, on the other hand, tend to focus on the bottom line immediately and to concentrate on political considerations.

Decks also tend to discourage interdepartmental consultations, since they only present, in point form, a relatively small part of the information. PCO officials now insist that all decks must be accompanied by a traditional Cabinet memorandum. However, ministers and other departmental officials still tend to look only at the deck and ignore the traditional memorandum.

The result is that the substantive debate on a Cabinet proposal increasingly takes place between the sponsoring minister and his department and central agency officials, who are often the only ones sufficiently well plugged in to a proposal to see it take shape, and who have the time and resources to focus on both the deck and the memorandum. The upshot is that decks tend to strengthen the hand of central agencies in their dealings with departments and to weaken the interdepartmental community. The abolition of several Cabinet committees has also had a similar impact.

Finance officials report that their minister, Paul Martin, has now taken decks to a new level. He prefers to brief Cabinet with power points rather than a simple deck. Power points are developed through the aid of the most modern computer techniques involving colour, large print, small print, and other forms of visual enhancement. The more substantive aspects of power points are captured in just a few words and, according to officials, do not lend themselves to in-depth policy discussions. They are, in the words of one, 'overheads with panache, a kind of Disney production.'[73]

What about the charge that if asked to ice a hockey team PCO would put six goaltenders on the ice? I put the question to several present and former PCO officials, and they all agreed that there was something to the observation. One explained, 'There is a misconception out there. PCO is not a policy shop. It is into operations. It is into transactions. It is not into coming up with new, grandiose policy solutions. The bottom line is that PCO is into risk management. That is its line of work. That being the case, you obviously try to minimize risks by stopping or derailing things that can go wrong.'[74] Another, who did not disagree with the goaltender analogy, added, however, that 'on occasions, PCO does take the lead. I can think of the transfer of human resources development programs to the provinces where we played a key role. Without us, I doubt if the initiative would have ever taken place.'[75]

There are other examples when PCO officials take charge of a file, having been instructed by the prime minister 'to make things happen.' One pointed to federal relief assistance for Manitoba flood victims in April–May 1997 as a case in point. He explains, 'We made things happen at extremely short notice. In fact, the prime minister told us at 4:00 p.m. one day to get the package done, and by 8:00 the next morning, everything was in place and we were pretty well ready for an announcement.'[76] At about the same time, another initiative, a $25 million package, was put together and announced, all in a matter of a few days. An official of the Western Economic Development Department who put the package together reports that in all his years in government he had never seen something happen so quickly. 'It became clear,' he reports, 'that the prime minister and the Privy Council Office had decided that this needed to happen. There was no sign of any interdepartmental meetings. In fact, I was effectively working for PCO when I prepared the initiative. I have never seen a Treasury Board submission getting approved so quickly. From start to finish, it took no more than seventy-two hours. Yet before and after, I attended countless interdepartmental meetings where Finance officials insisted that there was no money.'[77]

Another official mentioned the Oka crisis as yet another example of PCO taking charge of a file. He explains, 'The clerk, at the urgent request of the prime minister, essentially brought the file into PCO. Most mornings, Tellier [Paul Tellier, then clerk of the Privy Council] would meet with senior officials from the Department of Indian Affairs and Northern Development and from other relevant department, such as Justice and the RCMP, to manage the file. He did this until the crisis was over.'[78]

Foreign Affairs, Defence, and Security

Prime ministers traditionally have retained a special interest in foreign relations. Indeed, from 1912 until 1946, the prime minister also acted as his own secretary for External Affairs.[79] Even since 1946, the prime minister and his minister of Foreign Affairs have had to forge a close working relationship, and particularly in more recent years, the onus is on the minister to make it work. To be sure, if the two are always at loggerheads either in 'temperament or in policy,' the minister will have to go.[80] Other ministers, meanwhile, can get a 'look-see' in Canadian foreign affairs, but they do not have much of a say in its development. As noted above, there is no longer a Cabinet committee on foreign affairs and defence. Ministers will, from time to time, get a briefing in foreign affairs from the minister or the prime minister at Cabinet meetings, but these are quite general in nature and rarely focus on a specific point for resolution.

Canadian prime ministers, however, have, since Trudeau, sought to establish an independent source of advice on foreign affairs and to have a strong say in shaping policy. Trudeau appointed Ivan Head as international relations adviser in his own office from 1970 to 1978. We are now informed that 'during his tenure, Head usually exerted more influence on Canadian foreign policy than the incumbent secretary of state for external affairs.'[81]

Since the 1970s, the Privy Council Office has also retained a strong capacity to provide an independent source of advice. But this capacity is not simply reactive or a court of second opinion. It can also be proactive on selected files and shape new initiatives. Consultations with senior government officials reveal, for example, that the key organizers of the high profile land mines summit in Ottawa in late November 1997 were from PMO and PCO, not from Foreign Affairs. As he left the conference, Prime Minister Chrétien turned to the assistant secretary of Foreign and Defence Policy from PCO and observed, 'Congratulations, you have organized a very successful conference.'[82] The prime minister left little doubt as to who was the driving force behind the conference, and his comments were not lost on anyone, including officials from Foreign Affairs. A senior PCO official explained that 'the success of the treaty banning land mines had everything to do with the prime minister. Only the prime minister could make it happen in the Ottawa system and have access to the other heads of government to get them to focus on the issue. It is one case where [Lloyd] Axworthy [the minister of Foreign Affairs] gets a great deal of the credit, but where the prime minister is largely responsible for the success.' He added, 'One would have to be extremely naive about international relations to think that a minister could deliver the so-called Ottawa process which led 125 countries to sign a ban of land mines. Without the prime minister's direct involvement, we would still be trying to get 12 countries to sign.'[83]

Barbara McDougall, former minister of External Affairs in Mulroney's government, commented that heads of government 'talk to one another quite often. There is now such a thing as the telephone.'[84] The prime minister cannot control or even predict when and on what issue a foreign head of government will wish to communicate with him. The growing reliance on international regional summits ranging from the G7 to APEC and la francophonie meetings also places the prime minister front and centre in dealing with many international issues. But there are other reasons. An observer of British politics writes that 'Prime Ministers [also] have a more personal motive. Visits abroad and summit meetings have glamour. Every Prime Minister has devoted decades to seemingly intractable domestic problems. The world stage offers a different kind of politics where he automatically enjoys dignity and prestige ... At home, he is a politician. Abroad, he is a statesman.'[85]

Whatever the motive, it is clear that international summits, combined with modern means of communications, together with his or her power of appointment, provide the prime minister, his office, and the Privy Council Office with a strong capacity to shape Canada's position on many foreign affairs issues. Two observers of Canadian politics write that 'If someone sneezes within PMO, they sometimes said at the Foreign Affairs Department, everyone catches a cold at their offices at Fort Pearson.'[86]

The prime minister, PMO, and PCO will obviously pick and choose the international issues they want to influence, and when they do so, they will dominate the discussions and even shift the debate away from other issues at hand. In his comparative study of Canadian and Australian foreign affairs, Andrew Cooper writes, 'A tell-tale sign of how Canada's economic and diplomatic strategy were subordinated to political tactics in agricultural trade was the routing of all important decisions in this issue area in the later stages of the GATT negotiations through the central agencies of the Prime Minister's Office and the Privy Council Office. The decisive impact of the constitutional issue in this matter inevitably stymied the government's ability to perform effectively in the concluding phase of the Uruguay Round.'[87]

As in foreign affairs, so in defence. Here too the centre plays an important role. For one thing, diplomacy and defence are interrelated. For another, some of the most important defence issues now relate to the purchase of military equipment, ranging from fighter jets and helicopters to armoured land vehicles. These purchases are not only very expensive, having a considerable impact on the government's expenditure budget, but they also have international trade implications. The trade implications and the value of the contracts are such that foreign heads of government will get involved and will call the prime minister on the matter. Large military contracts also have regional implications as the provinces vie for a share of the pie. For these reasons and others, the prime minister and the Privy Council Office will invariably want to be directly involved in the decisions.

In addition, the prime minister, as head of government, 'cannot escape a special responsibility for the security of the country.'[88] Whenever there is a Cabinet committee on security and intelligence, it is the prime minister who chairs it. Though there are at the moment no operating Cabinet committees for security and intelligence, the Privy Council Office still houses secretariats in Foreign and Defence Policy, Security Intelligence, and Intelligence Assessment, all headed by assistant deputy minster level officials reporting to the clerk of the Privy Council through a deputy clerk who is a deputy minister level official.[89] These secretariats, along with the others in PCO, perform a variety of functions, but again, the most important one is to brief the prime minister on all significant developments in their areas.

PCO has two important policy instruments at hand to play a proactive role, and it never hesitates to employ them. One, the preparation of mandate letters, is a recent development, and the other, organizing the machinery of government, is virtually as old as Confederation, but it has gained a great deal of importance since the early 1970s.

A Mandate for Ministers

In the late 1970s, the Privy Council Office began the practice of preparing mandate letters for delivery to ministers on the day of their appointments. It has since become an integrated part of the cabinet-making process. Mandate letters are now handed to all ministers when they are first appointed to Cabinet and also when they are assigned to a new portfolio.

It is now extremely rare even for a senior minister to be reassigned without receiving a mandate letter signed by the prime minister. There are very few exceptions. One former PCO official explains, 'In the case of [Don] Mazankowski [deputy prime minister in the Mulroney government], it really did not make much sense to hand him a mandate letter when he received a new assignment in Mulroney's second mandate, and we did not prepare one. But in virtually all cases, we had mandate letters prepared.'[90] All ministers in the Chrétien government, for example, were handed a mandate letter at the time he formed the government in 1993 and again in his second mandate in 1997.

What are the contents of these mandate letters? The letters are brief in most cases, only about two to three pages in length. They are also tailored to the recipient. That is, a mandate letter to a newly appointed minister will be different from one to a veteran Cabinet minister. In the first instance, it will outline basic issues about becoming a Cabinet minister, including conflict-of-interest guidelines, and the need to respect the collective nature of Cabinet decisions. In all cases, the letters will point to issues the minister should attend to and identify priority areas, if any, for her to pursue. Here, again, there are two basic mandate letters. One states, in effect, 'Don't call us, we'll call you.' That is, the prime minister has decided that the department in question should not come up with a new policy agenda or legislative program. In these cases, the message is essentially: keep things going, do not cause any ripples, and keep out of trouble.[91]

In other cases, the letter will refer to particular policy objectives and major challenges. In these cases, they can be quite specific, singling out proposed legislation, a special concern that needs attending to or a program that needs to be overhauled.

Mandate letters are drafted in the machinery of government secretariat in the Privy Council Office. They are routed to the prime minister via the clerk. Things can get quite hectic at the time a new Cabinet is sworn in. The identity of the minister needs to be confirmed, the letters need to be drafted and, once approved, to be translated. In the past, there have been very few changes made to the letters either by the clerk or by officials in the Prime Minister's Office. To be sure, there is always discussion on the contents of the proposed letters so that the drafters are not working in a vacuum. But by and large, PMO staff do not substantially alter the letters once drafted. The one exception was the 1997 swearing in of the Chrétien Cabinet, where a number of the letters were returned by the Prime Minister's Office for revisions.

Where does machinery of government staff get its information to prepare the letters? First, from PCO officials with sectoral responsibilities – that is, those who are in constant communication with departments because of their work with the Cabinet committees for economic and social policies. Second, from the departments themselves. The deputy minister will be asked for his views on what needs to be accomplished and to identify the department's priority areas. The third source is PMO staff, who will bring a political perspective to the process and establish what is important politically and what is not. Other sources may be consulted, including officials in the intergovernmental affairs group. I asked current and former PCO officials if the election platform of the party in power was consulted. They said that it could be, but they certainly left the impression that if it were it would be at the bottom of the pile.

A mandate letter may also be prepared when a deputy minister is appointed. Unlike the case with ministers, until Jocelyne Bourgon became clerk not all newly appointed or reassigned deputy ministers received a mandate letter. It depended. It depended on the department, on the circumstances, and on the individual being appointed. When there was some uncertainty or when it was clear that a certain task needed to be undertaken, the clerk of the Privy Council directed that a mandate letter be prepared to the newly appointed deputy minister for his signature. Bourgon now insists that a mandate letter be handed to all newly appointed or newly reassigned deputy ministers.

Are mandate letters taken seriously? The answer is yes. Indeed, ministers consulted said that it is the very first thing that they will read after leaving the swearing-in ceremony at Rideau Hall. They also report that they take their contents quite seriously. They know, as one observed, that 'the prime minister can always dig out his copy and ask about the status of a particular point.'[92] More importantly, the letters reveal what the prime minister expects from them during their stay in their departments. In addition, present and former PMO and PCO officials report that all prime ministers, from Trudeau to Chrétien, take mandate letters to ministers seriously and that they spend the required time for the process to work properly.

I asked whether mandate letters inhibit the ability of ministers to come forward with a new idea, one not originally identified in the letter. The answer is no. Things do change, new ideas can surface anytime and anywhere, and ministers do not feel hobbled by the letters with regard to new proposals. Privy Council officials also confirmed that this was indeed the case. They report that no one, including the prime minister, would likely use a mandate letter to tell a minister that he could not look at a new idea or promote a new proposal. If the letters are employed to hold ministers accountable, and from time to time they are, it is in the sense that they may be asked to explain why they have not delivered on an issue identified in the letter as a priority matter. That said, letters to ministers in a new mandate make it pretty clear which departments will enjoy a priority status at the centre of government and which will not.

I asked both present and former senior PCO officials if mandate letters do not fly in the face of the collective nature of Cabinet decision making. How can priorities be established and major tasks identified even before Cabinet has held its very first meeting? Where, I asked, is the collective aspect of these decisions? The answer was that mandate letters are not from the Cabinet. They are from the prime minister. It is the prime minister who identifies priority issues for his government, and if a minister cannot accept them, then, as one former senior PCO official explained, 'He is free to leave or to resign on the spot. He is not, after all, forced to stay in Cabinet.'[93] The same can of course be said of members of the U.S. Cabinet.

Organizing the Machinery of Government

Some thirty years ago, the Privy Council Office established a new secretariat to advise the prime minister on the structure and functioning of Cabinet and the reorganization of departments, agencies, and crown corporations. The secretariat is somewhat peculiar to Canada. Other countries with a parliamentary system, like Britain and Australia, have officers at the centre responsible for such issues, but it appears that none has a secretariat headed by an assistant deputy minister level official and employing a dozen or so people.

Even within PCO, the machinery of government secretariat enjoys a special status. It reports to the prime minister through the clerk, and it does not readily share its information or its briefing material with other PCO secretariats. It is the prime minister's prerogative to organize the machinery of government as he sees fit. He may decide to consult a few advisers and ministers when contemplating changes, but he may not. One thing is certain. Such changes, big or small, are never submitted to Cabinet for consideration. When they are announced by the prime minister, they are already a *fait accompli*. Staff in the machinery of government secretariat never assume that the prime minister will, in the end, make the anticipated decision. Accordingly, they are always careful to protect and hold very close to their chests what they consider highly sensitive advice. They also argue that to have any chance of success in introducing the changes, the prime minister and they must operate in relative isolation and secrecy. They point out that 'adjusting the machinery of government raises all kinds of fear in line departments which, when threatened, tend to marshall their forces against proposed changes.'[94]

Why is it that changes to the machinery of government are the sole prerogative of the prime minister? One reason, no doubt, is that the prime minister prefers it that way. The thinking also is that ministers and their officials are hardly in a position to rise above the fray and contemplate changes in a detached fashion, ignoring their own interests and those of their departments. PCO, meanwhile, is directly involved not only because it is the prime minister's department, but also because it stands at the centre of government with no program responsibility or turf to protect. One former clerk of the Privy Council wrote that 'without input from the Privy Council Office, the outcome of interdepartmental boundary disputes may be determined by the relative negotiating strength of ministers and/or officials. Such outcomes may not reflect the wishes of the prime minister or all ministers.'[95] He also gives two reasons for the need for secrecy at the centre, including 'keeping the prime minister's options open until the last moment [and] protecting the change from preemptive attacks by those with other interests in mind.'[96]

The machinery of government secretariat is asked, again in the words of a former clerk, 'to cope with an endless stream of minor and major changes.'[97] The secretariat, together with the priorities and planning secretariat, for example, takes the lead on behalf of the clerk in all transition planning and in preparing or coordinating briefing books for the new or re-elected government.

The secretariat also advises the prime minister on a continuing basis on making minor adjustments to the machinery of government. These could involve sorting out overlapping jurisdictions or mandates between departments, such as moving regional development agencies under the 'Industry' portfolio or alternatively granting them a stand-alone and independent status.

But the secretariat also advises the prime minister on far-reaching changes. Two examples will make this point clear. In the early 1980s, Pierre De Bané, the minister of Regional Economic Expansion (DREE) in the Trudeau Cabinet, concluded that how a government organizes itself to promote regional economic development was as important to the success of its efforts as was the substance of its economic development policies. He felt that his department lacked clout in the interdepartmental policy community in Ottawa. He had fought and lost several battles with the then minister of Industry, Herb Gray, over the location of new automotive plants and the application of duty remission for certain automobile manufactures, notably Volkswagen, to locate in Canada.[98]

De Bané wrote to Prime Minister Trudeau to ask for his support for a complete review of the policy and also of the government organization in regional development. In his letter he suggested that 'DREE's responsibilities – to ensure that all Canadians have an equal chance to make a living with dignity – can't be handled by one department with one per cent of the federal budget.' Sadly, he wrote to Trudeau, DREE, an organization Trudeau had established in 1968, had been a failure because of the department's inability to muster a concerted federal government effort. De Bané's hope was that he would be asked to lead the review and then report to Cabinet with a series of recommendations.[99] Trudeau wrote back saying that De Bané had raised some valid concerns and that his officials in the Privy Council Office would now look into the matter.

Several months later, Trudeau announced a major government reorganization for economic development. The review was conducted in complete secrecy by machinery of government staff. Not only was De Bané not asked to lead the review, he was kept completely in the dark until two days before Trudeau's public announcement, when the prime minister briefed him and told him that he was being reassigned as a junior minister responsible for *la francophonie* and international development.[100] DREE was to be disbanded and a new Department of Regional Industrial Expansion (DRIE) established. As well, a central agency responsible for managing economic policy under PEMS was to be renamed the Ministry of State for Economic and Regional Development (MSERD) and given new provincial offices. The 'decentralized central agency' was geared to provide a greatly improved regional information base. But it proved short-lived. It, too, was disbanded a few years later.

Machinery of government officials at the time of the review had become deeply concerned with constant bickering in Cabinet committees between De Bané and Gray, the ministers of DREE and Industry. Indeed, shortly after the reorganization was announced, an official in the Privy Council Office described in a media interview the advantages of the new organizational structure: 'It [heated debates between two cabinet ministers] will never happen again ... DREE had its own ideas on Volkswagen and IT&C (Industry) had different ideas ... There was a lot of squabbling. Now that they're together, they'll have to resolve their differences internally and then go to Cabinet.'[101]

The machinery of government secretariat implemented far more ambitious and sweeping changes in 1993. On the day she was sworn in as prime minister, Kim Campbell unveiled a massive restructuring of the government's operations. Certainly by Ottawa standards, the move was radical. The purpose was to reduce the number of government departments from thirty-two to twenty-three, by reshaping eight departments, providing new mandates to three others, and merging or breaking up fifteen more.[102] Prime Minister Campbell declared that the move represented the 'first step toward providing Canadians with leaner, more accessible and more efficient government to meet the challenges facing Canada over the balance of the decade and into the 21st century.'[103] She explained that the Cabinet had been cut to its smallest size since 1963. 'A large cabinet,' she added, 'can be too bulky to be bold, too massive to meet, too diffuse to direct.'[104] The *Globe and Mail* reported that this would 'fundamentally alter the way the government operates.'[105]

Staff in the machinery of government had long been planning a major overhaul of government organization in the belief that how the government was organized had become in itself an important problem. They were not alone. Robert De Cotret, one of Mulroney's Cabinet ministers, had led such a review in the early 1992. De Cotret asked several former senior government officials, including a former clerk, a former associate clerk and secretary to the Treasury Board, and a former deputy minister of Agriculture and Employment and Immigration, to become members of an advisery group. Nick D'Ombrain, deputy secretary in the Privy Council Office responsible for the machinery of government and senior personnel, was also appointed to the group. Jim Mitchell, assistant secretary of machinery of government, was the main contact in the PCO for the review and also coordinated all the staff work.

Some advisery group members contributed think-pieces to the review. John Manion, former secretary to the Treasury Board and associate secretary to the Cabinet, for example, wrote a number of notes on the role of central agencies, forcefully making the case that some streamlining was urgently required. Manion looked to other countries and argued that in most instances central agencies are small and staffed with forward- and outward-looking experts who are strategically rather than operationally oriented. In Canada, he suggested, the federal government was heavily burdened with central agencies. He insisted that central agencies had a great deal to do with the success or failure of governments and that the De Cotret exercise should review their scope, size, and operations.

Manion offered a number of possible solutions. The Treasury Board secretariat could be renamed the 'Board of Management,' as the Lambert Commission had recommended, but he was opposed to this idea and he made his opposition clear. Treasury Board, he argued, should transfer its Bureau of Real Property Management to a line department, substantially cut down or even eliminate its Administrative Policy Branch, and become the sole authority charged with setting standards and policies in all areas of human resource management. He argued that the Office of the Comptroller General should be rebuilt and fully integrated in the Treasury Board secretariat. The office, he urged, should, among other things, be responsible for the 'functional direction of internal audit and program evaluation, special audits, monitoring the implementation of ministers' policies and decisions on management and administrative issues.' Consideration should also be given, he suggested, to having the board's Program Branch report to both the Finance department and the Treasury Board secretariat. This would eliminate serious problems of overlap and duplication in the work of both Finance and the secretariat. The Public Service Commission, meanwhile, should be turned into a small agency dealing solely with initial appointments to the public service. Other members of the advisery group meanwhile suggested that the Federal Provincial Relations Office should also be substantially reduced or, if possible, eliminated after the most recent constitutional storm had passed.[106]

The De Cotret review argued that government operations should be organized like a 'deck of cards.' He made the case that much like 'hearts should be with the hearts and the spades with the spades,' government programs designed to promote human resources development should all be brought under one roof, those with industrial and economic development under another roof, and so on.[107]

To be sure, there was concern not just in central agencies but also in the deputy minister community over the role De Cotret and his advisery group played in reviewing key issues of the machinery of government. Many were puzzled why the prime minister would ask a minister, occupying a junior portfolio at that, to lead such an exercise.

In any event, the ongoing constitutional problems, together with the staging of a national referendum on a proposal to renew the Constitution, not only dominated the media, but also the prime minister's own agenda. De Cotret submitted his report on time, but the one person who could give it life – the prime minister – had other preoccupations. The Constitution and dealing with the aftermath of the failed Charlottetown Accord remained priority issues for Ottawa throughout the summer and fall of 1992. In addition, the prime minister was considering his own future and was hardly in the mood to rethink his Cabinet, particularly its membership. The De Cotret report was put on hold.

Still, all was not lost. If nothing else, the exercise proved to be a good dry run for the Privy Council Office. It revealed that a widespread consensus existed among ministers and permanent officials that the existing machinery of government was lacking on several fronts. Finally, it confirmed, once again, the view held in the Privy Council Office that the best time to introduce sweeping changes to the machinery of government is during a transition – when there is a change of government, when a new leader is elected to lead the governing party, or following a general election even if the government is re-elected.

Machinery of government people had tried to make substantial changes to government organizations in 1988 at the start of Mulroney's second mandate. They felt that there were too many ministers and too many departments, with the result that the administration of government had become fragmented. Ministers took too many issues to Cabinet committees for resolution and all too often acted as the mouthpiece for some interest groups. This, in turn, was giving rise to all kinds of problems: there was interdepartmental bickering and a lack of policy coherence, officials were constantly fighting for turf, and government departments and programs were working at cross-purposes. In addition, there were too many spending ministers clamouring for a larger piece of the pie, a pie that was increasingly being financed through borrowed money. Lastly, it was felt that with a forty-member Cabinet, many interest groups could too easily pitch their message directly at the Cabinet table since they could easily identify one minister who would happily take up their cause if only because it was his departmental responsibility to do so.

PCO saw a chance to introduce change in the machinery of government in the 1992 or 1993 transition, in anticipation of a change of government or a change in prime minister. The then clerk of the Privy Council, Glen Shortliffe, opted for a strong hands-on approach in managing the transition planning exercise. The 1993 transition was special in that, as was the case in 1984, there would perhaps be more than one transition. Kim Campbell became the new leader of the Progressive Conservative Party (and, therefore, prime minister) in June 1993, but a further change of government was of course possible following a federal election that would be held no later than the fall of that year.

Glen Shortliffe and his staff identified four basic options to reform the government organization. Shortliffe submitted these to Prime Minister Campbell presenting the pros and cons of each. In the end, Campbell accepted Shortliffe's advice and opted for 'the most radical of the four viable options.'[108] She only added a few more ministers, to bring the total to twenty-four.

Though Campbell, as Cabinet minister, had in the past shown little interest in government organization issues, she embraced Shortliffe's transition recommendations on government restructuring. Much like John Turner, who in 1984 had abolished the coordinating ministries of state, Campbell was able to make a clear break with the past and show that a new hand was at the tiller. As Patrick Weller pointed out, 'She had nothing to lose from the dramatic gesture. If she lost, any difficulties would not be hers. If she won, there would be time to sort out the problems. Unlike most policy areas where the announcement long anticipates any consequences in the community, the public impact of machinery of government changes is immediate – even if the problems of implementation will be delayed, often not finally settled for some years.'[109] However, like Turner, Campbell went down to a resounding defeat at the polls only a few months after taking office.

The clerk of the Privy Council established an Implementation Board which he chaired and whose task was to oversee the early implementation phase of the restructuring. Again, the central agencies were well represented on the board. Peter Aucoin writes that the board included the 'Secretary of the Treasury Board, the Chair of the Public Service Commission, the Deputy Secretary to the Cabinet for machinery of government, and the prime minister's chief of staff. It was subsequently expanded to include a few deputy ministers.'[110]

The Treasury Board secretariat also played a key role in the first implementation phase. It was asked to provide a proposed program structure to the reorganized departments and new expenditure targets. It was also directed to develop 'savings targets' for all departments. In the end, the Program branch in the Treasury Board secretariat played an important role not only in the implementation phase but also in some of the events and the planning leading to the June 1993 announcement. The board's staff provided key information to PCO officials on budgets, staff complements, and departmental organization. The Public Service Commission subsequently played a critical role in human resource management in the implementation phase.

PCO officials envisaged three phases to the implementation: the first would involve the head office operations of the restructured departments and senior personnel issues; the second would deal with regional operations; and the third would review what the federal government should and should not be doing. A PCO document reads, 'A third phase will begin later this year and will include a fundamental review of roles and services.' The document was distributed to all federal government employees on 9 August 1993. In the end, phase III became the program review exercise launched by the Chrétien government shortly after it came to office.[111]

Some senior members of the federal Liberal Party were critical of the reorganization. Marcel Massé, a former clerk of the Privy Council but now a Liberal candidate, argued that the government should have first examined its activities and decided what it wanted to keep, shed, or reform. Massé was also critical of the secretive ways in which the changes were developed and planned, with no proper analysis and debate about the role of the federal government.[112] Massé was not alone in his criticism.

In his review of the 1993 reorganization, Peter Aucoin writes that the centre of government was far too secretive and heavy-handed in planning the reorganization. He was also critical of its part in the implementation phases. He writes, 'The centre reduced the discretion of departments by applying a number of conditions. Chief among these were directives and targets concerning the streamlining of corporate services and the rationalization of regional structures. This approach ran directly counter to the new philosophy of management that the centre, particularly the Treasury Board Secretariat, had been preaching ...'[113] Aucoin adds that PCO's decision to manage the restructuring in 'considerable secrecy' came at a price. For one thing, he argues that PCO 'denied' itself the advantages of having advice from a wide range of participants knowledgeable about government operations, notably senior officials from line departments. He also insists that the centre was sending out a signal to the senior executives (and presumably ministers) in line departments that they could not be trusted with state secrets.[114]

Notwithstanding Massé's criticism, the newly elected Chrétien government largely left the reorganization intact. The one exception was the decision to establish a Department of Public Security. This had been designed to bring together the former portfolio responsibilities of the solicitor general (the federal police, the security and intelligence agency, the federal prison system, and the parole service); immigration policy, selection, enforcement, and appeals from the former Department of Employment and Immigration; the passport office from the Department of External Affairs and International Trade; and the border inspection and control service from the Department of National Revenue – Customs and Excise.[115] Chrétien, in opposition, vowed to undo the change if elected. Once in office, he re-established the solicitor general portfolio and established a new portfolio of Citizenship and Immigration. With that exception, though, Chrétien essentially stayed with Kim Campbell's streamlined Cabinet and new government organization. He also pursued phase III, the program review phase.

In the end, Chrétien happily inherited what Kim Campbell delivered. What Campbell delivered in turn was something that the Privy Council Office had been envisaging for some time. Still, Glen Shortliffe, a key player in the reorganization and at the time clerk of the Privy Council, stressed that Kim Campbell alone made the call on the restructuring. He explained: 'Sure, I advised, but I didn't decide.'[116]

It is clear that PCO did not advise that the centre of government be restructured. Manion's advice produced for the De Cotret exercise was ignored. Central agencies were left largely untouched, except for the Office of the Comptroller General, which was merged with the Treasury Board secretariat. However, this development had already begun in 1987, when the comptroller general began to report to the president of the Treasury Board through the secretary of the Treasury Board. No attempt was made to rebuild the office along the lines suggested by John Manion. The Federal Provincial Relations Office was substantially cut back and what was left of it was moved over to the Privy Council Office. But the failed Charlottetown Accord essentially dictated this action. The office has subsequently been integrated in the PCO but it has again grown in size to its pre-Charlottetown days. The Privy Council Office, meanwhile, was left virtually untouched, as was the Public Service Commission, the Department of Finance, and the Treasury Board secretariat.

In an interview, I put the question to Glen Shortliffe – why did you not advise that central agencies also needed to be restructured? He was, of course, well aware of Manion's earlier work. He said that the decision to leave things as is was 'a judgment call.' It was essentially decided that one could blow everything up by overloading the agenda. He explained that Parliament had recently passed the first amendment to the *Public Service Employment Act* in twenty-five years. To rethink the role of central agencies would have required changes to legislation governing the Public Service Commission, and pressing the point could have compromised all the other changes.[117]

The above explains perhaps why no effort was made to change the Public Service Commission. But what about the other central agencies – PCO, Finance, Treasury Board secretariat, even the Prime Minister's Office? This too was a judgment call. One former senior PCO official explains that to have overhauled these central agencies, the clerk of the Privy Council would 'have had to bring onside the heads of these central agencies to make it happen. He decided not to do so.'[118] In short, there are two sets of rules and procedures, one for line departments and another for central agencies. The clerk did not think it was necessary to 'bring onside' the heads of the line departments being restructured. In fact, he did not even see the need to inform them beforehand of what was about to happen to their departments.

But on this point Shortliffe is no different than earlier clerks. For example, in the case of the 1982 government reorganization for economic development, neither the minister nor the deputy minister affected by the reorganization was informed – let alone consulted – before the reorganization was fully defined and ready for its public announcement.

Intergovernmental Relations

Briefing material for ministers prepared by the Privy Council Office makes it clear that 'the Prime Minister has direct responsibility for the conduct of federal-provincial relations.'[119] The reason, PCO officials explain, is that only the prime minister is in a position to intervene in an area assigned to one of his colleagues to assert the primacy of broader federal-provincial relations considerations over the specific programs or policies for which a minister may be responsible. They add that relations with the provinces have grown in such importance over the past thirty years or so that they now permeate virtually every area of federal government activity. Only the prime minister, they insist, can take a government-wide perspective and ensure that arrangements or programs that may appear to be highly desirable in a particular area do not have implications inconsistent with the general approach to intergovernmental relations.

The prime minister can hardly do this alone or on the back of an envelope before Cabinet meetings. He needs assistance, and the kind of help he needs goes beyond the expertise available in his own immediate office. For this reason, there has been a capacity at the centre since the mid-1970s dedicated exclusively to federal-provincial relations.

The head of the intergovernmental group cautions ministers to keep his officials informed of developments in their areas of responsibility that could affect the federal-provincial relationship. This is the only way, he argues, that his group can play the lead role in coordinating the prime minister's bilateral and multilateral meetings with provincial premiers. He also strongly encourages ministers and their departments to keep abreast of general developments in federal-provincial relations and the government's overall approach to the conduct of intergovernmental affairs by consulting his group. Lastly, he reminds ministers to address federal-provincial considerations in all memoranda and discussion papers submitted to Cabinet.

Trudeau established a stand-alone central agency dealing with federal-provincial relations in 1975 and appointed Gordon Robertson, former clerk of the Privy Council and secretary to the Cabinet, to head it up. Robertson essentially turned a relatively small unit housed in PCO into a full-fledged central agency – the Federal-Provincial Relations Office – and ever since federal-provincial relations have enjoyed a strong presence at the centre of Ottawa's decision-making process. This is not to suggest, however, that responsibility for federal-provincial relations has always enjoyed separate central agency status. It has alternately been a part of PCO or had its own separate status. It has never, however, shrunk to pre-1975 days, when it had only about eight officials dedicated to it. The most recent change occurred on 25 June 1993 when the Privy

Council Office was again given responsibility for federal-provincial relations through the reintegration of the Federal-Provincial Relations Office into PCO with the establishment of the Intergovernmental Affairs Office.[120]

Still, this office is headed by a deputy minister who serves 'the Minister of Intergovernmental Affairs and, through the Clerk of the Privy Council and Secretary to the Cabinet, the Prime Minister and Cabinet.' Though he has no direct program responsibility, he is responsible for four areas:

- policy advice and strategic planning related to national unity, the broad federal-provincial agenda, and constitutional and legal issues;
- liaison and advice on relations with the provinces, including assessment of provincial priorities, monitoring of policy files with important intergovernmental dimensions, and renewal of the federation;
- communications support on issues and initiatives with important federal-provincial dimensions; and
- aboriginal affairs.[121]

As Chart 2 shows, the head of the Intergovernmental Affairs Office directs the work of two deputy secretaries, one responsible for intergovernmental policy and communication and the other for intergovernmental operations. Accordingly, the organization is patterned on the PCO, which also has two deputy secretaries, one responsible for plans, the other for operations. The four deputy secretaries in PCO are on a scale ranging from DM1 to DM3, with the latter level reserved for the most senior level appointments, including the clerk of the Privy Council and secretary to the Cabinet.

The deputy secretary of Intergovernmental Policy and Communications is responsible for the development of strategic planning, integrated analysis, and options and advice on policy and communications issues related to Canadian unity and intergovernmental relations. The deputy secretary is supported by four directors general: one is responsible for intergovernmental communications, another for policy and research, another for constitutional affairs and intergovernmental policy, and one is responsible for strategy and plans.[122]

The deputy secretary (operations), like his counterpart in PCO, directs a hands-on team, and he is expected to work closely with the deputy secretaries of both operations and plans at PCO 'to integrate federal-provincial considerations in the assessment of policy options.'[123] He is also responsible for providing an integrated view of relations with the provinces across the government's broad policy agenda. In addition, the deputy secretary provides advice on the federal-provincial aspects of the aboriginal policy agenda. He also directs the work of a director general, provincial analysis, a director general responsible

Chart 2
Intergovernmental Affairs

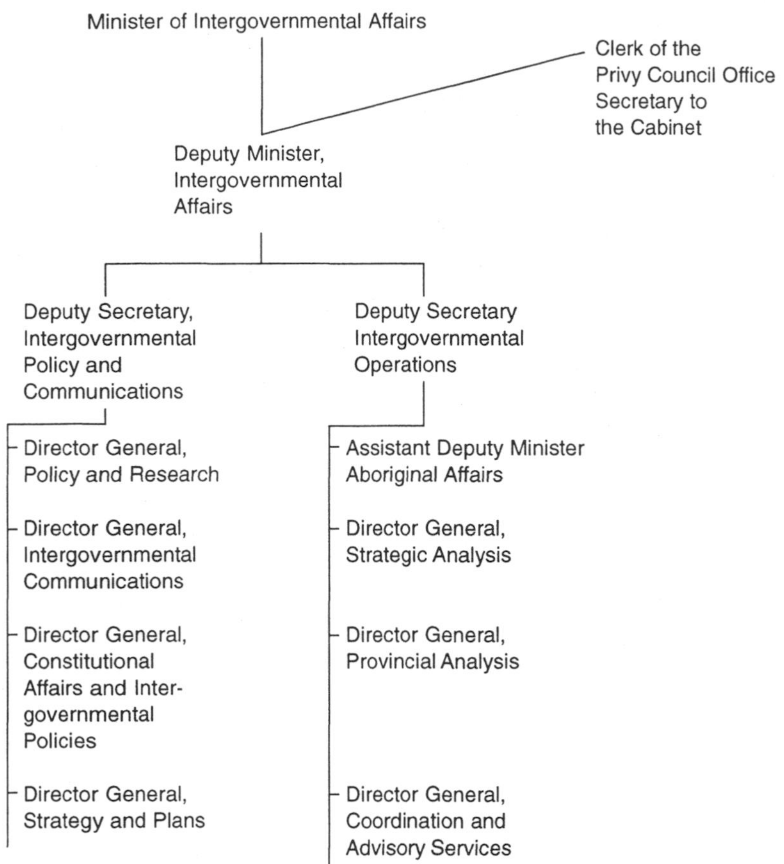

Source: Privy Council Office, December 1997

for coordination and advisery services, another for strategic analysis, and finally an assistant deputy minister of aboriginal affairs. These senior level officials, in turn, direct the work of at least several officials.[124]

There are striking similarities in the job descriptions of officials operating in traditional PCO units and those in intergovernmental affairs. Though officials in both claim that the concerns of PCO and intergovernmental affairs are basically different, there is no denying that there have been moments of tension over turf between the two. These will surface more readily when both groups report directly to the prime minister. At the moment, while the intergovernmental affairs group has a reporting relationship to the prime minister, it does so through the clerk of the Privy Council.

In the early 1980s, Trudeau became exasperated over 'duplications, repetitions, and occasional contradictions' in the briefing material sent to him by PCO and the Federal-Provincial Relations Office. He bluntly asked his senior officials whether he had to coordinate their activities himself or if they somehow could do the sorting out themselves.[125]

The Privy Council Office reminded the prime minister that it was responsible for advising him on the management of the government and in maintaining the integrity of the Cabinet. It pointed out that the federal-provincial relations aspect could be handled by adding a section on intergovernmental relations in all briefing material sent to him. This would serve to avoid duplication, and certainly any contradictions. The Federal-Provincial Relations Office meanwhile insisted that things could never be that simple. It had a mandate to advise the prime minister on the management of the federation, which had gained in importance in recent years and which was now equal in importance to advice on the management of the government.

The office insisted that management of the federation permeates, and at times even dominates, many aspects of government business. It could not be broken down into watertight compartments or contained in one government department. It could only work if the prime minister had a direct hand in its work and if federal-provincial relations generally fell under his purview. The office did not need to convince Trudeau on this point. On 12 May 1983 he had argued before the Miscellaneous Estimates Committee that 'the Federal-Provincial Relations Office is part of the Privy Council Office ... The purpose of that office is to ensure there is an overview which I have always believed should come under the Prime Minister or some ministers working directly with him, so that indeed ministers of energy, agriculture or public works who are having business with the provincial authorities know what the other ministers are doing and that there be a coordinated approach.'[126]

Prime Ministers Mulroney and Chrétien have followed Trudeau's lead and both established a direct relationship with federal-provincial relations or intergovernmental affairs. Mulroney had the secretary of Federal-Provincial Relations report either directly to him or indirectly through the clerk of the Privy Council and a minister. Chrétien has the head of intergovernmental affairs report to him also through the clerk and a minister. This enables the prime minister to have a hand in all important issues regarding federal-provincial relations.

The prime minister does not, of course, wish to be briefed on all federal-provincial issues. Many are resolved at the officials level and between the intergovernmental affairs group and one or several departments. Even line department ministers may or may not be informed of various developments.

But the prime minister will be directly involved in all important issues, particularly those that gain media visibility. The prime minister was firmly in charge of the failed Meech Lake and Charlottetown constitutional accords. The two initiatives were not born out of Cabinet's collective decision-making process. Similarly, Chrétien's Verdun speech on national unity was drafted by his key advisers and others at the centre. Cabinet was not consulted on its contents, let alone asked to make a contribution, and Chrétien read and approved every letter Stéphane Dion, the minister of Intergovernmental Affairs, sent to the Quebec government in the summer and fall 1997 which sought to establish a number of positions in the event Quebec voted for separation in a future referendum.[127] Cabinet was kept informed of developments in the exchange of letters, but it was not asked to agree to their contents.

Long-serving officials in intergovernmental affairs made the case in the consultations for this book that federal-provincial relations are both a 'substantive' and 'process' matter. By this they mean that advising the prime minister on whether, how, and when a specific initiative ought to be carried out is only part of the job. They also have to be fully conversant with the substance of a policy or program before advising on its implications. This, in turn, requires a capacity to gain a proper understanding of what departments are doing and proposing. Simply looking at what they write under 'Political Considerations' and 'Federal-Provincial Relations Considerations' headings in Cabinet documents is not sufficient.

Put differently, federal-provincial relations are no longer just limited to conferences and meetings. They cover virtually every aspect of the federal government decision-making process. Prime ministers invariably come to believe that provincial governments are much better at understanding this and applying it in their decision-making process than is the federal government. They believe that there is rarely any one-off initiative in provincial government decision making, particularly in the case of Quebec when sovereignists hold power. The thinking is that provincial governments have a game plan in their relations with the federal government and that everything fits into it. The prime minister, his office, and the Privy Council Office will push the federal government decision-making process to do the same thing. This, in turn, means that the Intergovernmental Affairs group and, in the past the Federal-Provincial Relations Office, will want to be present at departmental and interdepartmental meetings to shape policies and even decisions to promote more coherence, at least from an intergovernmental perspective, in federal government programming.

Senior PCO officials and several current and former deputy ministers insist that provincial governments are much better at coordinating their relations with the federal government than vice versa. One senior PCO official reports, for example, that 'all letters coming from the Quebec Government to all federal departments and agencies are written by two people. Imagine if we tried to do that.'[128] The federal government does not try to do that but it does from time to time ask one, several, or in some instances, all departments to check with the centre of government before it launches an initiative which could have implications for federal-provincial relations, particularly in Quebec.

It appears, however, that the federal government is constantly playing catch-up with provincial governments in their efforts to define a game plan for federal-provincial relations. Departments are for the most part left to manage day-to-day relations with provincial governments until a political crisis or a media report highlighting a problem come to light. Then the centre of government gets involved and, depending on the issue and the political circumstances, it can 'micromanage' the file, with senior line department officials essentially playing an advisery role.

The centre of government, however, has not been successful in defining an overall federal-provincial strategy for line departments. One line deputy minister reports that 'this has been a problem for us. We should be able to relate what we do to an overall government strategy. But that is not the case and we are paying the price for it.'[129] Senior PCO officials acknowledge that this is indeed the case but insist that it has been the case for some time. One reports that 'until I came here a few years ago, we did not even know what federal-provincial agreements existed. We had no inventory of them at the centre of government. At least now we have an idea of what is going on. Still, there is a problem of size. It is much easier for provinces to get their act together to establish a strategy than it is for the federal government.'[130]

The Centre Permeates and Dominates

Officials in the Federal-Provincial Relations Office in the early 1980s told the prime minister that they needed to brief him on many issues because the management of the federation 'permeates' and at times 'dominates' many aspects of government business. They could just as easily have argued that the centre of government 'permeates' and 'dominates' many aspects of government business and that they wanted to be a full partner at the centre of government, not a part-time one.

Any issue can be of interest to the centre. If the prime minister expresses an interest in any given matter, that is reason enough for the Privy Council Office to bring it into its own office, or at least to monitor its development very closely. The office also scans departmental activities to see if it should get involved, invoking an early warning system to identify issues that may create problems for the government in future that the prime minister may wish to review or that may gain notoriety in the media in the months ahead.

The centre holds in its own hands the key instruments of administration and policy. It holds the power of appointment which, as Mitchell Sharp once observed, is an important part of the structure 'by which the Prime Minister controls the operation of the federal government.' It now prepares mandate letters for ministers and deputy ministers that outline in broad terms what is expected of them as they assume new responsibilities.

The centre is responsible for policing boundaries dividing ministers and departments. It alone decides on mandates, on which department should be responsible for what. It can launch a major reorganization and fundamentally redesign the machinery of government in relative secrecy. Indeed, history tells us that that is usually precisely how major government reorganizations are conceived. History also tells us that, while the centre is quite prepared to recommend major surgery on line departments, it is much more reluctant to recommend major surgery on itself.

The centre is responsible for maintaining the integrity of the Cabinet decision-making process. A minister who wishes to modify his departmental policies or launch a major new initiative must do so through the cabinet process. Failure to do so can only invite problems for the offending minister and his department. It will also likely mean that the prime minister, a senior member of his staff, or the clerk of the Privy Council will have a word with the minister.

But here again there are two sets of rules – one for the centre and another for line ministers and departments. The prime minister can, at any moment, launch a new initiative, and he will decide if he will respect the Cabinet decision-making process. We also know that, traditionally, Canadian prime ministers have taken a special interest in certain areas of policy which can transcend the work of all government departments. These include federal-provincial relations, foreign affairs, and defence and national security.[131]

But prime ministers do not feel bound by their traditional areas of interest. During the consultations for this study, I was informed of many instances when they decided on their own or on the advice of one or two key advisers to undertake a major initiative in other areas, while completely bypassing the Cabinet decision-making process.

Prime Minister Chrétien, for example, decided in September 1997 on a new millennium scholarship fund for low- to moderate-income students. He decided to unveil the fund in his reply to the throne speech, and without consulting Cabinet. The cost of the fund to the federal treasury has been estimated at $2.5 billion and Chrétien labelled it the 'government's most significant millennium project.'[132] I put the question to Chrétien's senior advisers – why did the prime minister decide to ignore the Cabinet process in the millennium scholarship fund, given its importance both in political and financial terms to the government? The answer – 'If we had respected the process, the idea would never have come out at the other end the way we wanted it. Intergovernmental affairs would have argued that the matter was provincial, not federal; the Human Resources Department would have argued that the idea was in its jurisdiction, while Heritage Canada would have made a similar claim. The prime minister asked one of us [a PMO official] to call Paul [Martin, minister of Finance] and his deputy minister to let them know what we were doing. In that way he got what he wanted.'[133]

The minister of Finance could have pointed out that Chrétien not only ignored the Cabinet decision-making process, but also that his decision flew in the face of the program review exercise he, his department, and the Privy Council Office had completed a few years ago. Underpinning that exercise were five fundamental questions designed to determine if the federal government should continue delivering certain programs and activities. The millennium scholarship fund would not have met this test. A line minister coming forward with this initiative would have been told, as officials at the centre readily admit, that his idea would go nowhere.[134]

Yet, the minister of Finance, and for that matter the prime minister, are considered the 'guardians' in shaping the government's revenue and expenditure budget. They are the ones always ready to put the brakes on proposed new spending plans. They, together with the president of the Treasury Board, must confront the spenders – line ministers and their departments. There is now a whole body of literature describing the struggle between the guardians and spenders in shaping government budgets.[135] But as the next chapter argues, the relationship between guardians and spenders has evolved considerably in recent years.

6

Finance: Let There Be No Light

In discussing the budget process with some of his close advisers, Prime Minister Jean Chrétien once observed that he could not afford any light to show between his minister of Finance and himself.[1] Chrétien was not referring just to public disagreement. He also meant that there could not be any disagreement between the two before Cabinet colleagues. Accordingly, the bulk of the discussions between the prime minister and the minister of Finance over budget matters take place in private in the prime minister's parliamentary office or over lunch at 24 Sussex.

The Department of Finance and its minister occupy a position of preeminence in Ottawa. No minister of Finance has ever been fired, and the sudden resignation of John Turner as Finance minister in the mid-1970s caused, in the view of many, irreparable political damage to the Trudeau government, which went down to defeat in the next election.[2] The minister and Department of Finance cover the entire range of government activity. They are concerned with fiscal, and tax policy, federal-provincial relations, government expenditures, international trade and finance, and social and economic policies. In short, they are the guardians of the public purse.

They are also the government's economic adviser, a function they jealously guard. They do not easily tolerate other departments and agencies offering alternative views on economic policy. The department prides itself on holding 'quite firmly the reins of economic, fiscal, and financial policy' and on being 'considerably more influential than the US Treasury.'[3] It is well known, for example, that the Finance department was the key player in the undoing of the Economic Council of Canada in 1992. It will be recalled that Don Mazankowski announced the abolition of the council in his budget speech that year. Irving Brecher, emeritus professor of economics at McGill University and former vice-chairman of the council, writes that the 'Department of Finance, the self-proclaimed governmental fountainhead of economic wisdom ... had been uneasy about the Council's influence on economic policy, even though it was not designed to act – and did not act – as a competing source of ongoing advice to the federal cabinet.'[4]

The department's intellectual roots now firmly lie in the neoclassical school of economics. Certainly when Bob Bryce was its deputy minister (1963–70), the department had a Keynesian orientation. But Keynesian economics fell out of favour as the government's fiscal situation deteriorated alarmingly, and the department rediscovered its earlier roots.[5] It is now largely anti-interventionist, and there is no doubt that it has a great deal of confidence in the allocation of resources by the market. Its opposition to the great majority of proposed initiatives from departments is as predictable as its advice is inflexible. One deputy minister argues that 'the department has an economic theology. It is a theology that must not be challenged either from within the department or from other departments.'[6] Accordingly, not only should there be no light between the prime minister and the minister of Finance, the department's economic theology should not be exposed to a light other than its own.

The purpose of this chapter is to review the role of the minister and Department of Finance. They too operate at the centre of government. Arthur Kroeger, a former deputy minister who served in several departments, observed that 'through the budget, [they can] define the content of the entire government.'[7] He later wrote that 'governing is a continuous process of balancing aspirations and reality, of reconciling infinite wants and finite means. These are quite essentially the responsibilities of the minister of Finance, and in any cabinet only the prime minister occupies a more important position.'[8] Still, the power and influence of the minister and Department of Finance are not static. Their ability to define the content of government can vary, and this chapter explains why. It also outlines what the department does, explores the kind of relationship it has with other government actors, and discusses how it makes decisions.

What the Department Does

The Department of Finance outlines in considerable detail its organization, programs, and responsibilities in part III of the government annual expenditure plan.[9] This material is readily accessible, and there is no need to reiterate here the information contained in that document. Suffice it to note that the department employs about 700 full-time equivalents. It differs from most of its G-7 counterparts in that it does not review departmental spending in detail. The Finance or Treasury ministries in Japan, Germany, Britain, Italy, and France all not only prepare their government's, budget but also tend to carry out program-by-

Chart 3
Organization of the Department of Finance

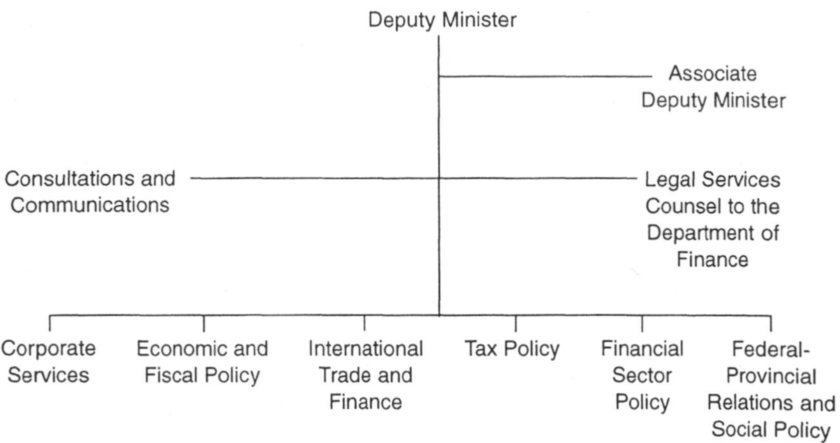

Source: Department of Finance, November 1997

program spending reviews and perform government accounting and financial control functions. In Canada, the Treasury Board secretariat reviews program spending and it is also responsible for accounting and financial control.

Accordingly, the federal Department of Finance is, comparatively speaking, smaller than its G-7 counterparts, and it tends to focus mostly on policy and program analysis. It also has very limited program administration. Unlike the case in France, for example, the Department of Finance is not responsible for revenue collection. Finance officials insist, however, that even though the department is 'small and focussed exclusively on policy and analysis ... [it is] as powerful as most of its G-7 counterparts in designing the economic agenda and moving it forward.'[10] They point out that there is very little policy content in revenue collection and that it does not matter a great deal where the capacity to add numbers is ultimately located in government. Moreover, they are quite happy not to be burdened with these functions since they would detract from the more important macroeconomic and budgetary issues. The department defines its organization along functional lines (see Chart 3).

The Economic and Fiscal Policy branch advises on the country's economic circumstances and prospects and on the government's fiscal framework, including the revenue and expenditure outlook and financing requirements. It also plays the lead role in preparing the government's budget. In addition, it defines the government's overall economic strategy and reviews and evaluates the programs and activities of government departments in the areas of industrial, regional, resource, environment, and science and technology policy. The branch also 'advises on the consistency of the microeconomic policy approaches in individual sector areas [and] provides advice on specific microeconomic policy and program issues.'[11]

The Tax Policy branch conducts ongoing reviews of existing tax measures and is responsible for developing new tax policies or adjusting existing ones whenever necessary. It also prepares analyses of federal-provincial tax measures and recommends what, if any, changes are needed to maintain or strengthen the effectiveness and efficiency of the national tax system. The International Trade and Finance branch prepares briefing material and recommends positions for the minister and the prime minister for their participation in various bilateral and multilateral negotiations and conferences. It is also responsible for program management of Canada's participation in the G-7, G-10, IMF, World Bank, European Bank for Reconstruction and Development, and APEC. The Financial Sector branch manages the public debt and advises on financial sector issues. It is also responsible for advising on the regulatory framework governing financial institutions.[12]

The Federal-Provincial Relations and Social Policy branch advises the minister and the government on fiscal federalism and social policy in general. It manages the federal-provincial transfer payments program and advises on federal-provincial fiscal arrangements. It is this branch, for example, that advises the government on the financing of the Canada Pension Plan.[13]

The department also has direct responsibility for several programs. It oversees transfer payments to the territorial governments, which are determined on a formula-based mechanism, and unconditional payments made to the provinces under conditions established by the terms of Confederation.

The department manages the fiscal equalization program, which consists of unconditional transfer payments to selected provinces. As is well known, the Constitution requires that Parliament and the government of Canada make 'equalization payments to ensure that provincial governments have sufficient revenues to provide reasonably comparable levels of public services at reasonably comparable levels of taxation.'[14] Payments are determined by a fairly complex formula which compares each province's per capita capacity against the average per capita capacity of five middle provinces. These five provinces exclude the richest province – Alberta – and the four poorest – the Atlantic provinces.[15] The department is also directly responsible for the government's fiscal stabilization program, which provides unconditional transfer payments to a province or provinces to accommodate 'over the year decline, exceeding five percent, in its revenues caused by changing economic circumstances.'[16]

Lastly, the department is responsible for managing the Canada Health and Social Transfer (CHST), transfers to the provinces and territories designed to support the provision of health, post-secondary education, social assistance, and services. The CHST program replaced the *Established Program Financing Act* and the Canada Assistance Plan in 1996–7. The transfers are now made through a combination of cash and tax points. They involve a substantial amount of public funds, amounting to about $27 billion in fiscal year 1996–7.[17] When these payments are combined with those made under the fiscal equalization program and transfers to the territorial governments, the Department of Finance spends over $20 billion in cash (i.e., excluding tax points) a year (1998–9), which represents about 15 per cent of the government's expenditure budget.

When one looks back ten, twenty, or twenty-five years, one is struck by the degree of stability in the organization of the Department of Finance. Indeed, its 1978 organization chart is not very different from the one above.[18] Department officials maintain that this should not come as a surprise, since the basic requirements of the government budget-making process has changed little. One former senior Finance official explains: 'We still need a capacity to look at the tax system, at economic circumstances, at projected revenues, at proposed spending plans, and at government programs. Sometimes things do not change because they should not change. There are not seven ways, or even two ways, to prepare a budget and to provide advice on economic policy.'[19]

The Department of Finance has also long prided itself as being the 'largest and best' department of economics in Canada. Many of its former deputy ministers were noted economists in their own right, and there is no denying that they have left their mark on Canadian public policy. They include W. Clifford Clark, Robert B. Bryce, and Tommy Shoyama.[20]

Twenty years ago, a Department of Finance official observed that 'we are the economics powerhouse in Ottawa ... I work in the best economics department in the country, have the type of resources and staff with which I can really do economic analysis, and, above all, have a chance to be in on decisions which have a tremendous impact on the economy. Departments are constantly coming up here with ill-conceived ideas which would either screw up the economy and/or employ an economic instrument, like taxation, for a social or cultural goal. I find it satisfying and exciting to see these policy proposals shot down ... purely on the grounds of economics.'[21] These observations are not dissimilar to what I heard from Finance officials ten years ago when I was carrying out research for a book on government spending, or from what I heard more recently from Finance officials while preparing for this book. They still maintain that the department is the best economics department in the country. One senior official suggested that 'the way we work in here is much like a graduate school. We argue, we debate issues at great length.'[22]

But this is not to imply for a moment that they do not stake out policy positions. In an interview in late 1997, the deputy minister of Finance said, 'In this department you can't be a shrinking violet in the public policy debate.'[23] It is made clear to all staff that there ought to be no sign of weakness in putting forward Finance's position at interdepartmental meetings. Tom Kent, a former head of the Prime Minister's Office, deputy minister in several federal departments, and a keen observer of government, writes that 'the Department of Finance can ... be a special problem. It regards its territory as involving, more than others, matters of policy as well as administration that professionals understand and amateurs, whether politicians or civil servants of lesser departments, do not. The attitude readily develops, among some Finance officials ... that everyone else should simply accept their word as to what will work and what will not.'[24] David Good, in his study of the budget process, quotes a former deputy minister of a line department who said that 'Finance has always had the strongest deputy ministers. They lecture the cabinet as if they were ministers themselves.'[25]

There is a strong corporate culture and firmly established ways of doing things in the Department of Finance that seem to survive changes in ministers and deputy ministers. For one thing, perhaps because the department has so few programs to manage, or because those it does have do not lend themselves to management, given that they are formula-based (e.g., equalization), the department and its senior officials do not attach much importance to management issues or even how best to manage the department's resources.

The federal government established in 1988 a new management centre, the Canadian Centre for Management Development (CCMD), to promote management development and also to conduct research in public sector management. The Department of Finance has scarcely been present in CCMD activities, and Finance officials will, much more often than not, avoid attending management courses. In consultations with present and former Finance officials, the New Public Management was hardly ever discussed, despite occasional efforts on my part to do so. It is not too much of an exaggeration to report that the topic is of no interest to them.

Finance officials, however, take great pride in their ability to work very well with their ministers. One is struck by the number of hours they spend briefing their ministers every week. This was as true when Marc Lalonde was Finance minister in the Trudeau government as it was when Michael Wilson was minister in the Mulroney government – and as it is with Paul Martin in the Chrétien government. Finance officials can spend anywhere between eight and thirty hours a week briefing their minister, with the length of time increasing as the budget date gets closer. No minister in a line department comes close to this level.

New employees in Finance quickly discover that they are in the business of saving public money, or protecting the public purse. This was true even when Bob Bryce, a Keynesian, was deputy minister, and it is even more so today. Bryce explained that 'much of the work of the Department of Finance is of the nature of a critical appraisal of the proposals of others.'[26] One former finance official recounted his early experience in the department.

> Shortly after I went to the Department, I was asked to prepare a briefing for the Minister on a proposal from the Department of Health and Welfare. I concluded that the proposal was a good one and I recommended that our Minister support it. I sent the note up the line but a few days later I was called into the Deputy Minister's office. He made it very clear that I had prepared a *stupid* note. 'What if the note had gone ahead and the Minister would have supported the proposal before his colleagues?' he asked. He then explained that there were many departments and agencies and thousands and thousands of officials whose job is to prepare spending proposals. Our job is to oppose them. We are the internal opposition in government. He concluded by asking, 'if we don't protect the Treasury, who do you think will?'[27]

Quite apart from its role in the budget process, Finance plays its opposition role to spending proposals in various ways. Officials will oppose new proposals at interdepartmental committee meetings, in bilateral meetings, or in exchange of correspondence with departments. You can always count on finance officials, reported one senior departmental official, to pour cold water on proposals. The minister, after having been properly briefed by his officials, will also voice his views at Cabinet committee or bilateral meetings with his colleagues and in discussions with the prime minister and his staff.

How the Department of Finance is organized and how department officials regard the role and importance of their department may not have changed much over the years, but how the department is regarded by others and how effective it may be in the Ottawa decision-making process has. Though it always operates from a position of considerable strength, the department's influence has waned and waxed over the years.

Finance's Changing Fortunes

Finance was different in the pre-Trudeau days. For one thing, the minister and Department of Finance, particularly from the end of the Second World War up to the first few years of the Trudeau government, were in the business of sorting out when to inflate, when to deflate, when to do nothing, when to cut spending, or when to increase it.

Moreover, the minister and the Department of Finance 'acted almost unilaterally' in preparing the budget.[28] Walter Gordon, Finance minister in the Pearson government, provides a detailed account of the budget-making process in the 1960s in his *A Political Memoir*. He writes, 'I went over the budget with the Prime Minister several times very carefully ... The budget was my responsibility, of course, but it was reassuring to know that the Prime Minister was so pleased with it. I asked him if he would like me to show it to Tom Kent, his personal adviser on policy matters, and whether I could properly do this under the general principle of budget secrecy. He instructed me not to do so.'[29]

It is important to note that Pearson's instructions applied not just to his own staff. Gordon also writes that he asked Pearson whether it would 'not be wise to discuss the budget proposals with a committee of cabinet, including Lamontagne and Sharp in particular, in view of the fact that it introduced so many new features. Pearson replied that if we brought in a group of Cabinet ministers, they would all want to make changes ... Therefore, the budget proposals were not discussed in Cabinet until either the morning of their presentation to the House or perhaps the day before. No one voiced any serious reservations about any of the proposals, although quite obviously they had no real chance to study them.'[30]

For his part, Pearson writes in his own memoirs that the budget was indeed prepared by Gordon and that he 'was shown in the course of two meetings the important aspects of what the Minister of Finance was proposing.'[31] Pearson does not report that anyone from his staff or from the Privy Council Office attended the briefings. Yet the opposition made an issue of the fact that Walter Gordon had hired three experts from outside the Department of Finance and had them sworn to secrecy as temporary officials. He later stood in the Commons to say, 'I take full personal responsibility for the budget.'

In his memoirs, John Diefenbaker does not spend a great deal of time dealing with the budget process in his government. He reports, however, on bilateral discussions with his minister of Finance, Donald Flemming, and on memoranda dealing with sensitive budgetary issues which he received from him. There is no indication that this information was shared further.[32]

Trudeau challenged Finance's preeminent position by not allowing it to escape his strong desire to introduce checks and balances in the Ottawa decision-making process, to promote rational debate in government, and to avoid the 'abuses and excesses of a monopoly of ideas advanced by a single authority.'[33] Looking back, it is now clear that the Department of Finance which

Trudeau bequeathed to his successors, and which they have largely left intact, is vastly different from the one that operated from Confederation to the early 1970s. Before Trudeau, powerful mandarins settled in the department and became virtually unchallenged experts in public finance and macroeconomic policy. An indication of this is the fact that in the 100 years from 1870 to 1970, there were only seven deputy ministers of Finance.[34] From 1970 to today, we have had ten, which means that they now stay in their position on average only three years.[35]

Trudeau looked to the Privy Council Office to introduce a number of specific measures to check the 'excesses of a monopoly of ideas' which emerged from the Department of Finance. When he was told that his proposed changes would upset the department, he is reported to have responded that Finance had to be upset. 'Otherwise the minister there would be as powerful as I am.'[36]

One of the greatest political strengths of the minister of Finance comes from the department's monopoly control of macroeconomic policy. Trudeau, in his desire to institute countervailing forces, broke Finance's monopoly, much to the dismay of the minister and his senior officials. Apart from introducing a capacity in the PCO to advise on macroeconomic policy, Trudeau later established two new central agencies responsible for managing the PEMS process, one on the economic side, and the other for social policy. These new central agencies would constitute new streams of policy advice at the centre of government and, if nothing else, would challenge Finance's monopoly of ideas.

Trudeau created a new position, 'Senior Economic Advisor,' in the PCO, a position which has remained on the organizational chart to this day. He made it clear that he wanted the PCO, on occasion his own office, and certain economic departments to come forward with new ideas and not to hesitate to voice opinions on the direction of the government's macroeconomic policies that challenged the Department of Finance. For example, Finance fought the PMO and the PCO over the introduction of price and wage controls in the mid-1970s and lost.[37] They also fought over a number of other issues, including the budget. A Finance official reported in the 1970s that his department had reached the point 'where the budget is going to have to be negotiated through the entire cabinet. Much of this is PCO's doing.'[38]

In addition, the Trudeau government launched a major priorities-setting exercise in early fall 1974, with staff from his own office and the PCO responsible for its coordination. The Department of Finance, meanwhile, was essentially left on the outside looking in. Staff from PCO and PMO were asked to interview each minister and to ask two questions: 'What does the government have to do during its mandate in order to win the next election?' and 'What do you want to be remembered for having done should the government lose the next election?' The hope was that these interviews would give rise to major new policy thrusts and that no more than about half a dozen overarching priorities would be identified by full Cabinet at a special Cabinet retreat in November. To ensure that the exercise was taken seriously, the prime minister met with all deputy ministers to stress its importance and to ask them for their full support.[39]

Richard French writes that 'the priorities exercise represents a rather heroic attempt to plan.'[40] He also writes, however, that the exercise failed badly. For one thing, PMO and PCO were never able to limit the number of priority areas to half a dozen, and in the end sixteen were identified. PMO and PCO officials quickly concluded that ministers and departments lacked 'vision' and simply reverted to a shopping list approach to the exercise by pushing their pet projects. They were also unable to keep the exercise on schedule and the process, as well as decisions, was continually pushed back. More importantly, 'economic and political events had evolved beyond it [i.e., the priorities exercise]. The wage-price spiral continued unabated. John Turner, the minister of Finance, pondered his political options and ... the Prime Minister's Office ... smelled disaster.'[41]

It was wage and price controls, not the priorities-setting exercise, that effectively redefined the public policy agenda. George Radwanski argues that wage and price controls, combined with the collapse of the priorities exercise, proved to be a turning point for the government. He argues, 'From that point on, Trudeau and his government found themselves doing exactly what the ill-fated and politically costly priorities exercise had been designed to avoid: they were reduced to stumbling along without a plan, racing to catch up to events, improvising desperately.'[42]

Ian Stewart, economic adviser in the Privy Council Office, and who acted as a counterweight to the Department of Finance, played a key role in the development of the anti-inflation program. He also wrote a discussion paper, *The Way Ahead*, published by PCO in 1976. The paper, widely read, at least in Ottawa, sought to outline 'the economic and social directions the government [intended] to take after controls end.'[43] The paper was middle of the road, stressing the importance of the market, but also pointing to the need for social goals and emphasizing public consultations.[44] It was also the kind of paper which the Department of Finance would not have produced, and Finance officials made no attempt to hide their disapproval. In any event, the document had limited impact. The unexpected persistence of stagflation – that is, inflation, slow growth, and high government deficits – were posing new problems for Ottawa, and some, in particular Finance officials, were calling for new stringent fiscal measures.

John Turner was not the only one to resign from the Department of Finance.

Simon Riesman, the department's deputy minister, also resigned in the mid-1970s. He felt that the department was being 'downgraded' because the government no longer relied on it for economic advice. Mr Riesman 'found himself unable to control the economic policy advice being tendered the government: sometimes he didn't even know what the advice was.'[45] Put differently, Finance's theology was being both challenged and ignored at the very centre of government. Light began to appear between the prime minister and his minister of Finance, and the minister decided to part company. The department's deputy minister also left, convinced that the department's credibility and *raison d'être* were being challenged not so much by spending ministers and their departments as by the centre of government itself.

It would not be the only time Trudeau would allow light to appear between himself and his minister of Finance. In 1978 it became clear the government had not been able to wrestle inflation to the ground as Trudeau had promised, and the government was still trying to deal with a stubborn deficit, despite four years of restraint. Trudeau returned from a trip to Bonn, where he had discussed government restraint measures with West German Chancellor Helmut Schmidt, determined to introduce new spending cuts to deal with the deficit rather than rely on restraint.

Trudeau's advisers had some bad news for him on his return from Bonn. They told him that the government would not be able to keep the growth in spending in line with increases in GNP unless spending cuts were made. In addition, they reported that the latest public opinion surveys revealed that he was widely perceived as having only limited interest in economic policies.[46] Trudeau decided virtually on the spot to deliver a speech on the economy on national television and to announce that 'we must have a major re-ordering of government priorities. We must reduce the size of government.' Unless this was done, he declared, 'Canadians within several years would almost certainly be faced with a fiscal crisis.'[47] He also announced that $2 billion would be cut from federal expenditures.

The cuts would later become known in Ottawa as 'the guns of August' because no one other than Trudeau and a few key advisers knew they were coming. Jean Chrétien, then Trudeau's minister of Finance, was left completely in the dark. Chrétien would later write that the cuts made him 'look like a fool. Normally, a minister of Finance would resign in such an embarrassing situation. I decided not to mainly because I was worried about the effect of a French-Canadian senior minister resigning when a separatist government was in power in Quebec.'[48] There is no doubt that this was one of the low points for the Department of Finance. A minister of Finance was again pondering his political future in light of Trudeau's initiative, a fact that did not go unnoticed in the department. In addition, the minister was losing a public relations battle with his Quebec counterpart, Jacques Parizeau, over a tax question, a fact that was open knowledge to the prime minister and his colleagues.[49] The deficit was also growing, and it appeared that there was little the department could do about it.

Things did not improve much for the department during the short-lived Clark government. Indeed, it was the Crosbie budget that brought down the Clark government and ended its brief hold on power. Many observers pinned the blame on the Department of Finance for the government's downfall by producing a politically naïve budget for a minority government.

The department was again in the ascendancy, however briefly, in the early 1980s. On returning to power, Trudeau decided to concentrate his energy on a few issues: national unity, energy, and, subsequently, an international peace initiative. He personally handled the national unity file together with a few key advisers, including Michael Kirby and Michael Pitfield. He asked his former principal secretary and now his Quebec political lieutenant, Marc Lalonde, to handle the energy file.

He appointed as Finance minister Allan J. MacEachen, one of his most senior and trusted ministers. MacEachen had masterminded Trudeau's return to lead the Liberal Party into the 1980 election campaign. It will be recalled that Trudeau had resigned as leader of the Liberal Party a few months before the Clark government lost a confidence motion in Parliament. MacEachen gave a passionate speech to caucus, urging its members to call on Trudeau to lead the party into the next election campaign. One minister who was present at the caucus meeting reports, 'MacEachen gave the finest political speech I have heard in my life. There was just no doubt after MacEachen spoke that caucus would ask Trudeau to stay.'[50]

Trudeau also appointed his economic adviser, Ian Stewart, as deputy minister of Finance. Officials who worked in the Privy Council Office report that it was 'obvious to everyone in the office that Trudeau was giving MacEachen and Stewart a completely free hand in preparing the budget and that he had full confidence in them.'[51]

But, as is well known, the 1981 MacEachen budget proved to be a 'political disaster.'[52] The budget called for significant tax increases resulting from the closing of tax loopholes on the assumption that the economy would continue to expand rapidly, despite high interest rates. But by the time the budget was tabled, economic growth had already come to a stop. Accusations of ineptitude and arrogance were hurled at the government from several quarters, and the government was soon on the defensive.[53]

Ian Stewart resigned as deputy minister of Finance, and in his letter of resignation to the prime minister he acknowledged that 'the Department of Finance and many of those who inhabit it have come under considerable public attack.'[54] Trudeau also asked Marc Lalonde to replace MacEachen in Finance.

The 1981 budget held considerable and lasting fallout for the Finance department. Many in Ottawa believed that the department lacked the necessary skills to protect the government's political interests in preparing the budget. Donald Johnston, then Treasury Board president, would later write, 'Who had been consulted? Certainly not Cabinet ministers. I can vouch for that. The budget documents had been preserved from the eyes of all except key officials in the Department of Finance and, I presume, the Prime Minister himself. I was both offended and amazed that, as the Treasury Board President ... I had not been consulted ... We had shot ourselves in the foot with the famous MacEachen budget.'[55]

An official in the PCO in the aftermath of the 1981 budget now reports that 'it became a defining moment for the budget process.' She adds, 'Never again would the prime minister and PCO give carte blanche to the Department of Finance to write a budget.'And, indeed, from that moment on, the prime minister and senior PMO and PCO officials began to review key issues in the budget before they were tabled. It became widely accepted in PCO at this time that the Department of Finance was 'too much economics, too technical, and not sufficiently political to be trusted to produce on its own a budget for the government.'[56] It is important to stress, however, that this did not signal a shift away from Finance to line ministers and departments. It simply meant that from that moment on it became standard practice for the prime minister, his staff, and senior PCO staff to receive fairly thorough budget briefings from the minister of Finance and his officials. In addition, PCO has retained an in-house capacity to generate its own numbers to test those of Finance in preparing the budget and in briefing the prime minister. When the numbers do not match, the prime minister will often ask the Finance minister to double check his, and to report back on them at a future briefing session.

But for ministers, even those in important economic portfolios, nothing had changed, and they continued to be kept in the dark over budget matters. In many ways, Don Johnston's criticism applies today as much as it did in the Mulroney years. Mulroney's senior ministers would, from time to time, express their displeasure over unpopular government measures which they only learned about a day or two before the budget speech and, in some instances, on budget day.[57] One PCO official reveals that 'I recall John Crosbie telling Mazankowski that he found it extremely hard to take not being informed of important budget matters until the last minute. I also recall Mazankowski reminding Crosbie that he was the minister for Alberta when Crosbie produced his budget, but that he only discovered one hour beforehand that he was increasing gasoline tax to .18 cents a gallon. So in other words, Maz was telling Crosbie, I am only doing to you what you did to me, except that in my case it was worse, since I was the minister for Alberta.'[58]

Consultations with current and former Chrétien ministers reveal that Paul Martin from time to time presents a deck to Cabinet on the state of Canada's public finances and on the government's fiscal framework. But important budget items are not presented to them, let alone discussed, until it is too late for any input. The one exception is the various spending decisions made during the government's program review exercise, discussed below.[59] Finance officials explain that ministers and Cabinet are not involved in preparing key elements of the budget because there are only three questions that need to be answered: how much of the public debt should be retired? What taxes should be cut or increased, and when? And should new spending initiatives be included, and if so, what should these be? They point out that only the prime minister and the minister of Finance can answer the first two questions, but admit that some balance and some discussions need to take place to answer the third.

New budget processes introduced in the late 1970s and early 1980s also served to weaken Finance's hand. As we saw in an earlier chapter, the Policy and Expenditure Management Systems (PEMS) sought to impose discipline on spenders by having Cabinet committees face the fiscal consequence of their decision. Richard Van Loon writes that PEMS was the result of the 'continuing attempts within the federal government to impose financial and qualitative discipline and a notion of collective responsibility on what was hitherto a rather undisciplined policy process.'[60] It will be recalled that two large central agencies were also established to manage policy envelopes and to oversee the operation of PEMS. Spending decisions were taken by Cabinet committees on the advice of these two central agencies.

The Department of Finance thus became one of several central agencies concerned with the government's expenditure budget. Accordingly, the department's focus for most of the 1970s and early 1980s was mostly on the revenue side, on taxation policy, and in preparing the fiscal framework. A former deputy minister who worked in several departments during this period reports that 'back then Finance would be mostly concerned with the revenue budget. I remember that Finance officials would make presentations on projected revenues. We always believed that the department was low-balling revenues for the years ahead. Ministers would then argue that revenues would be higher. It was all a bit of a game and we were all wise to it. But it was probably the only way

Finance thought that it could get a handle on the expenditure budget.'[61] All in all, however, the elaborate Cabinet committee process, PEMS, other central agencies, and the ability of some ministers and departments to make 'end runs' around all of these not only played havoc with the government's budget, but also weakened Finance's hand.

Finance, however, was able to regain some power when the two central agencies operating PEMS were disbanded and when Mulroney came to office. The Mulroney government was sworn to office on 17 September 1984, and within days it announced a freeze on staffing and discretionary spending and promised that more cuts were on the way. Mulroney appointed as Finance minister Michael Wilson, a one-time rival for his party leadership with strong ties to the business and financial communities. Mulroney made it clear early on that he would support Wilson in Cabinet and in preparing budgets. But we now know that he did not always respect that commitment.[62]

Mulroney had strong reservations about Wilson's political judgment. He felt that Wilson had too much Bay Street in him to appreciate 'real political problems.' In his briefings to Cabinet, Wilson came across as far too technical and bureaucratic, and he lost the attention of many of his colleagues who wanted a more political discussion.[63] Mulroney also had a tendency to strike bilateral deals with premiers and even with individual ministers, only informing Wilson after the fact that he had made new spending commitments.[64] In addition, he personally oversaw the development of major spending plans such as the establishment of two new regional development agencies for which over $2 billion of new money was allocated. Wilson knew full well that he could hardly fight this funding commitment in Cabinet and expect to win. In the end, the minister of Finance in such situations has two choices – to quit or pick up the pieces. Invariably, he picks up the pieces.

When Chrétien came to office, Finance was able to come full circle and regain its position of power. Without a doubt it has become the most important economic actor on the Ottawa stage. It does not have to contend with several Cabinet committees, including the powerful Priorities and Planning Committee, which had existed since the 1960s, but which Chrétien abolished on assuming office. Nor does it have to contend with other central agencies, as it did in the late 1970s and early 1980s. Other economic voices, like the Economic Council of Canada, have also been silenced.

Chrétien had once served as minister of Finance, one of only three such ministers to become prime minister. He had been minister of Finance in the late 1970s, just before PEMS was born and when spending ministers were challenging Finance numbers on the revenue side – and when they were often successful in using Cabinet committees or other means to secure approval for their pet projects. Chrétien came to office convinced that 'Prime Ministers and finance ministers must be seen as one' and that 'his finance's minister's authority [should not be] diminished.'[65] In short, experience had taught him that the most important ally the minister of Finance has is the prime minister.[66]

Chrétien's experience as minister of Finance, like others who have occupied the post, made him a fiscal conservative. Many in Ottawa are convinced that the Department of Finance can capture any newly appointed minister, and whatever his political beliefs may have been, turn him into a 'non-interventionist, nay-sayer politician.'[67] They point to Marc Lalonde, a free spender in Health and Welfare, and Allan MacEachen, one of the most interventionist liberals ever who after a stay in Finance became a fiscal conservative. The same is said about Jean Chrétien. A former colleague in the Trudeau Cabinet explains, 'Look at Chrétien. He was once prone to boast that he had established more new national parks than any minister in Canadian history. Even the Treasury Board could not stop his spending ways. As President of the Treasury Board, he launched a costly and ambitious government decentralization program. Trudeau appointed him in Finance and that was the end of him [i.e., as a strong spending minister].'[68] It is true that after Finance, Chrétien never again wore the spending hat in Justice, or Energy, Mines and Resources that he had so happily worn in his other pre-Finance portfolios.

If Trudeau looked to the Constitution, energy, and foreign affairs as his three priorities during his last mandate, Chrétien's 'holy trinity' would be the deficit, reforming Canada's social security programs, and national unity. He and his advisers would handle the national unity file and the Finance minister would deal with the deficit. Chrétien appointed Paul Martin, a former leadership rival also with strong ties to the country's business community, to Finance. Chrétien left no doubt in the minds of other ministers that he would stand by his minister of Finance whenever the need for it arose. Contrary to Mulroney, he did not back away from his commitment.

Martin's first budget, in 1994, was important. It presented tough spending cuts in areas previously shied away from. It introduced spending reductions to unemployment insurance and closed down some defence bases. Both came as a surprise to ministers. Martin, with Chrétien's full support, wanted no public consultation, nor did he want to deal with the lobbying of ministers and government backbenchers on either issue. Accordingly, 'Chrétien, Martin, and [David] Collenette [then Defence minister] agreed that it should be a budget decision: fast, clean, and hard to go back on. So, by virtue of budget secrecy, the information on which bases would go was held with a tight circle.'[69]

This budget was also noteworthy for other reasons. Martin included a $2.4 billion contingency fund and made full use of prudent economic assumptions in preparing his budget.[70] He also picked up on the last phase of Kim Campbell's restructuring of government operations and announced that a review of all departmental spending would be carried out to identify where savings could be realized through the elimination or reduction of low-priority programs.[71]

Program Review

Marcel Massé, for a very brief period clerk of the Privy Council and secretary to the Cabinet, was by 1993 a Liberal candidate in the Hull-Aylmer riding. He delivered a major address during the campaign – 'Getting Government Right' – in it declaring that, if elected, a Chrétien government would 'start by deciding what needs to be done by government, and what we can afford to do.'[72] The Liberal National Campaign Committee reproduced the speech and gave it wide circulation. In another speech a few months later, Massé referred to the earlier speech, revealing that 'Mr. Chrétien personally reviewed my previous speech before it was delivered. He has not only endorsed the ideas in it but has challenged me and my Cabinet colleagues to turn these brave ideas into action.'[73] In his second speech, Massé announced that 'over time, governments collectively have promised more than they could deliver and delivered more than they can afford.'[74]

Massé spoke to his public service rather than to his political experience in the speech. In fact, he had resigned as a senior deputy minister only a few weeks before the election. His last public service appointment was as head of the Federal-Provincial Relations Office, and he, like other deputy ministers, had lived through numerous across-the-board cuts introduced by the Mulroney government, all designed to bring down the deficit. He knew that Mulroney and his Finance minister on assuming power had been alarmed over the size of the government's accumulated debt and its $38.6 billion annual deficit. While in office, the Mulroney government had embarked on fifteen exercises to reduce expenditures and introduce restraint. These included several steps to limit federal transfers to the provinces, including a reduction in transfers for Medicare and post-secondary education. Yet at the time Massé was sworn in as a minister in the Chrétien government, the annual deficit amounted to $42 billion and the accumulated debt had tripled to $460 billion.[75]

Senior central agency officials (and Massé had been one of them only a few months before being elected to Parliament) had become convinced that the government had to find a new approach to tackle the deficit. Across-the-board cuts, the standard approach taken during the Mulroney and, for that matter, the Trudeau years, had failed to bring the annual deficit down.

Apart from across-the-board cuts, the Mulroney government had also sought to identify spending cuts. The deputy prime minister, Erik Nielsen, chaired a task force of nongovernment and government officials to review government programs. But the effort hardly proved successful.[76] One government official observed that the task force had 'generated a lot of work but that nothing was done.'[77]

Martin's first budget was very much in the Mulroney mould. It announced a series of spending cuts, but the media, particularly the financial press, dismissed it as just more of the same. Martin was taken aback by the criticism. He had just announced a series of tax increases, spending cuts in international assistance, in subsidies to business, in unemployment insurance, in defence, and in government operations. All in all, there were $3.7 billion in spending cuts in his 1994 budget. But the verdict from the media was still negative. Indeed, Martin discovered that the 'economic chattering classes and those ... who swapped bonds around the globe ... [turned] thumbs down on his first budget ... His tough approach to UI and defence demonstrated ... gutsiness ... but it was offset by mounds of mush elsewhere. The media saw little difference between the first Martin and past budgets from the Mulroney Government.'[78]

There was also a discernible shift in public opinion. During the early 1990s, a number of provincial governments, notably New Brunswick and Alberta, had aggressively pursued restraint measures. Balanced budgets were now a reality, or at least in sight. In addition, Finance officials held meetings with a number of interest groups in the wake of the budget and discovered a 'greater receptivity than they had expected to suggestions that government expenditures needed to be reduced.'[79]

In his budget speech, Martin announced that Marcel Massé would chair the program review. Officials report that no one, including the prime minister and the Finance minister, would have predicted the importance and scope the exercise was to assume. Public servants, one official reports, had grown tired of the 'axes, meat cleavers, and scalpels applied to departmental budgets during the past ten years or so.'[80] But at the same time, they had become quite concerned about Canada 'hitting the wall,' as New Zealand had done. A line deputy minister 'felt that the government couldn't simply continue tearing at the carcass, a more profound approach was required ... [he] dubbed several dozen copies [of a television news program on New Zealand's deficit experience] and sent them around town to the other deputies.'[81] The Department of Finance also made presentations suggesting that modest economic growth and low inflation, which is what it was forecasting, could never generate sufficient revenues to reduce the deficit substantially. They also maintained that there was only limited room for increasing taxes. Canada, they said, was close to a tax revolt, and as proof pointed to the political difficulty the Mulroney government had experienced in implementing a new Goods and Services Tax.[82]

In the immediate aftermath of Martin's first budget, the centre of government began to explore new ways to deal with the deficit and to develop an approach to undertake, as Martin had promised, a 'review of all departmental spending.' Between budget day and May 1994, they made a number of decisions. First, a review exercise would look at all spending except major transfers to persons (e.g., unemployment insurance and payments to senior citizens) and major transfers to governments (e.g., Established Program Financing and Canada Assistance). It was decided that these would be subjected to separate review processes. Second, the exercise would be 'designed and managed ... by three central agencies of the federal government: the Privy Council Office, the Department of Finance, and the Treasury Board secretariat.'[83]

The centre also established a Steering Committee of Deputy Ministers (SCDM) to guide the work of the review. Jocelyne Bourgon, the clerk of the Privy Council and secretary to the Cabinet, chaired the committee, and its membership included the deputy minister of Finance, the secretary of the Treasury Board, the deputy secretary (plans) at the Privy Council Office, and three deputy ministers from line departments. This committee was there not only to guide the work of departments, but also to advise ministers.

A Coordinating Group of Ministers (CGM) was also established. Marcel Massé chaired the group, which included Paul Martin, Treasury Board president Art Eggleton, the three Cabinet committee chairs Sheila Copps, André Ouellet, and Herb Gray, and three other ministers – Brian Tobin, Ann McLellan, and Sergio Marchi – to provide the regional perspective. The group was set up as an informal committee to advise the prime minister and the Finance minister. The prime minister was steadfast in his opposition to the proliferation of formal Cabinet committees and it was he who decided that the committee be ad hoc. Accordingly, the papers submitted to the group did not go through the formal Cabinet document process. They were, however, circulated to members of CGM, in PCO, and PMO. Two senior members of the prime minister's staff attended all CGM meetings. Initially, it was envisaged that the program review would apply from fiscal year 1995–6 to 1997–8. However, the exercise was extended, and a second phase was initiated in the summer of 1995 which extended the exercise to 1998–9 (see Table 2 below).

Early in the exercise, the Privy Council Office put together a series of tests against which the programs would be assessed. The office came up with six formal questions and circulated them to all departments. The questions were:

Public Interest Test:	Does the program or activity continue to serve a public interest?
Role of Government Test:	Is there a legitimate and necessary role for government in this program area or activity?
Federalism Test:	Is the current role of the federal government appropriate, or is the program a candidate for realignment with the provinces?
Partnership Test:	What activities or programs should or could be transferred in whole or in part to the private or voluntary sector?
Efficiency Test:	If the program or activity continues, how could its efficiency be improved?
Affordability Test:	Is the resultant package of programs and activities affordable within the fiscal restraint? If not, what programs or activities should be abandoned?

The Privy Council Office also established a secretariat to support the program review and to assist both the steering committee of deputy ministers and the coordinating group of ministers. The secretariat, with the help of the Department of Finance and the Treasury Board secretariat, prepared assessment notes and attached them to departmental submissions. It also sought to brief both groups on interdepartmental issues. The notes were circulated first to the committee of deputy ministers and subsequently revised and circulated to members of CGM and to the relevant ministers and departmental officials. Finance and Treasury Board officials also prepared briefing notes for their own ministers, but these were not circulated.[84]

Given that the program review was not directly tied to the Cabinet decision-making process, the interdepartmental consultation process was not as formal or as demanding as it usually is. Usually, when formal Cabinet memoranda are written, there is a requirement for sponsoring departments to hold interdepartmental meetings to inform other departments of the proposed measure and to seek their input. Indeed, the Privy Council Office usually insists on at least one interdepartmental meeting and often on a consensus recommendation before it will agree to place an item on a Cabinet committee agenda.

While the Privy Council Office was developing the six questions, the Department of Finance was busy determining the amount that needed to be cut from the expenditure budget. Once this was established, it then set out to break the total amount into notional targets for each department. The minister was directly involved in establishing these targets and did not hesitate to review questions and issues in some detail.

TABLE 2
Program Review Timetable

Phase I	
May 1994	Program Review official launch The minister responsible for the review, Marcel Massé, writes to his colleagues The clerk informs all DMs of the exercise
June–August 1994	Reviews begin in each department/portfolio
Fall 1994	The Coordinating Group of Ministers and the Steering Committee of Deputy Ministers begin work on the action plan drawn up by the departments/portfolios
February 1995	Budget includes results of Program Review I
Spring 1995	Each department/portfolio begins implementation of PR outcomes
Phase II	
September 1995	Program Review II official launch Minister Massé writes to all his colleagues DMs are officially informed
Early Fall 1995	Ministers Massé, Martin, and Eggleton meet with ministers whose departments/portfolios are expected to make major contributions
Fall 1995	Review begins in each department/portfolio
November 1995	The Coordinating Group of Ministers and the Steering Committee of Deputy Ministers begin their work
March 1996	Results of the reviews are incorporated in the budget
Spring 1996	Each department/portfolio implements the Program Review II outcomes

Source: Privy Council Office, November 1994

Arthur Kroeger, a former deputy minister, at the request of the Canadian Centre for Management Development, prepared a study of the role of central agencies in the program review exercise. He carried out numerous interviews with Finance officials and, on the issue of notional targets for line departments, he concluded that 'it is universally acknowledged by those who participated that this process was *utterly unscientific*. The reductions were broadly divided into three categories: large, being 25 percent or in some cases more; substantial – 15 percent; and token – 5 percent. The assigned reductions were to be implemented over a period of three years.'[85] Kroeger explains why the 'rough and ready' approach was adopted. He writes, 'There was not much alternative [and] ... there was no time for elaborate evaluation studies.'[86]

Finance officials, however, report that they did look to several sources to determine the size of proposed spending cuts. The Liberal campaign's 'Red Book' had pledged to bring the deficit down to 3 per cent of GDP and to cut defence spending and subsidies to business. Department of Finance officials also report that they had a very good sense of what departments did and an even better sense of the amount of spending cuts that were 'urgently needed.' One official explained, 'We were under the gun, there is no question about that. We did not have the luxury to wait twelve months for an elaborate study to tell us that expenditure cuts were required or where we should make the cuts. We knew two things for certain – we knew that we needed to cut spending and we knew that we had to do it quickly. In hindsight, we made some bad decisions. I do not think, for example, that we should have cut Research and Development as much as we did. But we had to move quickly and there was no time for sophisticated studies.'[87]

To be sure, line ministers and departments were taken aback by the size of the proposed cuts. Massé and Martin initially announced that the government would need to cut $10 billion out of the $50 billion under review. Several months later, Martin returned to the table and declared that he needed still more spending cuts, a great deal more, to deal with a possible impending crisis.

In December 1994 Mexico was plunged in a currency crisis and the Mexican economic miracle came to an abrupt end. Within weeks, the Canadian dollar came under attack. Given its high accumulated government debt, Canada also became the focus of scrutiny by international financial markets. In early January 1995, the *Wall Street Journal* described the Canadian dollar as a 'basket case.' The *Journal* ran an editorial on 12 January 1995 called 'Bankrupt Canada?' and declared that 'Mexico isn't the only U.S. neighbour flirting with the financial abyss.' It went on to argue that 'if dramatic action isn't taken in the next month's federal budget, it's not inconceivable that Canada could hit the debt wall and have to call in the International Monetary Fund to stabilize its falling currency.'[88] This editorial had a major effect on those in the Cabinet still hesitant to accept the general expenditure stance advocated by Finance; indeed, the deputy minister of Finance, David Dodge, later described it as a 'seminal event' in the politics of the 1995 budget.[89] In any event, the developments led to higher interest rates, which in turn led to higher public debt charges so that spending targets established several months earlier needed to be adjusted.

By most accounts, the three central agencies (PCO, Finance, and Treasury Board secretariat) were able to work well in developing and managing the program review exercise.[90] That is not to suggest that there were no disagreements. Initially, PCO officials wanted to avoid establishing notional targets, arguing that financial targets would come to dominate the discussions. Finance officials resisted, insisting that 'national government' or priority-setting exercises had been tried many times in the past and they had all failed.[91] Finance won the day.

Finance officials were prepared to go further and not only tell departments how much to cut, but also, at least in some instances, which activities should be cut. PCO officials resisted and this time they were successful. Arthur Kroeger argues that PCO's view prevailed 'because of PCO's primacy as the Prime Minister's department, but also because the Minister of Finance and his deputy saw merit in the broader approach ... At the same time, however, there was undoubtedly a widespread sense among Finance officials that they should keep their powder dry.'[92]

The Treasury Board secretariat meanwhile circulated 'perspective documents' to each department during late summer and early fall 1994. The objective was to point to possible future developments and their likely impact on the department's budget and programs. Opinions differ on the importance of these documents. Treasury Board officials suggest that though their quality varied, they were useful in putting the work of individual departments and their budget in perspective and in pointing to future challenges. On the other hand, line department officials claim that they were not a factor in the program review exercise; some even report that the documents added nothing and were utterly useless.[93]

Paul Martin met ministers individually in June 1994 to inform them of the target cuts for their departmental budgets. At the same time, Finance, Treasury Board, and PCO officials were already discussing with departments the amount of cuts needed and how they could be realized. Departments knew by early June that they were expected to produce either 'large,' 'substantial,' or 'token' cuts.[94]

A number of line ministers and their departments did not, at least initially, take the notional spending cuts seriously. Some felt that they were politically unrealistic and fully expected that the government would not go through with them. But by the end of June, it was a different story. At the last Cabinet meeting before the summer break, Prime Minister Chrétien left 'no doubt whatsoever that he was four square behind Martin.' He made it clear that he would 'do whatever was necessary to reach the 3 per cent deficit target.'[95] Though the prime minister did not participate directly in the work of the CGM, he was always fully aware of its deliberations. Two senior staff, members from his office, and the clerk of the Privy Council attended CGM meetings, and they regularly briefed the prime minister on the status of the program review. In addition, it had been agreed early on in the process that no decisions would be considered final until the prime minister had 'signed off on them.' My consultations reveal that while the prime minister agreed with most of the decisions, he also did not hesitate to overturn some and modify others. The consultations also reveal, however, that the prime minister 'stood firm at all times when ministers came calling to ask that he overturn Martin's decision on the proposed spending cut for their department or to plead for a special project.'[96]

One by one, ministers came to accept that Chrétien would not allow any light between himself and his Finance minister throughout the program review. Chrétien stood firm on notional targets and on program review decisions. Indeed, ministers came to recognize that the notional targets were not simply Martin's targets, they were also Chrétien's. And in many ways they were. After Finance had come up with the targets, PCO reviewed them and made some relatively minor adjustments to them on behalf of the prime minister.

Departments spent the summer of 1994 working on program review submissions, and by September they began meetings with the clerk and her committee. The committee of officials reviewed the proposals and offered advice to departments in preparing their ministers to appear before the program review group. It also enabled the clerk to see which departments would be able to put forward solid and well thought out proposals and which ones were simply going through the motions.

It became clear, for example, that John Manley and his Department of Industry officials would try to avoid the six questions altogether and make the case that their department should be spared.[97] But Finance had targeted the department for a 'large' spending cut. Manley took the unusual step of writing directly to the prime minister to inform him that Finance and the ministerial group were about to 'make a major political mistake' in cutting one of his programs.[98] It became, in the words of one Finance official, a game of 'political chicken and see who would blink first. We knew that this was a critical moment in the exercise, and if we were forced to back down on this one, there was no telling where the exercise would end up. We stood firm. The prime minister supported us completely and Industry had no choice but to play ball. Cuts to its budget would be made with or without the involvement of the minister of Industry and his officials.'[99] As it was, the prime minister did not reply until budget day, and when he did, he effectively supported the decision to strip the program in question of government funding.

Other ministers made impassioned pleas before their colleagues to protect their departmental programs. Ralph Goodale, the minister of Agriculture, asked his colleagues on the review group, 'What gives you the right to act as judges on what generations of other people have created? From what divine right do you derive the power to decide that fifty of my scientists will be without work tomorrow?'[100] Still other ministers, like André Ouellet, who had served under Trudeau, and who was also a member of the ministerial program review group, expressed deep concern that the program review would have grave political consequences for the government. Still, the prime minister stood firm.

In September 1994 the Coordinating Group of Ministers began to meet once a week, on Mondays at 3 p.m. The meetings lasted about three hours. Later the group started to meet two and three times a week for up to six hours. It tried to consider the work of three ministerial portfolios at one meeting. Relevant ministers accompanied by their deputy ministers attended the sessions and PCO staff provided the logistics for all meetings. Though the CGM did not constitute a formal Cabinet committee, the Cabinet was briefed on the outcome of the group's deliberations. The briefings in reality took the form of a summary of the group's recommendations, and detailed decisions were formulated, similar to normal records of decisions.[101] But again, this occurred only after the prime minister had signed off on all decisions taken by the Coordinating Group of Ministers.

By October–November 1994, it became clear that the review exercise would fall considerably short of the target established by Finance. Another round of spending cuts was planned, but in the end even this round would not be sufficient. As already noted, the Mexican currency crisis had pushed Canadian interest rates up, thus increasing public debt charges. Still more spending cuts would be needed to bring the deficit to its target of 3 per cent of GDP. Those officials interviewed now admit that the Mexican currency problem nearly plunged the government into full crisis mode between December 1994 and January 1995. One reports that 'Martin would literally be briefed on a daily basis, and he would tell his Cabinet colleagues that he needed more in spending cuts to accommodate higher interest rates.'[102]

The crisis atmosphere led Martin and Finance to take charge of the process. Indeed, they decided to put everything back on the table and to reverse earlier decisions. Cuts in defence spending would not be off limits as was initially envisaged, given the cuts the department had suffered in Martin's first budget.

More importantly, the social policy review headed by Lloyd Axworthy on a separate track and assisted by special task forces and a number of outside advisers and consultants would now be derailed. Martin lost patience with this exercise, wanting immediate decisions to deal with the emergency at hand. Martin got his way on this, and on several other issues. In his 1994 budget plan, he had warned his Cabinet colleagues that if the social security review did not generate the necessary savings, then 'other measures will be taken to achieve them.'[103] As is well known, there was limited progress on social review throughout 1994, and in the first week of January 1995, Martin, in concert with the prime minister, instructed the minister of Human Resources Development to produce $1.8 billion in spending cuts and to reduce his department's staff complement by 5,000 over a three-year period.

The result of the program review and spending cuts contained in the 1995 Martin budget are well known. Suffice it to note that under the program review 45,000 public service and military positions were eliminated. Long-established programs like Freight Rate Assistance and transportation subsidies for Western farmers were also eliminated, and major reductions were implemented in various agricultural and industrial subsidies. A further $1 billion in spending cuts were made in defence and $500 million in foreign aid. And the list goes on. New cuts were introduced to the unemployment insurance program and to federal-provincial transfers in the social policy area. Seventy-three boards, commissions, and advisery bodies were shut down. All in all, $29 billion in cuts were announced. By 1996–7 program spending would be reduced to 13.1 per cent of GDP, the lowest level since 1951.[104]

Phase II of the program review was launched as planned, but it never enjoyed the profile of phase I, nor the scope. Phase II was conducted between the 1995 and 1996 budgets. Finance did establish notional targets for each department, and these were met. There was, however, a much greater reliance on 'user fees,' costs recovery, and 'contracting out' to meet the considerably more modest targets in phase II than was the case in phase I.[105] In June 1995 the Cabinet approved a reduction of the deficit to 2 per cent of GDP by 1997–8 and vowed to bring down the government's borrowing requirements to zero by 1998–9. This in turn required another $2 billion in spending cuts by 1998–9.

The process for phase II was rather straightforward. Decisions were made to make further cuts in defence, foreign aid, and social housing. More importantly, phase II relied on across-the-board cuts; each department was to produce cuts of 3.5 per cent in their respective budgets. As already noted, many turned to user fees, cost recovery, and contracting out to meet this target. Finance decided on an across-the-board cut, even though a year earlier Paul Martin had declared that 'blind cuts are bad cuts.' Future responsibility for the program review was formally turned over to the Treasury Board secretariat following the 1996 budget.[106]

It is widely agreed that the program review was a success. Marcel Massé, in a special published report in 1997 called *Getting Government Right*, applauded the government's success in getting Ottawa's fiscal house in order. He maintained that 'these achievements in meeting the government's fiscal objectives result from a fundamental rethinking of priorities, programs and relationships through Program Review.'[107] The clerk of the Privy Council wrote in one of her annual reports to the prime minister that 'program review made a significant contribution to redefining federal roles and to deficit reduction.'[108] She added that the program review was necessary because it had become clear that 'past efforts to address pressure on public finances [which] took the form of across-the-board cuts and efficiency improvements' were no longer effective.[109] A year later she was even more direct in her praise of the exercise. She wrote, 'The magnitude and nature of the transformation underway and the period of time over which the transformation is occurring are unprecedented since World War II ... it is clear that an exceptional story about reinventing the role of government is being written in Canada today.'[110]

She credits the success of the program review to the full participation of public servants in identifying the cuts, rather than relying on outside consultants or outside expertise. She adds that the 'program review was a collective exercise of reform in which ministers, with the help of their departments, led their own reviews and were the architects of their own reform. Central agencies were the guardians of the process, ensuring that a consistent approach was used and that the underlying principles of the Review were sustained.'[111]

A former PCO official who worked directly in the review writes that 'the program review has transformed the traditional approach to reform, and the results have been significant.'[112] In explaining its success, she writes that the six questions had proved very helpful in focusing the effort, and incorporating program review in the budget process had provided momentum and a sense of importance to the exercise. She adds, 'The formation of a Steering Committee of Deputy Ministers, chaired by the Clerk of the Privy Council, also contributed to building a sense of importance about the exercise. The requirement for each Deputy Minister to appear before a peer review panel chaired by the head of the Public Service to explain the departmental submission acted as a motivator for reform. In addition to the power of her position, the Clerk of the Privy Council had demonstrated her desire and support for innovation in government in some of the early reform thinking that took place when she was the Deputy Minister at Transport Canada, prior to becoming Clerk.'[113] Finally, she argues that to have the Privy Council Office play a lead role in the exercise was important since 'it made sense that the department which provides support to the Prime Minister took charge of the exercise.'[114]

Several papers produced by academics on program review also gave the exercise a solid passing grade.[115] In addition, the Institute of Public Administration of Canada published a collection of papers on the program review and on the whole they too found it to be successful.[116] Some observers believe that the decision to spread the cuts over three years rather than just one year, or even a matter of a few months, as in the past, had also contributed to the exercise's success (it should be noted, however, that initially the cuts were to be made over a five-year period) .

A number of officials maintain that the prime minister's refusal to permit 'end runs' proved to be key to the eventual success. Some ministers, including Industry Minister John Manley, had tried to play under a different set of rules, but the prime minister made certain that they did not succeed. Once it was established that 'end runs' would not be tolerated, then everyone knew that the exercise was 'not only serious but that there was no avoiding it.'[117]

Still, the program review highlighted a number of problems, shortcomings, and flaws in the Ottawa decision-making process. One observer writes that while the program review did start off to 'reinvent government' by asking a number of fundamental questions, it 'degenerated into an exercise in fiscal restraint.'[118] Certainly, those persons charged with reviewing social policy would agree with this observation. There is no denying that the Mexican currency crisis and the jump in interest rates in December 1994–January 1995 shot the review into crisis management mode. Indeed, by early January, interest rates had reached a 'worst case scenario,' a scenario Martin had described only a few months earlier.[119]

One result of the currency crisis is that it placed the minister of Finance and his department firmly in the driver's seat. But the majority of the officials consulted for this book insisted that they had been there all along. One stated, 'When all is said and done about the program review exercise, the most important factors were the notional targets for spending cuts. They were produced by Finance and they established the ground rules for the review and they had everything to do with its final results.'[120] The other five questions were, by most accounts, of limited relevance. It also became clear that though the CGM played a significant role in promoting spending cuts, when it truly mattered it was still the prime minister and the minister of Finance who made the decisions. As one observer wrote, 'The final decision on where the axe will fall lies with Martin and the prime minister.'[121] For their part, Finance officials insist that the program review was critical to 'ensuring that ministers and departments would buy into the need to introduce large spending cuts on an urgent basis.'[122] By and large, however, their praise do not go further than this.

It is clear that the prime minister never lost control of the steering wheel. As already noted, two of his senior staff members attended meetings of the Coordinating Group of Ministers. The clerk chaired the meetings of deputy ministers and also attended the ministerial meetings. Early on in the exercise, the clerk, as already noted, made it clear to everyone that no important decisions would be considered final until the 'prime minister had signed off on them.'[123] Not only did this involve the prime minister directly in all crucial decisions, it also served notice to line ministers and their departments once again that 'end runs' were simply not on.[124] Accordingly, the prime minister was always well aware of the discussions around program review. He knew where the tension points lay and which ministers and departments were not delivering cuts. He also knew when to intervene in Cabinet and what to say. One central official summed up the exercise in this fashion: 'The prime minister and Paul Martin looked after the substance and everyone else looked after the process.'[125]

Still, the centre of government was found lacking in several respects. Departments complained that the notional targets were never firm until well into the exercise. One official remarked that 'there was more than one surprise from Finance through the fall and early 1995. Central agencies do not like surprises coming from us but they sure do not mind pulling them off.'[126]

The centre was also not clear or consistent when it came to numbers. In fact, a good many central agency officials consulted admitted that there is a serious numbers problem in government. This became apparent in the program review exercise. In developing notional targets for spending cuts, Finance turned to its own data. Many line departments, meanwhile, were operating from their own budget figures and from a different set of budget numbers. To add to the confusion, the Treasury Board secretariat, the keeper of the government's expenditure budget, had yet another set of numbers – and authoritative figures only for the current year. The program review and the notional targets, meanwhile, were for a three-year period. This proved to be very confusing for departments operating sunset programs, those which only had, say, a three-year life cycle. Were the notional cuts to apply on a department's sunset programs, to the ongoing 'A' base, or to both? If only to the latter, then how should sunset programs be treated?

The Department of the Environment and its Green Plan is an excellent case in point. Senior Environment officials report that they had a great deal of difficulty in determining from what base the cuts should be made. The Green Plan had (initially, at least) added $3 billion of new money to the federal government's expenditure budget. The Department of Environment was to receive about

40 per cent of the total by 1996–7. However, $1.2 billion from the total amount had already been cut within two years of the plan's inception. It will also be recalled that Green Plan spending was to be temporary – initially allocated over a five-year period, later to be spread over six years. The question was whether the money should be treated as 'A' base money for the purpose of the program review or as temporary spending. The Department of Finance and the Treasury Board secretariat argued that it should not be treated as 'A' base spending, but as temporary. In other words, the six-year Green Plan funding should not be included in the base and spending cuts should be made from the budget level established prior to the Green Plan. Accordingly, the central agencies wanted a 30 or 33.3 per cent cut (depending on the week, according to Environment officials) from a base of 72 per cent of the current budget, which actually meant a 50 per cent cut from the department's current base. Environment resisted, insisting that 'the Green Plan funds had become deeply integrated into the operations of the department's ongoing programs and ... they could not possibly be separated out. Fully 40 percent of the Green Plan budget over the previous five years went to DOE, with the result that 28 percent of DOE's budget came from Green Plan money.'[127] Environment eventually won the day on this issue. After several attempts, its minister, Sheila Copps, and her officials successfully made the case that Environment should not be treated like other departments because the Green Plan dominated their programs and had been fully integrated in the department. By contrast, they argued, other departments with Green Plan funding all had less than 10 per cent of their budget tied to the plan.

Copps was a member of the Coordinating Group of Ministers, but it was Martin, not the group, who made the decision. It has been suggested that Martin agreed with Environment's position because he had gained a strong appreciation for the department's programs while opposition environment critic.[128] In any event, Environment was the only department which had Green Plan funding calculated into its base; other departments had to make their cuts from their pre-Green Plan budgets. Though the final decision helped Environment in meeting its target, the confusion at the centre over numbers and the ensuing disputes, particularly in the summer of 1994, considerably frayed relations between central agencies and a number of line departments. Indeed, according to some officials, 'The difficulties in establishing accurate expenditure data for Program Review at one point threatened to put the entire exercise at risk.'[129]

The program review also demonstrated that the centre of government was extremely weak in managing horizontal or interdepartmental issues. Even observers who generally approved of the exercise acknowledge that horizontal issues were left unattended. The focus of the review had been on departments and there was a high price to pay for it. Line department officials explain that it was not always possible to take advantage of some opportunities to rationalize spending and operations because to do so would have required a multidepartment perspective. This became all too obvious in the case of the science departments, where closer cooperation among various research institutes could have given rise to significant savings. But untapped opportunities also existed in a number of ongoing programs. For example, the Department of Fisheries and Oceans (DFO) sought to redefine its role and responsibilities for freshwater fisheries. This had obvious implications for the Department of Environment but officials there were not apprised of what DFO was planning. Line departments blame the centre for this failure, insisting that it, not they, have the mandate and capacity to deal with horizontal or multidepartment issues.

A great number of line department officials consulted also argue that the centre of government was being self-serving in maintaining that the program review was a bottom-up exercise and that departments were relatively free to identify spending cuts. Although the program review largely made unnecessary a new round of across-the-board cuts, some insist that since all departments had to suffer cuts, it proved that the exercise was driven by fiscal realities, not by a desire to identify priorities.

The majority of the line department officials also claim that the reason the centre chose not to identify spending cuts is because it was incapable of doing so. It is worth quoting at length a former deputy minister who was a full participant in the exercise. He argues,

> Think back to the Joe Clark government when it was in office in 1979. The prime minister declared that his approach to the Quebec issue was for his government not to get involved. Clark said that it was largely a decision for Quebecers to deal with. The fact is that Clark simply came up with a rationale for his government's inability to get involved. He had one elected member of Parliament, Roch Lasalle, hardly a heavyweight, in his Cabinet and a handful of unelected senators with no credibility in Quebec or anywhere else. The simple fact is that Clark did not have the capacity to intervene, and rather than admit this, he came up with a rationale. The same logic applies to the centre's decision to turn to departments to identify the cuts. It simply did not have the capacity to do it, but it did not want to admit it.[130]

How well did the centre itself fare in the exercise? At the start of the review, the clerk of the Privy Council directed that the three central agencies, PCO, Finance, and the Treasury Board secretariat should all take 'a 15 percent cut to their staffs and to their budget. Central agencies were also asked to cut another 3.5 percent of their budgets as part of the phase II exercise.'[131] She argued that this was necessary if only to give the exercise credibility. The deputy minister of Finance strongly opposed the clerk's recommendation, arguing that it would weaken the department at a crucial time in the government's fight to reduce the deficit. He also pointed out that Finance was not a large department and that it could ill afford to take a spending cut. The clerk and deputy minister of Finance debated this matter on several occasions in the meetings of the Steering Committee of Deputy Ministers. Finance, however, decided not to pursue the issue in the Coordinating Group of Ministers. The clerk, with the prime minister's support, won the day on this issue.

In the end, however, PCO's budget did not suffer the same fate as the other central agencies. It needed new funding to build up its intergovernmental affairs group, and the office was provided with an additional $5 million over a two-year period, beginning in 1996–7, because 'the intergovernmental agenda is expected to be active with a number of major issues requiring extensive federal-provincial consultation.'[132]

Though the prime minister made certain that no light would appear to Cabinet colleagues between himself and his Finance minister throughout the program review, a glimmer became visible to those operating at the centre of government. Edward Greenspon and Anthony Wilson-Smith admirably document the disagreement that surfaced between Chrétien and Martin over old age pension reform.[133] At one point, officials in the Privy Council Office feared that Martin would resign over the issue. They were well aware that if the country's Finance minister were to resign on the eve of the budget the country could well be plunged into a serious financial crisis. Martin wanted to introduce old age pension reform in his 1995 budget by calculating benefits on a sliding scale based on family income, not an individual income. Poor families would receive more, while those with a family income above $40,000 would be worse off.

Chrétien believed that the 1995 budget would contain more than enough cuts as it was, and there was no pressing need to tackle the politically explosive issue of old age pension reform just yet. He was particularly worried about the impact of old age pension reform in the upcoming Quebec referendum. Martin, however, remained adamant. A senior policy adviser to the prime minister came up with a compromise at the last minute. Martin would not get his way in 1995, but the prime minister would agree to the reform in the following year. In addition, Chrétien permitted Martin to highlight the issue in his 1995 budget speech, which he did.

Cabinet was left completely in the dark, and at no time was it brought in to help resolve the matter. Indeed, very few ministers knew if or how the budget would deal with old age pensions until the last minute. Certainly, it was an issue with major political and policy implications, but it was also a budget issue, and it was left to the prime minister and his minister of Finance to resolve.

Now More Than Just a Budget

For many people, the word budget has come to conjure up images of a thick document crammed with obscure jargon understood only by economists and accountants. To be sure, Ottawa's budget documents have evolved greatly over the years. Today, the budget consists of much more than a speech accompanied by a document. In reality, it comprises several documents, though the minister's budget speech in Parliament remains the most important.

Traditionally, budget speeches have reported on the state of the Canadian economy, the government's fiscal health, its economic accomplishments, and any adjustments needed to the country's taxation system. Former deputy ministers who worked in Ottawa during the 1960s, 1970s, and even as late as the early 1980s, report that in their day these were the issues budget speeches were largely preoccupied with.

This was still true when Marc Lalonde was minister of Finance. His 1984 budget speech reported on the government's efforts to contain inflation, to reduce the deficit, to increase investment, and on new measures to simplify the taxation system. It introduced, for example, changes to the manufacturer's sales tax and amendments to the *Income Tax Act* and to the *Customs Tariff and Excise Act*.[134] No new major expenditure programs and no major policy statements were presented. In other words, the last Lalonde budget stuck to its knitting. This is no longer the case.

The Trudeau government, however, a year earlier had turned to Lalonde's budget speech to announce a $4.8 billion special recovery program designed to promote job creation. Half of that amount was made available to the private sector to support private investment, and the remaining $2.4 billion was to upgrade public facilities.[135] The initiative, however, had been discussed in Cabinet committee meetings, and Cabinet and regional ministers had been asked for their input in shaping its development before Lalonde made the announcement.

Michael Wilson and Don Mazankowski pushed back the traditional limits of budget speeches as Finance ministers in the Mulroney government. Budget documents under Wilson gained new importance in that they shaped specific economic and social policies. Indeed, both Wilson and Mazankowski used the budget to deal with microprogram decisions. For example, in 1992 Don Mazankowski's budget speech unveiled new measures to help small business and to support Canadians with disabilities. This budget also closed down twenty-one government bodies and merged another ten.[136] Senior Mulroney ministers admit that by the time they learned of these changes they were already a *fait accompli*.[137]

Paul Martin has pushed the scope of the budget document still further. It now delves into any policy area the minister and his department deem necessary. The budget is now the government's major policy statement, covering virtually the whole waterfront. If the minister and Department of Finance, for example, decide that a particular department is slow off the mark in reviewing a certain policy, they will move in and direct that action be taken in short order. And that is not all.

Budget speeches in recent years have announced new alternative service delivery measures, including new agencies, such as a single food-inspection agency. They have also restructured federal-provincial transfer agreements, established a new health services research fund, overhauled Canada's old age security system, provided increased assistance for child support, new funding for education and skills development, and increased education tax credits. And they have announced new funding for the Business Development Branch and for the Farm Credit Corporation. They have increased the number of communities receiving the necessary electronic infrastructure required to access new communications technologies. In the 1997 budget, the minister of Finance declared that $425 million in 'new' federal money would be added to the Canada Infrastructure program. Paul Martin also used his budget speech to announce the establishment of a Canada Foundation for Innovation. The foundation was provided with an up-front federal government investment of $800 million. The list goes on and on, and includes measures to update the government's equalization program and an overhaul of the Canada Pension Plan.[138]

In short, the budget has come to dominate policy and decision making in Ottawa as never before. This holds significant advantages for the centre of government. It enables the prime minister and the minister of Finance to introduce new measures and policies under the cover of budget secrecy and avoid debate in Cabinet – and perhaps, more importantly, long interdepartmental consultations and attempts to define a consensus.

This is not to suggest that all of the budgetary announcements come as a surprise to all ministers and departments. Ministers, for example, were well aware of the spending cuts produced by the program review exercise. But because they are budget measures, they are treated differently from regular run of the mill policy and program changes. Leaving aside the program review, many budget measures are presented to Cabinet ministers as a *fait accompli*, as part of the Finance minister's briefings, in the form of a deck or power points. Others can catch ministers and their departments totally unprepared.

In all cases, it is the prime minister and Finance minister who debate the options and make the final decision. The decision to create the Canada Health and Social Transfer program to replace other transfer programs was taken at the centre of government, not in Cabinet. Yet, it was an important decision involving $25 billion in transfers to the provinces in the form of cash and tax points. It also provided more flexibility to provincial governments to administer health care, post-secondary education, and social service programs.

This is not to suggest, however, that the prime minister and minister of Finance are always in agreement on measures contained in the budget. Consultations reveal, for example, that the prime minister insisted, over the objection of the Finance minister, that new funding be allocated to the Canada Infrastructure program. On the other hand, it was Martin's idea, not Chrétien's, to support the establishment of the Canada Foundation for Innovation and to give it $800 million of up-front money.

The above measures were not promoted by spending ministers, but by the guardians at the centre of government, and this change speaks to a different dynamic in the budget-making process. In brief, it means that the traditional guardians of the pubic purse have become the new spenders.

When Guardians Become Spenders

The key actors in my 1990 book *The Politics of Public Spending in Canada* were the guardians and the spenders.[139] The guardians were the prime minister, the minister of Finance, and the president of the Treasury Board. The spenders were the line departments. The guardians were pitted against the spenders in an effort to limit government spending. If the guardians, with the exception of the prime minister, wanted to promote a pet project, they would usually ask the relevant line department minister to come forward with the proposal. One former Trudeau minister explains, 'There was a kind of bartering system in place. I would propose something knowing that the Finance minister wanted it. There was an understanding that I could come back later for something for my region or my department.'[140] The abolition of the elaborate Cabinet committee system, including Priorities and Planning and the Operations committees, now provide fewer opportunities for the minister of Finance, the president of the Treasury Board, or even the prime minister, none of whom have direct access to programs, to work out deals with spenders. In their absence, guardians are now able to turn to the one document that matters, the budget – the one that they hold in their own hands – to advance their projects without having to strike side deals with spending ministers.

This change in the game plan has not been lost on line ministers and their departments. One theme that came up time and again in my consultations was the extent to which the centre, the budget, and the Department of Finance have come to dominate all policy areas. There are now two sets of rules, not just for the budget documents, but also the expenditure budget: one for the guardians and the other for the spenders.

The tension between the two erupted in the media in early December 1997. The minister of Finance had informed his Cabinet colleagues that autumn that $300 million in new spending would be available. The two Cabinet committees, the economic and social committees, held a joint meeting on 2 December 1997 to begin allocating Martin's 'fiscal dividends.' Neither the prime minister nor the minister of Finance attended the meeting.[141] A few months earlier, the Privy Council Office had issued a general call for spending proposals, a decision with which the Department of Finance did not agree. PCO officials wanted to see what departments would come up with in terms of innovative ideas to spend the newly found fiscal dividends. Finance officials felt that the call was premature and would only serve to raise expectations.

A number of ministers were quick to make clear their frustration, not so much with PCO's call for proposals, but rather with the government's overall policy and decision-making process. They were openly critical of Paul Martin, for example, for putting his own priorities outside the Cabinet review process and securing funding without consulting anybody except the prime minister. A government source explained that 'a number of ministers suggested that everybody but the Finance minister took their priorities through the Cabinet process as they were asked to do.' The *Globe and Mail* reported another source as saying that ministers felt that the UI tax cut, which the minister of Finance had recently announced, but which was not discussed in Cabinet, was 'not necessarily what Canadians are asking for.' A Finance official replied, however, that Paul Martin did not unilaterally make the UI tax cut, but in conjunction with the Human Resources minister and 'with the approval of Prime Minister Jean Chrétien.' Consultations with senior federal government officials for this book reveal that this is precisely what happened. The *Globe and Mail* quoted yet another source in its front page story, saying that 'while sceptical, they must live with Mr. Martin's [decision].'[142]

Ministers could just as easily have pointed the finger at the prime minister. He had only a few months before agreed to cost share a $300 million highway agreement, committing $150 million in federal funding without consulting Cabinet or Cabinet committee. Several months earlier he had committed $50 million to projects in British Columbia after meeting with Premier Glen Clark, and simply instructed government officials to look after the paperwork. The same is also true for the Canada millennium scholarships. Similarly, political commitments assembled by the prime minister and a handful of his advisers in the 1997 election campaign amounted to $1.1 billion. They too were not submitted to the Cabinet process. The list goes on. More than one minister at the 2 December 1997 meeting felt that they were left to allocate the crumbs, while the big ticket items were firmly in the hands of the prime minister and the minister of Finance.

Certainly, the prime minister and the minister of Finance have come to hold in their own hands all major and some minor decisions. They decide how the budget will take shape and the broad contours of government economic policies. They even decide which spending proposals should go forward, and this with or without Cabinet consent. Chrétien and Martin have taken this process to new heights but it is important to stress that it did not start with them. Mulroney did much the same. He did not, for example, bother with the Cabinet process when he decided to allocate over $2 billion of new money to two regional economic development agencies he established in 1987, or when he decided to support numerous bilateral deals he had struck with premiers and some of his own ministers.

It was Trudeau who launched a frontal attack on the power of the Department of Finance. It may well be that his original intention was to introduce checks and balances in the Ottawa decision-making process and to remove some of the powers of the Department of Finance in order to strengthen the hand of Cabinet. The actual results, however, proved different. He did not strengthen the hand of Cabinet, only his own, that of his advisers, and the Privy Council Office. Neither Mulroney nor Chrétien have turned back the clock.

The centre of government is not only concerned with macroeconomic decisions or even with developing spending proposals. It also has a hand in microprogram decisions and in management issues. The Treasury Board secretariat and the Public Service Commission both have a mandate to review microprogram and management decisions.

7

Treasury Board and the Public Service Commission: Pulling against Gravity

I asked a former secretary to the Treasury Board to describe his job for me in a few sentences. His answer: 'I do not know if I could describe what I do in a few sentences. But I do know what is expected of me and what ministers dislike immensely. They do not want any surprises and they somehow expect me to look after that.' He added, 'Treasury Board ministers will listen and usually nod their heads in approval when you talk about empowering departments and their managers, but let the media report on something that has gone wrong in a department and they are more than likely to ask or wonder where was the Treasury Board secretariat in all of this?'[1] I repeated the essence of these comments to another secretary of the Treasury Board for his reaction, and he responded 'Yes! That's about how it is in here.'[2] Both could have added that they too do not much like surprises.

The work of the Treasury Board and its secretariat go to the heart of recent reforms to modernize government operations and to the New Public Management movement. If anyone in government is in a position to encourage the manager to manage, it is the Treasury Board. To be sure, the Public Service Commission also plays an important role in human resources management, as do the Department of Public Works and Government Services in several administrative areas. But it is the Treasury Board that must take the lead and in concert with the Privy Council Office set the reform agenda and then pursue it. It is also the Treasury Board that lays down the rules on expenditure budgets, how human resources and real property are managed, and how official languages policy is applied.

In addition, it is the Treasury Board that sets in motion initiatives to devolve decision-making authority to line departments and frees managers from centrally prescribed administrative rules and regulations. Treasury Board, for example, has been leading the charge in introducing Special Operating Agencies (SOAs) which are designed to operate with less bureaucratic red tape than line departments. Its secretariat also provides support to the clerk of the Privy Council whenever he or she decides to launch reform measures, as was the case in 1989 in the implementation of Public Service 2000.

To the casual observer, it would seem that officials in the Treasury Board secretariat and, albeit to a lesser extent, those in the Public Service Commission lead schizophrenic lives. Certainly, on the face of it there ought to be a great deal of tension, if not outright contradiction, between the centre's need to limit 'surprises' and its responsibility to empower managers and bring the New Public Management to government operations. To remove or attenuate centrally prescribed rules may empower line departments, but it may well give rise to unwelcome surprises.

The purpose of this chapter is to review the roles the Treasury Board secretariat and the Public Service Commission play in financial and human resources management. These are, of course, the lifeblood of any government organization and they are also what drives the New Public Management. We should bear in mind that every government reform measure, starting with the Glassco Commission in the 1960s, has sought to modernize government operations by empowering line managers to manage their financial and human resources.

We begin by reviewing Treasury Board's role in several major public service reform efforts. We will pay particular attention to its responsibility for managing the expenditure budget process, knowing that 'budgetary decisions are the single most important factor that constrains and defines the delivery of programs and other nonfinancial issues such as human resources management.'[3] The chapter also seeks to answer a number of questions: what role has the centre played in introducing New Public Management to government? How successful has it been? What changes have been introduced to empower line department and agencies? How has the expenditure budget process evolved during the past thirty years or so? How well do central agencies, in particular the Treasury Board secretariat and the Public Service Commission, work together given that in human resources matters their mandates overlap? One would assume that they make every effort to work well together. After all, central agencies pride themselves on their ability to promote a horizontal or corporate perspective on issues.

The Treasury Board: Looking Back

The Treasury Board was established on 2 July 1867 and made a statutory committee in 1869. Unlike other Cabinet committees, much of its responsibility is specified in legislation under a number of acts, including the *Financial Admin-*

istration Act, *Federal Real Property Act*, and the *Public Sector Employment Act*. These acts empower the Treasury Board to speak for the government on matters relating to general administrative policy, financial and personnel management, and such other matters as may be referred to it by the governor-in-council.

Treasury Board is also the only Cabinet committee that does not rely on the Privy Council Office for secretariat support. It is served by its own secretariat. The modus operandi of Treasury Board differs from that of other Cabinet committees: its president and his or her ministerial colleagues sit on one side of the table while the secretariat officials sit opposite and present the cases to be considered. Only in exceptional circumstances are ministers and officials from the department under review invited to elaborate on the case, but even when they are, they are usually asked to leave before the Treasury Board ministers make their decision. In the case of other Cabinet committees, ministers present their own cases and, accompanied by selected departmental officials, they mostly sit where they choose.

Most Treasury Board decisions relate to the board's statutory authorities under the *Financial Administration Act*, and where they do not involve issues of general policy are not referred to Cabinet, but are reflected in a letter of decision from the Treasury Board secretariat to the deputy minister of the department concerned.[4] On matters of more general concern to the ministry, the Treasury Board produces committee reports for confirmation by full cabinet.

The Treasury Board secretariat does not enjoy the influence and glamour of either the Privy Council Office or the Department of Finance. Indeed, in many ways, the secretariat is Finance's poor cousin. One senior government official summed up the difference between the three central agencies in this way: 'PCO looks after the broad picture and resolves conflicts between ministers and departments. Finance looks after the big economic and budgetary decisions. The Treasury Board looks after the little decisions.'[5] But the little decisions do matter to departments. Indeed, while the decisions may appear to be 'little' from the perspective of some people at the centre, they are often big decisions for line departments and programs managers. In addition, the Treasury Board secretariat has the deepest knowledge of government programs of any central agency because it reviews in considerable detail departmental spending plans, or at least in more detail than is the case for the other two. The result is that PCO and Finance often have to turn to the Treasury Board secretariat for information and advice.[6]

A former secretary to the Treasury Board wrote nearly thirty years ago that the Treasury Board has two important responsibilities – the management of the public service and the expenditure budget.[7] The Glassco Commission, it will be recalled, sought to make the Treasury Board the management arm of the government by removing it from the Department of Finance and by giving it a new broader mandate than simply reviewing departmental budgets. The government adopted the Glassco Commission recommendation and the Treasury Board has ever since been expected to take the lead on management issues in government. But it has company. The Public Service Commission and the Department of Public Works and Government Services also play a part, the former in human resources management and the latter in several administrative areas.

When it was part of the Department of Finance, the Treasury Board secretariat was not only small, it was also largely concerned with the *Financial Administration Act* and managing the expenditure budget, and it was preoccupied with issues of financial and administrative details. The head of the Glassco Commission, Grant Glassco, a leading executive from the private sector, had been taken aback to discover that the public service, a large institution operating in Ottawa and in various cities and towns across Canada, had no management capacity at the centre. Essentially, the commission urged that the traditional concern with audits to ensure parliamentary control over resource inputs be supplemented with the authority to determine whether the purposes and results of programs were consistent with their legislated intents and stated objectives. The commission also recommended that departments and agencies have greater authority to administer their programs.[8] In short, Glassco's objective was to transform the Treasury Board and its secretariat into a modern central agency and to give it a management mandate.

When Glassco looked at the work of the Treasury Board and its secretariat, he discovered an institution which Prime Minister Bennett had essentially defined and provided with a central purpose. Indeed, before Bennett, the Treasury Board had never quite been able to find a solid footing. It never became the strong committee of Cabinet Sir John A. Macdonald had envisaged when he established it. For many years after Confederation, the board dealt mostly with the form of government accounts, the details of personnel administration, and the financial and administrative transactions criticized by the auditor general.[9] In his report on the federal public service in 1912, Sir George Murray even concluded that the Treasury Board should be abolished, believing that most of its work could be done by other officials and individual ministers.[10] Murray's recommendation was not accepted, however, and throughout the 1920s, the board 'continued to deal with a variety of subjects, apparently at a leisurely pace.'[11] The subjects brought before the Treasury Board were still relatively minor administrative matters, including superannuation questions and remission of some custom duties.

When Bennett came to power in the summer of 1930, he wanted urgent action to cut government spending to reduce the deficit and to maintain

Canada's credit ratings in financial markets abroad.[12] Bennett appointed himself minister of Finance and decided to overhaul the Treasury Board.

Bennett was taken aback by the apparent lack of financial control and the government's inability to tell him how much departments had already spent in the fiscal year. Indeed, it took officials six months before they could brief him on the government's financial position, and even then Bennett was not certain he had firm numbers. J.E. Hodgetts reports that 'Much to Bennett's horror, it appeared that the economic and social chaos in the country at large was hardly any worse than the administrative chaos which had reigned in the federal bureaucracy for years, insofar as financial control was concerned.'[13]

Bennett decided to overhaul the expenditure estimates, to establish an Office of the Comptroller of the Treasury, and to introduce an elaborate record of all expenditures and outstanding commitments. Cabinet also agreed to give the board authority to review a number of small administrative matters. For example, the Treasury Board would even review 'the installation of each new telephone in government offices and the purchase of each motor vehicle by government departments.'[14] These cases were presented to the board as 'routine,' so that ministers did not spend much time, if any, on them. Still, they were part of the material presented to the board so that an inquisitive minister was free to raise any question. This was in pre-Keynesian days. Government was small so that ministers did have the time to inquire about relatively minor administrative matters. Even by the mid-1930s, the Treasury Board had only a 'very small staff to assist the estimates and cases.' We are informed that the board had a clerk of the estimates, two other senior clerks, and three or four stenographers.[15]

The staff serving the Treasury Board expanded considerably between the mid-1930s and the early 1960s, when Glassco formulated his recommendations. But by and large, the Treasury Board continued to function along the lines Bennett had established. The federal government had grown substantially since the Bennett years, and Glassco concluded that it was time to turn over the operations of government to managers. Not only did he think that there was a need to promote a management perspective at the centre, he also concluded that the time had come to let the manager manage. The commission maintained that 'what was a relatively simple government organization in 1939 had become today a complicated system of departments, boards, and commissions engaged in a multitude of different tasks. Obviously, the methods found effective for the management of the relatively compact organization of the prewar days cannot control without extensive alteration the vast complex which has come into being in the past twenty years.'[16] It insisted that the government's financial controls were too cumbersome, with a wide variety of 'checks, counterchecks and duplication and blind adherence to regulations.'[17]

Though Glassco may have been the first to call for a new role for the Treasury Board, he would not be the last. The Lambert Commission, some fifteen years after Glassco, made a similar recommendation. More recently Prime Minister Chrétien declared, on appointing his new ministry for his second mandate on 11 June 1997, that 'the Treasury Board has been re-oriented to play an enhanced role as the government's management board.'[18] But, again, Chrétien was not the first prime minister to make such a statement.[19] Brian Mulroney, during the 1984 election campaign, had announced that the goal of his government would be 'to let managers manage,' and that his government would 'shift from reliance on regulations, controls, and detailed procedures towards greater reliance on managers' competence and their achievements of results.'[20] Thus, some twenty years after the Glassco report, Mulroney could still put forward deregulation of management and decentralization as important reform proposals and initiatives.[21]

The easy part, clearly, is to make the declaration. The hard part is to define what the shift actually means, and harder still, to make the new approach stick. To turn the Treasury Board into a management board invariably involves transferring more authority from the centre to line departments. The idea suggests that the Treasury Board should act more like a board of directors of a large corporation than a board concerned with financial and administrative controls.

The 1986 budget documents heralded the management board concept when they revealed that the government would give 'individual ministers and their departmental managers more latitude and more direct responsibility to manage the resources entrusted to them so that they can react quickly and effectively to the changing environment.'[22] A few months later, Robert De Cotret, the minister responsible for the Treasury Board, declared that the government 'will be more concerned with what departments do both in program results and in meeting service-wide policy objectives and less concerned with how well procedural rules are followed.'[23] Fast forward to 1997, when Peter Harder, the secretary to the Treasury Board, gave an interview to the magazine *Canadian Government Executive* in which he argued that 'results-based managing and a strengthened results-based accountability will become the order of the day within the Secretariat.'[24] Again, the kind of changes De Cotret and Harder proposed some ten years apart had already been proposed by their predecessors in one form or another ever since Glassco tabled his findings.

The Treasury Board Secretariat Today

The Treasury Board secretariat has witnessed important changes, if not a great deal of uncertainty, in its top management in recent years. Three individuals held the position of secretary in the span of about two years between 1994 and 1995 (Ian Clark, Robert Giroux, and Peter Harder). Peter Harder, not long after assuming his position in November 1995, decided to 'flatten' or 'de-layer' the organization. Until his arrival the secretariat had been organized into two major branches, both headed by deputy secretaries, one essentially responsible for the expenditure budget (the program branch) and the other for human resources.

Harder also decided to reorient what he labels the secretariat's 'business lines.' This is not to suggest, even for a moment, that many secretariat activities were jettisoned in favour of new and distinct ones. Indeed, even only a cursory reading of the secretariat activities contained in Part III of the document estimates for, say, 1988–9 and 1998–9, reveals that core functions remain largely as they were ten or even twenty years ago. To be sure, there are some new activities and some old ones, such as information technology, that have been recast and given a much higher profile. But it would not be too difficult, for example, for Gérard Veilleux, secretary in the late 1980s, to recognize his old department. He would, however, be struck by the number of new approaches the board had introduced to strengthen management since he left. This chapter reports on them. He would also see that departments have to bring far fewer cases to the board for consideration than when he was secretary.

Yet he would discover that, as Al Johnson observed nearly thirty years ago, the Treasury Board remains in essence the Cabinet committee 'on the expenditure budget' and 'on management.'[25] The secretariat's organization still reflects this dual mandate, as indeed it has ever since it was broken off from the Department of Finance.

Harder's reorganization had a number of purposes. As already noted he wanted to de-layer the organization. But he was also seeking to move the Treasury Board 'towards a management board role ... to modernize the way in which it exercises its responsibilities ... [and to place emphasis on] a much stronger strategic and results-oriented focus and away from an emphasis on individual transactions and approvals.'[26] In addition, he wanted to deal with the often-heard criticism in Ottawa that the Treasury Board secretariat 'can never get its act together,' that 'there is not one but several Treasury Boards,' or that 'the Secretariat is a series of silos hardly connected to one another.'[27] But Harder was not the first secretary to try to deal with this criticism. Gérard Veilleux, for example, had it at the top of his priority list in 1986. Al Johnson also probably had this problem in mind when, in 1971, from his vantage point as secretary, he authored a paper, 'The Treasury Board of Canada and the Machinery of Government in Canada.' He began his paper by comparing the Treasury Board secretariat to Kafka's Castle.[28]

Harder is not the sole architect of the modern Treasury Board secretariat. Ian

Clark, one of his predecessors, established a new position in July 1993, 'Chief Information Officer,' and made the incumbent, together with his staff, 'responsible for developing policy and standards for information management and technology and related telecommunications activities.'[29] The then president of the Treasury Board, Jim Edwards, reported that his goal was 'to eliminate paper from the government's internal administrative processes by the end of the decade [and] along with the paper, I hope I will have eliminated a great deal of red tape.'[30] The first person appointed to the position had previously been head of the Office of the Comptroller General. That office was fully integrated into the Treasury Board secretariat in Kim Campbell's 1993 restructuring, so that establishing the new post of chief information officer only a few weeks after Campbell's announcement proved to be convenient in more ways than one. The two secretaries before Peter Harder had also introduced other changes to the organization. Indeed, there were several changes to the Program and Human Resources branches in 1993 and 1994. For instance, consolidation took place in several branches and some management de-layering was introduced in all branches.

But Peter Harder, more than anyone, shaped the organization from below. He had, while deputy minister of Citizenship and Immigration, overhauled that department by substantially de-layering its management levels. He would do the same at the Treasury Board secretariat. There are now at least twelve individuals reporting directly to the secretary. As was the case for the other central agencies reviewed in earlier chapters, there is no need to describe in detail the work of the various levels. This is available elsewhere, particularly in Part III of the Estimates for the Treasury Board secretariat and in a number of other documents published in recent years by the secretariat.

Evert Lindquist writes that 'for many observers inside and outside the government, the Treasury Board's Program Branch *is* the Treasury Board Secretariat.' The Program branch produces the expenditure budget and deals with departments and agencies on all budgetary and financial matters. The argument is that budgetary decisions, more than any other, define what departments do and how they do it.[31]

The Program branch has recently been reorganized into five sectors, each headed by an assistant secretary reporting directly to the secretary. The functions performed by these five sectors are little different than those performed in the past by the Program branch. One assistant secretary is responsible for the economic sector, another for the social and cultural sector, and the other for government operations, which includes foreign affairs and defence. While the functions of the old branch may have been spread around a bit, they remain essentially unchanged. Policy and multiyear program requirements still must be

Chart 4
Treasury Board of Canada Secretariat

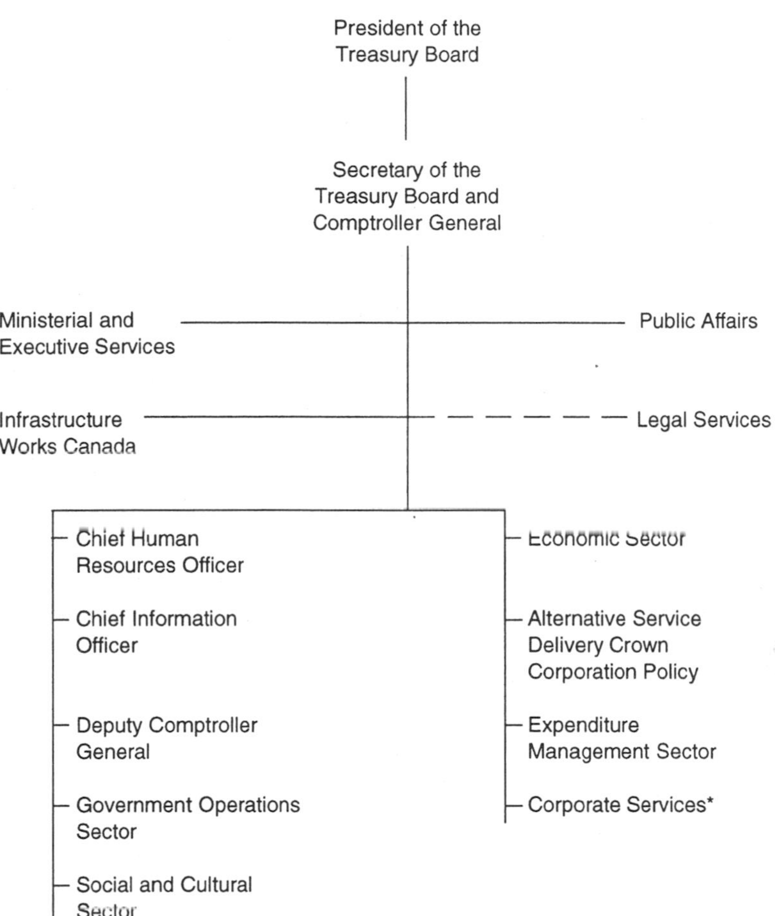

* Joint services with the Department of Finance, 1 November 1997

Source: Based on information provided by officials in the Treasury Board Secretariat, November 1997

analysed to enable the secretariat to advise the Treasury Board on the allocation of resources. There is also a 'requirement to provide technical support to departments – in the preparation of business plans, main estimates submissions and to maintain an up-to-date account of planned government expenditures.'[32] There is an assistant secretary, again reporting directly to the secretary, responsible for the management of the estimates and expenditures. He and his staff work closely with Department of Finance officials to finalize expenditure budget numbers, particularly in the weeks leading up to budget day. Finally, there is an assistant secretary charged with identifying and promoting alternative service delivery approaches. It is this group that is responsible for the SOA concept, discussed below.

Another part of the organization handles what the secretary describes as the 'second line of business – Human Resources Management.'[33] This group is responsible for developing a 'human resources management framework' and for a good part of its implementation. The framework consists of 'legislation and policies related to job evaluation, compensation, terms and conditions of employment, training and development, labour relations, employment adjustment, the human resources framework of Alternative Service Delivery, the pension program, pay equity, employment equity, and official languages.'[34] The staff also has a number of duties related to job classification and collective bargaining. During the early and mid-1990s, for example, they produced a number of options on how to plan and implement government downsizing and, subsequently, on how to retain competent managers at a time when their salaries were frozen for several years. The Treasury Board secretariat has produced a detailed report for Parliament which outlines the various activities carried out by these five assistant secretaries.[35]

Secretariat officials are increasingly convinced that new information technology holds the key to improved service delivery, and have established a group to promote its use in government. The group carried out, for example, a review of the government's information and technology standards program 'to ensure the application of standards supports shared infrastructure, software and data across government.'[36] It also works with departments to review a number of issues, including Internet access, and to identify means to address the year 2000 problem.

The Office of the Comptroller General, established in 1978, was fully integrated in the Treasury Board secretariat in 1993. Its function in the secretariat has been guided by the following framework – the operation of a single consolidated fund; an estimates and supply process consistent with parliamentary rules; a solid body of financial and other administration policies; a professional financial, material, property, and review staff; efficient and effective management practices within departments; and effective performance reporting. There are signs, however, that things could be changing on this front. The current leadership at the Treasury Board would like to sharpen the existing accountability and performance reporting regime, insisting that in management 'what gets measured, gets done.'[37] Both the president and the secretary of the Treasury Board have recently expressed a strong desire to 'renew' and 'modernize' the comptrollership.

The president, Marcel Massé, established an independent review panel drawn from the private sector in November 1996 and asked it to identify 'critical success factors ... to achieve successful comptrollership modernization.'[38] The panel reported that 'many of the fundamental conditions and assumptions of the past no longer apply [and] that embracing modern comptrollership will involve dramatic further change and a quantum leap.'[39] It then stated that 'the single most important change proposed in this report is a move to a new guiding philosophy for comptrollership. In very general terms, it is proposed that the philosophy guiding comptrollership move from a "command/control" orientation to a more contemporary one, sometimes called "loose/tight." A "loose/tight" orientation combines a strong commitment to central standards and values and achievement of planned results, with flexibility regarding processes and operational approaches.'[40] But the centre of government, and more specifically the Treasury Board and its secretariat, have been pursuing a 'loose/tight' approach virtually since it was established, and in particular since the mid-1980s.

If You Stand Here Long Enough, It Will Go Around Again

To be sure, the Glassco Commission had a substantial impact on government operations. A long-time student of government observed that Glassco brought 'a sort of managerial revolution in the bureaucracy.'[41] Many of the previously strict controls exercised by central agencies over administrative matters such as salaries, travel, and office equipment were removed. In addition, the government began the shift towards program-based budgeting and away from line item budgeting. Moreover, a number of people who worked with the commission later came to occupy senior positions in government. They were joined by others with private sector experience in financial and personnel management who were brought in to implement the radical reforms.

But while officials were still busy implementing the Glassco recommendations, the government came under attack for 'waste, extravagance and other abuses in the spending of government money.'[42] A special debate was held in the Commons on the government's apparent inability to protect the public Treasury in refitting the aircraft carrier *Bonaventure*. In the debate, specific cases were identified, such as the awarding of two separate contracts – for different amounts – to remove fifty-two chairs from the *Bonaventure*'s briefing rooms. Glassco's call to 'let the manager manage' was now being put severely to the test in the political arena.

In response, the then Treasury Board president unveiled new measures to improve efficiency in government. One of the most important of these was the establishment of a special administrative policy branch in the secretariat. The branch was designed to draw up administrative norms for departments, covering fields like accommodation, construction contracts, travel, material acquisitions, and to develop an accounting system for these expenditures. In a circular, Treasury Board made it clear to all departments that the work of the branch would be directed towards ensuring qualities of probity and prudence in government. The new branch quickly identified two types of administrative activities: those dealing with the quantity and quality of goods and services (such as accommodation and furnishings) and those dealing with acquiring them (contract regulations). The Treasury Board would have a direct hand in both. To implement the new approach, the branch employed three instruments: legislation (such as the *Financial Administration Act* or *Access to Information Act*), regulations (mandatory instructions approved by the governor-in-council), and directives (mandatory instructions approved by the Treasury Board that are normally to be followed).[43]

The auditor general also pressed the federal government in the mid-1970s to establish a new deputy minister level position, that of comptroller general. He wanted a chief financial officer to oversee how money was being spent in government. Jean Chrétien, then Treasury Board president, resisted the suggestion because he did not want two deputy ministers reporting to him. He observed, 'I do not want to be caught between two men.'[44] Convinced that the government would never follow up on his recommendations, the auditor general put the cat among the pigeons in 1976 when he wrote in his annual report that 'Parliament and indeed the Government – has lost, or is close to losing effective control of the public purse.'[45] Again, the notion of letting the manager decide was being put to the test in the political arena.

On the very day the auditor general made his annual report public, the president of the Treasury Board rose in the Commons to announce the setting up of a royal commission on financial management and accountability with a mandate 'to ensure that the departments and agencies meet the highest attainable standards.'[46] Robert Andras was the new Treasury Board president. Unlike his predecessor, he decided to negotiate directly with the auditor general the creation of a new position – that of comptroller general. Andreas tried unsuccessfully to persuade the auditor general to agree that the comptroller general should be the associate secretary to the Treasury Board. The Office of the Comptroller General, headed by a deputy minister reporting directly to the president of the Treasury Board, was established in 1978.

To Treasury Board officials, the Office of the Comptroller General represented a purely political move to placate the media, the auditor general, and the Public Accounts Committee. One official explained that 'the problem they wanted resolved was a political one; their intention was not to institute greater financial controls in government or to improve public administration generally. The consideration that went into all this was – "we've got a political problem. Now, how do we get out of it?" The answer was "if we do appoint a comptroller general – we will make a good number of people happy, so let's do it – and to hell with the rest."' He went on to argue, 'We knew right from the start that his office would not do much.'[47]

The Office of the Comptroller General had many problems during its fifteen-year existence. In 1984 Mulroney directed Robert De Cotret, the president of the Treasury Board, in his mandate letter to clarify the role of the Office of the Comptroller General and to focus or limit its activities to financial management. The Privy Council Office and the Treasury Board secretariat had concluded that the Office of the Comptroller General was not playing the strong financial role envisioned and that it was focusing too much on general management issues.

In terms of the expenditure budget, its most important shortcoming has been in evaluating programs. It assumed full responsibility for the coordination of evaluation planning, for policy guidance, and for assessing the quality of evaluation findings in studies carried out by departments. Shortly after the office was set up, it served notice that it would urge all departments to establish program evaluations and that it would conduct studies on issues of interdepartmental or government-wide concern. It would also take the lead in developing the appropriate methodology and procedures for such evaluations. A keen student and practitioner of public administration predicted shortly after the office was established that the growing concern over increased government spending would lead to 'a new industry, *The Evaluation Industry*.'[48] We now know that program evaluations did indeed develop into a growth industry, one that grew around the Office of the Comptroller General. It remains today an important and largely Ottawa-based industry.

Some observers felt that the establishment of the Office of the Comptroller General had pulled the rug out from under the new Royal Commission on Financial Management and Accountability, or as it became known, the Lambert Commission. But the commission kept at it and soon concluded that there were still two other problems that needed fixing. First, it expressed the urgent need 'to avoid waste' in government. It declared that 'in the context of today's fiscal situation and the pervasiveness of government activity, managers in the public service are being challenged to rediscover a sense of frugality and a commitment to the careful husbanding of resources.'[49] The message from Lambert was clear enough – government managers are not sufficiently competent to let them manage.

Second, it argued that the serious malaise in management stemmed from 'an almost total breakdown in the chain of accountability.'[50] It then sought to repair this situation and to restore a sense of frugality and good management practices. It presented over 130 recommendations, ranging from a restructuring of the Treasury Board secretariat and the Public Service Commission to the transfer of the government's day-to-day cash management to the Department of Finance from Supply and Services. To strengthen accountability in government, the commission urged, among other things, that deputy ministers be appointed for three to five years and that goals be set for all managers to meet. Moreover, it recommended that the goals should provide 'an objective basis for measuring the manager's performance.'

The commission noted with great concern that ministers, deputy ministers, and senior managers were far more interested in policy issues than management ones.[51] Deputy ministers, the commission concluded, were largely deficient in management skills. It then argued that central agencies should take the lead in evaluating the performance of deputy ministers and that new importance be attached to their management functions.

To ensure a proper evaluation of senior managers and that increased emphasis be placed on management rather than policy, the commission recommended a complete overhaul of the central agencies. It reported,

> The deficiencies in the central management of government today relate in no small measure to a failure to plan thoroughly at the top. Accepted, instead, is a planning process too often dependent on trying to marry uncoordinated proposals coming up from the bottom. There is a consequent failure to budget rationally, and a confusion of responsibility for control and evaluation. The follow-up by central management to see if commitments have been met or indicated levels of performance attained has been lacking. The shortcomings of the existing system stem as well from a failure to define precisely and distinctly the tasks and responsibilities of the central agencies. Accountability of the central agencies themselves for the way in which they have performed their own roles is incomplete.[52]

The commission also recommended that the management of governmental functions be 'consolidated.'[53] Specifically, it suggested that the Treasury Board be renamed the Board of Management, and that it assume new responsibilities for overseeing all aspects of management in government. The Board of Management would be supported by two secretaries of the board, one the secretary for personnel management and the other the comptroller general. The former would assume responsibilities for 'government-wide policies on manpower planning, appraisal of senior management personnel ... collective bargaining, classification and official languages.'[54] The latter would essentially lead the expenditure budget process at the officials level. The role of the Public Service Commission would, in turn, be substantially reduced, with most of its responsibilities transferred to the Board of Management. The commission recommended that the Public Service Commission be reconstituted as a 'Parliamentary Department with the duty of ensuring that selection and appointment to the public service are made on the basis of merit.'[55]

The government in the end rejected most of the commission's recommendations. To many senior officials, the Lambert Commission 'had a very naive view of how government operates. It had a strong private sector bias in its work. What works in the private sector does not necessarily work in government and no doubt what works in government would not apply in the private sector.'[56] One senior official reported that when the Lambert report was released, 'we [senior departmental officials] went away for a day and a half session to study the report. We were able to finish the review after only just a few hours. The report did not measure up in any way and it was far removed from the quality and substance of the Glassco Commission. The Lambert report was simply fluff, pure fluff, with no practical application.'[57]

Many senior government officials felt that the commission even lacked a basic grasp of how parliamentary government works. They argued that in describing a process in which departments are held accountable 'through the Board of Management to Parliament,' the commission confused the roles of the executive and legislative branches of government and the manner in which individual ministers are directly answerable to Parliament for the exercise of their responsibilities. They point out that the president of the Treasury Board answers to Parliament for the exercise of *his* responsibilities, including that to develop good management practices and standards. Other ministers, however, are not, and cannot be, responsible *through him*, or through the Treasury Board which he chairs, to Parliament.[58]

One of the Lambert recommendations, however, did strike a chord with a good number of senior officials – that the role of the Public Service Commission be substantially reduced, and that most of its responsibilities be transferred to a newly constituted Board of Management.[59] But the Trudeau government, only months away from calling a general election, decided that it would be unwise to be seen to be tampering with the merit principle in the public service, fearing that it could turn out to be a politically charged issue in the campaign. The role of the Public Service Commission was left unchanged.

Shortly after coming to power, the Mulroney government, wishing to deliver on its campaign commitment to let manager manage, declared that it 'will be more concerned with what departments do both in program results and in meeting service-wide policy objectives and less concerned with how well procedural rules are followed.'[60] Robert De Cotret, the then president of the Treasury Board, announced that the government was introducing a new approach to decision making – Increased Ministerial Authority and Accountability (IMAA).

There is no need to review in detail here the workings of IMAA.[61] Suffice to note that if IMAA was implemented through two complementary initiatives – a general review of Treasury Board policies, and the development of individual memoranda of understanding (MOUs) between departments and the Treasury Board.

The policy review was designed to identify the potential for greater flexibility, deregulation, and delegation, to reduce reporting requirements to the board, and generally to simplify policy. The review prompted some changes. Among other things, departments could now sponsor conferences without having to secure Treasury Board approval, the ceiling on competitive contracts for construction and consulting without reference to the board was doubled, departments could classify positions, except in the management category, and approve organizational changes. The number of reports required under various administrative policies was reduced by 65 per cent, and the delegation of authority in certain areas of human resource management reduced departmental requests to the secretariat by about 1,000 a year. Moreover, departments were allowed to carry into the next fiscal year 5 per cent of their capital budget, to a maximum of $25 million in 1988–9, rising to $75 million in 1990–1. There is no denying that these changes, among other factors, served to reduce Treasury Board's involvement in the day-to-day operations of departments.

The second major activity was the negotiating of MOUs with departments and agencies. The memorandum of understanding outlined the department's increased authority and flexibility in delivering programs and established an accountability framework against which performance can be assessed. The MOU covered the responsibilities of all the branches in the Treasury Board secretariat and the Office of the Comptroller General, and it spelled out in one place the levels of authority delegated to deal with all Treasury Board policies. Further, any savings realized by departments as a result of more efficient operations under IMAA would remain with them for reallocation to priority initiatives.[62]

But IMAA did not live up to expectations and it eventually petered out. For one thing, only eight departments signed a MOU. To make matters worse, those that did sign were disenchanted with IMAA, claiming that the paperwork involved and the reporting requirements were not compensated for by the limited freedom they received from central agency controls.[63] In short, the paperwork practically equalled that required to process their former submissions to Treasury Board. Word quickly spread, and departments simply stopped asking the Treasury Board secretariat to sign MOUs.

In any event, IMAA was soon overtaken by yet another approach. On 12 December 1989, Prime Minister Mulroney unveiled Public Service (PS) 2000. Its purpose was clearly stated: to cut red tape, empower managers and their employees, and improve service to the public. One could only be left wondering, however, what the purpose of IMAA had been, given the stated objectives of PS 2000. Only a few years after Treasury Board had completed a general review of its policies and requirements under the IMAA initiative, the Privy Council Office declared in introducing PS 2000 that 'the personnel and administrative management regimes are encrusted with barnacles of rules and procedures that are wasteful and hamper efficiency.'[64]

The then clerk of the Privy Council and secretary to the Cabinet, Paul Tellier, led the PS 2000 exercise and became closely identified with it. The fact that PS 2000 was seen as the clerk's initiative sent a signal throughout the system that it should be taken seriously. And it was, at least initially.

Tellier appointed John Edwards, a long-serving senior public servant, to establish and lead a secretariat to develop and promote PS 2000. Ten task forces were assembled, with a total membership of 120 deputy ministers and senior managers to review specific management areas, including administrative policy and common service agencies; classification and occupational group structures; compensation and benefits; management category; resource management and budget controls; service to the public; staff relations; staffing; training and development; and workforce adaptiveness. PS 2000 was designed to be an internal public-service-driven exercise, and it was largely an attempt by the public service to reform itself. John Edwards explained, 'This is indeed an unabashedly management-driven exercise, and is based on a gamble: that we can do better than a conventional Royal Commission, that we know the problems, we are capable of finding the solutions, and perhaps most important we will be around to inculcate the changes into the public service.'[65]

PS 2000's main finding was that the public service needed to undergo a fundamental cultural change. The secretariat produced a table to contrast the 'old culture' with the desired 'new culture' (see Table 3 below). It is clear that the shift from the 'old' to the 'new' culture was inspired by the New Public Management Movement which was by the early 1990s starting to take root in the United States.[66]

TABLE 3
Changing Civil Service Culture

Old Culture	New Culture
Controlling	Empowering
Rigid	Flexible
Suspicious	Trusting
Administrative	Managerial
Secret	Open
Power based	Task based
Input/process oriented	Results oriented
Preprogrammed and repetitive	Capable of purposeful action
Risk averse	Willing to take intelligent risks
Mandatory	Optional
Communicating poorly	Communicating well
Centralized	Decentralized
Uniform	Diverse
Stifling creativity	Encouraging innovation
Reactive	Proactive

Source: Public Service 2000 Secretariat, Ottawa

The PS 2000 secretariat said that the transition from the old culture to the new would require a 'shift centred on prudence and probity, to one which recognizes the primacy of service to clients while accepting the need for reasonable prudence and probity.'[67] It put together more than 300 recommendations for 'delayering,' reducing central controls, reducing the number of job classifications from seventy-two to twenty-three, and making it easier to staff positions. The PS 2000 secretariat also put together a number of 'broad strategies' to support the change: decentralization of decision making, empowerment, the notion of trust and confidence in a nonpartisan, objective, and professional public service, a reduction on controls on managers, more flexible organizational structures, upgrading the skills of government managers, and a stronger sense of service to the public. Departments were also encouraged to launch their own PS 2000 review exercises to identify 'useless' red tape and to 'delayer' management levels.

To implement these strategies required changes, especially to ensure that centrally prescribed controls were attenuated, if not eliminated. More specifically, the centre of government would again have to change its ways and to review its own policies and practices. It was made clear, for example, as it had been before, that the Treasury Board secretariat would have to overhaul many of its requirements and in future act less as a treasury board and more as a management board preoccupied with good management practices rather than rules and regulations. Another key target was the Public Service Commission, with its elaborate rules and regulations governing staffing, training, promotion, and dismissal. The secretary to the cabinet, in his J.J. Carson Lecture delivered on 8 March 1990, argued that, 'For the Public Service Commission, the changes will mean getting out of the management business and focusing on its role as Parliament's agent in protecting the integrity of the personnel system.'[68]

Changes such as these require not only alterations to the machinery of government but new legislation. On 18 June 1991, the president of the Treasury Board, Gilles Loiselle, tabled legislation 'to support Public Service 2000 and to overhaul the federal public service.'[69] The background briefing material in support of the legislation reported that the government would be delegating more authority down the line, reducing levels of management, and simplifying government budgets and the classification of positions. The new legislation provided for a number of changes, including measures to make it easier for departments to hire casual workers, to 'release' poor performers, and to contract out activities to the private sector. The legislation restated the merit principle as the fundamental rule for public service hiring and promotion. While collective bargaining also remained largely unchanged, departments were given a greater role in collective bargaining and in handling grievance adjudications for cases that do not have a service-wide impact. The proposed changes made clear that employees could be 'released' on grounds of 'incompetence, incapacity, and unsatisfactory performance.' This was a necessary step 'to let the manager manage.'

Indeed, Treasury Board secretariat officials insisted at the time that the PS 2000 legislation was tabled that in future managers would be free to manage. However, the performance of managers would also be evaluated. They wrote that a 'manager's performance evaluation will reflect how she or he has recruited and developed women and minority groups – members of visible minorities, aboriginal peoples and persons with disabilities.'[70] These were not the only criteria to be used in assessing a manager's performance, and as already noted, determining the performance of a government manager is hardly an exact science. Some would even question whether it is at all possible, given the varied criteria and the many reasons why one can be successful or not in managing government operations.

In the early months of PS 2000, it was widely assumed that significant changes to central agencies would be introduced. The thinking was that they would be cut back substantially. The clerk of the Privy Council and secretary to the Cabinet pointed out, for example, that the mandate of the Public Service Commission would be reformulated to perform essentially an audit role. Line-department managers were arguing that if there were to be any real meaning this time to 'letting-the-manager-manage,' then it was important to cut back central agencies. However, the legislation did not attempt to do this, not even with the Public Service Commission, which mounted a concerted defence of its organizational interest, and which was left intact.[71] Nor was any administrative reform introduced to cut back the size of the other central agencies. It will also be recalled that a few years later, Kim Campbell, in a massive restructuring of government, also left the central agencies virtually unchanged.

PS 2000, as noted earlier, did formally designate the clerk of the Privy Council and secretary to the Cabinet as head of the Public Service. This, however, simply cast in legislation what had become clear for some time, at least to officials in the Privy Council Office. Still, the Treasury Board remained the 'employer' and continued to monitor public service performance. Some inside government wondered why the secretary to the Treasury Board was not formally designated head of the public service.[72] The authors of the PS 2000 report, who were senior PCO staff members, explain that the clerk is 'the most senior deputy minister ... who takes the lead in policy and issues of management ... [and who is the] leader of the Public Service.' They add that the clerk 'is responsible to the Prime Minister for the overall effectiveness of the public service's support to the Ministry.'[73]

Did PS 2000 live up to expectations? By most accounts, no. The government declared a wage freeze and announced that it would cut the number of senior executives by 10 per cent at about the same time PS 2000 was unveiling its recommendations. In addition, the notions of letting the manager manage and of risk management were given a sudden jolt when it was discovered that Al-Mashat, Iraq's ambassador to the United States until January 1991 and Iraq's principal spokesman during the Gulf War, had been permitted to enter Canada as a landed immigrant.

The Mulroney government refused to accept responsibility for the decision to admit Al-Mashat, pinning the blame on the bureaucrats instead. In the aftermath, three observers wrote, 'Senior executives now heard a mixed message from the government: We want you to take risks, we expect you to make mistakes sometimes; but if you screw up, we may hang you out to dry publicly. The refusal of ministers Joe Clark and Barbara McDougall to take responsibility in the traditional manner for departmental errors reinforced public service caution and scepticism about taking risks.'[74] In a seminal article on the issue, Sharon Sutherland wrote that the controversy 'led the Clerk to fire on the troops in order to give comfort to the government of the day.'[75] The message was clear: the concept of 'letting the manager manage' had its limits. Suddenly, Tellier's PS 2000 exercise began to ring hollow.

Gradually, observers, politicians, and even public servants began to make the case that PS 2000 had not delivered 'the goods.' Marcel Massé, as newly appointed minister responsible for public service renewal in the Chrétien government, but a senior deputy minister when PS 2000 was developed, wrote that 'while PS 2000 did achieve some important successes, notably the passage of legislative changes which have helped to remove needless red tape and provide more flexibility to managers, it became tainted through a series of events starting in 1991 ... For these and other reasons, PS 2000 put its tail between its legs. In many government departments, managers no longer refer to it, as it has lost credibility as a symbol for reform and renewal.'[76]

In his review of PS 2000, the auditor general reported that he encountered a great deal of cynicism among managers about the initiative.[77] Meanwhile, a line deputy minister reported, 'I continue to modernize my operations but I do not call it PS 2000. It now lacks credibility.'[78] Another deputy minister claimed that PS 2000's inability to deal head on with the work of central agencies explains its modest success. She explained, 'Unless you are prepared to deal with the structure and role of central agencies, the PS 2000 will be little more than an exercise of finely crafted words. So if you are not prepared to deal with this problem – and obviously PS 2000 is not – you are not prepared to deal with the real problems of government operations.'[79] John L. Manion, former associate secretary to the Cabinet and secretary to the Treasury Board, wrote that 'the abiding impression of PS 2000 is that it dealt with marginal issues. It did not come to grips with the need for institutional reform, particularly at the core of government.'[80]

In the end, there was virtually no one left in Ottawa singing the praises of PS 2000, not even those who earlier had been its most ardent supporters. Even Paul Tellier began to speak about its shortcomings. He left his position to became president of CNR, a crown corporation, and after about eighteen months in his new job, he gave a provocative and remarkably candid speech on public service reform. It is worth quoting at some length his views on the matter. He wrote, 'When I was at the Privy Council Office we had a vision of re-engineering the bureaucracy: PS 2000. I deplore letting some of my colleagues convince me to go slow in reforming some processes.' He insisted that for re-engineering to work, you require *bold implementation* (Tellier's italics). Government, he implied, does not move in bold ways even when the clerk of the Privy Council, the most powerful person in the public service, is leading the charge. He reported, 'I introduced and implemented more change in the last 12 months at CN than I was able to do in my last seven years in the public service.' He echoed the views of many line deputy ministers when he observed, 'In my 13 years as a deputy minister, I spent far too much time having to justify my decisions to the comptrollers of the comptrollers. The problem was never at the deputy or associate deputy minister level, but rather at the lower ranks [where] I had to answer irrelevant questions from individuals who were just trying to justify their existence.'

He then took aim at the Treasury Board secretariat, asking, 'What is the added value of the bureaucracy of the Treasury Board Secretariat? I don't mean the Committee of Ministers, which has the responsibility of reviewing financial or personnel transactions. I mean the very large bureaucracy which supports that Cabinet committee. But I use the Treasury Board Secretariat as an example because, perhaps better than any other agency [it] reflects a lack of added value.' He concluded by saying that 'had I known then what I know now, I would have introduced more radical changes.' As a case in point, he wrote, 'PS 2000 involved a radical, bold and rapid change of the classification system. It could have been completed in six months. Instead, we adopted a slow, gradual approach that focused on the executive category. The end result? Very small, modest changes. What's the big deal in combining the SM and EX-1 groups! And today we still have a system where senior managers hire consultants to write 10-page job descriptions that nobody reads.'[81]

Ian Clark, at the time secretary to the Treasury Board, decided to respond to Tellier's stinging criticism. He reminded him that in government 'collegiality' is important and that Tellier himself had made an important contribution in promoting it within the ranks of the senior public service while he was clerk (Tellier, for example, had initiated the weekly deputy ministers' breakfast). He also reminded Tellier that only politicians can take decisions on structural or machinery changes, and that ultimately they also have to decide whether one can move on government reform or not. Clark wrote, 'Public service reform must obviously compete with other government priorities. In this context, one can see why Public Service 2000 was not more boldly implemented by senior public servants. During the early 1990s, the federal government had a very full policy agenda, including the attempt to secure an agreement with the provinces on a new Constitution. Negotiations with the provinces and other groups, and the extensive public consultations, taxed the energies of many of the best policy and managerial minds throughout the Public Service. This affected the progress that could be made on other major initiatives, including management reform. To evaluate progress on public sector reform without acknowledging such pressures is to unfairly assess the true possibilities for success.' He added that 'the initiatives launched under Mr. Tellier's leadership came close to the boundaries of what could be achieved without risking the ire of Parliament. To have accomplished more, in my view, would have required a consensus within the government, and among the opposition parties, on the goals and the mechanisms for public service reform.' Clark concluded that 'while it is fashionable to deride the Public Service 2000 exercise, its impact has been lasting and its principles have been reflected in many subsequent initiatives.'[82]

Though admittedly it did not meet expectations, PS 2000 undeniably had an impact. As Marcel Massé suggested, it did remove at least some 'needless red tape.' PS 2000 also introduced the operating budget concept to government operations, and a number of senior officials I consulted certainly approved of this. The concept enables managers to pool funds allocated for salaries, operating costs, and small capital projects and then decide the most cost-effective ways of getting the work done. In implementing the operating budget concept, the Treasury Board secretariat dropped its person-year control. Departments are now free to use salaries for other operating costs and, conversely, resources earmarked for other purposes can be employed to pay salaries. Still, departments are still expected to do a head count and report the number of their full-time equivalents to Parliament.[83]

PS 2000 also reintroduced an old IMAA concept under which enabled departments could carry forward 2 per cent of their expenditure budgets into the next fiscal year. In the past, there was always a rush to find ways to spend resources towards the end of every fiscal year, since any unspent resources lapsed. Under PS 2000, the amount allowed to be carried forward into the next fiscal year was increased from 2 per cent under IMAA to 5 per cent. PS 2000 also did away with many centrally prescribed administrative and financial requirements. Deputy ministers were given new authority to delegate some staffing decisions to their senior managers in the departments, to award competitive contracts, to approve hospitality expenditures, to purchase goods, and so on.[84]

In the summer of 1991, while PS 2000 was still in the implementation phase, the Treasury Board secretariat decided to introduce yet another new approach, the shared management agenda. It had four objectives: to improve communication between the Treasury Board and line departments; to improve service to the public; to encourage better 'people management'; and to promote empowerment. The shared management agenda worked as follows: the secretary of the Treasury Board and deputy ministers agreed – either in the form of a letter or a memorandum of understanding – on the management issues and objectives the departments wanted to address over a one- to three-year period. They then agreed on the steps required to meet these objectives. Such steps included, for example, decentralizing more authority to the department and improvements in the operations and policies of the Treasury Board.[85] The shared management agenda, according to Treasury Board officials, was essentially another attempt at transforming the 'command-and-control' model of government decision making into an empowered business-management model. In short, it was yet one more attempt to let the manager manage.

Again, however, the approach was met with a high degree of scepticism. Officials in line departments called it a 'paper exercise,' and a 'make-work' project designed to keep central agency officials busy. One deputy minister maintained that there was little to be gained in the exercise for line departments, with all the 'information going one way, and that is to central agencies. We still have not been able to figure out what advantages it holds for departments. Still, we go through the motions, not so much because it will accomplish anything. What it does, however, is avoid creating problems with the Treasury Board.'[86]

The Treasury Board secretariat introduced still another new approach by looking to Margaret Thatcher's 'Next Steps' initiative for inspiration. The secretary to the Treasury Board explained, 'Canadian interest in special operating agencies [SOAs] was spurred by the Executive Agency, or *Next Steps* initiative in the United Kingdom.'[87] Members of the Treasury Board secretariat staff were sent to London to study the agency concept and returned with ideas on how to adapt it to Canada.

Government officials report that one of the main reasons for establishing SOAs was to provide 'the first clear break with the traditional control and command model and to offer concrete evidence of the beginnings of a culture for government services that emphasizes the practices of management in place of the systems and processes of program administration.' The Treasury Board secretariat made it clear that SOAs should be 'business units oriented to good management' and should, over time, promote more 'business-like services, improve service to the customer, and demonstrate concern for efficient management.'[88] At the risk of sounding repetitive, SOAs are also designed to let the manager manage.

The SOA initiative did not attempt to deal with the principle of ministerial responsibility. Unlike in Britain, where there is a direct relationship between the agency head and the minister, in Canada the deputy minister remains the key point of contact. The Treasury Board simply reported that 'no change is contemplated in the current accountability relationship. If anything, accountability will be strengthened and made more transparent under the Agency approach. Similarly, the establishment of an Agency will not change the status of an employee as a public servant, nor will it change union representation.'[89] Still, the Treasury Board insists that it is possible to decentralize a number of management authorities. This includes, among other things, the power to introduce organizational change without going to central agencies for approval, to establish a pay-for-performance plan, increase staffing authority, provide more flexibility in assigning tasks and duties to employees, and give the head of the agency freedom to move funds around to different tasks within an existing budget.

But the implementation of the SOA concept has not been without problems and a fair dose of cynicism. One deputy minister argued in print that it was 'a bureaucratic version of a halfway house. It is neither a jail, nor is it total freedom. It is part of a department, yet separate from it.' He added that SOAs 'are still very much part of the federal family. Staff in agencies are still public servants. SOAs still report to the department, to the Minister and to the Treasury Board.' The secretary to the Treasury Board wrote that 'SOAs are not quasi-Crown corporations. They remain a distinct part of the home department, albeit with enhanced operational authority.'[90]

The uncertainty over what precisely an SOA is gave rise, at least at first, to some confusion. Senior officials readily admit that 'some Deputy Ministers are concerned about accountability and what might be called the *balkanization* of a department.' This, in turn, has led to tension between the agency head and the parent department, with agencies pushing for more authority and departments resisting it.[91] Senior SOA officials complain about a lack of 'authority,' 'empowerment,' or overall support from the system. Unlike in Britain, where the head of the agency is the chief executive officer, in Canada the chief executive officer is the department's deputy minister, while the head of the agency is the chief operating officer. This, they insist, places the deputy minister in a conflict between the set of rules stemming from the department and those established internally by the agency. There are all kinds of incentives for a deputy minister to favour the department over an agency that is continually striving to secure arm's-length status. In any event, they argue, deputy ministers are far too busy with their own jobs to give much time to SOAs. Agency personnel also report that the lines of accountability for SOAs have never been properly defined.

The biggest complaint one hears, however, is that SOAs have changed precious little. Central agencies continue to exercise some control as formal rules and guidelines still apply – in the name of accountability. In the early years of development, middle-level officials in the SOAs became very critical of how the agencies were being established. One reported in 1994 that 'the rules are the same and the senior executives are the same. We have seen no new blood coming from outside. If anything, the home department has made things more difficult, perhaps because they do not like part of their empire hived off. For me and my colleagues, SOA no longer stands for Special Operating Agency; it stands for Screwed Once Again. If anything, we have less freedom than before.'[92]

During my interviews for the research for this book in the fall of 1997 and winter 1998, I still heard essentially the same kind of criticism. A number of senior federal government officials met in early 1997 to review 'critical management issues and central agency intervention/withdrawal' and asked 'what would happen to central agencies if you went the route of executive agencies like in the United Kingdom?'[93] They also concluded that 'in Canada we are cautious and timid. We have 16 SOAs which critics say combine the worst of the private and public sector.'[94] I put a question to a senior government official who had been directly involved in the late 1980s in identifying alternative service delivery models for the government, and that is, 'Why is it that there are still only nineteen special operating agencies in operation?' His response, 'Because we never had the courage to introduce real change. We did not do like the British and say here is a new way of doing things; it is vastly different, there is some risk, but we are prepared to take those risks. We have been far too tentative. We have lacked the required political will and political interest to introduce real change, as opposed to cosmetic change.'[95]

But there have been other problems. A government-sponsored review of the SOAs suggests that there has been a 'lack of coordination among central agencies' in developing SOAs. It goes on to report that 'central agencies other than Treasury Board have been virtually absent in the initiatives.'[96]

The lack of a coherent view from the central agencies explains why the SOA concept has evolved in an unfocused manner. Indeed, it has not been possible for anyone to sort out precisely why the centre of government would want to establish SOAs. Thatcher's rationale for establishing executive agencies was never in doubt, nor was her desire to have them operate from substantially different rules than regular government departments.[97] The federal government, unlike Britain, has been tentative in both the number of SOAs established and in the actual changes it has been willing to allow.

In short, Treasury Board decided to apply to Canada a scaled-down version of Thatcher's innovative approach, and on a much more modest scale. One government official writes,

> Several different perspectives inspired the establishment of the initial five SOAs. Some viewed the initiative as a way of delaying pressures to privatize or as a half-way station to privatization. Others viewed SOAs as pilot projects or 'laboratories' for public sector reform, responding to the same impulse that led to Public Service 2000 – to improve service to the public, to unleash the creativity of people, and to introduce accountability for results. From yet another perspective, the SOA concept offered a 'prototype' for the public service, an alternative approach to delivering government operations similar to the Executive Agencies in the United Kingdom. Given the range of expectations attached to the initiative from the start, it is not surprising that as additional SOAs were named, each for its own particular reasons, the rationale for the initiative became even more cloudy.[98]

One thing is clear, however. It is only the Treasury Board secretariat which has actively promoted the SOA concept. It is the Treasury Board which granted

SOAs flexibility in managing financial and 'person year' resources. But the others at the centre of government have been less forthcoming 'in administrative policies and common services, and least willingly in the personnel area. The tendency has been to use existing ground rules and not concede much more. Salary freezes, however, have applied to SOAs as they have to the rest of the public service.'[99] Though SOAs recently have been granted more financial independence, the 1991 budget, for example, subjected SOAs, like everyone else, to a 10 per cent cut in the management complement, even though they were all operating on a cost-recovery basis.

The SOA concept did give the Treasury Board secretariat a chance to test new opportunities. SOAs were the first in government, outside of crown corporations, to produce business plans for the Treasury Board. The thinking behind business plans is that they enable the Treasury Board to focus on the larger issues, on broad directions, and leave administrative-type decisions to the front line managers, where they belong. In addition, properly prepared business plans serve to strengthen the board's hand in its efforts to establish performance targets for government activities and determining whether standards or commitments are being met.

The Treasury Board has now adopted the business plan approach for its dealings with all departments. At the same time, the board decided to do away with Multi-Year Operational Plans which departments had to submit every fall as part of the annual estimates process, as well as the shared management agenda and the IMAA initiative. That said, departments still have to produce Annual Reference Level Updates and their Part III of the Estimates.[100]

The business plans are designed to be different from past approaches on a couple of fronts. Unlike, for example, IMAA, they do not focus on operational details. In addition, the secretariat declared that it would make every effort to bring down its 'silos' mentality. For this reason, it decided to create teams to deal with individual business plans. Teams, it was argued, would create a 'single window' at the Treasury Board for line departments so that they would not, as in the past, go from branch to branch to sort out different Treasury Board requirements.

Evert Lindquist has reviewed the business plans approach and writes that thus far it has met with 'qualified success.'[101] He also writes that 'the adoption of business planning is generally a promising, overdue development.'[102] Though departments believe that much more can be done, they are pleased with the secretariat's efforts to establish a 'single window.' They also approve the board's decision to focus on broader issues and not on questions of detail.

But there are problems. Again, there is some cynicism about yet another approach designed, in Peter Harder's words in his correspondence to a deputy minister, 'to better articulate the evolving management board role for the Treasury Board and its Secretariat.'[103] The fact that the business planning concept is being implemented in the immediate aftermath of the program review exercise does not help matters. In addition, in light of the criticism levelled at previous approaches, including IMAA, PS 2000, and the shared management agenda, one can appreciate that government managers will keep their enthusiasm in check. The fact that Robert Giroux, the Treasury Board secretary who played a key role in promoting the approach, quit and left the public service after less than two years on the job did not help matters.

There is also a great deal of concern that business plans will become little more than a paper-pushing exercise. Three years after the introduction of the plans, we are hearing about the need to move from 'business plans' to 'business planning.'[104] The implication is that both departments and the Treasury Board have been far too preoccupied with the need to publish a document called 'Business Plan' than with producing strategic thinking or identifying ways to assess the success or performance of departmental plans and programs.

Questions have also been asked about the capacity at the centre to review business plans and to make some contributions to their development. Departments have complained that there has been a lack of 'substantive feedback from the Treasury Board' both from secretariat officials and ministers. All too often, they report, the feedback has been in the form of 'the plan is helpful or of a superior quality, but little else.' Someone at the centre also needs to answer the question – what are the consequences for ministers and their line departments when they do not produce solid business plans?[105] Thus far, at least, business plans have had no or very little impact on the government expenditure budget.

Managing the Expenditure Budget Process

At the time the Treasury Board secretariat was established, the expenditure budget process was fairly straightforward. Treasury Board ministers were handed a series of documents from the secretariat which included 'A,' 'B,' and 'X' budgets. 'A' budgets represented ongoing programs at current levels of services, 'B' budgets were new proposals or measures that were yet to be approved, while 'X' budgets were low-priority programs which could be dropped to make room for high-priority new programs.[106]

When new approaches were introduced, notably PEMS, Treasury Board's hand in trying to manage the expenditure budget was weakened. Decisions on new expenditures were taken elsewhere in other Cabinet committees followed by routine ratification in full Cabinet. The proposal was then referred to Treasury Board 'for consideration of resource aspects.' Treasury Board ministers then could either challenge a Cabinet decision or agree to the new spending. A former secretary of the board once observed to the board ministers that 'with this system you don't need a Treasury Board, you just need an adding machine.'[107]

In February 1995, the then Treasury Board president, Art Eggleton, in somewhat of an overstatement, announced that the government was 'revamping, for the first time in 15 years its Expenditure Management System.'[108] (After all, doing away with PEMS, establishing an expenditure review committee, among other changes, also constituted new approaches.) Eggleton explained that 'Under the [new] system, departments will now provide Outlook documents to Parliament every spring. The Outlook will be drawn from the department's business planning on program priorities and expenditures. It will show how departments will adjust their programs over the next few years to operate within the resources set out in the Budget.'[109]

The new system does not have policy reserves for funding new initiatives between budgets. The current system leaves no doubt whatsoever that the budget is the key document for decisions on funding major new initiatives. If departments have any new proposals they wish to bring forward between budgets, they need to fund them from their own budgets through reallocation. They are also asked to lead the process to identify options for reallocation 'with advice and assistance of the Treasury Board Secretariat.'[110]

The Treasury Board published a document to explain the new system. It outlines in some detail the roles of all the key players in the expenditure process from the Privy Council Office to line departments (this part of the document is reproduced in appendix A at the end of this chapter). The document also outlines the expenditure budget cycle. It notes that the process begins in the spring with a general briefing to Cabinet on the 'results of the last budget' and a review of 'high' priorities. Cabinet policy committees are asked to 'oversee' the design and implementation of initiatives unveiled in the previous budget. Departments, meanwhile, prepare their business plans while the Treasury Board secretariat begins the review process.

In the summer months, the Department of Finance, in consultation with the Privy Council Office and the Treasury Board secretariat, prepares strategies and identifies options for the minister of Finance to manage the consultation process. At the same time, Finance updates its fiscal and economic outlook. In the fall, the minister of Finance briefs Cabinet on his public consultation strategies and the department prepares a series of consultation papers. The Department of Finance, again with the assistance of other central agencies, identifies prospective fiscal and expenditure targets. In November–December, the Finance minister and his department develop the overall budget strategy.

In the winter months, or between January and March, the budget documents are fine-tuned and 'put to bed.' The minister of Finance provides a general overview of his budget strategy to Cabinet. The government document makes it clear, however, that 'the Prime Minister and the Minister of Finance make the final decisions.'[111] The Department of Finance finalizes the budget documents and the Treasury Board secretariat produces the main estimates, 'incorporating Budget decisions to the extent possible.'[112] The minister of Finance then delivers the budget speech and the president of the Treasury Board tables the estimates. The Treasury Board will also require departments to prepare their business plans consistent with 'Budget targets, strategies and new spending and reduction initiatives.'[113]

The current expenditure management system differs from earlier approaches on several fronts, but it also has a holdover from the past. Like several previous approaches, most notably the PPBS, the new system is designed to promote performance evaluation and productivity. It also calls for decentralizing management and at the same time improving financial management in government departments. The Treasury Board secretariat now stresses performance evaluation at every turn, and departments are expected to identify ways to measure program performance in their submissions to Treasury Board.

The secretariat has launched a major effort to report performance reviews to Parliament as part of its effort to strengthen accountability. The president of the Treasury Board secretariat now tables an annual report to Parliament called *Improving Results Measurement and Accountability.*[114] The report is part of a broader effort to promote 'a results-based culture in the Public Service while at the same time continuing to ensure appropriate controls.'[115] The secretariat explains that in the years ahead it will continue to explore 'which [performance] indicators are most useful; how they should be selected, measured and reported ... how to link the indicators back to the actual programs and initiatives.'[116] Long-serving federal public servants can no doubt recall that the Treasury Board secretariat made precisely the same observations over twenty-five years ago in introducing PPBS.

In addition, the board's desire to redefine or modernize the comptrollership function is tied directly to the secretariat's desire to place stronger emphasis on performance evaluation. The trade-off in having less control from the centre on financial, administrative, and personnel matters is to have departments be more forthcoming in evaluating their performance and that of their programs. Performance evaluation is also a central feature of the new public management movement and its desire to focus on results rather than process. Much of what the Treasury Board secretariat is doing in performance evaluation squares with the new public management literature.[117]

Managing the expenditure process is an important activity of the Treasury Board secretariat, but it is not the only important activity. We saw earlier that a substantial part of the secretariat's organization is responsible for the management of human resources. However, it is not alone at the centre of government in having this responsibility.

Public Service Commission

The Public Service Commission is a central agency but it is fundamentally different from the others. As already noted, as a parliamentary agency it enjoys a degree of independence from the government that the others do not. The PSC is accountable to Parliament and 'then only for its overall performance, not for specific actions. The PSC is headed by a chair and two other commissioners, all appointed for a ten-year term and who can be removed prematurely only by joint resolution of both the House of Commons and the Senate.'[118]

The *Public Service Employment Act* gives the commission 'exclusive' responsibilities to make appointment to or from within the public service, to develop processes and standards for the selection of candidates for position in the public service, to operate an appeal system for appointment, to audit staffing activities, to investigate allegations of irregularities or inequities in staffing, to oversee or protect the political rights of public servants, and to recommend to the governor-in-council exclusions from the *Public Service Employment Act*. The Public Service Commission also has responsibilities which are not exclusive or which are shared or delegated from the Treasury Board. These include middle management, supervisory and specialty training, language training, development courses, audit of certain personnel management functions, investigation of complaints of harassment, and a series of activities in the fields of human resources planning, counselling and career development for the executive group, and measures to promote the participation of under-represented groups.[119]

The commission has defined four business lines, namely resourcing (i.e., staffing), learning, recourse and policy, and research and outreach. The organization (see Chart 5 below) reflects the commission's four business lines.

The staffing program accounts for about 40 per cent of the commission's operational expenditure and total workforce and has a strong presence both in Ottawa and the regions. The program covers a wide range of activities in support of delegated staffing authority to departments and nondelegated authority. These activities include policy and program development, monitoring, establishment of tests and standards for selection, and recruitment.

The training program concerns both language training and staff development.

Chart 5
Organization of the Public Service Commission

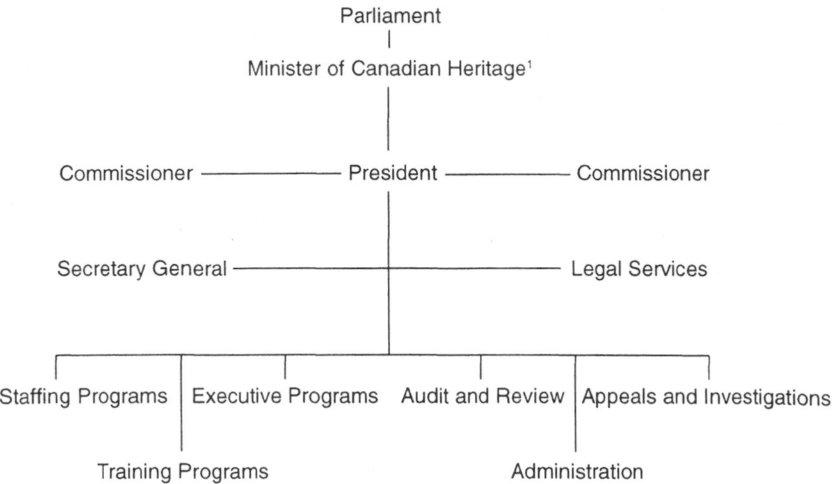

[1] In matters dealing with the Public Service Employment Act, the minister of Canadian Heritage is designated as spokesperson for the commission in Parliament and is also the appropriate minister within the context of the *Financial Administration Act.*

The language training component assesses the potential to succeed of employees who are eligible for language training. It provides mandatory and discretionary language training in both official languages and related orientation and language-training services in conformity with government policy to meet the needs of departments and agencies in the federal public service. It also provides second-language courses designed to meet job-related linguistic requirements, and a range of advisory, informational, and coordinating services related to language training. The staff development component provides professional, technical, policy, middle management, and supervisory training and related specialized training and training services to public servants across Canada in response to Treasury Board policies and departmental demands. It also provides courses designed to meet the job-related training and developmental requirements of departments and a range of advisory, informational, and coordinating services related to training.

The appeals and investigations program, through the establishment of independent boards and investigators, sees that appeals by public servants against internal appointments and complaints against deployments are heard with respect to alleged breaches of the *Public Service Employment Act* and regulations. The program also provides for an investigation into complaints of irregularities in staffing and in certain other personnel actions. In addition, complaints of alleged personal harassment in the workplace are also investigated. Training, advice, and assistance are provided to departments, employees, unions, and other interested individuals and organizations. An audit and review program reviews departmental and PSC staffing practices and procedures in order to determine that appointments conform with the *Public Service Employment Act* and regulations and commission policy. It reviews the manner in which departments administer selected aspects of their personnel services for which Treasury Board has policy responsibility.[120]

The mandate and activities of the Public Service Commission have been remarkably stable over the past fifty years. This is true despite repeated calls from royal commissions for change. Ted Hodgetts writes that in the administration of 'private concerns' it goes without saying that management responsibility for effective performance carries 'with it full command over [human] resources.' He adds, 'In the public administration the situation is not so clear cut.'[121] In public administration, there is the need to think in terms of a unified public service with at least some standardized conditions of employment. In addition, we saw in an earlier chapter that the fight against political patronage in public service appointments gave rise to a capacity at the centre of government which would be imposed on departmental managers.

Over twenty-five years ago, Hodgetts argued that 'the need to preserve uniformity and the need to protect the so-called merit system have encouraged the growth of an ambivalent attitude towards personnel management which has resulted in a confused sharing-out of this function.'[122] Hodgetts could write that same sentence today and it would ring as true now, if not more so, than it did in 1973. More importantly, the same point was made earlier in a 1946 royal commission report, and again by another in 1979 – not to mention by a countless number of senior public servants in between and ever since.

As early as the 1930s, observers were writing about a cold war between the Treasury Board and the Public Service Commission.[123] In 1945 the government established a royal commission to review the classification and pay of senior public servants. The Gordon Commission, however, extended the scope of its inquiry beyond these two administrative matters and sought to resolve turf issues between the Public Service Commission and the Treasury Board secretariat. The commission borrowed a page from the British experience, where the Treasury controls much of the personnel management field. Accordingly, it urged that the Treasury Board assume more authority while the Public Service

Commission be given less. The government, however, did not accept this recommendation. Had it done so, the role of the Public Service Commission would have been confined to recruitment from outside and a review of departmental recommendations for promotion and transfers.[124]

Some sixteen years later, the Glassco Commission also urged a redefinition of the role of the Public Service Commission. Glassco wanted the commission's emphasis to be on auditing, reviewing, and appellate functions: 'personnel decisions – on appointment, promotion and disciplinary matters.'[125] The Treasury Board would have, in turn, inherited many of the functions of the Public Service Commission.

In 1979 the Lambert Commission expressed concerns over the ambiguities lying between the Treasury Board and the Public Service Commission. It pointed to numerous specific problems, reporting, for example, that 'the levels of authority delegated by the Public Service Commission and the Treasury Board [to departments] are uneven. The PSC has delegated less authority for staffing senior positions than the Treasury Board has delegated for classifying senior positions. The Treasury Board, in turn, has delegated less authority for classifying senior positions than it has for organizing the management team. Not only is this situation confusing, it also reduces the real authority of the 'deputy head.'[126] Lambert recommended that a new board of management take over much of the personnel function for the Public Service Commission and that in turn 'the Public Service Commission be reconstituted as a Parliamentary Department with the duty of ensuring that selection and appointment to the public service are made on the basis of merit, and that the PSC report annually to Parliament those instances where personnel policies, procedures and actions fail to support the merit principle.'[127] The government, as already noted, did not accept the Lambert Commission recommendations.

PS 2000, it will be recalled, was designed to empower managers and remove needless red tape. Some senior public servants, even at the centre of government, strongly urged the clerk of the Privy Council to recommend to the government that the Public Service Commission be reconstructed as a small statutory body which would be responsible only for initial appointments from outside. They insisted that the 'competition and overlap' between central agencies dealing with personnel issues should be confronted once and for all.[128] The importance of personnel issues and the problems associated with them was brought home in the PS 2000 initiative when seven of the ten task forces established to come up with recommendations to modernize government operations focused on this issue. PS 2000 did not, however, introduce any significant changes to the Public Service Commission.

The architects of the massive 1993 government restructure were also urged by some senior officials at the centre such as John L. Manion, who had recently left his position as associate clerk of the PCO, to deal with the 'overlap' and 'confusion' between the Treasury Board secretariat and the Public Service Commission. Manion told the Privy Council Office that 'past efforts to reform administration in the federal government have all crashed on the rocks of the Public Service Commission.'[129]

Consultations with both central agency and line department officials between September 1997 and January 1998 reveal that relations between the Public Service Commission and the Treasury Board secretariat remain in a state of 'cold war.' The impact is felt at the centre of government and in line departments over both big and small issues. Examples will make this clear.

The Treasury Board and the Treasury Board secretariat in their role as the employer decided in the late 1980s that the government should recruit recent university graduates with the potential to excel as managers. A management trainee program (MTP) was first introduced in 1990–1. Recruitment has varied from year to year, given the need to cut spending. But in the 1994–5 recruitment campaign, for example, some twenty external candidates and seven internal candidates were recruited. The selection process was rigorous, with all candidates subjected to a series of tests and interviews. Once enrolled in the program, MTP participants were given a series of special assignments in central agencies, in line departments, and in regional offices. They were also given special lectures and courses. Participants graduated from the program after five years, at which point they would take up a permanent appointment in a central agency or line department. The Public Service Commission objected, pointing out that 'MTP participants should not have a leg up on others and that the merit principle should apply.'[130] One Treasury Board secretariat reported, 'You cannot begin to appreciate the number of high-level meetings that were held between us and the PSC on this issue. It was plain crazy. At one point, we even had MTP people declared surplus so that they could be appointed. It really did not make any sense whatsoever. We wanted it one way, departments agreed with us, MTP individuals agreed with us, but not the PSC. It is true that we finally did solve the problem, but at a tremendous cost to taxpayers and to good management.'[131] She added, 'The fundamental problem is that the PSC wanted to administer what we rightly regarded as an employer issue. In any event, I never heard anyone even hint that MTP participants were politically partisan. So what was the problem?'[132]

Jocelyne Bourgon, the clerk of the Privy Council Office, led the charge in launching a high-profile initiative which she labelled *La Relève*. *La Relève* is designed to be 'a new way of thinking' in human resources management, to ensure that 'every public servant has the competencies and tools required to maintain a world-class public service' and to 'help shape the public service of the future' by making sure that competent people are available to assume leadership roles.[133]

Bourgon devoted a full chapter to *La Relève* in the clerk's fourth annual report to the prime minister on the Public Service of Canada. She referred to 'La Relève' as 'Our Greatest Challenge.' She summed up the problem in this fashion: 'For the first time [public servants] are questioning their career choice: [they] would not advise their children to follow in their footsteps; some students would not consider a career in the Public Service if presented with other options.'[134] Much of the work to promote *La Relève*, she argued, should be in line departments. But, she insisted, 'Central agencies owe it to departments to support their efforts and act decisively in areas requiring corporate attention.'[135] She provided a list of things central agencies needed to do, including 'accelerated executive development, prequalification of potential assistant deputy ministers, appointment to level for assistant deputy ministers, compensation and retention, support for professional communities [e.g., the policy community inside the government] and external recruitment.'[136]

Three central agencies have a direct hand in promoting *La Relève*. The Privy Council Office, in part because of the clerk's strong and visible leadership role in its development, but also because the clerk is now formally head of the public service. In addition, PCO has, as we have seen, a legitimate role in advising order-in-council appointments, including all those at deputy minister and associate deputy minister levels. The Treasury Board secretariat has a role in *La Relève* because of its status as an employer and its responsibilities in the areas of classification, pay, collective bargaining, medical and pension plans for public servants, and so on. Finally, the Public Service Commission has a role because of its responsibilities in the areas of staffing and training.

The consultations reveal that *La Relève* has been down a bumpy road and the level of cynicism is as great as it was for previous reform initiatives, such as PS 2000. Even strong supporters now acknowledge that *La Relève* has not been as well received as was at first envisaged.[137]

There are many reasons to explain these difficulties. Some officials report that the decision to identify winners through its assistant deputy minister prequalifying and its accelerated executive development programs created problems and fuelled cynicism. Some 450 senior public servants applied under both programs, but only 20 qualified for the assistant deputy minister prequalifying program and 55 under the accelerated executive development program. Moreover, the opportunity for senior managers to apply under the programs were for nearly everyone the first opportunity for advancement in several years, given various cuts to government programs and the program review exercise. Few at the centre had foreseen the need to manage expectations or to match 450 expectations with only 75 opportunities. The 'losers,' as some began to refer to themselves, could hardly be expected to praise *La Relève*. In fact, they did the opposite, claiming that the selection process invariably favoured individuals who had worked or were working in central agencies over those with line department experience.[138] Central agency officials insist, however, that this criticism is unfair and that, *toute proportion gardée,* there have been as many from line departments who qualified under the program as from central agencies. One explained, 'We have pretty solid balance in both programs in terms of gender, linguistic, regional, head office, central agency, and line department.'[139]

But there were other problems. There had been a great deal of tension between the three central agencies, tension which became all too apparent to line departments. PCO and Treasury officials became convinced that PSC was moving much too slowly to promote *La Relève* properly. They argue that PSC always challenges new ways of doing things and that in any event it unnecessarily complicates things.

Officials in both PCO and TBS insist that the Public Service Commission is on a never-ending process to 'reinvent itself' but that, in the end, very little actually changes. The PSC, they argue, can never focus properly on the immediate task at hand. Some were highly critical of a series of 'search conferences' on governance sponsored by the Public Service Commission which had nothing to do with *La Relève*, and which they considered to be extremely abstract, impractical, and costly.[140] The search conferences and other such initiatives sponsored by the PSC in the mid- and late 1990s served to distract the commission from the purposes at hand, such as *La Relève.* They also diverted precious financial and human resources away from priority issues to, in the words of one senior PCO official, 'exoteric initiatives which were outside the PSC's mandate, parliamentary or otherwise.'[141] The fact that the chair of the Public Service Commission can only be removed by a joint resolution of both the House of Commons and the Senate limits the centre's ability to change the commission's leadership prematurely.

For their part, Public Service Commission officials report that their mandate is unlike that found anywhere else, whether in other central agencies or departments. Their purpose is to act as guardian of the merit principle on behalf of all Canadians. 'Sometimes,' one senior PSC official argued, 'we have to say, hold it a minute, we need to square this idea with our parliamentary mandate. This may well upset people in government, but after all, we have a specific mandate to pursue.'[142]

In any event, the criticism that the Lambert Commission levelled at the Treasury Board secretariat and the Public Service Commission over their inability to delegate the same authority still holds. In a letter sent to all deputy ministers in April 1990, the secretary of the Treasury Board announced a 'particularly significant decision concerning the delegation of Management Category Classification authority ... Effective July 1, 1990, Deputy Heads will be empowered to exercise classification authority for positions [up] to the EX3 levels inclusive.'[143] The Public Service Commission, meanwhile, as part of its staffing reform for *La Relève*, announced in late 1997 that deputy ministers would now be empowered to 'design, manage [and be] responsible for *internal* staffing up to the EX level (or for positions below the EX, that is the senior executive level).'[144] The Public Service Commission also announced that an accountability mechanism would be introduced to ensure that departments 'respect and defend merit' and 'establish meaningful, timely, reasonable performance and outcome measures as they assume new staffing authority for non executive positions.'[145]

The commission provided a written explanation to the other central agencies and line departments as to why it would not agree to 'get out of EX staffing and give it to departments.' It argued that 'EXs are a corporate resource, things [which] are done on behalf of the system need to be managed in a coordinated, systematic way ... The PSC believes that it must be able to provide Parliament with special assurances on political non-partisanship of this group. Its involvement in EX appointments is a visible way of doing so.'[146]

The Public Service Commission, as already noted, is a different kind of central agency in that it is a parliamentary agency. It enjoys a degree of independence from the prime minister, Cabinet ministers, and the Privy Council Office like no other agency; notably, Finance and the Treasury Board secretariat. The chair of the commission is appointed for a ten-year period and can only be removed by a joint resolution of the House of Commons and the Senate. This means that the commission, if it so wishes, can walk to the beat of its own drummer and ignore much of what the Privy Council Office and the Treasury Board secretariat may have to offer. That said, staffing and training are key components of human resources management, and the Privy Council and Treasury Board secretariat insist that all the actors in the field should coordinate their efforts.

The above explains in no small measure why the Privy Council Office decided to launch the *La Relève* initiative. Many officials consulted for this study suggested that the initiative was designed to strip the Public Service Commission of some of its responsibilities in order to get things done, given that PCO could not direct it to action. A few years after the *La Relève* initiative was launched, PCO unveiled yet another measure in human resources management and located it outside the Public Service Commission and the Treasury Board secretariat. The prime minister announced on 4 June 1998 the creation of a 'Leadership Network,' which he described as a 'new horizontal organization ... [to] support the collective management of Assistant Deputy Ministers.'[147]

The new organization was established through an order-in-council and designated as an agency with its own spending estimates. It reports to the clerk of the Privy Council and COSO. The clerk explained why the network was being established when she wrote that assistant deputy ministers were 'being asked to play many roles – that of expert manager, strategist, and visionary leader. You are also expected to operate in an environment where issues are increasingly horizontal and service delivery must be seamless.'[148] The centre concluded that a new capacity was needed at the centre itself, but outside of PSC, to meet the challenge.

Under the collective management approach, new assistant deputy ministers are appointed to level, not to a position. 'Corporate exercises' are conducted to prequalify assistant deputy ministers. Candidates can self-identify or be nominated by a deputy minister and are assessed against leadership competencies. There is now one 'corporate pool' of assistant deputy ministers so that 'Assistant Deputy Ministers in the Department of Foreign Affairs and International Trade will be considered for assignments outside the Department. Conversely, Assistant Deputy Ministers will be considered for assignments in the Department of Foreign Affairs and International Trade.'[149]

The decision to shift to a collective management of the assistant deputy minister community and to promote to level rather than to a position is a significant development for the public service. It means a fundamental shift away from the classical Weberian public service organization. Weber insisted that the requirement of the position was of paramount importance. For him, everything turned on the job, not the individual.[150] Under the new approach, everything turns on the individual who prequalifies and not the requirements of the position.

The new approach will favour 'generalists' for promotion to the assistant deputy minister level, and from there to the deputy minister level. The various background documents published in support of the new approach speak to this issue through many references to the need to 'diversify experience' and to 'work in an environment where issues are increasingly horizontal.'[151] Accordingly, in future more senior officials will make it to the top because of their general knowledge of the system, because of their ability to manage a difficult situation, and because of their capacity to work with the centre of government. Specialized knowledge of a particular sector or the policies and programs of a given department will become less important for those wishing to rise above their peers.

The new approach also strengthens the hand of the clerk of the Privy Council in deciding who gets promoted and weakens that of the chair of the Public Service Commission. COSO will play a role in the management of the network, but it is the clerk, not the chair of the Public Service Commission that chairs COSO. In government, securing promotions is the one indicator of success understood by all. In the absence of market forces to decide who wins and strictly objective criteria about who should get promoted, the ones who hold in their hands the ability to appoint individuals to a level will inevitably also hold considerable influence within government. It is also interesting to note that the establishment of the network and a stand-alone agency reporting to the clerk and COSO can, potentially at least, weaken the Public Service Commission, a parliamentary agency. Yet, the matter was hardly raised, let alone fully debated, in Parliament.

Has Anything Changed?

It would be easy for the reader to conclude that those in Ottawa who wish to reform the system are kept busy turning cranks not attached to anything and that in the end nothing changes. One senior government official offered this telling observation. 'Shortly after I joined the public service, I was told of a new approach and I got pretty excited about it. My manager, who had been around for some time, said, "Don't get too excited. If you stand here long enough, it will come around again under different buzz words." I thought then, "This guy is pretty cynical." But, you know, I look back and I now know where he was coming from.'[152] We have seen one major reform measure after another introduced in quick succession, most of them pursuing essentially the same objective – to empower managers and get rid of needless red tape.

There has not been one reform effort introduced in recent years that has lived up to expectations. Indeed, if one is to believe consulted officials or former public servants like Paul Tellier or John L. Manion, who have written about their experience in government, none ever succeeded in meeting even modest objectives. Another former senior deputy minister, Arthur Kroeger, writes that 'the roll-call of innovations launched during the 1970s and 80s includes Programming, Planning and Budgeting, Management by Objectives, cost-benefit analysis, effectiveness evaluation, Operational Performance System, strategic overviews, and Multi-Year Operational Plans. Each had a certain plausibility in its time, but in the event none lasted for more than a few years, and it is striking how little difference any of them actually made in the end, despite the efforts of many talented people.'[153] The innovations during the 1990s such as PS 2000 and *La Relève* could now be added to the list. By all accounts, then, there has been no fundamental change.

Still, there is no denying that some things have changed. Both central agency and line department officials agree that there is now much less need to go to the Treasury Board than, say, eight or fifteen years ago. Departments and managers have a great deal more freedom than they have ever had to move financial resources around and to manage human resources. One has only to look at the number of Treasury Board decisions over a period of fourteen years to see that there have been some changes. In 1983, the Treasury Board issued 6,000 decisions.[154] By 1987 the number had dropped to 3,500.[155] By 1997 the number had dropped still further, to about 1,100.[156]

Treasury Board and line department officials admit that there is more than one reason to explain this sharp drop. For one thing, there is little or no new money available at the Treasury Board for departments to apply for. That was not the case in the early 1980s, in the mid-1980s, or even in the early 1990s. One senior Treasury Board official reports, for example, that she had 'to handle six or seven cases a week in the late 1980s–early 1990s to approve funding under the Green Plan.'[157] This, she reveals, had more to do with financial resources being available than to a lack of delegated authority to departments.

But it is clear that the Treasury Board has, at least since PS 2000, freed departments from many controls and administrative requirements. This is as true in the area of human resources management as it is in financial management. Ministers and senior officials now have much more authority to approve spending from their own approved budgets than was the case several years ago. An assistant deputy minister from a line department explains, 'We now have in essence two budgets – one O & M (salaries, consultants, travel, etc.) and another Grants and Contributions (program spending). If we want to move money from one budget to another, we need to get Treasury Board approval. Failing that, we are pretty well left alone to do what we want. Our signing authority is sufficiently high that there is very rarely a need to go to the Board.'[158]

The Atlantic Canada Opportunities Agency (ACOA) is a case in point. At the moment, the head of the agency (the deputy minister) can approve all spending up to $1 million without even having to go to his minister. Meanwhile, the junior minister responsible for ACOA has signing authority to approve all spending up to $3 million. The senior minister, the minister of Industry, can approve all spending up to $20 million without having to go to the Treasury Board. There is, however, one exception to this pattern. ACOA was the government's implementing agency in Atlantic Canada for both phase I and phase II of the Canada Infrastructure programs. For this program, all projects had to be submitted to the president of the Treasury Board for approval, but not, however, to the Treasury Board.[159]

It is important to note that departments have varying degrees of signing authority so that department X can approve spending up to, say, $20 million while department Y can only do so up to $5 million. There is no longer any authority that applies to all departments at all times.

Treasury Board officials also report that the great majority of cases submitted to the board are 'appendix' (about 65 per cent) or 'routine' cases (25 per cent) rather than 'considered' cases (about 10 per cent). Routine cases are very rarely discussed by ministers and their approval is usually straightforward. A Treasury Board minister can ask to speak to a routine case but this is also very rarely done. The majority of routine cases are from the human resource side of the secretariat, and they are submitted to the board often simply because an act requires it. It could involve, for example, declaring somebody a common-law spouse for pension purposes or even declaring someone dead in order to stop pension payments.

There are two kinds of routine cases, those that are flagged and those that are not. Flagged cases suggest that they may be of interest to a Treasury Board minister because they have the potential to be of interest to the media, or because of regional or other concerns. The secretariat always ensures that an official is available to speak to the case should a minister wish to pursue it. An appendix case, meanwhile, could involve a proposal to reclassify an EX4 position to the EX5 level. Treasury Board ministers are handed a précis of appendix cases for consideration, but not the full submission.

Considered cases are major proposals, and in some instances they may require more than one Treasury Board meeting to arrive at a decision. Considered cases could involve a proposal to restructure the personnel classification system, to establish a new approach to service delivery, or to reallocate a substantial amount of funds from one program to another.[160]

Treasury Board officials do not believe that delegating authority to departments has lessened their own influence. They point out that 'delegation of authority can be a moving target' and that 'track record matters a great deal.' One senior official explained, 'We do not blindly transfer authority to departments. We know exactly what is being transferred to whom. We know departmental track records. A couple of screwups matters a great deal and we do monitor closely what goes on in departments.'[161] In any event, they insist that delegating more authority to departments has actually strengthened their own hand in managing government operations from the centre. They claim that all they have lost to departments is the authority to nitpick and that there is no value for anyone, including the centre, in having 'nitpicking' authority. 'What difference does it really make,' one Treasury Board secretariat official asked, 'if we have the authority to review a proposal to reclassify a position from an EX1 level to EX2?'[162]

The Treasury Board and its secretariat can always reinstitute its authority to nitpick. In many instances, there is no need to do so. A simple telephone call from the secretary to a line deputy minister asking that a certain initiative be stopped or reviewed will suffice. An example will make this point clearer. An official with the Canadian Centre for Management Development (CCMD), a federal government agency, worked for nearly one year on a project to develop a management course and a series of special events or projects on management-labour relations. The then secretary of the Treasury Board telephoned the head of CCMD suggesting that the whole initiative should be dropped because of high-profile management-labour disputes, including a strike over a wage freeze. The initiative was dropped.[163]

In 1992 the auditor general delivered a 'broadside' to the government for its administration of payments to employees under its workforce adjustment policy.[164] The policy, it will be recalled, was introduced to assist those employees whose positions were being cut from the public service. The secretary of the Treasury Board came under attack before Parliament's Public Accounts Committee for the secretariat's apparent inability to monitor properly how departments had managed the board's workforce adjustment directive. Some employees, for example, had received special payments when their positions were abolished but were rehired to another position only a few weeks later. At the next deputy ministers' breakfast meeting, the secretary made clear his displeasure with the turn of events, his inability to answer questions at Public Accounts, and particularly over the fact that he was 'caught by surprise.'[165] Departments, he argued, should have alerted the secretariat of the potential problem. He also made it clear that the secretariat would be putting in place 'a system which will never again put me in a position of having to say I do not know.'[166] We are informed that the fallout from this 'put added pressure on human resources staff [at the Treasury Board secretariat] to assess its capacity to monitor complex human resource policies for which it was responsible, and to clarify the accountability relationships among TBS, Parliament, and operating departments.'[167]

The Public Accounts Committee or, for that matter, question period, will not always search out precisely to whom questions should be asked if political points can be scored. The president of the Treasury Board can find himself in the direct line of fire if a question involves government spending or personnel management issues. Ministers may not insist that a system of administrative and financial controls be firmly in place to prevent all potentially politically embarrassing situations. They will insist, however, that they are well briefed on potential political problems before walking into the House of Commons for question period facing a media scrum.

This and the preceding chapters, however, raise a number of questions. One of these is how ministers and line departments view the centre. We noted in the introduction that a senior central agency official observed that 'much of what we do is related to the need to keep corralling bouncing politicians and bouncing departments.' How do ministers and line departments view central agencies? Do they regard them as a positive or a helpful force in their work? If yes, how? If no, why not? The next two chapters seek to answer these questions.

Appendix

Roles within the Expenditure Management System

Parliament

The changes to the House rules in February 1994 enhanced the role of Parliament in the budget process. Through the operations of standing committees, Parliament will review the departmental Outlooks and provide its views on future spending priorities. In addition, these committees will continue their traditional role of reviewing and reporting on spending proposals in the Estimates for the current fiscal year. The Standing Committee on Finance will discharge its responsibilities to review and report on the budget consultation papers.

The Public

The release of budget consultation papers in the fall will give various groups and individuals the opportunity to provide input to the minister of Finance on the budget. Similarly, the public can be invited to comment on proposed spending plans to the parliamentary standing committees when they consider departmental Outlooks in May and June.

Cabinet

As the executive decision-making body, Cabinet will review budget strategies, policy priorities, and fiscal targets based on advice on various reallocation and expenditure reduction options that the minister of Finance and the president of the Treasury Board have provided.

Policy Committees of Cabinet

The policy committees will:

- formulate strategic sector priorities for input into the budget and expenditure planning processes;

- oversee the design and implementation of new programs announced in the budget; and
- take the lead in putting together reallocation packages to fund any significant new initiatives that, due to exceptional circumstances, were not identified during the budget planning cycle.

The Privy Council Office

The Privy Council Office will:

- focus on overall government and prime ministerial priorities and the integrity and functioning of the system;
- provide support to Cabinet and its committees and coordinate Cabinet review of budget consultation papers and strategies; and
- advise the prime minister, Cabinet and policy committees of Cabinet on specific proposals in the budget and budget consultation papers.

Finance

The minister of Finance, assisted by the Department of Finance, will:

- set the fiscal framework;
- focus primarily on the economic outlook, macroeconomic management, and tax and fiscal policy;
- ensure that decisions on the macroallocation of resources are compatible with the government's economic and fiscal policies;
- prepare the budget consultation papers and the budget documents, a process which includes updating the economic outlook and fiscal plan and recommending fiscal targets; and
- focus on expenditure management at the macro level with the primary emphasis on major statutory expenditures, debt management, the financial policy framework, and guidelines for loan and guarantee programs and Crown corporation borrowings.

The Treasury Board

The Treasury Board, assisted by its secretariat, will:

- exercise its statutory responsibility for accounting for expenditures, including the preparation, based on Cabinet decisions, of the main estimates and their tabling;
- advise Cabinet on the extent to which departments are using their resources efficiently and effectively through its 'budget office' functions – namely, the costing, design, and performance of programs and the management of resources within specified targets;

- assist the Cabinet policy committees and departments in developing any reallocation options that were not identified during the budget planning process and provide advice to the policy committees of Cabinet on the viability and costing of identified options;
- review departmental business plans;
- manage the operating reserve; and
- focus primarily on all expenditures other than major statutory payments and public debt charges. This includes grant and contribution programs, defence spending, payments to crown corporations, operating and capital expenditures, and public sector compensation.

Departments and Agencies

Ministers and the deputy heads of departments and agencies will:

- deliver effective and efficient programs and services to their clients;
- inform the Treasury Board about the effective and efficient use of resources within their departments in keeping with the corporate framework and Treasury Board authorities and seek advice and assistance from the Treasury Board on intradepartmental reallocations;
- develop, in consultation with the appropriate policy committees, new departmental initiatives to be funded through reallocating internal resources;
- develop departmental business plans and release Outlooks that reflect the budget and report on key strategies and plans their departments have developed so that they can manage within their resources; and
- prepare departmental estimates, including Part III, which provide, in relation to stated objectives, performance expectations for the estimates year and performance information on the results of previous years.

8

Ministers: Knowing When to Land

In their book *Double Vision*, journalists Edward Greenspon and Anthony Wilson-Smith tell us a story. Prime Minister Chrétien was reading a newspaper on an airplane flight early in his first mandate when he came across an article quoting one of his ministers, Ralph Goodale. Goodale was quoted at some length on a sensitive trade issue, without uttering a word of substance. Chrétien told one of his assistants, 'Now that's how a minister should talk!'[1] Chrétien should know. Before becoming 'the boss,' he had spent sixteen years as a minister in the Pearson and Trudeau Cabinets. The secret to being a successful minister, thus, is to know how to circle an issue without landing or, better yet, perhaps, to know when to land.

The purpose of this chapter is to consider the role of ministers and how they work with the centre of government. Ministers, in theory at least, should constitute the centre of government, not just in form but also in substance. Gordon Robertson explained nearly thirty years ago that the nature of our executive is very 'different from that in countries like the United States ... the first and most obvious [difference] is that each member of the executive must know what is involved in the policy and program decisions for which he shares responsibility ... The second is that each must have an opportunity to participate in those decisions.'[2] Robertson went on to argue that for the collective executive to function properly, 'it should involve awareness of problems and relevant considerations and discussion of lines of solutions at a stage early enough that a minister can share in shaping the final result. Either to accept or to reject a finished product may be totally unsatisfactory.'[3] Robertson summed it all up: 'The ministers are responsible. It is their government.'[4]

This chapter explores a number of issues. How do ministers work with the centre? Has their role changed in recent years? How do ministers make it 'their' government? How successful are they? In an earlier chapter, we noted that a prime minister must make the government 'his' or 'hers.' This begs the question: is it possible for both the prime minister and ministers simultaneously to make the government theirs?

What Makes a Minister Successful?

I asked several present and former Cabinet ministers what makes a minister successful. One replied, 'The first thing one must do to become a successful minister, and I am not trying to be funny here, is to become a minister. It is part skills and part luck. What matters first is the election, what matters second is re-election, what matters third is for one's party to win, and what matters fourth is to make it in Cabinet. The point is that you can only become a successful minister if you are a successful politician. In other words, you do not become a successful politician by becoming a successful minister. There are some exceptions, like Marc Lalonde, but they are very, very few.'[5] Another replied that 'being a successful minister is like being successful at something else. You look for a role model, or to someone who has been there before and who was successful.' When asked what makes a good role model, he replied, 'Someone who was able to have been in there a long time without getting either himself or the government in too much political trouble.'[6]

John Reid, a former Trudeau minister, writes that 'there is no system in the federal Parliament to test whether a person is able to perform the job of Minister, and most Ministers lack any background or preparations for the task they must perform as Minister. The first year of a Minister's existence is taken up with on-the-job training. Many do not survive, even though they may linger on. They find out what they can do and try to stick to that area.'[7] Not only is there no training available or any test possible to determine whether a person will be able to perform the job, no job description exists (or could exist) outlining what ministers should be doing and how they should go about their work. Apart from getting elected to Parliament on the winning side and the fact that the prime minister wants you as minister, about all that is required to become a Cabinet minister is a security check to see if any criminal charges are pending. Overnight, then, it is possible for a teacher, a small town lawyer, an entrepreneur, or a medical doctor to be appointed to Cabinet and find himself in charge of a large, sprawling government department.

To be sure, not all ministers are created equal. This point was made in virtually every interview we had. There are always some ministers who, as John Reid observed, simply 'linger on.' That is, they are not particularly strong in any policy area, prefer to ride the political wave wherever it may lead, and are not inclined to make too much of an effort to shape its direction. In short, they never land on a policy issue. Their hope is to gain a positive media profile, to stay out of political trouble and try, as best they can, to secure new initiatives for their constituency or their province. Still, these ministers can be successful, at least in the eyes of their riding and province, simply by lingering on and taking care of the people who elected them. In Ottawa, they may well be viewed as parochial, but back home they will be seen as able to look after their constituency and region. Their power is manifested in securing an appointment to a government board for a long-standing party member or in getting new funding, however modest, for a high-profile initiative in their region. This kind of activity sends out a signal that they have influence in the corridors of power in Ottawa. As well, although it is the prime minister who appoints senators, there is nothing to stop a Cabinet minister from taking the credit for the appointment.

What matters to ministers who linger on is that they are Cabinet ministers, that they are able to win the prized possession and hold on to it. In many ways, this should not come as a surprise. We saw in an earlier chapter that political candidates in Canada organize around leaders rather than around political principles and ideologies.[8] In the absence of principles and ideologies, sitting in Cabinet becomes the end rather than the means. For these ministers, the centre of government or the prime minister and his senior advisers are pretty well all that matters in Ottawa. The key is to stay out of trouble with the media and to handle question period with dexterity. Their focus is on the prime minister. One long-serving deputy minister (over ten years) observed, 'You have no idea what kind of power the prime minister holds over ministers. He has in his hands the minister's car, his chauffeur, his office, his job, his ego, and so on. I have been in the public service for nearly thirty years in the Privy Council Office and line departments, and I can tell you that the grovel count in the great majority of ministers has always been quite high and, if anything, it keeps getting higher as the years go by.'[9]

There is no question that those who choose to linger on, or who, for any number of reasons, are forced to linger on, can still be very busy and give the appearance, at least to those outside of the centre of government, that they are making a difference. There is never a shortage of things for them to do. They must spend time in their constituencies and province. They have to attend to party matters, attend caucus, prepare for question period, and be accessible for media interviews. They also have House duties, including attending to committee matters. They must meet regularly with their senior departmental officials. There are also always any number of reasons to travel to different parts of Canada on behalf of the party or their department. Powerful or not, ministers always have specific projects to promote or some government funding to secure for one reason or another. If the funding requirement is modest and can be secured from within his or her department, so much the better. If the relevant program is in another department, then the minister and his office will have to lobby or negotiate to secure the project or the funding. This too takes time.

Ministers, independently of the portfolio they may hold, put in extremely long hours, especially when Parliament is sitting. We were shown weekly agenda for several Cabinet ministers in the fall of 1997. There was hardly an open spot in any of them. Nor did the agenda chronicle all that ministers do in the course of a week. There are always last-minute meetings to be arranged, telephone calls to return (often in the evenings), correspondence to deal with, documents to read, and so on. As two students of politics wrote over twenty-five years ago, politicians 'miss meals, neglect children, and lose sleep for politics. For them, politics is a central, vibrant and continuing preoccupation. Formal statements of purpose cannot adequately account for their involvement.'[10]

A former clerk of the Privy Council and secretary to the Cabinet, Gordon Osbaldeston, once issued a warning to Cabinet ministers that 'having many roles, you will be under constant and unremitting pressure to allocate some of your time to this or that worthy endeavour. [Ministers] must establish priorities and the time frame within which they want to accomplish them and allocate their time accordingly. If they don't do this, and do it well, they will be lost.'[11] He added that ministers work between seventy and eighty hours a week, but that 'surveys indicate that they often have only three hours a week to spend with their Deputy Ministers.'[12]

There are no hard and fast rules to determine if a minister is successful. To be sure, winning one's own riding at election time is the unambiguous measure of success for politicians, and ministers are, of course, no exception. As already noted, longevity in politics is its own reward. But beyond that there are precious few unambiguous signs of success other than having the confidence of the prime minister.

Success for ministers is in the eye of the beholder. As many ministers, members of Parliament, and senior public servants observed in the consultations, 'in politics, perception is reality.'[13] For example, a former minister of Agriculture was praised by his Cabinet colleagues for his ability to 'connect' with Canada's farming community. But the minister, it transpires, was not effective in Cabinet or even in leading his own department. One former official from the Privy Council Office confesses, 'I remember the very first Cabinet meeting I attended as a note taker. The minister spoke at length about nothing. Frankly, he did not make much sense. When I came back to my office, I reported this to a senior PCO official, well versed in the ways of cabinet. He said, "Now you understand why many important decisions are not taken in Cabinet."'[14] Still, when Trudeau wanted to promote his government and his party to Canada's farming community, he would invariably turn to this minister. But when he wanted someone to sort out a complex political problem, he would turn to Marc Lalonde or Allan MacEachen. When he wanted someone to play political hardball with Quebec sovereignists, he would turn to Jean Chrétien. Chrétien, in his own words, became 'Trudeau's firefighter.'[15]

Mulroney was much the same. When he wanted someone to fix a political problem, he would turn to Don Mazankowski because he was particularly adroit at finding a compromise or a solution. When he wanted someone to tackle a difficult sectoral problem, like the crisis on the east coast ground fishery, he would ask John Crosbie, a strong, articulate minister from Newfoundland and Labrador, to handle it. When Chrétien decided early in his mandate to deal with the deficit problem, he turned to Paul Martin, a successful businessperson with a strong personality and strong ties to the Liberal Party. When he wanted the Department of Transport to be overhauled, and later to introduce far-reaching changes to the Department of Defence, the minister he called on was Doug Young, a no-nonsense politician who, the consultations reveal, was always ready to carry out any tough assignment on behalf of the prime minister.

But for every Marc Lalonde, Don Mazankowski, and Paul Martin, there are other ministers who leave little or no trace of their accomplishments during their stay in government. Think, for example, of Fred Mifflin, Lucienne Robillard, Diane Marleau, and Lyle Vanclief in the Chrétien government. Or of Pierre Vincent, Shirley Martin, Robert Layton, and Gerry Weiner in the Mulroney government, and of Charles Lapointe, James Fleming, Patrick Mahoney, and Joseph Philippe Guay in the Trudeau government. Even politically knowledgeable people could be left scratching their heads trying to associate these names to government departments or to political events.[16]

In an earlier book we wrote that one could group federal Cabinet ministers into 'four broad categories: *status, mission, policy* and *process* participants.'[17] The argument is that in the absence of political ideology to guide them, one must look at what it is that motivates ministers.

The main preoccupation of status participants is visibility. Maurice Lamontagne summed up it well when he observed, 'If a minister enjoys a good press, he will be envied and respected by his colleagues. If he has no press, he has no future.'[18] Status participants, however, take public visibility to the extreme. At the same time, they are the least troublesome ministers to the prime minister or to their departments, rarely questioning ongoing policies and programs. If anything, they are likely to encourage their departments to do more, if only to capture attention. Status participants and their staff are continually on the prowl in search of new initiatives. If Treasury Board approval is required, they will happily take up the challenge and lobby their colleagues on the board. They will volunteer to make announcements and give speeches.

Status-participant ministers also try to avoid confrontations with their own staff, their Cabinet colleagues, or even their departments. They will not want to jeopardize any opportunities to be cast in a favourable public light. A long-running debate with the department over policies and programs (over which they usually have only a limited interest in any event) could well divert attention from initiatives involving the media and public relations. Examples of status participants include Sergio Marchi in the Chrétien government, Tom MacMillan in the Mulroney government, and Gerald Reagan in the Trudeau government.

Mission participants make quite different Cabinet ministers. They will certainly seek a favourable press, like all politicians, but that is not their all-consuming purpose. They have strongly held views and usually do not avoid confrontation. While their views are not always politically or ideologically inspired, they do 'seek to serve a cause' which is brought to the Cabinet table. Examples of mission participants include Eric Kierans and Monique Bégin in the Trudeau government, Jake Epp in Mulroney's government (if only because of his strong religious convictions, which he brought to bear on a number of public policy issues), and Lloyd Axworthy in the Chrétien government.

Policy participants, meanwhile, are rarely numerous in Cabinet and they usually have limited success. One former deputy minister explained in a study on management in the federal government, 'My experience as often as not was that the minister had no view [on policy].'[19] The few real policy participants in Cabinet, however, profess to be in politics precisely to influence and shape public policies. These ministers usually welcome long policy debates with their officials. They often have a specific area of expertise and come to office equipped with more than the generalities of their own party election platforms. These credentials, however, do not automatically ensure their making it to Cabinet, let alone being appointed to the post for which they are best suited. Don Johnston, one of Trudeau's ministers, for example, was a policy participant. He had some definite policy views and is an expert in tax policy. He was never, however, appointed minister of Finance or even of National Revenue. Other policy participants would include Marcel Massé, a former senior deputy minister in the Chrétien government, and René-Robert De Cotret in the Mulroney government.

There is a tendency for Cabinet colleagues to dismiss policy participants as politically naïve and as 'policy wonks,' far too preoccupied with the finer points of public policy. There are other reasons why policy participants have limited success. Having an interest and even some expertise in public policy is one thing. Knowing how the policy process works is quite another. Along with the machinery of government, it is now a field of specialization in its own right.

It usually takes several years for permanent officials to understand the process fully and to feel at ease working in it. The result is that most ministers must rely on their own departmental officials to help them through the maze.

Those policy participants who have been Cabinet ministers and who have later written about their experiences often speak of their disenchantment and the deep frustration they felt over their inability to change policy.[20] They point to officials in the Prime Minister's Office, the Privy Council Office, Finance, and elsewhere as inhibiting their efforts to introduce real change. Those who claim some success report that they had to go to extraordinary lengths to bypass the formal policy process.

The most successful and the most numerous Cabinet ministers are (for want of a better term) the process participants. Ministers that linger on are mostly found in this category. They rarely question policy or the policy process itself. Their purpose is to make deals for a designated clientele. They usually understand how Parliament works, enjoy parliamentary jostling, get along well with most of their colleagues, and take particular delight in striking deals. They are often politically partisan and willing to help out one of their own who might be in some difficulty in his or her constituency.

Policy content, political ideology, government organization, management issues – and even government programs themselves – are all of very limited interest to the process participants. The notion that a government policy should be overhauled may make for an interesting discussion, but it holds little real appeal. Projects are what matter and the more the better. Process participants will look to their own departments to come up with specific projects for their own ridings or for the regions for which they are responsible. They generally view their departmental officials as allies in getting their projects through the approval process. They will have difficulty only if the officials are uncooperative in putting deals together. Process participants are generally easygoing extroverts. Nothing pleases them more than having a project to announce at the end of the week. Like mission participants, process participants will, when possible, collaborate with each other and seek to strike alliances among themselves. Such alliances, however, are never as solid as those between mission participants, in part because they do not relate to a fundamental purpose, as do those of mission participants. Examples of process participants include Diane Marleau or Ralph Goodale in the Chrétien government, Elmer McKay in the Mulroney government, and Charles Lapointe in the Trudeau government.

The program review did make life difficult for most ministers. Process participants, for example, had virtually no opportunity to identify new projects throughout the exercise. In addition, ministers from all categories had no choice but to challenge their departmental policies and programs. But as noted in chapter 6, the consultations reveal that many sought to sidestep the program review. At the risk of sounding repetitive, the atmosphere generated by the Mexican currency crisis and the media, combined with Chrétien's firm decision to stay the course, forced the hand of all ministers to play by the rules. Unable to get a sympathic hearing from Chrétien, some ministers even organized leaks to let their constituents or interest groups know that they were not comfortable with the exercise. The *Globe and Mail*, for example, reported in a front page story at the time of the program review that Ralph Goodale's struggle was straightforward. 'How much can he save now, how successfully can he slow the pace of reform and what programs can he introduce in the meantime to smooth the transition?'[21] A friend of Goodale was quoted as saying that he had always wanted to be the federal minister of Agriculture, but that 'unfortunately he reached his objective just when a fiscal crisis loomed.'[22] Another suggested that Goodale was trying to persuade Finance minister Paul Martin to ease up on the cuts, and yet another insisted that Goodale 'might be perceived as the messenger who has to deliver the bad news, rather than the bad guy.'[23]

In addition, it is clear that a number of ministers temporarily became mission participants during the program review exercise. Paul Martin did not avoid stating his case clearly, nor did he avoid confrontation with his Cabinet colleagues in pushing for substantial spending cuts to reach the 3 per cent deficit to GDP target. But he was not alone. Brian Tobin and André Ouellet, who in more normal times would fall squarely in the process participant category, became mission participants. Tobin, for example, went 'after the deficit with missionary zeal.'[24] One senior government official reports that 'Tobin in opposition when the Mulroney government was trying to introduce spending cuts was a far cry from Tobin as a member of the Cabinet committee on program review. It was like night and day.'[25] Tobin himself told his colleagues during the program review exercise, 'I've become the right-wing fiscal conservative of this government.' He also reported that he became a right-wing conservative while on a trip to Japan which had impressed upon him Canada's vulnerability to the 'whims of foreign leaders.'[26] Some consulted officials scoffed at this observation, saying that if Tobin could add, he would have known long before he went to Japan that Ottawa was in serious fiscal difficulties. They argued that it was simply convenient for him to oppose spending cuts when Mulroney was in government but to change his tune when Chrétien was in power.

But no sooner was the deficit brought under control than ministers reverted to their previous categories – albeit with only limited success. When Martin declared in 1997 that the fiscal framework would provide for $300 million of new spending money, they began to line up with spending proposals, just as in the old days. Paul Martin summed up the difference in this fashion, 'Bringing the deficit down to zero is tough – but there is a consensus on the need to do it. It's what comes after that no one can agree on.'[27]

Ministers came forward with projects, all of them, with the exception of the prime minister and the minister of Finance (who, in any event, play by a set of different rules), as soon as the centre gave them the green light to do so. By the end of the exercise, some $298 million had been allocated. Senior government officials report that the exercise was an 'extremely difficult one,' with some ministers arguing 'very hard for their corners, whether it was their region or their department.'[28] One minister argues that 'the odds that we would somehow reach agreement on how to spend $300 million were not high. In fact, we did it because we knew that Martin and his officials were saying that the process would never work. Well, we proved them wrong.'[29] The process was managed by the Privy Council Office, not the Department of Finance, and it became clear to ministers that PMO was keeping a very close eye not only on the process but also on the recommendations being made. One minister reports, 'We know that PMO was directly involved and that the prime minister was keeping an eye on things. Some of us got messages that we could not ignore.'[30]

Few argue that the various projects, taken together, add up to a coherent or an overarching government strategy. Ministers simply borrowed a page from the past to find ways to promote their pet projects or their departmental agenda, including timely leaks to the media. Some ministers even gave media interviews shortly before two Cabinet committees began allocating funding to make a case for their own departments. John Manley, the Industry minister, for example, told the *Globe and Mail* that his department wanted a share of the new spending pie and pointed to the need to allocate new funding to a special program, the Industrial Research Assistance Program, which had suffered substantial spending cuts in the program review.[31] His efforts proved successful. One by one ministers got one or two spending projects approved and every single project was assessed on its own merit. One senior PCO official observed that 'what we wanted was to avoid seeing ministers slowly reinstitute programs and initiatives cut by the program review exercise. We really could not aim much higher than that in terms of overall strategy. If you look carefully, you will see that we were not completely successful in that some of the preprogram review exercise activities have reappeared. But a good part of the $298 million also went to new activities. We can only manage the process and then leave it up to the politicians to make the decisions.'[32]

Looking back, two things need to be stressed in any attempt to classify ministers in set categories. First, though one can discern a dominant characteristic, a good number of ministers can be found in two or more categories – for instance, a mission participant can also be seen by departmental officials as a status participant. Second, whatever category he may fall into, a minister will need the strong support of his department to be successful at virtually anything he tries to do. Accordingly, no matter however one defines success for ministers, they can always use a helping hand from their departments.

Ministers and Their Departments

Ministers do not manage their departments. J.W. Pickersgill, a former Cabinet minister and former clerk of the Privy Council and secretary to the Cabinet, explains, 'No one with any experience expects a minister to manage his department. That is the duty of the deputy minister.'[33] He adds, 'Except in periods of revolutionary upheaval – something never yet experienced in Canada – at least ninety percent of the activity of government follows a relatively set pattern, which tends to be highly repetitive ... In the normal course, ministers do not, and should not, concern themselves with these large areas of day-to-day administration.'[34] Pickersgill could have added that, in any event, there are many areas in the running of the department in which the minister is virtually powerless.

The most obvious example is in the personnel field, which is beyond the work or the mandate of any single minister. A minister does not have the authority to hire, fire, promote, demote, or even transfer *anyone* in the department. The only staff over which he has some control is his very small ministerial staff.

There are also a host of other centrally prescribed or even departmental rules and regulations which inhibit or in some instances prohibit ministers from getting involved in certain financial and administrative issues. The *Financial Administration Act* and government policies on public tendering, for example, simply take decisions out of the hands of the minister. In addition, the minister, as political head of the department, has precious little, if any, say on issues such as salaries and bonuses paid to senior officials.

Accordingly, one can hardly describe the minister as the chief executive officer of the department. Nor is he akin to the chairman of the board. No CEO would agree to lead an organization unless he had a relatively free hand to manage the personnel field. Similarly, few would accept to serve as chairman of the board of a large private firm without access to some levers of management authority, including the capacity to appoint a new CEO when the position becomes vacant and to establish the salary and bonuses of the CEO and other senior members of the management team.

A former Trudeau Cabinet minister described the sensation of being appointed minister and coming to terms with what it meant – or did not mean. He observed, 'It's like I was suddenly landed on the top deck of an ocean liner and told that the ship was my responsibility. When I turned to the captain [i.e., the deputy minister] I was told that he was appointed there by someone else and any decision to remove him would be made elsewhere. When I turned to others on the ship, I soon found out that they all report through the deputy minister, owe their allegiance to him and their future promotions. When I asked for a change in the ship's course, the ship just kept on going on the same course.'[35]

To be sure, ministers have a relatively free hand to organize their own office. They are free to employ a handful of politically partisan staff members who serve the minister and retain their positions only so long as the minister retains his.[36] Ministers, however, have strict limits on the size of their exempt staff budget and the salary they can pay to individual staff members.

It will be recalled, however, that Brian Mulroney decided to strengthen ministerial offices. As part of the transition planning exercise, key political and policy advisers convinced him to let ministers appoint a chief of staff in their offices and to increase their exempt staff budgets. Salary levels for chiefs of staff were established at the assistant deputy minister level, a level immediately below deputy minister in the Canadian public service. Mulroney's decision to establish a chief of staff in each ministerial office had one purpose – to check the permanent officials' influence on policy. Government press releases even described the position as an 'official in the American style.'[37]

All ministers had a chief of staff within days of Mulroney's coming to power. His transition team had put together a list of potential candidates for ministers to pick from as they were appointed. The chiefs of staff, however, had a mixed reception, often dependent on the quality of the incumbent. They introduced a new level between ministers and permanent officials, which gave rise to a number of misunderstandings and complications. In some instances, the chief of staff acted as a mediator between the minister and permanent officials, screening advice going up to the minister and issuing policy directives going down to officials, much to the dismay and objections of deputy ministers. Many chiefs of staff took a dim view of the competence of permanent officials, while senior officials took an equally dim view of chiefs of staff. The arrangement, one senior permanent official said, had 'on the whole hardly been a happy or a successful one.'[38]

One of the first things Chrétien did after assuming power in 1993 was to abolish the chief of staff position in all ministerial offices except his own. Chrétien's objective was to promote a better working relationship between his ministers and the public service. Under the Chrétien government, the senior official in a minister's office is the executive assistant, as it was under Trudeau. However, the executive assistant is a relatively junior position and enjoys neither the salary nor the status that the chief of staff position enjoyed in the Mulroney years. In the Prime Minister's Office, for example, there are about twenty staff members who occupy more senior positions and more status than does the executive assistant in a minister's office.

Typically, executive assistants to ministers are young – anywhere between twenty-seven and thirty-five. They are well educated but most have little government experience. Often, they have fought election battles, either on behalf of a candidate for the party's leadership, for the party in the national election campaign, or in provincial elections. In virtually all cases, they have well-established track records as supporters of the party in power.

The Chrétien government has, however, decided to carry on with at least one practice established by the Mulroney government. Under Mulroney, the Prime Minister's Office was directly involved in the selection process for a minister's chief of staff. Indeed, PMO had a list for ministers to consult in selecting a chief of staff, and in some instances more junior-level ministerial assistants.[39] Chrétien's office is also involved in selecting executive assistants for ministerial offices. This is not to suggest that all ministers must accept a candidate from PMO. But some do, and PMO is always there to provide suggestions.

Looking to PMO for an executive assistant holds a number of advantages. If the incumbent doesn't work out, blame can be shared or even shifted to PMO. In addition, consulting PMO for your closest political adviser means that you are a team player.

Some ministers, however, have little option but to accept PMO's choice of an executive assistant. If a minister is experiencing continuing political difficulties (e.g., David Anderson in Chrétien's first mandate or Fred Mifflin in his second), then PMO will simply select the executive assistant, and for all practical purposes the minister must accept PMO's candidate for the job.

In addition, PMO now arranges briefing sessions for new ministerial staff. The sessions are said to be 'useful, particularly for those who did not have government experience.' They also provide an opportunity for new ministerial staff to 'get to know each other' at an event organized at the centre of government.[40]

An executive assistant to a minister in the Chrétien government wrote about her experience as she left her position. She broke down her responsibilities under four broad headings: political adviser, office manager, time manager, and crisis manager. As policy adviser, she reports that the executive assistant is expected to bring a 'political perspective' to the minister's departmental agenda, analyse Cabinet items to brief the minister on 'regional, provincial, and constituency responsibilities,' and provide an 'appropriate spin' before the media to 'reflect the minister's political interests ...' The executive assistant is also expected to establish contacts with PMO, party members, provincial caucus, and with the minister's constituency.[41]

As manager of the minister's office, the executive assistant is responsible for staffing, for the budget, for the minister's correspondence, and for organizing and scheduling the work of the office 'to emphasize the minister's priorities.'[42] As time manager, the executive assistant organizes the minister's crowded agenda. Question period, she writes, 'calls for lengthy preparation.' The minister may also need briefing material for 'full Cabinet meetings, and at least one and usually two Cabinet committees ... national, regional and provincial caucus meetings ... House or senate committees when steering legislation through the system ... departmental [meetings], preparing speeches.' She provides a long list of possible weekly meetings and concludes that it is 'an environment where the urgent always displaces the important.'[43]

She also writes that every minister 'experiences crises' and that 'it is important to predict which issues are one-day wonders and which will become full-blown crises.'[44] For all crises, she explains that 'a plan' must be 'drawn up' to identify the 'actions required.' She concludes by arguing that 'it is of utmost importance for the plan to be relayed to the PMO.'[45]

The focus of ministerial offices, as the above makes clear, is clearly on the minister, partisan politics, the media, and working closely with the Prime Minister's Office. The focus is not on the minister's department or on departmental matters. To be sure, executive assistants are in constant communication with the deputy minister's office. Consultations reveal that relations between a minister's office and senior departmental officials are rarely easy, and in some instances they are extremely difficult. This was particularly true under the Mulroney government, but it appears that 'things have only improved slightly, if at all, under Chrétien.'[46] There is also evidence to suggest that relations between ministerial staff and senior departmental officials were not much smoother under Trudeau, particularly in his later years in office.[47] The reasons for the conflicts have remained fairly consistent from the Trudeau years to Chrétien's second mandate in office – a widely held perception among ministerial staff is that senior departmental officials from the deputy minister down are not sufficiently sensitive to their minister's objectives and his political interests.

There is no question, however, that the department's manager is the deputy minister, or the permanent head of the department. His counterpart in Britain is called the permanent secretary, a term which better describes the position, even here in Canada. Someone unfamiliar with Canadian public administration may well assume that, given his title, a deputy minister has a partisan political connection to the minister. He does not.

As a rule, federal deputy ministers are nonpartisan, and the great majority of them are products of the federal public service. In almost all cases, they intuitively shy away from partisan politics. As one former minister explained, 'It is a cultural thing with the bureaucrats. You will never see them in a church basement attending a party meeting. In fact, they would be, extremely uncomfortable if ever they would land there all of a sudden.'[48] Senior career public servants would not disagree with this observation, insisting that this is the way it should be, and for valid reasons. A report prepared by senior federal public servants on 'Values and Ethics in the Public Service' makes the point that it is very important to 'reassert neutrality as one of the fundamental values of the Canadian public service ... in our view the non-partisan character of the public service is inextricably linked to other essential values such as loyalty, integrity, impartiality, fairness, equity, professionalism, and merit.'[49]

Though ministers do not as a rule have a say in the selection of their deputy ministers, they must learn to work with them. As one senior Privy Council Office official explained, 'There can be no competition, no interviews by ministers to determine who can be a deputy minister. In addition, deputy minister appointments are not a matter to be discussed in Cabinet. It simply does not belong there. It never has, and as far as I am concerned it never will.' The official also explained, 'We simply cannot let ministers appoint deputy ministers. The reason is clear – a deputy minister's loyalty must be to the government, never to a minister.'[50]

The above begs the question how do ministers work with their departments? It is often taken for granted that somehow ministers will learn how to work well with their deputy ministers. Yet there are no courses available to assist them in working with a large organization, in particular with the organization's permanent head. Still, it can be the determining factor in how well a minister will perform in government, however one may wish to define the criteria for success.

At the risk of sounding repetitive, more often than not ministers come to their position from a law firm, a small business, or a teaching position. Thus, the learning curve for a newly appointed minister obviously has to be steep. In addition, as a minister learns to work with the public service, he must also at the same time learn the ways of the centre of government and the Cabinet decision-making process. If ministers are to make it 'their' government, they need to gain an appreciation of what other ministers and other departments are doing or proposing. Indeed, if Cabinet is to be truly a collective decision-making body, these ministers, as Gordon Robertson explained, need to be aware of relevant considerations and the proposed lines of solution at a relatively early stage.

At the first Cabinet meeting of his government, Jean Chrétien told his ministers that they needed to establish a strong working relationship with their deputy ministers. In the same afternoon, he met with their deputy ministers and essentially gave the same message – ministers and deputy ministers need to strike a strong partnership.[51] For Chrétien, 'there is a community of interest between' the minister and his deputy minister. He adds, 'If a minister doesn't trust his officials, he won't get anywhere ... Many Ottawa bureaucrats are extremely well-educated, well read, and nobody's fool. Knowledge is power, and in many cases these people got to power because of their knowledge. The Canadian bureaucracy has a tradition of great loyalty to the system and the institutions ... [but] in my experience, if you tell the bureaucrats what you want with no ambiguity or confusion, there's no problem.'[52] This is not to suggest that senior government officials, notably deputy ministers, will run with every idea or suggestion from their minister. If a minister states his ideas and preferences clearly enough, however, his senior officials should either promote them or explain the difficulties in doing so.[53]

It is one thing for Chrétien to stress that ministers and deputy ministers should establish a strong working relationship. It is quite another to put it into practice. In fact, central agency officials report that both Mulroney and Trudeau made precisely the same pitch time and again at Cabinet meetings.

Public servants also have minds of their own and many do not hesitate to voice their views. Ministers arriving in a department, and even those who have been in a department for some time, should not expect that permanent officials will accept their ideas on a particular subject without judging their merits. Senior government officials pride themselves on being politically sensitive rather than politically partisan.[54] Being politically sensitive essentially means having a sense of what is possible, and what is not.

Deputy ministers will assess what is possible by looking to the department's capacity, including its financial resources, but especially by looking to the centre of government for guidance. They can begin by reading the mandate letters from the prime minister to their ministers and from the clerk of the Privy Council and secretary to the Cabinet to themselves. These are quite clear on whether the department is expected to generate new ideas or policy and program proposals or whether simply to manage the status quo.

No deputy minister wants to be accused of 'going native' – that is, of pursuing his own or his minister's agenda with little regard for what the centre thinks. A deputy minister who does this runs a very high risk of seriously hurting his career prospects.

One senior deputy minister explained, 'When a new minister is appointed, I make it very clear that he should not ask me to do something which our legislation does not allow or to try something knowing that the prime minister is against it. Other than that, I make it clear that I am open to suggestions.'[55] Other current and former deputy ministers were asked if they also made the same points to their ministers. It is clear that they did, though some said there is no need to spell it out, in particular to a minister who has served in Cabinet for any length of time. One explained that 'it was simply understood that is the way things work.'[56]

In the pre-Trudeau days, strong ministers would strike an alliance with their deputy minister and together decide if, when, and how departmental policies or programs should be overhauled or adjusted. The minister would then bring the matter to Cabinet to get a green light to proceed.[57] Cabinet, Trudeau and his advisers maintained, did not have the capacity to challenge the minister, to identify and debate the various options. This is what Gordon Robertson was getting at when he wrote in the early 1970s that ministers as a collective body needed to be aware of problems and discussion of solutions at a stage early enough that they could share in shaping the final decision. As already noted, a simple yes or no, in his opinion, 'may be totally unsatisfactory.' In order for ministers to make it their government, the argument went, they needed a capacity and support at the centre of government and in Cabinet to discuss the 'lines of solutions' and make policy. Michael Pitfield was even more explicit on this point when he wrote that 'I think we should be very leery of casting our lot towards a system of bureaucratic decision-making ... through the arbitrary imperialism of a minister-spokesman who may but usually would not understand his file, whose colleagues would never be given the chance [to understand the file].'[58] For Pitfield, ministers collectively would stand a better chance of understanding a series of files from across government than an individual minister working directly with the deputy minister on one or a few files.

The Trudeau changes, as already noted, had a considerable impact on government policy and decision making, which is still being felt today. Ministers are now less likely to strike a partnership with their deputy ministers. For one thing, deputy ministers are now more likely to look to the centre of government for guidance than was the case in the pre-Trudeau days. Many of them now, much more often than not, come to their position after working at the centre of government. It was common up to the late 1960s for deputy ministers to rise through the ranks of their department and stay in that position until retirement. To be sure, these long-serving senior public servants had enormous clout.[59] Mitchell Sharp suggested that 'in many cases, they [had] a greater influence upon the course of events than have ministers, particularly the weaker and less competent ministers.'[60]

Trudeau's decision to curb the power of the mandarins gave rise to a new breed of deputy minister. Have-policy-will-travel became the new credential that created deputy ministers capable of serving in virtually any department. It is now not uncommon for deputy ministers to serve in several departments before they retire. One former official I consulted, for example, served in four departments in an eight-year period. Deputy ministers are no longer specialists in one sector or in the policies and programs of a single department. They take pride in being able to manage any department and any situation. They are what one former senior public servant labelled 'careerists, and their careers are paramount.'[61] Moreover, the single most important determining factor on career prospects for current and aspiring deputy ministers is how well they are perceived at the centre of government.

The Privy Council Office also attaches a great deal of importance on 'being corporate' when it looks at the work of a deputy minister. One former deputy minister reports that at one of his performance reviews a senior PCO official observed, 'You are doing great, and everybody is saying so from your minister to other deputy ministers. You are strong on both the policy and management front. But you are not being corporate enough.'[62] It is important to note that in this case the individual became a senior deputy minister without having worked in a central agency, a rare occurrence.

The Privy Council Office also stresses in print the importance of being 'corporate.' In its document *Responsibility in the Constitution*, it states that 'Deputy ministers are, of course, responsible to their respective ministers, but their appointment by the Prime Minister reinforces their commitment to ensure the successful functioning of ministerial government.' It then adds that 'the system would be unstable without the collective responsibility necessary to Cabinet solidarity, and the deputy must also play a role in and be affected by means that are used to ensure the maintenance of collective responsibility among ministers.'[63]

The centre also makes it clear that deputy ministers should not 'allow their ministers to go off on a tangent or get too far ahead of the government with any idea, however brilliant.'[64] Ministers are well advised to look to their deputy ministers for guidance on whether, when, and how they should broach an idea.

Ministers also spend less time with their deputy ministers or on departmental matters than was the case thirty or forty years ago. Arthur Kroeger writes that 'whereas the commonest complaint of deputy ministers of my generation was the difficulty of getting time with our ministers, with bilateral meetings once a week being the best that most of us could manage, the normal practice in both Mr. St. Laurent and Mr. Pearson's government was for ministers and their deputies to meet at the beginning of every working day. Consequently, ministers could be kept fully informed about work that was in progress, and were able to provide guidance to their officials on a regular basis. I have yet to meet anyone with first-hand experience of this period who is in any doubt that ministers, such as Mitchell Sharp, Paul Martin Senior, Bud Drury, and Allan MacEachen were fully in charge of what happened in their departments.'[65]

My consultations reveal that most ministers now only meet their deputy ministers and other senior departmental staff on average for about three hours a week. Some spend no more than an hour a week with their deputy ministers. Both ministers and deputy ministers were quick to point out, however, that they are often on the telephone with one another in the course of a week. The problem, they insist, is simply an overcrowded ministerial agenda.

I put a question to both ministers and deputy ministers – why is it that the prime minister can find the time to meet with his deputy minister, the clerk of the Privy Council, for at least half an hour most mornings when he is in Ottawa, but that they cannot do the same? How is it, I asked, that the minister of Finance can spend up to three or four hours a day, nearly every day, in briefing sessions with his senior departmental officials, particularly in the months before he tables his budget, but that they cannot do the same? After all, officials in PMO, PCO, and Finance also reported that the prime minister and the minister of Finance can be on the telephone on numerous occasions in the course of a week.

The reaction to my question in many cases was a puzzled look. Some said, 'That is a very good question,' and essentially left it at that. Others argued that line ministers probably have more interest groups to meet than either the prime minister and the minister of Finance. However, if one takes the number of interest groups the minister of Finance must deal with as an example, from the banks to antipoverty groups, there clearly must be other reasons. In addition, we saw in chapter 4 that the prime minister and his office are always in constant battle to manage the prime minister's agenda.

It may be that both the prime minister and the minister of Finance consider that the time spent with their deputy ministers is time well spent. Decisions are made, things get done, major initiatives are planned and launched, and policy is established. Both are prepared to sacrifice other important meetings to invest the time where it truly matters. The same cannot be said for line ministers.

Many departmental decisions from personnel to financial matters simply do not belong in meetings between the minister and deputy minister. Policy issues can be discussed at such meetings, but only to bring the minister, or on some occasions the deputy minister, up to date. Policy matters are rarely ever resolved at these meetings.

I asked what was usually discussed at a typical weekly briefing session between the minister and his deputy minister. The answer was that it varied and it depended. It varied by department and it depended on personalities. Departments with a high policy content require a different agenda than, say, Revenue Canada, which has only a limited number of possible policy issues to discuss with the minister. Meanwhile, the deputy minister of a department like Fisheries and Oceans, which often has to deal with various crises, will produce an agenda for his weekly briefing meeting with the minister which focuses on hot issues. Personalities matter in that deputy ministers who have an easy relationship with their ministers will be much more willing to put everything on the table than will those who don't. In fact, if tension between the two is strong, both sides might find a reason to postpone a briefing session or a meeting unless it is absolutely essential. However, the same is not true at the centre of government. We saw earlier that if tension should exist between the prime minister and the clerk of the Privy Council, or between the minister and deputy minister of Finance, then changes will very likely be made.

In most instances, the deputy minister will prepare an agenda of issues he wishes to discuss with his minister at a regularly scheduled weekly briefing session, usually informing the minister or the executive assistant ahead of time of the issues he wishes to raise. In most cases, the executive assistant attends the session, and one, two, or at times, all assistant deputy ministers will also participate. The minister will also at least from time to time raise issues he wants to review with the department. These can be any number of issues involving the department or may have very little to do with the department. The latter may involve an issue discussed in Cabinet committee or elsewhere on which he would like his officials to use their contacts to track down some information.

Deputy ministers will adjust briefing sessions to accommodate the minister's personality. A minister who falls into the mission participant category will want the department to explore new policy options with far more tenacity than, say, a process participant. Similarly, a deputy minister will know that a status participant will always be on the lookout for the department to identify projects or new initiatives for him to pursue. Process participants, meanwhile, will very rarely focus on questions of policy, or the policy process. They will be quite prepared to act as the department's ambassador before their colleagues or Cabinet committees and happily take up any message put forward by the department. 'Going with what the department wants,' one minister explains, 'is the road of least resistance. It also makes life easier for everyone.'[66]

As noted earlier, most Cabinet ministers are process participants. If the department can generate positive media visibility for its minister and deals for him to strike with his Cabinet colleagues, the process participant will be happy, as one minister observed, 'to sell the department's salad in the system.' He added, 'It is very easy for ministers, especially new ones, to be captured by arguments from his officials, such as, "We know that you have special access with the prime minister and that you can promote this project or this funding for the department." It happens. I have seen it more than once.'[67] But selling a department's salad is not likely to either surprise or upset the centre of government.

The above is not to suggest that relations between ministers and their senior officials have improved over the past thirty years. In fact, there is plenty of evidence to suggest that they have deteriorated. Though many admitted that they were in no position to say how ministers and deputy ministers worked together in the 1940s, 1950s, and 1960s, they did acknowledge that it is very likely that the situation is much worse today. A number reported that, for the most part, relations between senior public servants and ministers during the Mulroney years were difficult, and that things were not much better during the Trudeau years, particularly from 1975 onward. Moreover, the great majority of senior public servants consulted claimed that things have not improved or have only improved slightly under the Chrétien government.

Without insisting that there is a firm link between the time ministers and deputy ministers spend together on the one hand, and how well they get along on the other, it is clear that the atmosphere has changed a great deal. Reading the political memoirs of ministers from Walter Gordon to Paul Martin, one is struck by the positive things they had to say about the great majority of senior public servants who worked with them.[68] While former prime ministers and the current prime minister, Jean Chrétien, at least from time to time, sing the praises of senior public servants, we no longer find ministers, even senior ministers, doing so.[69]

The British television satire *Yes Minister* became highly popular with some politicians and public servants in Canada. Sandford Borins writes that it became 'something of a cult program, exceedingly popular with a small following that is intensely interested in public affairs.'[70] Some of the things said in the program rang true, at least with some politicians. The not-so-subtle message of *Yes Minister* was that public servants were actually running the country, their deference to politicians was pure pretence, and that the Sir Humphreys of the bureaucratic world yielded considerable power. The series did serve to give evidence of bureaucrat-bashing. There is now a veritable who's who of former and current senior ministers from all sides of the Canadian political spectrum who have publicly questioned the work of their own public servants. The list includes, among many others, Allan J. MacEachen, Lloyd Axworthy, and André Ouellet from the Liberal Party and Bernard Valcourt, Sinclair Stevens, and Otto Jelinek from the Progressive Conservative Party. This list is certainly not complete.

Though the phenomenon is not limited to Canada, we have seen in recent years the rise of macho ministers. Though macho ministers are very rarely effective, they do not make for easy, productive relations with their departmental officials. Macho ministers will decide, at least on occasion, not to rely on their deputy ministers for advice. Under Mulroney, ministers had chiefs of staff and a growing cadre of highly paid and often politically partisan lobbyists always at the ready to offer advice. Though the chief of staff position no longer exists, the lobbying industry in Ottawa is still alive and well. Macho ministers take delight in challenging or even overturning departmental positions or decisions.[71]

Macho ministers, by definition, also suspect their senior departmental officials of not only having too much influence but of being too close to the centre of government. In the consultations, a number of deputy ministers reported that they have been in the past instructed by their ministers not to discuss a particular issue with PCO or to keep PCO officials in the dark over a specific matter. One deputy minister reported, 'My minister was about to say something in a speech that could annoy PMO. She knew it and I knew it. She instructed me not to discuss the matter with PCO. I really had no choice but to alert PCO. The next time I saw her, I could sense that she knew that I had done so. Nothing further was said, though.'[72]

Sergio Marchi, minister in the Chrétien government, boasted that he had more influence in Ottawa than his deputy minister because of his own connections to the centre of government. He observed, 'My deputy minister is all right, but he knows that in any showdown, I can get to the prime minister a lot faster than he can.'[73] One can hardly imagine a minister making a similar observation thirty or forty years ago at a time when he met with his deputy minister every morning. If there was a showdown to be had, it was more likely to involve him and his deputy minister working as a team.

Though a macho minister may well take delight in challenging his deputy minister over a program decision after lobbyists get to him, there is a price to pay. When all is said and done, a minister's main policy adviser is his deputy minister. This is true not only on departmental matters, but also on broad government policy issues. If anyone in the system is able to brief a minister on policy issues coming before Cabinet and Cabinet committees, it is the deputy minister. Without his strong support, a minister will find it extremely difficult to be an effective participant in Cabinet. In short, there is nowhere else in the system that a minister can turn for help. Wise ministers will come to term with this and do what they can to ensure a smooth working relationship with their deputy ministers, but others never do and they pay the price.

The Minister in Cabinet

In Canada, a fundamental theory of government is that ministers decide. The Privy Council Office tabled a major statement, 'Responsibility in the Constitution,' in 1977 and reissued it in June 1993. The then clerk, Glen Shortliffe, explained in the preface to the 1993 edition that the document 'has been used as a basic reference work within and around the Privy Council Office ever since

[1977].' He added that it deals directly with the 'foundations of our system of responsible government and of the principles and conventions that underlie it.'[74]

The document makes it clear that the Privy Council Office 'must respect the confederal nature of the system in which power flows from ministers.'[75] It adds that the Privy Council Office, 'like its master [the prime minister] exists primarily to promote consensus by maintaining the equilibrium among ministers, and this raison d'être remains valid so long as neither the secretariat nor departments lose sight of the essential differences in their respective roles, the one co-ordinating and the others initiating.'[76] The document sums up the role of central agencies as one of enabling 'the confederacy to work.'[77]

The Privy Council Office also explains in some detail how our theory of government should work. It states that 'the tone of the government may be set by the Prime Minister and the cabinet, but most of the policies of the government flow from the exercise of the individual responsibilities of ministers. With rare exceptions, these policies are initiated by ministers and their deputies, co-ordinated at the official level through a network of interdepartmental committees, and by other means, discussed by ministers and deputies in committees of the cabinet, finally resolved by ministers themselves in the cabinet, and given effect through the exercise of the individual responsibilities of the minister and ministers involved.'[78]

How does this square with the findings of my consultations? Boldly stated, it does not. For the most part, ministers, starting with those who served under Trudeau, and continuing with those who served under Mulroney and now under Chrétien, say that Cabinet is no longer where the important decisions are made, and that, in any event, decision making in the federal government can hardly be described as Cabinet operating in a 'confederal nature.' They also say that it is no longer the case that 'power flows from ministers.' Very early in interviews for this book, a Chrétien Cabinet minister observed that 'Cabinet is not a decision-making body. Rather, it is a kind of focus group for the prime minister.'[79] Shortly after this interview, a former minister in the Mulroney Cabinet observed that 'Cabinet was more like an advisory committee to Mulroney than an effective decision-making committee.'[80]

I then decided to start every other interview with current and former ministers and some senior PCO officials with the question: 'A Cabinet minister has described Cabinet as a kind of focus group for the prime minister rather than a decision-making body. Do you agree with this observation?' The responses varied, but no one suggested that the observation was wrong. One said, 'I don't agree completely but I know where he is coming from.' Another, 'There is some truth to it, but it is not the whole truth.' Yet another, 'While one can make the case, the problem is that there are too many large egos at the Cabinet table to think that we were only there as members of a focus group. Not many of us will care to admit that we are a kind of a collective focus group.'[81]

Ministers, however, dismissed virtually out of hand the theory of a 'confederal nature' of decision making or that 'power flows from ministers.' Power, they believed, flows from the prime minister to ministers – unevenly at that – and is always subject to change, depending on circumstances. It also flows to a handful of his or her most senior advisers in his office and in the public service.

I asked present and former Cabinet ministers and officials who attend Cabinet meetings what goes on in Cabinet. One of those I put the question to was a senior minister who served in both the Trudeau and Chrétien Cabinets. He had also served in a minister's office during the Pearson years. I wanted to see if things had changed a great deal over the years. Based on discussions with his then minister, he was able to compare the workings of Cabinet under Pearson, Trudeau, and Chrétien, with the caveat that his information on the Pearson Cabinet was secondhand.

He reported that by all accounts Cabinet operated quite differently under Pearson than under Trudeau or Chrétien. The Pearson Cabinet, he revealed, was more 'free wheeling, more chaotic, and more open. Strong ministers got their way unless Pearson and other senior ministers were dead against it, but even then it did not happen often.' The Trudeau changes, he adds, 'completely turned things around. Cabinet became a highly structured process and frankly quite bureaucratic. We would spend hours and hours in Cabinet committee, pretending that we had all read these lengthy documents. Chrétien got rid of most committees, leaving only two [the actual number is four, but no doubt he was referring to the Economic and Social Policy Committees].' But leaving aside the number of Cabinet committees, he reported that Cabinet today operates much as it did under Trudeau. He pointed out, however, that Trudeau and Chrétien have very different personalities – and this came out in Cabinet. Trudeau, he claims, liked to read long Cabinet documents; Chrétien does not.[82]

Ministers, senior PMO staff members in the Mulroney government, and senior public servants report that during Mulroney's leadership Cabinet operated essentially as it did under Trudeau and as it does under Chrétien. To be sure, Mulroney's personality also had an impact on the Cabinet. He, like Chrétien, was not as willing to read Cabinet documents and briefing material to the extent Trudeau was, and unlike Trudeau, but like Chrétien, he also enjoyed telling stories and anecdotes about his meetings with world leaders and past political experiences. Chrétien, unlike Trudeau and Mulroney, 'does not like to waste time in Cabinet, and if you want to say something to Cabinet it better be brief and not something that has already been said. Chrétien will not hesitate to cut you off if he senses that time is being wasted.'[83] PCO officials reveal that the nature of Cabinet deliberations and even decisions has changed a great deal from the pre-Trudeau days. One former PCO official reports that she decided to go to the archives and read all Cabinet minutes and decisions to prepare herself shortly after she was asked to attend Cabinet meetings to take notes and prepare Records of Decisions. She reports, 'I was struck by how Cabinet dealt with the important issues back then compared to now.'[84]

So what actually goes on in Cabinet meetings? By all accounts, the Cabinet agenda has changed very little since the early Trudeau years. The first item on the agenda is 'General Discussion,' which the prime minister opens and leads. He can raise any matter he chooses, ranging from a letter he may have received from a premier to a purely partisan matter to diplomacy. The Privy Council Office prepares a briefing note of possible talking points for the prime minister to speak from. But prime ministers can, of course, completely ignore it. Trudeau relied on PCO briefing material to lead the 'General Discussion,' Mulroney somewhat less so, and Chrétien even less than Mulroney. 'With Chrétien,' one senior PCO official reports, 'we have no idea what he can come up with. Often it is as much a surprise to us as it is to ministers what he will raise.'[85]

There are a few issues, it appears, that come up time and again, whether it is Trudeau, Mulroney or Chrétien in the chair. The prime minister will invariably remind Cabinet ministers every month or so that they have to pay attention to caucus and backbenchers. One senior PCO official reports, 'I heard the "pay-attention-to-backbenchers-because-they-are-the-reason-why-we-are-here-speech" perhaps a hundred times.'[86]

Federal-provincial issues often appear on Cabinet's weekly agenda under the General Discussion. The prime minister will present his views on the state of federal-provincial relations, on Quebec, or on a specific file which has received media attention. Ministers can then offer their opinions, and here, according to a senior PCO official, 'there is no doubt that it has a kind of focus group characteristic to the process. The prime minister will listen and he will then do whatever he pleases with the views being offered.'[87]

Ministers who have served under Trudeau, Mulroney, and Chrétien all report that the prime minister is always *de facto* the minister of Intergovernmental Affairs and the minister responsible for the Constitution. Ministers can voice their concerns at Cabinet meetings, but even those who do, and by all accounts they are not numerous, know full well that the prime minister will 'call the shots pretty well as he sees it.'[88]

One or two ministers, however, will on some occasions dare to offer a different view to the prime minister's on federal-provincial relations. One former and long-serving PCO official reports that the prime minister always has 'a kind of burr in the saddle. There is always one or maybe two ministers that will raise awkward questions, or make points that, however softly, will question the prime minister's position on federal-provincial matters or other important issues. In the end, they usually have no impact other than being annoying to the prime minister. I am thinking of Jean-Luc Pépin and Trudeau, John Crosbie and Mulroney, and in the case of Chrétien, perhaps David Dingwall.'[89]

The second item on the Cabinet agenda is called 'Presentations.' Ministers accompanied by their deputy ministers are on occasions invited to make presentations or briefing sessions on various issues. The minister of Finance and his deputy minister might present a 'deck' on the government's fiscal position. Or the minister of Industry and his deputy minister might make a presentation on Canada's productivity or competitiveness in relation to the United States. At the end of the presentation, ministers are free to raise any question or to ask for further classification or explanation.

The third item is 'Nominations.' Government appointments, ranging from a Supreme Court judge, to a senator, to a deputy minister, to a member of the board of a crown corporation require an order-in-council. There is always a list of appointments to be confirmed at every Cabinet meeting. However, the nominations have all been sorted out well before the Cabinet meeting is actually held.

The Prime Minister's Office and the Privy Council Office manage the appointment process. For non–public service appointments (deputy ministers and ambassadors), the Prime Minister's Office will consult regional Cabinet ministers and others in the party. The extent to which individual ministers are consulted varies according to the prime minister's wishes. In his early years in office, Trudeau was guided by the wishes of his regional ministers. Later, he started to look to his own counsel and to the advice of senior PMO officials for certain appointments, particularly Senate appointments.[90] Mulroney had a trusted assistant with deep roots in the party, Marjorie LeBreton, who looked after appointments. She would consult a fairly elaborate party machinery at the provincial level to secure advice on virtually all political appointments. Mulroney, however, would reserve the right to appoint his own person, particularly when it came to the Senate, or high-profile board appointments.[91]

Chrétien keeps a tight control on appointments, and it appears that ministers now have less influence than was the case under Mulroney, and certainly under Trudeau. For one thing, Chrétien spends more time on reviewing appointments than either Mulroney and Trudeau did. For another, certain appointments are pretty well declared off limits to ministers, notably Supreme Court judges and senators. One minister who served in both the Trudeau and Chrétien Cabinets points out that 'Trudeau, especially in his early years, did not want to decide who should get what in terms of appointments. That was patronage, and it was better left to regional ministers. In time, however, he began to get directly involved in certain appointments. Chrétien runs it very tight and he and his office decide many appointments. If regional ministers had full say in our first mandate, I can tell you that we would have seen different kinds of appointments.'[92]

To be sure, prime ministers do not seek a Cabinet consensus when appointing either Supreme Court judges or senators. They, and they alone, decide, and everyone else is on the outside looking in, whether it is Cabinet, caucus, first ministers, or Parliament. Individuals may be consulted, including the minister of Justice and individual premiers, in the case of Supreme Court judges, but there is no pretence – the decision belongs to the prime minister. The Ottawa *Citizen* had it right when it wrote that 'Mulroney's Supreme Court may soon become Jean Chrétien's court' because of 'an unusual confluence of expected retirements.'[93]

The fourth item is Cabinet committee decisions presented as appendices on the agenda. In overhauling the Cabinet decision-making process, Trudeau made it clear that all decisions taken in Cabinet committee could be reopened for discussion in Cabinet. A former Trudeau Cabinet minister reports that in his early years in office Trudeau would quite willingly let ministers reopen a Cabinet committee decision in full Cabinet. In time, however, he became annoyed with the practice, and he did not hesitate to show his displeasure whenever a minister sought to review an appendix item. Cabinet simply did not have time available to discuss Cabinet committee decisions. In any event, by the late 1970s and the early 1980s, Trudeau would automatically send a Cabinet committee decision back to the committees for review whenever a minister would raise questions about it in full Cabinet.[94] Mulroney did much the same or relied on the Operations Committee of Cabinet, chaired by Don Mazankowski, to sort out problems with Cabinet committee decisions. Chrétien, as already noted, does not react well whenever a Cabinet committee decision is challenged, and like Trudeau in his later years, he automatically refers the decision back to the Cabinet committee without any discussion in full Cabinet. For Chrétien, challenging a Cabinet committee decision simply indicates that the committee did not do its job right the first time and it should try again. The result is that Cabinet committee decisions are very rarely challenged in full Cabinet (it only happened three times between 1993 and 1997). Mulroney had little patience for the Cabinet process and at one point said that he 'favoured any decision-making system that minimized the time he spent in cabinet.'[95] He preferred to deal with the big issues outside of Cabinet, preferring to operate outside the constraints imposed by the system. The telephone and face-to-face conversations 'were his stock in trade.'[96] Indeed, we are now informed that 'under Mulroney important matters such as energy mega-projects were often decided without benefit of any Cabinet documents at all.'[97] The point is that Mulroney, like Chrétien and Trudeau, did not easily tolerate ministers querying Cabinet committee decisions, consequently it was rarely done.

What Goes on in Cabinet Committee?

Cabinet committee meetings in the Trudeau and Mulroney years took up a great deal of ministerial time. One former minister reports that they dominated his agenda from Tuesday morning to Thursday evening.[98] Things are different under Chrétien, with only five Cabinet committees, including the Treasury Board, in operation.

The prime minister appoints all Cabinet committee chairs. Prime ministers themselves chaired the key Priorities and Planning Cabinet committee when it existed, largely because it performed a kind of 'inner cabinet' role. Chrétien, however, does not chair any of the five Cabinet committees, nor does he participate in their discussions. Still, he does, as we saw in earlier chapters, keep a close watch on their work and their decisions. In addition, while he does not appreciate ministers challenging Cabinet committee recommendations in Cabinet, he does not hesitate to do so himself when he sees one that he does not like. In addition, he may well ask that a particular Cabinet committee decision not be included as an appendix item because he may disagree with it or because he is not comfortable with it and wants to think about it before letting it go forward. Officials in the Prime Minister's Office argue that the prime minister has every right to review any Cabinet committee recommendation or hold them up since he is not a member of any Cabinet committee.

The prime minister can also direct the work of Cabinet committees in various ways. The Privy Council Office will prepare briefing notes to the prime minister on virtually all proposals well before they are submitted to Cabinet committee. The clerk of the Privy Council Office can also raise any Cabinet committee proposals in his daily morning meetings with the prime minister.

Prime ministers appoint all Cabinet committee chairs, a task that they do not take lightly. From Trudeau to Chrétien, they invariably, in the words of a senior PCO official, turn to a *personne de confiance*, someone they can trust, with good judgment and a capacity to look at more than one side of an issue, to appoint as chair of a Cabinet committee.[99] Strong-headed, highly opinionated, and independently minded ministers such as Jean-Luc Pépin, John Crosbie, and David Dingwall, by all accounts, do not make good chairs, and consequently, they are seldom chosen.

Put differently, prime ministers do not want mission participants to chair Cabinet committees. Process participants are much better suited to the job. Chrétien, for example, in his second mandate, appointed Ralph Goodale, he who knows when to land, as chair of the Cabinet committee on the economic union.

What is discussed in Cabinet committees? In an earlier chapter, we reviewed the work of the Treasury Board and Treasury Board secretariat. The Special Committee of Council performs essentially a housekeeping role and ensures that all the 't's are crossed and i's are dotted and reviews in considerable detail proposed legislation and regulations.'[100]

The Economic and Social Union committees review proposals from departments in their respective sectors, including program changes and virtually any matter a minister and his deputy minister consider appropriate to bring before Cabinet.[101] In addition, PCO will ask ministers and their departments to come forward with proposals or even issues which cut across the policies and programs of more than one department.

The above could mean that most, if not all, of the new measures a department is contemplating should be submitted to a Cabinet committee. When asked to present his department's policy agenda to his colleagues at a regular deputy minister breakfast meeting, a deputy minister writes that his department did 'not have an agenda. I only had my department's manifestation of the government's agenda, and I put down each of the policy files that we were working on and beside that I put down the other departments that I needed as partners. There was not one issue I could take forward – either to ministers, to the public interest groups that we were dealing with, or to my minister alone – without bringing along another department. I don't think there are very many of those issues left where you can say "I am sorry, it's none of your business! I've got this one."'[102] In addition, departments somehow want the cachet of a Cabinet decision even for things over which they already hold full authority. 'One can only assume,' one central agency official suggested, 'that writing or working on Cabinet documents gives midlevel officials a certain amount of credibility or prestige.' He adds that some highly technical issues which no Cabinet or Cabinet minister would ever want to understand, let alone challenge, should be dealt with elsewhere than Cabinet, but that somehow they make it on the agenda.[103]

The point here is that a number of Cabinet committee decisions are noncontroversial and fairly straightforward. This is true for highly technical issues such as specific trade or tax agreements with another country. It is also true for some program revisions which are quite straightforward and for which it is not difficult to secure a consensus for its approval.

An example will make this clear. In late 1997 the Central Mortgage and

Housing Corporation (CMHC) decided that it could find the necessary funding within its own budget to extend for five years three programs to improve housing conditions. The programs were designed to assist low-income Canadians, as well as those living in rural and remote areas, to improve their homes.

The Residential Rehabilitation Assistance Program provides loans to low-income homeowners and landlords of properties targeted to low-income Canadians to bring homes up to health and safety standards. The program can also be used to make homes accessible for disabled residents, enabling them to live independently. The Emergency Repair Program provides nonrepayable contributions to homeowners in rural and remote areas of Canada to undertake the emergency repairs required for the continued safe occupancy of their homes. The Home Adaptations for Seniors' Independence assists low-income elderly Canadians whose difficulties in daily living can be addressed by certain adaptations to their homes. These programs also benefit many aboriginal households.[104]

The total funding for the three programs amounts to $250 million over five years. However, in discussions with central agencies, CMHC, made it clear that it would not seek new funding to finance the program extensions. It prepared a Cabinet memorandum for the minister responsible for CMHC, and officials accompanied the minister to Cabinet committee to answer any questions.

The minister had little difficulty in securing Cabinet committee approval. CMHC officials had done plenty of background work with PCO and even PMO officials to explain the proposal and its political appeal, and to insist that it would entail no new cost to the Treasury. It was described as a win-win proposal. No minister and no department would oppose the proposal since any impact it had on their own programs was positive. PMO officials and ministers also saw that their own backbenchers would applaud the initiative since it would give them something to promote to their constituents. When the Cabinet committee decision went to full Cabinet on an appendix item, no one raised any questions, and CMHC officials were then free to prepare a press release and promote the program extension to its clientele. There are a number of similar proposals that go to Cabinet committees, including the Treasury Board, in the course of a year.

At the risk of stating the obvious, not all Cabinet committee decisions are this easy. PCO officials report that the more difficult ones surface when ministers and departments have fundamentally different views on a proposal, whenever new funding is made available and when a minister gets ahead of the process by announcing a measure before it has been considered by Cabinet committee.

PCO's role in the Cabinet committee process is to sort out issues that are potentially difficult to manage, to settle the conflicts, seek out the compromise solution, and essentially 'fall on the hand grenades.' If PCO officials have a measure of their own success, it is how well they manage conflicts between ministers and departments, and more importantly, how successful they are in ensuring that they never get any play in the media.

For many of them, not surprisingly, process rather than the substance of the issue is key. They make sure that the prime minister is always fully informed of potential conflicts and may well seek guidance from him on what to do. On occasion, the prime minister may decide to bring the issue to his own office and settle the matter himself. Trudeau, Mulroney, and Chrétien have all done this.[105]

At times, the prime minister may simply decide to go against the wishes of one of his senior ministers, and this happens probably more often than is generally assumed. A case in point: in the early 1980s, Trudeau instructed his then minister of Transport, Jean-Luc Pépin, to reverse his decision to transfer subsidies under the Crow's Nest program from transportation firms to the producers in Western Canada.[106] Pépin had secured Cabinet committee and even Cabinet approval for his decision, but when it became public there was fierce opposition from farmers in other regions of the country. Producers in Ontario and Quebec feared that Western producers would simply apply the subsidies to create new capacity rather than putting them to transportation costs. Pépin wanted to stand firm. Trudeau, however, simply informed Cabinet that Pépin would have to reverse his decision and, in the words of a former Cabinet minister, 'That was that.'[107]

Mulroney and Chrétien have both turned to key ministers or advisers to manage potentially difficult situations. Mulroney used his deputy prime minister, Don Mazankowski, to manage conflicts and issues in which he had only limited interest. Chrétien has established ad hoc committees of Cabinet to review politically difficult issues. In the course of a single year, Chrétien can set up 'six, seven, or more' such committees.[108]

He established a five-member ad hoc Cabinet committee, for example, to review recommendations from his minister of Defence on the purchase of new rescue helicopters in early 1998. Art Eggleton and the Defence Department made it clear that they wanted the EIX-101 helicopter. Chrétien, however, had made highly publicized commitments during the 1993 election campaign to cancel the purchase of a similar helicopter produced by the same manufacturers. On establishing an ad hoc Cabinet committee to review Eggleton's recommendation, Chrétien, in the words of one of Eggleton's colleagues, 'left his Minister of Defence out to dry.'[109] Chrétien finally accepted the recommendation from his minister of Defence only after the ad hoc committee told him that the government could well face serious legal challenges from the winning bid if it were turned down in favour of another manufacturer or that the bidding process might even have to be reopened. In addition, the Department of Defence forcefully made the case that the competing bids were offering helicopters that were too small to do rescue work in Canada and that they would only be able to serve a limited purpose. The controversy, the delay, and the establishment of an ad hoc Cabinet committee to review the work of the Defence minister, according to observers, had as their source the Prime Minister's Office. The *Globe and Mail* quoted a government official, insisting that 'all the PMO is worried about is the Prime Minister's political capital and credibility.'[110] It is important to note that ad hoc committees of Cabinet only meet a few times – sometimes only once – before they are dismantled, and that they report directly to the prime minister, not Cabinet.

However, in most cases when there is disagreement between ministers, the prime minister will let PCO officials manage the situation, and he will intervene personally only when PCO, his advisers, and he himself conclude that it is necessary for him to do so. PCO's objective is to identify a common ground when there is sharp disagreement between some ministers and to promote a consensus. Strong ministers, in particular the mission-participant-type, find this difficult to accept. Paul Martin explained his own frustration with the PCO process when he observed, 'The bureaucracy is very process-oriented and I'm not. Nobody who has been in business is. I basically want to get a job done. I don't give a goddamn about the process. For the bureaucracy, what's interesting is that as long as the process is working, everybody is happy ... You know, as long as the meeting breaks up with nobody throwing a punch, everybody in the system is happy. And my view is you're a lot better off to have the meeting end with somebody throwing a punch because at least something gets decided.'[111] Martin's views are close to Chrétien's. Chrétien explains, 'The PCO gains power from using its information-gathering system for real influence. Coordination becomes more important than the action. Compromise, the way to protect everyone's interest, becomes more important than a good solution; and the quickness, the responsiveness and the freshness of departments are lost to empire building. Even important ministers came to fear the PCO.'[112] The only one in government, it appears, allowed to throw a punch is the prime minister, and when he does not, PCO is left to find common ground among competing ministers and departments.

The above explains why mission participants do not make good chairs of Cabinet committee and why they are rarely appointed. Chairs of committees have a special relationship to the prime minister and the Privy Council Office. PCO officials prepare briefing material for the chair and are always available to advise or assist them. Committee chairs are also in a better position to influence the process and even tilt some decisions to their way of thinking or to pursue their own goals. When he was president (and chair) of the Treasury Board, Chrétien reports that he 'made it a point not to cut the arts or foreign aid. I knew that pleased Trudeau, and it also pleased me. At one point, Trudeau mentioned to me that the National Gallery wanted to buy a masterpiece by the great Italian painter, Lotto, and it needed a million dollars from the Treasury Board. I got the message and the National Gallery got the painting.'[113] One would assume that Chrétien, as prime minister, would expect no less from his Treasury Board president or other chairs of Cabinet committee.

I asked a former chair of Cabinet committee whether he shared briefing material from PCO with his Cabinet colleagues. The answer was no. I asked present and former PCO officials whether they would be willing to share their briefing material and advice with all Cabinet ministers, given the collective nature, or even the confederal nature of Cabinet decision making. They responded that though it is not done, they would have no objection to sharing 'some' briefing material. Some of the material and recommendations, they explain, are *only* for the prime minister, and cannot even be shared with the chairs of Cabinet committee. This material contains information on where certain ministers stand, where precisely are the points of disagreement between two or more ministers, where a consensus may lie, and recommendations to resolve the matter.[114]

A former chair of the Cabinet committee on economic development reports that neither PCO nor the prime minister would ever agree to share briefing material and recommendations. He explains, 'The question you are raising goes to the heart of the art of governing. Information is power and information shared is power lost. I knew all along that I only got from PCO part of the information and advice the prime minister was receiving. But there was no way I was going to share the bit I got with members of the committee.'[115] I also asked what kind of briefing material and advice he received from PCO. He reports, 'It was a brief summary of the issues and it usually led you to one possible decision, one possible consensus, not two.'[116]

The above begs the question of where ministers get the information and advice that enables them to participate fully in the Cabinet process. One former PCO official explains, 'Ministers can read the Cabinet document and look to their deputy ministers for advice.'[117] For their part, ministers report that they simply do not have the time, and some even the inclination, to read Cabinet documents. Indeed, the consultations suggest that only a handful of ministers, such as Pierre Trudeau, Otto Lang, Jean-Luc Pépin, Marc Lalonde, John Crosbie, Michael Wilson, and Paul Martin, were or are prepared to commit the time to read the documents.

This may explain in part why ministers who have served on the Treasury

Board and other Cabinet committees report that, looking back, they rate their Treasury Board experience better than that of other Cabinet committees. They point out that members of the Treasury Board have access to briefing material prepared by secretariat staff. The discussions at Treasury Board meetings are also somewhat more free-wheeling than in the other Cabinet committees in that ministers can engage Treasury Board staff in a discussion about any proposal under review.

Ministers also report that they feel much more in control at Treasury Board meetings than in other Cabinet committee meetings. To be sure, the fact that membership on the board is considerably smaller than is the case of other Cabinet committees (about one-third), is a factor. But ministers argue that the most important factor is that Treasury Board actually makes decisions about specific cases. 'Other Cabinet committees,' one former minister insists, 'are into long intellectual discussions about a number of subjects. They are never quite sure if a decision is being made or had been made. At Treasury Board meetings, things were to the point and decisions were made and we knew it.'[118]

Whose Government Is It?

In the introductory paragraphs to this chapter, I asked how do ministers make it 'their' government? In an earlier chapter, we noted that a prime minister will want to make the government 'his' or 'hers.' Can both simultaneously make it their government?

The prime minister has all the instruments to make the government 'his' or 'hers' while ministers have very limited capacity to do the same. The prime minister is the only minister with full knowledge of what goes on in the Cabinet decision-making process and who knows through briefings from PCO where ministers sit on a particular issue. It is he or she who appoints not only the ministers but also their deputy ministers, who controls the Cabinet, and whenever necessary, Cabinet committee agenda.

Decisions taken by Cabinet committee are submitted to Cabinet as an appendix item for ratification. But, again, prime ministers, from Trudeau to Mulroney and now Chrétien, do not react well when Cabinet committee decisions are challenged in Cabinet, and as we have already noted, it is very rarely done. But there is another perhaps more important problem with the Cabinet committee process. Ministers do not sit on all Cabinet committees. In the case of the Chrétien Cabinet, about half of the Cabinet sit on the Economic Union Committee and the other half on the Social Union Committee. Accordingly, half of the Cabinet has to accept what has been decided by a Cabinet committee of which they are not members and based on discussions in which they did not take part.

Moreover, ministers have very limited means of securing advice on matters discussed in the Cabinet decision-making process other than from their own departments. It is asking a great deal for, say, the minister of Heritage Canada to request briefing from her senior departmental official on a proposal put forward by the minister of Fisheries and Oceans. Briefing material from the centre, whether it is produced by PCO or the Department of Finance, is off limits to ministers. Ministers are, of course, free to read Cabinet documents, but we know that very few actually do. Even if they did, they would be reading a document prepared by a department pursuing a particular policy, program, or funding objective, hardly representing all viewpoints.

The machinery of government is such that ministers are still encouraged to fight for their corner. The view from the centre or from the top is limited to the prime minister, and to some extent to the Finance minister and the president of the Treasury Board. Cabinet committees exist more to take the pressure off the Cabinet than to promote a horizontal perspective for ministers. In any event, committees react to specific proposals that come to them from individual departments. They still do not, as a rule, request that department X come forward with one proposal and department Y with another. PCO manages the process on behalf of the prime minister, not the Cabinet, to ensure that interdepartmental conflicts do not get out of hand and to identify a consensus among competing ministers and departments.

The Trudeau Cabinet reforms, which have in essence lasted to this day, were designed to remove power from the hands of strong ministers and their mandarins and bring it to the centre to strengthen the hand of Cabinet ministers as a collectivity, but have fallen far short of the mark. In explaining the Trudeau reforms, Gordon Robertson wrote that 'ministers now, in many cases, have to give up some share of their authority and control to other ministers if the totality of policies is to be coordinated ... ministers have less chance to appear in roles of clear and firm decision.'[119] There is no doubt that beginning with Trudeau, and continuing to this day, strong ministers and their mandarins have lost power. But as this and previous chapters point out, the power has not shifted to Cabinet. Rather, the reforms have strengthened the hand of the prime minister and central agencies, notably PCO.

The focus group analogy which one Chrétien minister employed to describe Cabinet may not be too much of an overstatement. In fact, Chrétien himself wrote before he became prime minister that a minister 'may have great authority within his department, but within Cabinet he is merely part of a collectivity, just another adviser to the prime minister. He can be told what to do and on important matters his only choice is to do or resign.'[120] It is ironic to note that participants in focus group exercises are also 'just advisers.' This is not to suggest for a moment that ministers in Ottawa are without influence. Advisers to prime ministers can have a great deal of influence. In addition, ministers like Marc Lalonde, John Crosbie, and Paul Martin, among others, through their force of personality alone, can take charge of a government department and give it direction.

Chrétien is not the only one to argue that if ministers disagree with the prime minister they can always resign. It will be recalled that when I asked a former senior PCO official to explain how the prime minister could possibly be in a position to sign mandate letters to his ministers to outline priorities and what is expected of them before Cabinet has even met once, his response was, 'Ministers can always resign.' The fact is that very few ministers are prepared to put their jobs on the line because they are not happy with a government policy. It is simply too much to expect that at least a status, policy, or process participant will resign over a specific policy issue, and prime ministers and their senior advisers know this better than anyone else.

Sharon Sutherland looked at the causes of ministerial resignations from confederation to 1990. She reports that 'solidarity' problems caused only 19 per cent (or twenty-eight cases) of all resignations. By 'solidarity' problem she means ministers unable or unwilling to agree with Cabinet colleagues or 'with the Prime Minister in particular.'[121] In more recent years, she documents the resignations from the Diefenbaker government: Douglas Harkness, Pierre Sevigny, and George Hees (1963); Judy LaMarsh (1968); Eric Kierans (1971); Jean Marchand (1976); and James Richardson (1976). From the Mulroney government: Suzanne Blais-Grenier (1985 – here, however, former senior PMO officials report that she jumped just before she was going to be dropped from Cabinet); and Lucien Bouchard (1990). There have been no resignations for reasons of solidarity since Bouchard left. It is interesting to note that, in contrast, 41 per cent of ministers who left Cabinet did so to accept a political appointment offered by the prime minister.[122]

What this chapter suggests is that the idea of Cabinet as a collective, confederal-type decision-making body no longer applies. The notion was invented at the time the prime minister was *primus inter pares* and both concepts now belong only to our history books. Only the prime minister and, to a lesser degree, the minister of Finance, through the budget, can decide when and how to land on a policy issue or even on a new spending commitment. Other ministers must know either not to land or, if they strongly want to do so, they have to look to the prime minister, not Cabinet, for permission to land and guidance on when and how to go about it.

9

Departments: Running on the Track

On the face of it, central agencies should be no match for line departments, which, after all, are in daily contact with citizens and which ultimately manage government programs. They also employ a large number of policy specialists who have direct access to information from the front line employees who actually deliver the programs and services. Central agency officials, meanwhile, must cover the waterfront and, by definition, become policy generalists. They also often have to rely on the policy specialists in line departments for their information. In contrast, departmental policy workers can focus exclusively on their own sectors and become experts in their areas of responsibility.

Line department officials maintain, however, that things are not as simple as they may appear, although the centre, in particular the Treasury Board, has given them more authority to manage their own financial resources. But, they explain, one must recognize two distinct categories of activity in any effort to assess the balance of influence between central agencies and line departments. Line departments are on the whole left to their own devices when managing ongoing programs and maintaining the status quo. All in all, it is not too much of an exaggeration to suggest that, as far as central agencies are concerned, line departments are at their best when they are at rest. But the moment they want to introduce change or when the minister or the department become embroiled in any controversy, interdepartmental conflict, or disagreement – especially if the media gets wind of it – then we are looking at a very different picture. They add that since there is hardly an issue left which can any longer be neatly compartmentalized in a single government department, the centre can always find a reason to intervene should a department decide to introduce change or challenge the policies or activities of another department.

They also claim that relations between the centre and line departments have changed in more recent years. Jocelyne Bourgon, at the time deputy minister of

Transport, shortly before she became clerk of the Privy Council Office and secretary to the Cabinet, wrote in 1993 that it was time to 'rethink the relationships between the centre ... and departments.' She pointed out that the expression the 'centre' of government did not even exist as recently as ten years before. Rather, she claims 'we had a concept of central agencies with different mandates bringing different checks and balances to the decision-making process.'[1]

The purpose of this chapter is to look at the centre of government from the perspective of line departments. It seeks to answer a number of questions. How do departments regard the centre of government? How do they work with the centre? What forces are at play shaping relations between the two?

What Matters to Departments

The Canadian Centre for Management Development (CCMD) offers a variety of courses and management development seminars to federal government managers, and in some instances to aspiring managers. The centre decided in 1997 to retain a highly reputable American firm to carry out a survey of managers for the purpose of assessing the 'organization's culture, as seen by individuals and groups within it.'[2] By organization, CCMD meant the federal public service, not its own institution.

The survey reported on the 'major elements of the current Public Service culture as perceived by managers,' and revealed that they include 'obedience to chain of command, dedication and loyalty to the organization, reinforcement of authority, rules and regulations, restraining individual desires for organizational goods, self protection and self interest.'[3] My consultations confirmed the survey's findings, and indeed much of the literature on Canadian public administration has for quite some time focused on these very characteristics in defining the organizational culture of the federal public service.[4]

To be sure, deputy ministers attach a great deal of importance to protecting the interests of their department. In this respect, for example, the deputy minister of Finance was no different than, say, the deputy minister of Industry in the program review exercise in urging that his department be excluded from the proposed spending cuts. The fact that all departments suffered significant cuts made it easier for deputy ministers to explain to their departments that they had fought the good battle on behalf of the department before the committees of deputy ministers chaired by the clerk, and before the committee of ministers.

While one can speak of a public service culture in Ottawa, it also became clear in consultations with line department officials that there are some differences, even some sharp ones, in the way public servants regard their department and their role as one goes up the organizational chart or if one occupies a line versus a staff position. Discussions with present and former line deputy ministers pointed to different preoccupations, and to some extent to different values, than those expressed by public servants at the EX1 to EX3 levels, or at the director to the director general levels. As could be expected, assistant deputy ministers (i.e., EX4 and EX5 levels) did bridge the two groups and spoke to the preoccupations of both. Similarly, public servants in line positions viewed their work in a different light than those occupying staff positions.

I am not alone in sensing this division. The Task Force on Values and Ethics in the federal public service also reported that its 'dialogue with public servants revealed to us a certain divide between levels in the public service, perhaps especially where public service values are concerned. Many at the middle and lower levels of the public service to whom we spoke or from whom we heard do not feel connected to the senior levels, and they are not sure whether they necessarily share the same values as those at higher levels.'[5]

There are also important differences in how deputy and assistant deputy ministers and other managers view accountability. The more senior managers believe they are accountable to the prime minister, Cabinet, their ministers, and the Privy Council Office. As one goes down the hierarchy, however, this view is much less apparent. Program managers are more likely to look to the public, their 'clients,' and their immediate superiors for a sense of how well they are performing.[6]

Some observers, including the Task Force on Values and Ethics, speak about a fault line in the accountability structure.[7] Deputy ministers, it appears, are much more willing to accept the traditional view of accountability. That is, since the public service has no constitutional personality or authority in its own right, they are there to serve the government of the day and to support its members in performing all the functions for which they are liable to answer to Parliament.[8] The same is not true for program managers, who, as already noted, tend to look more to their 'clients.' When asked to explain why such a fault line exists, a senior government official pointed to the New Public Management, 'You tell them [the program and front line managers] that the way ahead is empowerment and to focus on clients, and you repeat that message over and over again, as we have during the past several years. You also explain that the inside of government operations is not very healthy. It is full of red tape, rules, and controls. Now we wonder why our people are looking mostly out to clients and less and less to within government.'[9]

The Treasury Board secretariat commissioned a study in 1997 to determine why managers were leaving the federal public service at a higher rate than in the past. The study 'clearly showed' that pay was not the main problem. Rather, 140 current and former managers consulted in a focus group explained that their work was being constantly 'distorted' for political reasons. The more senior officials (deputy ministers and assistant deputy ministers) stood accused of turning the public service into a 'ministerial service' and of being overly preoccupied with the political interests of the government, not in a partisan sense, but rather in making every effort to make the government look good.[10]

The study also reported that the concern was more 'acute' among managers in Ottawa, 'especially among those who have already quit.'[11] It adds that in the regions where many of the programs and service are actually delivered, managers were less concerned. It should be noted that though close to 70 per cent of all federal public servants work in regional offices, about 65 per cent of all executives or senior managers are located in the National Capital Region.

Deputy ministers now constitute a club in Ottawa circles and, to be sure, peer pressure matters. Deputy ministers do not wish to lose face before their peers, and this factor alone promotes close collaboration among club members. How does one lose credibility in the club? Certainly, all deputy ministers prefer walking into their breakfast or luncheon meetings knowing that their minister is in no political controversy or difficulties. All pride themselves on being able to keep their minister out of political trouble. This has become a key criteria within the club to measure success, as indeed it is to the centre of government. To be sure, deputy ministers cannot always deflect a potential crisis, but depending on the circumstances, the centre and members of the club may wonder if the deputy minister could have done so. On the other hand, when it is apparent that he has been able to keep his minister from embarrassment in the media or in question period, the club's praise is unstinting.

Deputy ministers operate under a different set of rules than do other senior public servants. Other public servants are appointed by the Public Service Commission, while deputy ministers are appointed, as we have seen, by the prime minister on the advice of the clerk of the Privy Council, and they can be removed by the prime minister at the stroke of the pen. Officials revealed in the consultations that both Prime Ministers Mulroney and Chrétien reminded them of these terms of their appointment from time to time, pointedly mentioning that deputy ministers work for the prime minister. I asked two current and two former senior officials from the Privy Council Office why it was that Jean Chrétien, as minister of Justice or of Finance, could not be fully trusted to appoint his own deputy minister but that Jean Chrétien as prime minister could be trusted to appoint all deputy ministers in the government. One said because 'he is the boss'; another said because 'he is the prime minister'; and, interestingly, two said because 'he is king.' One claimed that the monarch holds the right of appointment because he is 'king and not for any other reason.'[12] Yet another explained, 'You have to understand that the prime minister is the government.

Ministers and deputy ministers serve at pleasure, and if the prime minister falls, or leaves, the government falls and a new government takes over. That is why the prime minister can say to deputy ministers that they work for him.'[13]

Deputy ministers enjoy a number of administrative perks not available to other public servants. They have access to a chauffeured departmental automobile. They also enjoy a special pension plan which can pay up to 90 per cent of their salary based on their six best salary years; the plan is indexed and tied to the country's inflation rate. They have much larger offices than other public servants and a great deal more administrative support than do officials down the line.

The club now meets regularly over breakfast, luncheon, and at special retreats, all chaired by the head of the public service, the clerk of the Privy Council Office. It has its own rules – deputy ministers may have sharp differences with one another but there is an unwritten understanding that you do not voice that difference outside of the club or, in some instances, even inside. A recently retired deputy minister explains, 'The department produced a letter for me to sign to the deputy minister of Public Works, which was very testy, if not harsh. I turned it back. I simply could not send that kind of letter to my colleague, although my people had every reason to be upset at Public Works.'[14] As is the case for most other clubs, members are also expected to remain loyal to the club itself. Indeed, a deputy minister may not always support her minister in a disagreement with another minister or another department. They know full well that they will have to live with other members of the club for as long as they are deputy ministers, but that the minister's tenure in the department can be short-lived. In any event, the clerk will intervene if the differences between ministers or departments get too sharp, and deputy ministers will usually take the wise decision and walk to the beat of the clerk. As one deputy minister observed, 'You pay attention to your dealings with the clerk of the Privy Council unless you are about to retire or leave government for the private sector, and even then you should still pay attention.'[15]

Deputy ministers must look in several directions at once in their day-to-day work. They have to be flexible and to learn to deal with various forces. They must operate 'like a hinge between the political and bureaucratic world.'[16] Again, although they are appointed to the job by the prime minister, their main responsibility is to support their ministers.[17] The Privy Council Office has in more recent years provided in print the reasons why it is the prime minister, not ministers, who appoints deputy ministers. Quoting the Glassco commission, PCO maintains that the appointment of deputies by the prime minister provides 'a reminder to them [deputy ministers] of their need for a perspective encompassing the whole range of government' and 'emphasizes the collective interest of the Prime Minister in the effectiveness of management in the public service.'[18]

But what if a conflict should surface in the department between the minister and the deputy minister? On this issue, the Privy Council Office maintains that 'conflict between the deputy's loyalty to the minister and his or her responsibility to the prime minister will be symptomatic of a failure of the confederal principle [of Cabinet government]. If it occurs, the clear line of responsibility passing between the minister and the deputy minister may be destroyed and in the extreme will only be restored through the resignation of one or other, in which event who goes will depend on the particular circumstances.'[19]

But all this aside, the deputy minister 'is, in reality if not in principle, accountable to the Secretary to the Cabinet.'[20] The Privy Council Office makes it clear in its guide that if a disagreement between a minister and a deputy minister cannot be resolved between them and that 'it appears to affect the operations of the department, the deputy may wish to discuss the matter with the Secretary to the Cabinet. One of the accepted roles of the Secretary to the Cabinet has been to discuss with a deputy matters related to a department and the deputy's relationship with his minister, when the deputy is uncertain of the proper course of action. Similarly, a minister might prefer to discuss a concern with the Secretary to the Cabinet first before seeking the consideration of the Prime Minister.'[21] Thus, deputy ministers are expected to manage as best they can a kind of *ménage à trois*, which, if nothing else, explains the need for them to be flexible. This makes them as much a part of the centre as the administrative head of their departments.

But there is more. A deputy minister must also take account of the Treasury Board secretariat, the Public Service Commission, the commissioner of Official Languages, the Office of the Auditor General, and parliamentary committees, including the Public Accounts Committee, in her day-to-day work. All government managers, notwithstanding the rhetoric of the New Public Management and the repeated calls to let the manager manage, are still confronted by a myriad of complex procedures and regulations which make it extremely difficult for them to manage. Some insist that, by definition, the government cannot let managers manage, and that in the end only the process, not true management authority, can be delegated to managers. Accordingly, management accountability can only be based on how well the process is respected, rather than on results.

It is important to recognize that a good number of the procedures and regulations are beyond the immediate hand of the government to fix. The government can only change the mandate and the work of the Offices of the Commissioner of Official Languages and the Auditor General, the *Access to Information Act*, and the Public Service Commission[22] by going to Parliament with new legislation, and it is very likely that this could only be achieved at a political cost. In any event, those procedures and regulations also serve an important purpose for the prime minister. They protect ministers, especially those whose political judgment is suspect, from the media and question period in the House.

For deputy ministers, however, the various procedures and regulations hardly provide for quick, decisive, imaginative, or flexible management decisions. But quite apart from the restrictions of centrally prescribed procedures and regulations, deputy ministers must also always keep a watchful eye on the media, special interest groups, and provincial governments. Finally, they should be in constant contact with the department's client groups. In brief, anyone who wants a clear mandate should not accept an appointment as a federal deputy minister.

Though their mandate is not always clear, deputy ministers are very busy people. A detailed study of their workload published in 1997 reveals that on average they work eleven hours and twenty-eight minutes a day, or fifty-seven hours a week. The study also reveals that on average they spend one hour out of every three on interdepartmental issues. It is interesting to note that typically a deputy minister allocates nearly twice as much time to meetings with his peers than on matters involving his own minister.[23] With respect to issues, deputy ministers on average allocate more of their time to crisis management (16 per cent) than to human resources management (15 per cent). The study also reveals that the deputy minister is at the very centre of departmental activities and that he is always trying as best he can to accommodate 'the urgent,' the 'important,' and the 'unforeseen in his daily agenda.' 'Planning,' the author argues, 'is always left wanting.'[24]

It may well be that deputy ministers in Ottawa allocate more of their time to meetings with other deputy ministers and on interdepartmental issues because that is the way ministers prefer it. Indeed, a comparative study of the satisfaction of ministers towards their deputy ministers in Ottawa and Quebec reveal that federal ministers attach a great deal of importance, certainly a great deal more than their Quebec counterparts, on the ability of their deputies to influence the interdepartmental decision-making process.[25] My consultations with current and former federal Cabinet ministers also suggest that the 'ability to play the interdepartmental game,' as one former minister called it, ranks very high, if not at the very top of what ministers expect from their deputy ministers.[26] In fact, when discussing what they expect from their departments and deputy ministers, every minister consulted made at least one reference to their ability to influence the interdepartmental process, in particular PCO and the Department of Finance. Lewis Mackenzie insists that one's ability to work the Ottawa system has now become an important factor for promotion, even within the military. He writes, 'Regrettably, the mastery of the Ottawa games became one of the criteria, if not the key criterion, for selection as the Chief of Defence Staff. This reinforced the opinion of field soldiers that senior field command was not the route to follow if one aspired to be CDS – a most unfortunate and uniquely Canadian development.'[27]

To be able to work well with the centre of government and other departments, one must learn, as one deputy minister explained, 'to roll with the punches, learn to take things in stride, learn to be a bit detached and not too dogmatic about things.'[28] While carrying out an interview with a deputy minister for this book, we were interrupted by an urgent telephone call. By coincidence, the call came from someone in PCO. As he hung up the telephone, he turned to me and said, 'Boy, things can sure turn on a dime around here.' Without letting me in on the issue raised by PCO, he did observe that his understanding of the matter 'had been turned on its head.' But, he explained, one should 'not be surprised by this. That is the nature of our work. We walk on quicksand most of the time. No one is particularly at fault for this. This is just the way things work in government.'[29]

As federal deputy ministers juggle with forces from above, they must also manage departmental operations and activities from below. The Privy Council Office has produced a document designed to outline the 'duties and responsibilities of a deputy minister.'[30] They fall into three main categories: managing the internal operations of the department on behalf of the minister; supporting the collective management responsibilities of the government; and providing policy advice to the 'minister and the government.'[31]

Much of the responsibility for managing the internal operations of the department which can be delegated by government is delegated directly to the deputy minister, not to the minister. Each departmental act generally includes a standard declaration that the governor-in-council may appoint a deputy minister and explicitly delegate power to her for the independent exercise of her authority in specified areas, not just in management issues, but also, in some instances, in managing programs. This is particularly true in the case of departments that have regulatory functions in such areas as customs, excise, and immigration. But while the authority gives deputy ministers a certain independence from their ministers, it is never absolute. All deputy ministers, regardless of the departments, must abide by the requirements outlined in the *Financial Administration Act*, *Public Service Employment Act*, the *Official Languages Act*, and so on.[32]

Audrey Doerr, a former PCO official in the machinery of government directorate, writes that 'in many respects the changes and reforms of the Trudeau administration had the most dramatic impact at the departmental level efforts as top-down coordination activated a number of different developments and processes within departments. Departmental mandates were pushed outward as the range of activities increased. Lines of responsibility and hence accountability for senior officials often became blurred. From the perspective of the deputy minister, in particular, the job environment became both more complex and more constrained.'[33] A sure sign that departmental mandates were indeed pushed out in the Trudeau years was the phenomenal growth in the number of 'coordination,' 'liaison,' or 'integration' units in government departments. Comparing the government telephone directory from the early 1960s to the 1990s is revealing. In the early to mid-1960s, there were no units within departments called liaison and coordination and very few called policy. By the late 1960s and early 1970s, we saw the birth of coordination or liaison units whose very purpose was to monitor and participate in the interdepartmental consultation process. By 1987 the Department of Industry alone had twenty-five organizational units devoted to policy, liaison, coordination, or evaluation, or to a combination of them.[34] By 1996 and notwithstanding the program review exercise, the number stood at thirty-five. Nor does this figure include units containing the words planning or economic analysis, of which there are several. It should be noted, however, that because of the 1993 government reorganization, the Department of Industry in 1996 was a great deal larger, encompassing far more activities than was the case in 1987.

What do interdepartmental coordination and liaison units actually do? I put the question directly to many line department officials, but did not get a standard response. Such units, I was told, perform a variety of tasks. They seek information from other departments and central agencies which can be of interest to their own department and senior managers. They also represent the interest of their departments at interdepartmental meetings called either by a central agency or another department to review a proposal. At the risk of oversimplification, they can be said to perform a kind of lobbying function. People who work in these units readily admit, however, that they are rarely, if ever, present at meetings where policy issues actually get sorted out. That is left to others much higher in the organization. In any event, it is virtually impossible to hold coordination, liaison, or integration units accountable for their performance. How one could possibly determine, for example, if a coordination unit was successful in influencing another department or a central agency? Was it a specific meeting, a memo, a letter, or a development completely outside the department which shaped a particular interdepartmental position on a given issue? No one is in a position to know for certain.

Coordination and liaison units are now found not only in large departments like Industry or Human Resources Development, but in relatively small departments as well. Beyond the deputy and associate deputy ministers, the interdepartmental coordinating units, and policy shops, not many other officials look to other departments or to the interdepartmental consultation process in their day-to-day work, at least with much enthusiasm. Concerns over turf and the 'stovepipe' mentality are usually directed at other units, mostly those actually delivering programs and services.

The great majority of government employees down the line identify first and foremost with the interest of their department. Gordon Osbaldeston explains why, 'First, many of those who work in government organizations are first attracted to a particular department because it promises an opportunity to work in a field – regional development, the environment, health care – for which they have strong personal feelings and in which they have a special expertise. Their primary attraction is not to government per se, it is the policy field. Second, each organization's leaders will normally try to instil values and attitudes in their staff that are consistent with the mission of the organization. Consequently, even those who do not share these values and attitudes when they arrive may adopt them over time.'[35]

A government department, as J.E. Hodgetts explained, is an administrative body 'comprising one or more organizational components.'[36] Hodgetts sought to group departments based on general policy fields or functions carried out by the department. Bruce Doern, on the other hand, suggested that we should group departments by developing a system based on such things as the size of budgets, the responsibility for coordination, and the research capacity.[37]

Regardless of how we might group or classify them, most government departments are organized along the same lines. They are hierarchical, they have units responsible for policy, planning and coordination, others for specific functions in the areas of human and financial resources, and still others for actually delivering programs and services. In many instances, regional offices deliver the programs. This standard structure is found in both large and small departments.

J.R. Mallory maintains that government departments 'are carved out of no coherent principle of organization.'[38] Still, we do know that some are organized according to the classes of person to be served (e.g., Veterans Affairs), functions (e.g., Health), and regions (e.g., Western Development or the Atlantic Canada Opportunities Agency). Whatever the basis for organization, units and officials in the department are organized hierarchically with a 'clear chain of command running from the Minister through the deputy head to the lowest level of official.'[39]

The Department of Citizenship and Immigration is a case in point. Though all departments have their distinct organizational features, Citizenship and Immigration (see Chart 6 below) is somewhat typical of the departmental form

Chart 6
CIC Management Structure

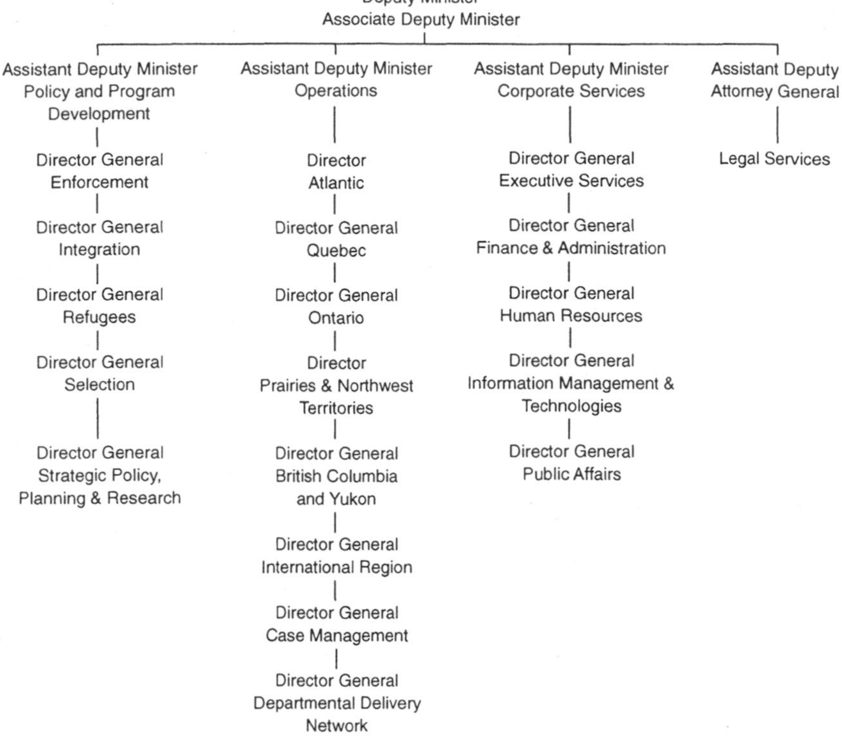

in the federal government, despite its being much smaller than perhaps Human Resources or Industry.

The Department of Citizenship and Immigration was significantly reorganized in October 1997. The purpose was not to change its responsibilities, to define new functions, or redefine its mandate – in any event, as we have seen, only the Privy Council Office can redefine a departmental mandate. Rather, its purpose was to regroup the existing responsibilities into new units, and its major objective, according to the deputy minister, was to promote 'horizontal integration in policy development and program management.'[40] The department has a deputy minister, an associate deputy minister, and four assistant deputy ministers, and the responsibilities are grouped under 'policy,' 'programs or operations,' and 'corporate services, including financial, administrative, and human resources.' All units report up the organizational chart through various management levels to the deputy minister.

The internal functions of government departments can be broadly defined as *line* and *staff*. Richard Van Loon and Michael S. Whittington summed up the difference between the two very well. They wrote, 'The goal of the Department of Revenue is tax collection. Those branches involved directly in collecting tax revenues are said to be performing line functions ... there are branches involved in matters such as personnel administration, finance and legal advice, none of which directly involves the performance of the line function. These branches are said to perform a staff function, and they exist to assist line managers in an advisory capacity or through the performance of a service.'[41] A good number of line managers continually question to what extent people who perform staff functions are being truly helpful to them. They also maintain that it is only what they themselves do that constitutes the department's true *raison d'être*.

In the consultations, I was not surprised to hear line managers, including some deputy ministers, insisting that there are still far too many people in government performing a staff function. They also argued that 'staff people' tend to complicate things unduly and slow down decision making. The charge is, of course, not new, and the New Public Management is designed, at least in part, to strengthen the position of line management.[42] As is well known, the public service culture and traditions have not favoured strong line management. As the preceding pages have made clear, the federal government has, over the years and for a variety of reasons, decided to fragmentize responsibility for various functions, including personnel, finances, and policy.

Managers in staff functions tend to look to the centre of government while line managers look mostly to their clients, their own operations, their own staff, and to line managers up the organization line to the deputy minister. There was a tendency among line managers consulted to lump many of the staff functions together with the work of central agencies and to make the case that the contribution of staff personnel did not compensate for their costs.

It is beyond the scope of this study to determine how many individuals in government occupy staff versus line jobs. In any event, a senior Treasury Board secretariat official suggested that a 'detailed and accurate count' may not be possible, even within government.[43]

Still, this much we know. In the late 1980s, a comprehensive review was carried out to identify all positions that were involved in providing services to the public. Some 221,434 positions were surveyed in an attempt to identify all jobs that had at least some responsibility to deal with the general public, even if that 'some' amounted to only 10 per cent of the total work. It found a total of 92,488 such positions.[44] I asked a Treasury Board secretariat official if, in his opinion,

I would be wrong if I were to write that well over half of EX positions (EX1 to EX5, or all managers below the deputy minister and the associate deputy minister level) were in staff positions. His response was, 'It is very difficult to always know when a position is truly staff or line, but I would say that you would not be wrong to say that over half of the EX positions are staff.'[45] In any event, we know that the great majority of EXs in the regions are line managers but that a high number of those in Ottawa occupy staff positions. Indeed, as already noted, about 65 per cent of all EXs are located in Ottawa. Though he did not provide a breakdown of staff versus line positions in his study of the structure of the Canadian government, J.R. Mallory did observe that 'only a small fraction of the total strength of the public service is directly engaged in carrying out administrative decisions. The rest of the public service is engaged in staff functions.'[46]

Some line managers believe that there are in reality two governments in one: they and their staff who actually deliver programs and services, and everybody else. They argue, for example, that the decision to establish new special operating agencies and other agencies such as the Food Inspection Agency was simply to give them more management autonomy. 'Someone in Ottawa,' one regional manager claimed, 'decided that there was something very wrong with how government was organized. We can no longer play at the margins, and new agencies were established to free line operations from a lot of the nonsense. We have known this for years.'[47]

The fact that the SOA concept has not been successful has more to do with the central agencies, the deputy ministers, and their staff people in line departments than the agencies themselves. There is evidence to suggest that, while central agencies have delegated some management authority to enable SOAs to operate more in the private business mode, line departments have not in turn done the same. In fact, line departments have simply retained in head office some of the management authority delegated by the Treasury Board secretariat. It is clear that, as a former secretary to the Treasury Board observed, 'Deputy ministers are concerned about accountability and what might be called the *balkanization* of a department.'[48] This, in turn, has led to tension between the agency head and the parent department, with agencies pushing for more authority while departments resist. Deputy ministers readily acknowledge that they have added a new set of rules and controls in the name of accountability. One deputy minister explains, 'I would like to delegate more authority, but I do not like bad surprises. After all, I am the one who has to live with the consequences.'[49]

I consulted line managers in regional offices in the departments of Human Resources, Corrections Canada, Indian and Northern Development, Fisheries and Oceans, Industry, and the Atlantic Canada Opportunities Agency, and I was struck by the similarities in how they regard the work of Ottawa-based staff people and central agencies. Much like ministers, line managers have also come to rely on staff people in the departments to get things done in the system. Indeed, knowing how the system operates and how to navigate in it has become a much valued competence even inside the federal public service. One line manager explains why, 'I simply do not have the time to deal with all the nonsense central agencies keep throwing at us. That is what our staff people in Ottawa are paid to do. When there is a problem with the Treasury Board secretariat, Finance, or PCO, they take over. I attend some of the meetings when I have to or when I am in Ottawa. Frankly, it is just another world. It is so far removed from what I do, it is unbelievable. Sometimes I think that they speak in tongues.' But, he adds, 'You need these people sometimes if you want to get things done.'[50] Another reported that he 'tries to avoid involving head office or central agencies' as much as possible. He explains that it is important in a line operation to 'keep your head down, keep things under control here, and don't involve Ottawa people unless you absolutely have to. They will leave you alone if you don't give them a reason to call you. My measure of success is how often that phone rings and someone in Ottawa is on the line. If it rings often, we are doing something wrong. If it doesn't ring, we are doing fine. From time to time, you get head office people introducing a new approach. You know they have to keep busy so that they come around with a new Treasury Board approach in this or that area. We just go along filling their forms while we deliver the programs.'[51]

For line managers, it appears that there is yet another club in Ottawa – staff people in line departments working with central agencies. This club also has its own rules. Integrity of the system and due process often matter more than the substance of what is being proposed. That is, what is done in one situation often dictates what ought to be done in another similar situation. If you delegate authority to one region, you do the same for another, whether or not circumstances differ. Put differently, if the head of human resources, finance, or even policy in department X decides on an issue in consultation with the Treasury Board secretariat, the Public Service Commission, or the Privy Council Office, then either that decision or a similar approach will be applied to other issues in other regions or elsewhere in the department. In brief, line managers insist that most staff people will try to apply the central agencies view to their problems or circumstances rather than try to adjust it to fit the program or front line perspective.

I asked respondents in senior staff positions in line departments whether line managers had painted an accurate picture of how things work in their departments. The majority of them thought not. 'It is much too simplistic,' an assistant deputy minister in a staff position argued, 'and it does not take into account the many occasions when we do everything we can to accommodate the special circumstances of our program people.'[52] She added, 'It may come as a surprise to some of them, but we also have many problems and disagreements with central agencies and what we often do here is fight on behalf of our program managers. We win some, we lose some. But on the whole, we are no more impressed with central agencies than they are, I can assure you of that. The fact is, that is the system and we all have to learn to live with it.'[53] Another assistant deputy minister (Policy) suggested that regional and front line officials often forget that they operate in a political context and 'what they do, especially if they go off on an tangent, can have important consequences for my deputy and my minister.'[54] Yet another pointed out that 'we would love to let our people go free and do their things. In most instances, it would make a great deal of sense from where they sit. It may not, however, make much sense from where our minister or deputy sit.'[55]

Essentially, staff people in Ottawa insist that their preoccupations have more to do with protecting their minister and deputy minister than with promoting central agency prescriptions in managing human or finance resources or even policy. We saw earlier that deputy ministers spend an average of 16 per cent of their time managing crises. The assistant deputy ministers (Policy) I consulted believed that 16 per cent appears low and that the figure probably does not include managing potential crises that never become full blown. One explained, 'A lot of what we do here is managing crises, putting out fires, or preventing fires.'[56]

Staff people also say that a crisis can surface from anywhere in the department, but that it is usually from the program side. Line officials deal directly with Canadians and citizens unhappy with the service can always appeal to their members of Parliament. In any event, programs are in the public eye, and there is a greater potential for problems in this area to become visible than is the case for staff people working on a position paper. Closing down an office in the regions, for example, is much more difficult than closing one in Ottawa. Not only can Ottawa more easily absorb the closing down of one government unit, but closing an office in the region also usually means that the level of services to people in that community will be affected. In any event, closing a government office in, say, Corner Brook, will be widely reported in the local and provincial media while shutting down a staff unit in Ottawa will hardly be mentioned, if at all.

A crisis can take various forms, and it is hardly possible for a deputy minister to predict where the next one will come from. Examples will make this clearer. On 11 February 1998, officials at Heritage Canada knew that they would be in for a rough day when they read a front page article in the *Globe and Mail* titled 'Ottawa flunks own quiz history.' The opening paragraph began, 'They're singing "Don't Know Much About History" at the Department of Citizenship and Immigration and Canadian Heritage.' A glossy brochure distributed to Canadian schools stated that 'The Act of Union' rather than the 'British North America Act,' had created Confederation in 1867. An official with Heritage Canada explained to the media that it was too late to correct the 90,000 copies of the brochures, but that the Web site was being corrected.[57] One can hardly describe this error as a major policy issue, but it made the front page of the *Globe and Mail* and left senior officials from two departments and officials in the Communications directorate at the Privy Council Office scrambling to manage the political fallout.

The deputy minister of Fisheries and Oceans also knew that he would be walking in a minefield all day when on 5 March 1998 he read on the front page of the *Globe and Mail* that the House of Commons' fisheries committee reported that it wanted 'bureaucrats removed' because of the collapse of the ground fishery in Atlantic Canada.[58] The deputy minister of Defence no doubt had the same feeling when he read, a few weeks earlier, that an opposition MP had scored political points in question period by suggesting that the government was putting military personnel at risk by not providing inoculations before sending them to serve in the Middle East. The troops were being sent to the region in support of possible military intervention against Iraq, given Saddam Hussein's unwillingness to let UN inspectors visit sites where it was believed that Iraq was producing and storing chemical and biological weapons. This story also made the front page of the *Globe and Mail*.[59]

The three incidents described above all happened in a three-week period. The list goes on, and hardly a week goes by without the national media reporting on a screw-up somewhere in a government department. Rarely, if ever, is it in a central agency, not least because they do not deliver programs. Again, even within departments, screw-ups are more often than not found in line operations than on the staff side. It goes without saying that there is less interest in a position paper being prepared by policy specialists at Corrections Canada than in someone with a dangerous criminal record escaping from a correction facility. But even policy papers can prove to be an embarrassment if they make controversial statements that are leaked to the media.

No deputy minister looks forward to the day when the auditor general tables his annual report. It always commands media attention, highlighting, as it does, administrative breakdowns, program overspending, the construction of a road to nowhere, or irregularities in the expense accounts of senior officials.[60] Again, the auditor general's report focuses on programs, government operations, and line managers rather than on the work of people occupying staff positions.

The *Access to Information* legislation has also generated a demand for good political firefighters in Ottawa and has made policy people cautious. Giles Gherson, former policy adviser in the Human Resources Development, explains, 'To address the access to information issue ... I saw it myself that officials are extremely leery of putting things on paper that they wouldn't like to see made public or find its way to the media, several months later, that could be embarrassing to the minister.'[61] Conrad Winn, a pollster, argues that access to information has seriously inhibited the ability of government departments to ask the right question when commissioning a survey. He explains, 'The bottom line for the average public servant is don't embarrass the minister, that is the surest way to have your career stopped or slowed down. If you have polls that ask all kinds of questions that would reveal the truthful complexity of what people think ... then [the polls] will inevitably show the public doesn't like something the government does.'[62] Hugh Winsor, a *Globe and Mail* journalist, readily admits that the media often takes advantage of access to information to get at a story. But, he argues, it does that 'not so much to find out what the people dislike about the government ... but to try to get an advance look at what the government's agenda might be ... [and get an early look] at the next budget or the next Speech from the Throne by making an access to information request about a public opinion survey which is being commissioned.'[63]

For their part, government officials in both central agencies and line departments report that Access to Information legislation has made them reluctant to commit their views and their recommendations to paper. The fear is that these could well appear in the media and force them to either support or defend them in public. This, in turn, flies in the face of public service traditions in Ottawa. The point, as Herman Finer explained in his classic essay, is that the views and advice of civil servants are to be private and their actions anonymous, so that 'only the Minister has views and takes actions. If this convention is not obeyed, then civil servants may be publicly attacked by one party and praised by another and that must lead to a weakening of the principle of impartiality.'[64]

Senior staff officials in Ottawa in the areas of policy, personnel, and finance may not view themselves in the same light as line managers do, but they admit that there is a kind of club with its own code of behaviour and even its own language which differs from that found in line operations. In government, they argue, 'you stand where you sit,' and if you sit in a senior staff position, your concerns will be different than if you manage a program in a region. You monitor new developments closely, not only in terms of your department's clients, but also at the centre of government, at the political level, and in the media. It is very much in your interest to have close ties with officials in central agencies, if only because if there is a crisis to manage, they will be involved, whether you desire it or not. One assistant deputy minister policy in a line department summed up well the view of many officials I consulted in line departments. 'There are occasions when things get off the rail and you are forced to operate in a crisis atmosphere. Central agencies, particularly PCO, can be with you or against you in getting things back on track. It is much better if they are with you.'[65]

Though senior staff officials in line departments will want close working relations with their counterparts in central agencies, this is not to suggest that they will always applaud the work of central agencies. By and large, they do not. Indeed, the great majority of them made the point that officials in their regional offices do not appreciate the extent to which they, too, have some difficulties with the work of central agencies.

The View from Departments

In many instances, when meeting with line department officials I began the interviews with the question, 'How do you regard the work of central agencies?' On several occasions, respondents started their reply with the comment, 'Central agencies are a necessary evil,' which made me think that there is a kind of *mot d'ordre* among line departments when discussing the work of central agencies. In any event, I heard very little praise of the work of central agencies without important reservations.

But there were exceptions. Every deputy minister I consulted observed, at least once in the interview, that the clerk of the Privy Council has a very difficult job and that it is much easier to criticize the incumbent than point to success stories. One deputy minister said, 'What people outside government and even a number of public servants often fail to appreciate is that it is not easy to work for the prime minister. This is as true in the case of Chrétien as it was for Mulroney. The clerk can be blamed for things that are simply not her doing. She does not control the agenda. The prime minister does.'[66]

A number of line department officials from director to assistant deputy minister levels also argued that central agencies, like line departments, have to operate in a highly charged political environment. Priorities can change very quickly, they report, and central agencies have to respond. They expressed some understanding, if not sympathy, for those in central agencies trying to make sense of continually changing political priorities. Lastly, I could easily tell in the interviews if a line department official had central agency experience. Those who did were not as critical of the agencies' work as those who had never worked in a central agency.

However, the criticism, even from those with central agency experience, far outweighed positive comments. The criticism was varied, but there was an underlying theme: central agencies are still far too preoccupied with individual 'transactions,' with day-to-day issues, with interdepartmental disagreements, and with 'micromanaging' specific files whenever a crisis flares up.[67]

But here again there were exceptions. Senior line department officials report that the presence of an intergovernmental affairs group in the day-to-day work is never steady. At times, it can be heavily involved in transactions or specific files, as it was in the months leading up to the Charlottetown Accord; at other times, one would hardly know that it exists. At the time of my consultations for this study, the latter situation prevailed. One deputy minister observed that it 'is not visible on my radar screen. I have no idea what they are up to.'[68] Another made a similar observation, but said that it was 'unfortunate.' He added, 'We need somebody at the centre to paint a broad picture of federal-provincial relations and draw out some implications for us. I can tell you that provincial governments do it.'[69]

Some line department officials also report that there is strong evidence that the Treasury Board secretariat is changing its role away from transactions, and that there is some confusion about the board's future role. They sense a great deal of tension even within the secretariat itself between those who would like to turn back the clock and those, including senior management, who would like to shift even further away from transactions and towards a business planning approach. There are also a number of line department officials who believe that it is still too early to say that the new approach will stick. One senior departmental official observed, 'Come back to see me in five years to see if there have been real changes. I have been in this business a long time, and when someone tells me that he has introduced change, I tell him – right, wait five years to see if any of it has survived.'[70]

To be sure, the Treasury Board has changed some of its ways, and one only has to consult the appendix at the end of this chapter to see that important changes have already been introduced and implemented. From the perspective of line departments, some changes have already survived, and there is no need to wait five years to see their impact. The Treasury Board Circular 1995–3 outlines a series of specific initiatives designed to reduce the number of transactions between the board and line departments. However, when reforming the mandate of the Treasury Board secretariat, it is much easier to detail what the board should stop doing than to define and agree on what it should continue or start to do. Line departments approve of the board's many decisions designed to reduce transactions, but for the most part they are holding back judgment on the board's new role.

In discussing the emerging role of the Treasury Board secretariat with line department officials, one very quickly understands why Treasury officials would like, as we reported in chapter 7, to make the transition from 'business plans to business planning.' Departments regard the preparation of business plans as just more 'bureaucracy' under a different name, and 'much of it is paperwork and process like it was the case in previous approaches.'[71] Indeed, business plans are viewed more as hurdles to be jumped over than as strategic documents designed to help plan or even to assist central agencies in gaining a better understanding of what departments do and what their major challenges are. The preparation of business plans is delegated down the line, and senior officials allocate no more of their time to their preparation and review than they did for documents required under past approaches.

The most frequently heard criticism of central agencies from line departments is that they do not do what they ought to be doing, and they do things that they ought not be doing. The role of the centre of government, it is argued, should be to help ministers manage the government-wide policy-making process and resource allocation systems, to set standards, and to hold line departments accountable for their decisions and activities. They should paint the 'broad picture' and 'bring coherence to what departments do' by 'defining a strategy for the government.'[72] Accordingly, many line department officials argue that central agencies should be small, outward-looking, and more strategic than they have been in the past and are at the moment. Instead, they insist, central agencies tend to look inside the government, and more specifically to line departments, and to focus on specific issues, in an attempt to manage conflicts between departments that may otherwise turn into political crises played out in the media.

Central agencies, despite the rise of cross-cutting problems and issues, remain too oriented towards the activities of line departments, to the detriment of issues that require broader attention. All in all, their role has changed very little during the past thirty years. The 'goalkeeper' analogy used to explain their work still applies. Pierre Gravelle, a deputy minister from the late 1980s up to the mid-1990s, and a former associate secretary to the Treasury Board, wrote that 'it is after all the task of central agency officials to ensure that ministers are not caught by surprise with a new policy or a new initiative ... [it explains why] central agency officials are great goalkeepers, that is, they are excellent at stopping things, but are rarely themselves capable of successfully launching new initiatives.'[73]

Line department officials believe that central agencies are at their best when they sit in judgment of what line departments do or propose. Their track record, meanwhile, is not impressive when they take the lead on a major initiative. Line officials offer the examples of PS 2000 and *La Relève* as cases in point. Both were conceived at the centre and neither can be described as a success. Paul

Tellier, former clerk of the Privy Council and architect of PS 2000, wrote, as we have seen, about the shortcomings of PS 2000. But he has not been alone.[74]

La Relève has also come under strong criticism, not least from line departments, whose officials point to 'turf wars' between the Treasury Board secretariat and the Public Service Commission, wars that have been as intense as any between two line departments. In addition, human resources officials in line departments argue that the selection process in *La Relève* had serious shortcomings. For one thing, it had no game plan in place to deal with those who did not qualify, which made an already serious morale problem in the public service even worse. For another, they report, one of the questions asked of those applying for a promotion under the initiative was to describe their 'track record,' something no large private firm would ever ask of its executives in a competition. 'Track records,' it was argued, 'would be obvious to everyone in the firm.'[75]

Line departments are also critical of the centre for its role in the program review. They claim that the centre simply sat in judgment of what they were proposing to cut and that it offered very little in the way of ideas on where cuts should be made. Worse still, the centre, as we have already seen, failed very badly in defining, let alone promoting, a horizontal or multidepartment perspective to the exercise. That, line officials argue, is precisely what the centre ought to have done because it could only be done by the centre. Moreover, line departments accuse the centre of not even getting its act together over fairly straightforward issues, recalling the sharp disagreement between the Finance department and the Treasury Board secretariat over the exact budget figures for departments, expenditure budgets for ongoing programs. That dispute almost compromised the program review exercise.

Departments insist that these shortcomings at the centre are not due to a lack of staff. The centre employs more EXs (from director, director general, assistant deputy minister level) than several line departments combined. Indeed, there are more EXs in the four central agencies (278) than there are in the departments of Justice, Defence, Agriculture and Agri-Food, Citizenship and Immigration, and Western Economic Diversification (252).[76] As well, some of the assistant deputy minister positions in the Privy Council Office are classified at the deputy minister 1 level and so are not counted as EXs. The highest classification of the EX group is EX5, and there are thirteen positions classified at this level in the four central agencies. The departments of Agriculture and Agri-Food, Communications, Environment, Natural Resources, Solicitor General, Public Works and Government Services, and Fisheries and Oceans combined only have twelve EX5 positions. It is also important to bear in mind that the above line departments deliver programs and services directly to Canadians while central agencies do not. They also have regional operations (with the exception of the Public Service Commission, which has some small regional offices), while central agencies do not.

More importantly, the centre of government was left virtually intact in the massive 1993 government restructuring. Yet the number of departments was reduced from thirty-two to twenty-three. The number of line deputy ministers was also cut from thirty-two to twenty-three and, the number of assistant deputy ministers in line departments was cut from 319 to 266.[77] There were no comparable cuts at the centre.

Assistant deputy ministers in line departments report that the restructuring has had a profound impact on their work and on the work of line departments. One observed, 'I am now occupying a position whose responsibilities were handled by 2.5 assistant deputy ministers before the restructuring. I now only have time to move things along. I certainly don't have time to sit back and think about the more important issues. In fact, I came in over Christmas holidays, knowing that it would be quiet around here and I would have time to think.'[78] It also means that staff assistant deputy ministers cannot encourage strong communication with interest or client groups. In fact, a typical government department must now deal with several interest or client groups. The old Department of Secretary of State, for example, had only a handful of client groups. Heritage Canada, its successor since the restructuring, must deal with three- or fourfold the earlier number. Thus, not only do line deputy and assistant deputy ministers have less time to spend with client and interest groups, there are now more groups with whom they should be meeting. At the same time, the centre of government has not shrunk nearly as much, given the establishment and expansion of the intergovernmental group in PCO. And, by all accounts, demands on line departments to feed it information have not lessened.

Departments always have to be ready to respond to requests from the centre for briefing material for the prime minister. But that is as it has always been. What is different is the information required by the Treasury Board secretariat for departmental business plans. The plans cover not only financial and human resources, but also outline how departments intend to strengthen their ability to deliver services in both official languages, to promote employment equity, and to deliver initiatives for minority language groups. The list goes on.

More importantly, however, there has been an explosive growth in the evaluation industry in Ottawa, fuelled in large part by the Office of the Auditor General and the Treasury Board secretariat. Program evaluation, as we have already seen, came into fashion in Ottawa in the 1970s. To this day, its record has been dismal. Indeed, a recent review of the government's evaluation efforts reports that in 1992–3, $28.5 million was spent on program evaluations carried out by both departmental staff and external consultants. Out of 168 evaluations, only

1 per cent resulted in program termination, 9 per cent in reform, and 20 per cent in modification.[79]

Departments have simply learned to cope with program evaluations and a stream of outside consultants, appreciating that one does not bite the hand that feeds one without consequences. Not a single deputy minister I consulted believed that program evaluation is of much assistance to them. Departments still regard evaluation more as a kind of 'gotcha' tool for the benefit of the auditor general and, albeit to a lesser extent, the Treasury Board secretariat, than as a management tool for departmental managers. The auditor general himself acknowledged this when he wrote in his annual report that 'it is too often as though departmental managers are saying – if central agencies want us to provide financial and program information and measurements of our efficiency and effectiveness, we will of course provide them. But we don't see that information as being at all relevant to the day-to-day job we are being asked to do. So, providing it is a tiresome task that we will perform in a desultory manner.'[80] In short, many government managers regard program evaluation as a means to generate information for someone outside the department to come back and point out where they have failed.

Departments must also deal with a number of other oversight bodies. The commissioner of official languages, for example, annually passes judgment on how well departments are doing. The Treasury Board secretariat plays the lead role at the centre on official languages matters and constantly monitors the performance of departments. A line deputy gave me a copy of a letter the secretary to the Treasury Board had recently circulated to all departments. The letter is accessible under Access to Information, and the deputy minister assured me that I could quote from it. It is worth quoting at some length:

> ... the preliminary conclusions of a survey of points of service by the Commissioner of Official Languages, and observations by the Treasury Board Secretariat, cast doubt on the data provided by federal institutions. This issue has already been discussed at the Deputy Ministers' breakfast on December 10, 1997. These contradictory results suggest that not all federal institutions are monitoring compliance with the official languages requirements with equal effectiveness. Under these circumstances, I am sure you will appreciate the potential for embarrassment of the government. Therefore, I would ask you to undertake a rigorous and ongoing review of all your designated offices and points of service so as to establish the availability and quality of services in both official languages. I would also request that you make all your managers responsible for those offices aware of the official languages obligations. In your future annual reports on official languages, I would be obliged if you would include the results of your monitoring and awareness-raising activities as well as an action plan to correct the situation in those

locations where problems have not yet been resolved ... I also want to inform you that the Treasury Board Secretariat will be visiting a number of offices to confirm the availability of services in both official languages.[81]

A good number of line department officials I consulted, spoke about a double standard, one for themselves and another for the centre. One official explained, 'I admit that market forces do not discipline line departments, or provide a check on our power or size. Central agencies do. But who checks the power and size of central agencies? As far as I can see, no one.'[82] He has a point, as we saw in the 1993 restructuring exercise. But there are many other examples.

In the early 1990s, the government announced that all government departments were to de-layer their management levels so that there would only be four levels of manager between the working level and the deputy minister. The Department of Finance has long had several levels, ranging from the deputy minister to associate deputy minister, senior assistant deputy minister, assistant deputy minister, general director, director, and managers. To de-layer, Finance simply declared that, henceforth, three of the levels would be considered staff positions and would no longer constitute management levels.[83] Everybody stayed in their positions doing precisely the same things as before. Line departments, meanwhile, had to play by a different set of rules and actually de-layer management levels to the desired objective.

Deputy secretaries in the Privy Council Office are now classified at the deputy minister (1) level. They are virtually the only assistant deputy minister level officials who enjoy this classification. When I asked why this was so, I was told that it resulted from 'classification creep'; that is, from positions in the Privy Council Office being 'slowly but surely reclassified up.'[84] When asked why this was allowed in PCO, but not in line departments, I was told, 'It also happens in line departments, though not as badly. I suppose that it is a lot easier for the secretary of the Treasury Board to say no to a deputy minister than to the clerk of the Privy Council.'[85]

One can easily make the case that central agencies operate in a similar fashion to the prime minister and the minister of Finance. They, too, operate from a different set of rules when they wish to get things through the decision-making process (see, for example, the Canada Millennium Scholarship Foundation fund and the Foundation for Innovation).

A former deputy minister maintains that a significant part of the problem in government now is that 'the centre of government is both too big and employs too many bright young people.' He explains, 'I could have worked a lot better with the centre had it employed incompetent people. But it does not. It employs bright, young, highly educated and ambitious people. That is the problem. They want to be seen to make a difference. How do they do that? By getting in the way, by finding problems with what departments do or propose to do. It is much easier for them to find problems with what we do than come up with new solutions.'[86]

Another recently retired line deputy minister spoke about the size of central agencies as a key part of the problem. He commented, 'You are doing research on central agencies. Why don't you do this? Senior central agency people take great pride in saying that the size of the public service is back to what it was in the late 1960s. Why don't you compare the current size of the central agencies to what they were then?'[87] The size of the federal government is actually smaller than it was in the late 1960s, given that several major crown corporations like Air Canada and Canadian National Railways have been privatized. Still, it is indeed revealing to compare the size of central agencies over several dates. In 1997 the Privy Council Office employed 662 people; the Department of Finance, 584; the Treasury Board secretariat, 837; the Public Service Commission, yet another 1,344. In 1993 (the year the government announced its restructuring plans and before program review), the Privy Council Office and Federal-Provincial Relations Office employed 446 people; Finance, 729; the Public Service Commission, 2,226; the Treasury Board secretariat, 979; in all, a total of 4,380 people.[88] In 1969 the Privy Council Office employed 209 people; Finance, 372; the Treasury Board secretariat, 414; and the Public Service Commission, 1,048.[89]

Certainly, from the perspective of line departments, the centre's workload has decreased substantially in recent years. Line officials also insist that if the shoe were on the other foot the centre would have imposed cuts in their budgets. In any event, departments point out that PCO has far fewer Cabinet committees to service than was the case in the 1970s and 1980s. The number, as we have seen, is down to five from a high of fifteen. We saw in an earlier chapter that the number of Treasury Board submissions had dropped from 6,000 in 1983 to 1,284 in 1996. In addition, partly because the government had essentially shut down the spending tap until recently, the Cabinet system is much less busy today than was the case in 1983, as Table 4 below shows.

Still other line department officials argue that the problem is not just size. They point out that the centre controls 'all the levers' to change things and that departments are at its mercy with no right of appeal. One official, until recently a director general official in the Department of Industry, argues that central agencies

> hold all the cards to control the agenda and what departments do. They hold the key on who gets to the top. They also control very tightly the decision-making process. Here is how. In the late 1980s, my associate deputy minister asked that I accompany her to a Cabinet committee meeting. We had an important proposal before the committee and

TABLE 4
Annual Throughput of the Cabinet System (Approximate)

	1983	1996
Meetings of Cabinet and of committees	300	107
Memoranda to cabinet examined	900	176
Records of decision produced	750	216
Orders-in-council passed	4,000	2,087

Source: Privy Council Office, November 1997

she asked that I attend to take notes on the discussion. After about ten minutes, a senior PCO official came over and asked what I was doing. I said 'taking notes.' He said that I was not allowed and that only he could take detailed notes of the discussions. I looked over to my associate deputy minister and she just rolled her eyes. I left the meeting. The point here is that only the Record of Decision of Cabinet matters. What is said in Cabinet committees is just talk, and only PCO officials can have a formal and, for that matter, practical say about what has been discussed and decided.[90]

But the ability of the centre to control the Cabinet agenda, to decide who becomes a deputy minister or a high flyer, and the size of central agencies still only tell part of the story. There have been some important changes to line departments that have served to weaken them in relation to the centre.

The changes are most visible at the deputy minister level. A detailed study, 'Changing Profile of Federal Deputy Ministers, 1867 to 1988,' is very revealing. It reports that deputy ministers' prior experiences in the department of appointment has declined to three years from twelve years in the early period of confederation. In addition, deputy ministers now spend about four years at that rank and on average change departments once during that period. Unlike their predecessors, deputy ministers no longer stay with and retire in their department, and as one study of the profile of modern day deputy ministers argues, 'They can no longer head the same department for many years.'[91] When compared with other national public services, it is clear that federal deputy ministers have less seniority in government on average than, say, British permanent secretaries. Moreover, in Ottawa, recruitment of deputy ministers easily crosses the boundaries between departments, while countries such as France and Germany have remained loyal to the tradition that the permanent head of the department is chosen from its senior ranks.[92]

Former federal public servants, the only ones allowed to speak out on this issue, are now arguing that the government would be better served if the appointment of deputy minister took more into account the 'knowledge of the business.'[93] Gordon Osbaldeston maintains that knowledge of the department should be an important criteria in the selection process and explains, 'under such a policy, every effort would be made to appoint qualified Deputy Ministers to a department where they had previous administrative experience.'[94]

Frank Swift, a former senior federal public servant, carried out a study of the background and work experience of deputy ministers. His conclusion reveals that 'experience in a central agency, most notably in the Privy Council Office, is now a virtual prerequisite for deputy-level appointment. Almost two out of three deputies have no previous experience in program management in a line department. Although there is evidence that more deputies have management experience outside of central agencies, this increase is more typically in policy and process management positions. Previous experience in the department is not usual for deputy appointees. It has been considered less important in line departments delivering services to the public and more important in central agencies providing policy advice. Most deputies have no federal public service experience in Canada outside the National Capital Region.'[95]

The above is not without implications for the government and the public service. The 'Have-Policy' and the 'Have-Central-Agency-Experience' will-travel types have a different perspective than someone who has come up through the ranks of the department to become its deputy minister. For one thing, the former will be preoccupied with 'managing up' – that is, looking up to their ministers and to the centre of government rather than down the organization to establish priorities and a sense of direction. A federal task force recently argued that 'many senior public servants have made their careers because of their skills in managing up. They have been valued and promoted because they were adept at providing superiors with what they needed ... But if they [i.e., skills of managing up] are nourished in excess, to the exclusion of other important values, they can obscure the importance of managing down.'[96]

A well-honed capacity to manage up is much valued at the centre of government, particularly in the Privy Council Office. The office, as we have already seen, has a unique relationship with the prime minister. The office has several roles that it plays on behalf of the prime minister, and an important one, particularly since Trudeau came to power, is to operate an early warning system to alert the prime minister and his staff of any political danger ahead. The system is designed to highlight departmental issues which are or may become politically 'sensitive or controversial because of their political ramifications.'[97] A deputy minister known for his ability to manage up will know not only when to alert the centre, but also how to work with it to bring any potentially controversial issue back on track.[98]

Those who have limited capacity to manage up do not usually survive. If they do survive, it will be only in the department from which they were appointed, and PCO will invariably appoint an associate deputy minister with a strong central agency background to provide a helping hand. A case in point is Art May, appointed deputy minister of Fisheries and Oceans in 1982. Mr May had come up through the ranks of the department, where he had gained the respect of his colleagues as someone who knew the fishery sector well. But the sector went through a painful adjustment in the early 1980s – one of several it has gone through in recent years, given that there are always too many fishers and not enough fish. The situation gained a great deal of visibility in the media in the early 1980s, and PCO became convinced that the department was stumbling from one political crisis into another. The centre appointed an associate deputy minister who had a great deal of central agency experience to assist May. Art May was later transferred to head the Natural Sciences and Engineering Research Council and was thus moved outside the deputy minister club.

It is interesting to note, however, that Art May had a very strong relationship with the full confidence of his then minister, Roméo Leblanc.[99] But that would not come as a surprise to those familiar with federal government operations in the 1960s. In the pre-Trudeau days, this situation was common, in part because ministers and their deputies spent a great deal more time together every week than has since become the case, but also because deputy ministers then looked more to their ministers and less to the centre of the government in their work. Jake Warren, appointed deputy minister in 1964, explains that back in those days 'you were allowed to feel that you had the confidence of the minister.'[100]

Ministers have come to appreciate the advantages of having some of their senior officials possess an intimate knowledge of how the system works and an ability to pilot department initiatives through the approval process. The system has become so complicated and the centre so omnipresent that having such a capacity in their departments is important for both the minister and the department to get things done.

But ministers, if they could, would happily turn back the clock to the days of Jake Warren and to the time when senior departmental officials had an intimate knowledge of their sectors and the policies and programs of their departments. Roméo LeBlanc, reflecting on his days as minister of Fisheries and Oceans, observed, 'I shared with many Ministers a somewhat jaundiced view of the idea that you can be a good ADM in anything, the moment you're transferred there by the system ... I still think that being able to talk with fishermen on the wharf or with farmers in their barns is important ... It is essential to have direct experience.'[101]

I was told during the course of my research for this book by both present and former senior public servants that Mitchell Sharp had said that he had had more influence as deputy minister in the St Laurent government than as minister in the Trudeau government. In an interview with Mr Sharp, I asked him whether this was in fact true. His response, 'I do not know if I actually said that, but I probably came very close. You see, back then [in the St Laurent and the Pearson governments], deputy ministers were clearly responsible for policy and for working with the minister to define policy in your area of responsibility. Your minister would of course challenge your ideas, but then he would agree on a position with you and take the ideas to Cabinet and have it out with his colleagues. Things did not work quite like that under Trudeau. It was different.'[102] He added that 'you have to understand that the art of governing was different then (i.e., pre-Trudeau days). Ministers had a strong base and had strong personalities. They would go to Cabinet and take on even the prime minister. Some ministers would threaten to resign over policy, and some actually did. So it was different then for a deputy minister working with a minister. I am not sure that we bothered too much with PCO. Putting aside Pickersgill, secretaries to the Cabinet were rather low-profile people and they didn't much bother you.'[103]

A retired deputy minister discussed the changes at the centre of government from the time he became a public servant in 1958 to when he retired in the early 1990s. Much like Mitchell Sharp, he reports that during the 1960s the clerk of the Privy Council and secretary of Cabinet did not dominate things in Ottawa until Michael Pitfield's appointment. When my respondent became deputy minister in the early 1970s, he claims that he 'would not have recognized one-third of my colleagues had I come across them on the street.' He adds, 'It was very rare that you had dealings with the clerk perhaps a couple of times a year. You had a job to do with your minister and you went and did it.' There was no such thing, for example, as a mandate letter from the clerk. But things began to change in the 1970s, particularly when the clerk started to chair monthly luncheon meetings with deputy ministers. Things changed again in 1985, when the clerk added weekly breakfast meetings and again later when deputy ministers' retreats were organized.[104]

Deputy ministers, in many ways, have thus become as much a part of the centre of government as they are the administrative heads of their departments. It should be expected that if they are selected for their knowledge of how the system works rather than for their sectoral expertise or their knowledge of a department and its policy history, then their value will be confined to an ability to manage the policy process and the system. However, the importance attached to their 'knowing their way around the system' to their ability to avoid 'surprises' and to manage real or potential political crises, have led some former and even present senior public servants to doubt whether senior officials can now 'speak truth to power.'[105] One former deputy minister, for example, wrote that 'the honest public servant is in danger of being superseded by the courtier.'[106]

Anxiety, Blame, and Risk Avoidance

Line department officials argue that if the federal government is to have a strategic vision, it can only be constructed at the centre of government. Similarly, if coherence and coordination are important concerns to the government, then the centre should be held responsible for their promotion and their success or failure. They argue, as this chapter makes clear, that the centre has failed on both fronts. In brief, they suggest that the centre may be able to corral bouncing ministers and their departments, but when it comes to taking the lead on a file, in establishing a strategic vision for the government, or even in providing a sense of coherence and coordination, it fails.[107]

Departments, meanwhile, are left to manage their programs and operations, all the while trying to keep their ministers out of trouble, coping with oversight bodies of one kind or another, and constantly feeding requests for information from the centre. The purpose of these oversight bodies, most notably the Office of the Auditor General, can hardly be described as being helpful to departments. Rather, their purpose is to find fault.

James Q. Wilson's observation on public service culture is as valid in Canada as it is in the United States. He writes, 'When a culture of forbearance and forgiveness descends on Washington, please alert the FBI at once, for it will be evidence that somebody had kidnapped or anaesthetized the entire legislative and judicial branches of government.'[108] If nothing else, this suggests that political institutions need to be reformed before politicians can truly set out to reform national civil services.

Line departments generally do not believe the centre of government, particularly the Treasury Board secretariat, when it argues that they are encouraged to take risks. One line official explains that 'risks are tolerated so long as nothing goes wrong. Should our minister be asked a question in the House, or should the media get on to something that has gone wrong, then all bets are off for getting any kind of support.'[109] On this point, the Treasury Board secretariat commissioned a study to understand why managers are leaving the federal public service. It reports that 'there's a new emphasis in the federal government to encourage risk-taking among its employees. But the reality remains that when mistakes are made the individual is hoisted up the flag pole.'[110]

A good number of line department officials singled out the Al-Mashat affair as an example of the hollowness of the talk of empowering autonomous risk-taking managers. Here, it was the Privy Council Office itself which hoisted a public servant up the flagpole. Sharon Sutherland makes the point that Raymond Chrétien – at the time associate deputy minister – was without minimal rights throughout the incident. She writes,

> It is interesting to reflect upon how the episode began for him. He was called to the Privy Council Office in the evening to meet with a senior PCO official with the responsibility for personnel management, Mr. Glen Shortliffe. In the presence of two other PCO officers [but no witness or counsel for Mr Chrétien], he was told to read a document which contained a report of an apology to Mr. Clark [Joe Clark, the then minister]. In Mr. Chrétien's case, the chain of command from Marchand [the deputy minister] to Chrétien was apparently disregarded, and here was the Privy Council Office doing what its code of behaviour says it never does: telling other officials what to do. Mr. Chrétien's words describe the impact on him: 'My reaction was one of astonishment. I could not believe what I was witnessing ... there I was ... presented with a chronology that I had never seen ... to have to react in a matter of 15 minutes or half an hour.' A common sense view might suggest that an apology from Mr. Chrétien would constitute an admission of professional negligence. Yet Mr. Shortliffe explicitly stated that he was personally 'very comfortable' in what amounts to imposing a statement on Mr. Chrétien: 'at one point in the exchange, as I recall it, I said to Mr. Chrétien, "Yes, you are being asked to apologize. The apology is being given to me. I will convey it, and you don't need to discuss it any further."'[111]

Such incidents do not occur daily. But for many officials in line departments, the Al-Mashat case was a defining moment. Though the incident took place in 1991, public servants still raised it in my consultations in 1997 and 1998. It demonstrated that when a political crisis flares up in a department, it is the centre, in particular the Privy Council Office, which intervenes to bring things back on track. In most cases, the PCO is not as heavy handed as it was in the Al-Mashat instance. A simple phone call from the clerk to a deputy minister, a word from the clerk to the deputy minister club at the weekly breakfast meeting, or an appointment of an associate deputy minister with a strong central agency background to a problem-prone department will suffice.

Appendix

Appendix to Circular 1995–3, Treasury Board Secretariat, 13 July 1995

1. **Policy Amendments**
   The board approved the following nine policy amendments.

(i) It raised contracting thresholds in three departments, the Canadian International Development Agency (CIDA), National Film Board (NFB), and Revenue Canada, to signal that the government supports more open competition.

(a) CIDA: for competitive aid contracts: 'entry into' from $4 million to $10 million, and 'amendments to' from $2 million to $5 million.

(b) NFB: for contracts for producer services in making films from $100,000 for 'entry into' and $25,000 for 'amendments to' to $250,000 for 'entry into and amendments to' combined.

(c) Revenue Canada: for competitive contracts for printing using the Open Bidding Service for 'printing': 'entry into' from $400,000 to $1 million, and 'amendments to' from $200,000 to $500,000.

(ii) It increased departmental approval authorities for capital projects below an appropriate limit.

This removes the requirement for departments to seek Treasury Board authority, except when the board specifically requests them to do so, for capital projects below an appropriate limit. For departments with separate capital votes, this should generally be around $20 million or 10 percent of their capital budget, whichever is smaller. For departments that do not have separate capital votes, the threshold would be $3 million.

The board will examine authorities department by department at the first opportunity with a view to approving a long-term capital plan or reviewing a business plan.

To give the Treasury Board the opportunity to request submissions below these levels, departments must briefly describe prospective capital projects costing above an appropriate floor [i.e., generally $2 to 5 million for departments with capital votes and $1 million for others] in an appendix to their business plans. Based on this information, the secretariat will recommend to the board which, if any, projects require a submission seeking preliminary, or some other form, of approval. The following criteria will have major influences on the secretariat's recommendations: whether a department has a sufficiently viable and accurate long-term capital plan; whether it has an appropriate internal approval process; and whether the project entails significant government-wide risks or touched on the interests of other departments.

If a department did not identify a prospective project in its business plan and the project cannot wait until the next plan, it must ask the secretariat to determine whether a submission is required.

(iii) It has delegated authority to the appropriate ministers to approve certain technical changes and exceptions to the terms and conditions governing grants, contributions, and other transfer payments.

(a) Authority to amend terms and conditions previously approved by the Treasury Board *except for*:
- the program objectives of the grant(s) or contribution(s);
- the identification of the recipient or definition of the class of eligible recipients;
- basic financial parameters (e.g., the total amount payable under a class of contributions, if applicable, or the total amount payable annually, if applicable);
- the maximum amount payable to any recipient;
- all conditions under which a contribution is repayable; and
- any conditions that the Treasury Board specifies may not be changed without its approval.

(b) Authority to extend the applicability of terms and conditions for up to one year as long as the fiscal consequences stay within the department (i.e., no adjustments to reference levels required).

(c) All amendments to terms and conditions made under authorities delegated to the appropriate ministers must be consistent with government and Treasury Board policies.

(d) Authority to approve exceptions to the maximum amount payable to any recipient up to 25 percent in excess of the maximum amount approved by the Treasury Board as long as any such exceptions are consistent with government policies and cabinet policy decisions and the fiscal implications stay within the department.

(e) Departments must: consult the secretariat about whether Treasury Board approval is needed before implementing changes under these delegations; and inform the secretariat in writing of any amendments or exceptions approved under these provisions within one month after the appropriate minister has approved them.

(iv) Departments may seek approval for Vote 5 paylist shortfalls by a letter from their senior financial officer to the director of the Estimates Division of the Treasury Board secretariat, which would then seek approval annually from the Treasury Board through an aide-mémoire.

(v) Departments may include non-controversial technical items (e.g., year-end vote transfers, increases in appropriations required solely to comply with the policy on accounting for non-monetary transactions) in a Supplementary Estimates submission without the board's prior authorization if a secretariat official at the director level or above has agreed to it beforehand.

(vi) The Treasury Board secretariat must ensure that current procedures in the Treasury Board Submissions Guide (part of the *Treasury Board Manual*) for handling orders in council authorizing federal-provincial agreements are carried out in order to limit the board's involvement to substantive issues or to where it has to make recommendations before the order may go to the Privy Council Office.

(vii) The board amended its Material Management Policy as follows:

(a) It amended the policy statement to include the following: 'Departments provide employees with material required to carry out their work in an efficient, economic, productive, and safe manner.'

(b) It amended the policy requirements to include the following: 'Automated information systems and supporting technology must be used to manage material resources and material management functions when investments are cost-effective and can improve the material management function. The full cost of inventories (purchasing and holding costs) must be visible and distributed to the end-user. Furniture, material, and equipment must be provided to employees in an equitable manner consistent with the services being provided.'

(viii) It directed the Treasury Board secretariat to ensure, as specified in the policy, that progress reports on major crown projects are submitted only at key events or milestones.

(ix) The annual submission of the cash management report by Treasury Board secretariat is discontinued, and correspondingly, departments are no longer required to submit cash management information annually to Treasury Board for that purpose.

2. **Legislative and Regulatory Amendments**

The Treasury Board invites the appropriate ministers, if the opportunity presents itself, to put forward the following legislative and regulatory amendments.

(i) Change sections 23(1) and 23(2) of the *Financial Administration Act* (FAA) dealing with the remission of taxes and penalties as follows:

(a) Amend section 23, as appropriate, to remove the requirement for the Treasury Board to recommend the approval of orders in council authorizing the remission of premium payments into the Unemployment Insurance Account, the Canada Pension Plan, or any similar government program; and

(b) Introduce, pending an opportunity to amend the Act, streamlined procedures for seeking the board's approval of these orders in councils – specifically, to process these submissions in the routine way (i.e., only the front page of the submission and the order itself would be included in ministers' books; there would be no précis) and that departments use a very brief form for these submissions.

(ii) Change the *Prairie Farm Rehabilitation Act* to remove anachronistic requirements for the board's approval of threshold limits as follows:

(a) Amend section 9 to remove the requirement for the Treasury Board to approve any project or scheme under the Act involving an expenditure of more than $15,000 in any fiscal year by deleting the sub-section that reads 'No single project or scheme under sub-section (1) involving an expenditure in excess of fifteen thousand dollars in any fiscal year shall be undertaken without the consent of the Treasury Board.'

(iii) Amend the *National Capital Act* and *Government Contracts Regulations* to give the NCC comparable flexibility to other crown corporations.

Alternative 1: Introduce legislative change and a consequential amendment to the *Government Contracts Regulations* as follows: eliminate sub-section 15(3) of the *National Capital Act* (NCA) and make a consequential amendment to the Regulations (i.e., remove the NCC from the definition of 'contracting authority' on page B-3). As a result the NCC would no longer be subject to the Regulations and would not have to seek the board's approval to enter into, or amend, any of its contracts.

Alternative 2: Introduce new regulations under the NCA and FAA and a consequential amendment to the *Government Contracts Regulations* as follows: introduce regulations under sub-sections 15(3) of the *National Capital Act* and 41(1) of the FAA with a consequential amendment to the Regulations (i.e., remove the NCC from the definition of 'contracting authority'). As a result, the NCC would be subject to its own contracts regulations.

(iv) Amend the *National Capital Act* (Real Property) to give the NCC the latitude to enter into real property transactions without the approval of the governor-in-council as follows: amend section 15 to eliminate the requirement for governor in council approval of real property transactions and to delegate to the Treasury Board the power to establish thresholds beyond which transactions would require the board's approval.

(v) Amend section 46 of the *Public Service Employment Act* (PSEA) to allow the Public Service Commission to authorize persons to administer oaths and to take and receive affidavits, declarations, and solemn affirmations for any purposes of the PSEA or regulations made under it:

(vi) Amend the *Harbours Commissions Act* (Real Property) to give the minister of Transport the authority to approve all land leases as follows: amend section 15(2) to remove the requirement to seek governor in council authority to lease land for a term of more than 25 years. An amended section 15 would delete sub-section (2)(b) and amend sub-section (a) to provide the minister of Transport with the authority to approve all leases.

(vii) Amend section 27 (1) of the *Public Harbours and Ports Facilities Act* (Real Property) to remove the requirement for the department to seek the authority of the governor in council to lease land for a term of more than 25 years.

3. **Blanket Authorities for Approving Pension Benefits**

The board has granted the following blanket approvals under the *Public Service Superannuation Act*:

(i) Payment of pension benefits in misconduct cases;

(ii) Validating elections for prior pensionable service; and

(iii) Authorizing the president of the Treasury Board to enter into reciprocal pension transfer agreements.

Contentious or unusual situations will continue to be referred to the board to prevent an individual's rights from being prejudiced.

4. **Policy Rationalization**

The board has approved the continuation of the review of its policy instruments to ensure that they focus on results, give departments more flexibility, and clarify the scope of the board's accountability.

The initial review has resulted in the cancellation of the following:

(i) The Furniture and Furnishings Policy;

(ii) The Works of Art Policy; and

(iii) The directive on Increased Ministerial Authority and Accountability (IMAA).

5. **The Treasury Board Secretariat's Strategic Policy and Program Monitoring System**

The board approved the following three elements of the system:

(i) A proactive risk-based monitoring capacity in individual policy areas to ascertain whether the policy is the most cost-effective instrument for achieving favourable results, and to determine the extent to which those results are achieved.

(ii) An evaluation, audit, and review function that analyses the effectiveness of high-risk, strategically important programs and that ascertains the effectiveness of existing monitoring systems; and

(iii) government-wide studies, when necessary, to examine urgent government priorities such as the issue of year-end spending.

PART III

THE DENOUEMENT

10

Governing by Bolts of Electricity

Jean Chrétien maintains that 'the art of politics is learning to walk with your back to the wall, your elbows high, and a smile on your face. It's a survival game played under the glare of light. If you don't learn that, you're quickly finished. The press wants to get you. The opposition wants to get you. Even some of the bureaucrats want to get you. They all may have an interest in making you look bad.'[1] Mulroney had to learn the hard way as prime minister what Chrétien had learned as minister – when in power, a politician is constantly walking in a minefield.

Mulroney stumbled on his first mine within months of coming to office. His government had announced a partial deindexation of the old age pension. Shortly after the announcement, Mulroney ran into a group of seniors on Parliament Hill holding a vigil to protest the decision. Mulroney decided to engage the group in a 'relatively harmless banter for a few moments,' but Solange Denis shot back at him, 'You lied to us.' She added, 'You made us vote for you, then Goodbye Charlie Brown.' The words 'you lied to us' and 'Goodbye Charlie Brown,' according to two journalists, became some of the 'most famous television clips in Canadian politics.' Mulroney sought to recover some of the lost ground by saying, 'I'm listening to you, Madame.'[2] And barely a week had gone by when the then Finance minister, Michael Wilson, announced after a private lunch with Mulroney at 24 Sussex that the government was reversing course. But the damage had been done, and in the words of a former Mulroney minister, 'It became a kind of defining moment for us.'[3] In brief, the best-laid plans by the 600-person-year strong Department of Finance, including hundreds of senior economists, came crashing down all because of a fifteen-second sound bite. It is also interesting to note that, when Paul Martin also wanted to change the old age pension early in Chrétien's first mandate, he decided to pay Solange Denis a visit to her home to outline the proposed changes.[4]

Reading the memoirs of former federal Cabinet ministers or listening to interviews with them reflecting on their years in office, one is struck by the number of references to what they consider relatively minor issues which came to receive a great deal of media attention and to dominate the government agenda, if only for brief periods of time. Erik Nielsen writes about 'tunagate' and John Crosbie about his 'Pass the tequila, Sheila' comment, which, he claims, gave Sheila Copps prime air time on national television two nights running. Crosbie insists that had he given a major 'speech of substance dealing with intricate policy issues' at the conference where he had said, 'Pass the tequila,' the media would have completely ignored it.[5]

Reading Don Johnston's book *Up the Hill*, one quickly senses his deeply felt desire to speak to a broad political agenda and to offer specific policy prescriptions. Yet reflecting on his experience as a minister in the Trudeau Cabinet, he maintains that 'politics,' 'political institutions,' and the 'centre of government' let him down in his efforts to influence public policy. He writes, 'Television exposure of the posturing of MPs during Question Period has not helped; nor have the annual reports of the Auditor General. Government management has improved, but the media naturally highlight those juicy parts of the Auditor General's report which sell newspapers and stop viewers from switching channels. It will be ever thus.'[6] As for the centre of government, he claims that the Privy Council Office played havoc with his proposals for change. He cites, as an example, his proposal to improve the accountability and management of crown corporations. This, he reveals, was 'intercepted and unceremoniously disembowelled by PCO ... on its way to Cabinet.'[7]

All ministers, whether they are status, mission, policy, or process participants, it seems, are convinced that politics is not about substance and intricate policy issues, but about sound bites and perceptions shaped by the media and by politicians trying to score points in question period, all hoping that they will make it on the national TV evening news. Virtually every current or former Cabinet minister I consulted made at least one reference to the fact that governments are defeated by sound bites, not by major policy issues. Former ministers in the Conservative Mulroney government took pleasure in the consultations in reporting that the Chrétien Liberal government has continued to pursue the Conservatives' policy agenda, from NAFTA and fiscal restraint to regional economic development. The point they were making was that it was not the big policy issues that defeated the Mulroney government, but the small issues and the sound bites.

Public servants, particularly deputy ministers, either become well versed in the survival game or they lose their membership in the deputy ministers' club. A former deputy minister reported on his deep sense of relief the day he left government, saying, 'From the first day I became a deputy minister, I could never walk into my office in the morning without a knot in my stomach, always thinking what could possibly blow up in my face today.'[8] Deputy ministers, unlike ministers, do not get dumped in the glare of publicity, but some do get dumped. This exchange between Senator John Stewart and John Edwards, the head of PS 2000, is revealing:

Senator Stewart:	What will happen to the deputy minister who goofs up?
John Edwards:	They ... quietly move on.
Senator Stewart:	How many deputy ministers have been fired in the last six years?
John Edwards:	The firing of deputy ministers happens in the same way as the firing of many vice-presidents in the private sector. It happens reasonably quietly. People get moved into early retirement or go off to other challenges in the private sector ...
Senator Stewart:	Do you have a record?
John Edwards:	No, I certainly do not. The Clerk of the Privy Council may have, and I doubt that he would share it. These things are best done quietly as opposed to having a roaring battle in public.[9]

The above begs the question of what goofing up means. In the deputy ministers' club, it means not being able to manage an accident-prone minister or turn around an error-prone department. The centre of government, in particular the Prime Minister's Office and the Privy Council Office, will always keep a watchful eye on ministers and departments, and if they should stumble too often, then changes will be made. Put differently, if a minister and his deputy are associated with several visible problems that are highlighted in the media and raised in question period, then one of them will go. If it's a minister, then the firing (e.g., Michel Dupuy) or the demotion to a more junior portfolio (e.g., Sheila Copps and Diane Marleau) will be done in full public view. If it's a deputy minister, it will be done quietly (see, for example, John Edwards himself at Corrections Canada over a report suggesting that Corrections officials had mishandled an incident at the women's penitentiary in Kingston).

Tom Axworthy, former principal secretary to Pierre Trudeau, argues that the political leadership is not only concerned about implementing a policy agenda; it also wishes to 'master events.'[10] He adds that as principal secretary to Trudeau he spent a great deal of time dealing with crises. He explains, 'Only crises came to the PMO – the easier problems got solved elsewhere.'[11] Daily morning meetings in PMO 'often dissolved into tactical fire-fighting sessions,' and he writes that 'the only compensation was knowing that the ability to diffuse a crisis ... is among the most important characteristics of a central policy staff.' He concludes, 'Mistakes avoided are just as important as bills passed.'[12] How did he go about ensuring that the government would avoid mistakes? 'My foremost objective,' he explains, 'not often reached, was to avoid surprises.'[13]

The highly charged political environment ministers and their deputies operate in, the Trudeau reforms of the centre of government implemented in the 1970s, developments in federal-provincial relations, and at the international level, weekly, monthly, and special retreat meetings of deputy ministers convened by the clerk of the Privy Council and secretary to the Cabinet have all served to strengthen considerably the centre of government. But the hand of the centre has been strengthened not just in dealing with crises but also on major policy issues. Don Johnston summed up the view of many former and present ministers I consulted when he wrote, after he heard for the first time about a major initiative in a telephone conversation with a PCO official, 'I thought "Are my views irrelevant? Does cabinet no longer count?"'[14] Johnston had every right to ask that question as a member of the Trudeau Cabinet. Ministers in the Mulroney and Chrétien governments could also ask the same question and get the same answer. The role of Cabinet in the federal government has been marginalized considerably over the years, as has that of ministers as the political heads of their departments.

The New Public Management, which by most accounts has had substantial impact on government operations in Britain, Australia, and New Zealand, has been much talked about in Ottawa, but its actual presence has, thus far at least, hardly been felt.[15] To be sure, when government assets and activities are turned over to the private sector, obviously things change. The federal government has done this on numerous occasions since the mid-1980s, and if all of it was done under the New Public Management banner, then it *has* made a difference. But the sale of government assets and the contracting out of activities by the federal government, at least in Canada, have had more to do with the need to raise cash and reduce spending than a desire to pursue the New Pubic Management agenda.[16] But when activities remain inside government, things change very little, if at all.

In this chapter, we look at how major policy initiatives are decided and how the centre goes about managing potential or real crises. There are two types of major policy decisions in government – the ones that are made at the centre with little or no adjustment and those made by the formal decision-making process which inevitably are shaped to accommodate a consensus. The fundamental problem here is that the federal government must continually contend with an overload problem. Accordingly, for a prime minister to succeed in promoting an agenda for change, he must pick and choose a handful of major initiatives and put aside most of the other policy issues for the system to cope with.

While he is busy pursuing his own carefully selected priorities, others reporting to him will keep a careful watch on the policy process and government operations. Policy initiatives born out of this process are adjusted to accommodate interdepartmental concerns. This, in turn, explains why government measures are rarely bold. In brief, only when the prime minister is directly involved or in moments of crisis is the government capable of bold action and decisions. When either of these two circumstances exist, the overload problem is held in check. We saw in earlier chapters that the federal government was capable of bold decisions and even great things in planning the war effort or in managing the program review exercise.

The overload problem is not limited to various policy issues. It also involves coping with government operations which have in recent years become more transparent and better understood by outsiders, notably the media.

Prime-Ministerial Priorities

In earlier chapters we saw that whenever the prime minister wishes to focus on an issue, he or she will get their way. In addition, it is clear that he and his minister of Finance have a free hand to establish their own priority projects. The prime minister's priorities will always see the light of day pretty well as they were first envisaged. As for the rest, the centre of government monitors, decides, and lays all the groundwork for a consensus to emerge to resolve outstanding issues or to decide on a course of action. One minister in the Chrétien government explained, 'The prime minister and Martin [minister of Finance] are allowed to have their projects approved with the bark still on. The rest of us will see the bark taken off before we can announce anything, assuming that we can get something through the system.'[17] What he meant was that any proposal from a line minister must go through the interdepartmental consultation process and the PCO and Finance review and adjustment requirements. What comes out at the other end doesn't always look anything like what went in. It will be recalled that this is precisely the reason Prime Minister Chrétien decided to bypass the Cabinet process in launching his Canada Millennium Scholarship Foundation. He feared that his idea would look different by the time it reached the other end if it had to go through the formal decision-making process. If a prime minister can have such fears, one can only imagine what must go through the mind of a typical line minister as he gets ready to bring forward a proposal.

At the risk of stating the obvious, the prime minister and his handful of advisers are only able to focus on a few priority issues. As already noted, there are countless decisions taken every day inside the federal government. The challenge for the centre, then, is to keep a lid on things that do not enjoy the prime minister's attention, to corral bouncing ministers and departments, and in the words of a senior Privy Council Office, to fall on hand grenades before they explode. The centre has a full arsenal of instruments to deal with these needs.

I put this question to a former senior adviser to Brian Mulroney: 'Where is the centre of power in the federal government?' His answer, 'On issues we cared about, or on the big issues, the prime minister had all the power he needed. On the other issues, it was the Privy Council Office.'[18] The issues they 'cared about' included the Constitution, national unity, the Canada–United States Free Trade Agreement, relations with the United States and several other countries, and specific initiatives for the prime minister's riding. To be sure, some issues came on and off Prime Minister Mulroney's radar screen and included special economic problems at the regional level, including the establishment of regional development agencies, ministerial resignations, and the budget deficit. The adviser added that when Mulroney focused on an issue, 'no one stood in the way inside the government and we always got what he wanted.'[19]

Mulroney was no exception. Trudeau also focused his attention on a select number of issues, and when he did, we are told that success followed.[20] Trudeau's priorities, as is well known, were the constitution, the Quebec referendum, energy policy, inflation, official languages, and foreign affairs – including his peace initiative in the final months of his last mandate. Nor would Trudeau hesitate to employ levers of power that were available to him, though not to his ministers, in pursuing his agenda. The power of appointment is a case in point. Trudeau explains why he appointed Michael Kirby to head federal-provincial relations in his last mandate in office. Trudeau had decided to concentrate aggressively on constitutional reform, and 'I knew that he [Kirby] had no feel for the subject, but that he would know what pieces to cover, which tactics were needed with the premiers, the other Cabinet ministers, and so on. He was a very good Executive Assistant on this subject.'[21]

Don Johnston provides a scenario of Trudeau's tactics. He writes, 'The NEP [National Energy Program] was developed by Marc Lalonde and a small coterie of officials. It was accepted by Trudeau and [Allan] MacEachen and imposed upon the country as the centerpiece of Allan's first budget rather than as a Bill introduced by the Energy minister. Through this technique, much of the content was hidden from Cabinet until it was a *fait accompli*. Certainly, the tax implications belonged in the budget but hardly the entire program ... no one was willing to come down from the ivory tower to find out what was going on in the world below. They had not even bothered to consult with the oil and gas industry, nor the provinces.'[22] He concluded that during the Trudeau years the 'combined power of PMO and PCO had grown far beyond anything reasonable in a parliamentary democracy.'[23] Things have not changed under Mulroney and Chrétien.

Prime ministers do not need the cover of the budget to get their pet initiatives going. Trudeau, for example, decided to establish a Royal Commission on Canada's Economic Prospects without consulting anyone in his Cabinet. When word of this leaked to the media, Trudeau responded to a question in the House by admitting that he had 'not even consulted my colleagues in Cabinet ... on this project.' But he added, 'I think this Royal Commission will be extremely important in terms of the change in thinking regarding the future of the country. I hope it will play a role as important as that played by the Rowell-Sirois Royal Commission.'[24] Don Johnston writes that, as the minister for Economic and Regional Development, hearing Trudeau's statement, and especially that the commission may be as important as the Rowell-Sirois Commission, 'the Prime Minister's announcement struck me with the force of a lightning bolt.'[25]

Trudeau had many other lightning bolts in store for his ministers. Former ministers revealed in the consultations that they learned about such things as the National Art Gallery, the international peace initiative, and many government appointments, including the nominations of their own deputy ministers, either 'at the same time as any other Canadians did,' or as '*a fait accompli*.' Both Mulroney and Chrétien also have their own catalogues of specific projects or lightning bolts.[26] Apart from specific projects, Prime Ministers Trudeau, Mulroney, and Chrétien all pretty well decided on their own and on the advice of their senior advisers at the centre of government what needed to be done in foreign affairs and federal-provincial relations.

Prime ministers, at least since Trudeau and likely before, have had to deal with a political overload problem. James Douglas described the problem: 'Modern democratic governments are overwhelmed by the load of responsibilities they are called upon ... to shoulder.'[27] The term 'political overload' speaks to a sense of urgency in government matters and of being overwhelmed by both events and things to do.

The overload problem is at least as serious today, if not more so, than it was in the Trudeau years. To be sure, the program review exercise, privatization, and contracting out have all contributed to a smaller government. But this does not tell the whole story. For one thing, the federal government remains a large institution to manage. In contrast to the present situation, in 1873 Prime Minister Alexander Mackenzie functioned without a secretary, answering all correspondence himself.[28] In 1909 the newly created Department of External Affairs was entirely housed above a barber shop in Ottawa.[29]

Moreover, the Prime Minister's Office and central agencies do not only deal with new policy issues. Their work also involves keeping tabs on government operations, monitoring federal-provincial relations, meeting with provincial premiers and international trade representatives, participating in a growing number of international conferences, and meeting with visiting foreign heads of government. Governments themselves have now become an important source of what governments do. This is particularly true in a federal system. Federal, provincial, or intergovernmental coordinating groups do not manage programs but they generate a great deal of work, as well as expectations that solutions can be found to any number of federal-provincial disagreements.[30] The centre of government must now also cope with different issues that require a great deal of attention. For example, the Access to Information legislation requires time to monitor and to plan strategies for, especially if a particular request can give rise to a political crisis.

The machinery of government at the centre also requires the attention of the prime minister, and it too generates a great deal of work. Arnold Heeney reports that he had ten officers working with him in the Privy Council Office in 1945. Gordon Robertson writes that he had, in 1971, fifty-five officers engaged in work relating to the secretariat and another thirteen processing Cabinet documents and orders-in-council. Today the number of officers in the PCO is more than five times that of 1971. Robertson, however, warned of the dangers of increasing the size of PCO. He explained that, given its role at the centre of government and the potential for 'misunderstanding and bruised feelings,' PCO should operate on the basis of a few important principles. One such principle is that the office should be kept deliberately small. He writes, 'By recruiting versatile officers who work hard *not* to be encumbered by program responsibility, a large staff is avoided. I have indicated their present number. To expand beyond a certain critical size would be to deny the other principles that help control the Privy Council Office.'[31] Among the 'other principles' Robertson cites is 'staying off the field' by always remembering that 'it is the minister who is responsible and his department that acts.'[32]

For his part, John L. Manion, a former associate clerk of the Privy Council under Mulroney and secretary to the Treasury Board under Trudeau, argues that we now need to strip central agencies 'of their operational responsibilities or those which duplicate the functions of departments.'[33] He writes, 'In most other countries, central agencies are small and strategically-oriented. In Canada, central agencies employ a large number of people, and yet, there is little evidence of long-term strategic and outward-looking thought in these agencies. They have also largely escaped the impact of restraint.'[34]

Looking back, Robertson's caution was fully justified. Line ministers and departments certainly made clear in the consultations and, at least in the case of ministers, through their writings and public comments after they left office, that the centre no longer stays off the field.[35] Playing on the field requires political direction, and there is always a constant flow of memoranda and reports going to the prime minister from PCO officials. To be sure, there is a high degree of satisfaction if you are a PCO official to see the prime minister responding with comments in the margin to a memorandum you drafted. After all, their 'boss' is the prime minister. But every memorandum, every report sent by PCO officials obviously takes up prime ministerial time. It also often means that departments must spend time preparing briefing material for the Privy Council Office.

In chapter 4, we saw the never-ending demands on the prime minister's time. The question, then, is how does the prime minister successfully pursue his agenda? Tom Axworthy offers this advice: 'Only with maximum prime ministerial involvement could the host of obstacles that stand in the way of reform be overcome.' A strategic prime ministership, he writes, 'must choose relatively few central themes, not only because of the time demands on the prime minister, but also because it takes a herculean effort to coordinate the government machine.'[36]

The government machinery became part of the problem on the road to Trudeau's trying to get things done. As Christina McCall and Stephen Clarkson point out, all of the major policy initiatives in Trudeau's last mandate, including the National Energy Program, the Constitution, the 'Six and Five' wage restraint, and the peace initiative, had to be organized outside of the formal decision-making process.[37] Trudeau practised the art of adhockery in policy-making better than any powerful minister from C.D. Howe to J. Gardiner ever did under either the Pearson and St Laurent government. If a line department did not cooperate fully, Trudeau simply established an 'ad hoc group of officials' at the centre to advise him. He did precisely this, for example, in the case of his 1983 peace initiative 'largely because of the skepticism of the Department of External Affairs about the enterprise.'[38]

Both Mulroney and Chrétien followed in Trudeau's footsteps. In their attempts to establish a strategic prime ministership, they too focused their efforts on a handful of policy issues. The need for a prime minister to do this has now become accepted wisdom in Ottawa, even among line department officials. When the Privy Council Office asked a senior Human Resources Development official what was needed to launch a successful social security review, he answered that having a 'strong minister would be necessary, but not sufficient condition for success. The prime minister ... would have to be willing to give the effort his or her full backup ... [and] limit the policy clutter in order to concentrate all [of the government's] firepower on such a major undertaking.'[39]

It is not sufficient for the prime minister simply to declare that a given initiative enjoys his highest priority. He must also give it his time and energy. Mulroney's decision to establish a new Expenditure Review Committee of Cabinet in 1989 is a case in point. Both Mulroney and his Finance minister, Michael

Wilson, had served notice shortly after securing a second mandate in 1988 that deficit reduction would rank high on the government's agenda. The media picked up the cue and both print and electronic journalists ran story after story about Ottawa's precarious fiscal position. Typical headlines reported on the 'Crushing deficit,' 'Getting to the root of the federal deficit,' 'The debt: Where does all the money go?' 'Are we sinking or just swimming in debt?' and so on.[40]

Initially at least, Mulroney made much of his new Cabinet committee on expenditure review and its prospects for success. There was a consensus within the government that deficit reduction could only be possible by attacking the expenditure budget. Wilson argued, for example, that 80 per cent of any deficit reduction 'should come from spending cuts, not taxes.'[41] It was widely reported inside government and in the media that Mulroney borrowed from Britain's Margaret Thatcher and Australian Prime Minister Bob Hawke in 'centralizing absolute power for spending cuts into a new committee.'[42] Government officials at the centre explained that the new committee would 'wage preemptive strikes against ministers [and departments who are believed] to be spending too much.'[43] The Montreal *Gazette* ran the headline 'Mulroney to crack down on government spending.'[44]

To be sure, the new committee was quick off the mark. With Mulroney in the chair, it held its first meeting within a few days after it was established and it initiated a thorough review of the government's expenditure budget. The perception inside government was that the new committee would not hesitate to make tough decisions. When asked whether committee members were 'biting the bullet,' a senior Privy Council official who attended the meeting responded that 'they are not only biting the bullet, they are chewing it.'[45] The major difference between the work of this committee and earlier efforts to cut spending was that the prime minister himself had decided to chair the committee. At no time before, or at least since the days of R.B. Bennett, had a prime minister personally taken the lead in reviewing the expenditure budget.

The 1989 Wilson budget did contain some spending cuts, but nowhere near the level that was first envisaged when the committee was set up. In addition, contrary to Michael Wilson's wishes, the bulk of the measures introduced to deal with the annual deficit were on the revenue side. The budget brought a series of tax increases, including raising the federal surtax by 2 percentage points, an additional 3 per cent on high-income individuals, an increase in the federal sales tax, as well as an increase in excise levies on tobacco and a one-cent-per-litre tax hike on gasoline. Total tax increases amounted to $3.3 billion for 1989–90 and over $5 billion for 1990–1.[46] The budget also moved the full cost of the unemployment insurance program to employee-employer premiums.

What about the expenditure budget? Wilson reported spending cuts of $1.5 billion for 1989–90 and $2 billion for 1990–1. The cuts were spread over several departments, agencies, and crown corporations. However, a close look at some of the cuts reveal that they scarcely constituted expenditure reductions.[47] For example, a cut of $215 million for 1990–1 is identified as repayment of social transfers. In fact, however, this had no impact whatsoever on the government's expenditure budget, thus hardly qualifying it as a spending cut. Other cuts were in reality only delayed expenditures. For example, the construction of a new prison for Newfoundland was simply delayed, not cancelled. The call for tenders to build a new headquarters for Transport Canada was cancelled. However, employees continued to be housed in leased buildings; cancelling the contract could hardly be described as a true spending cut.[48]

It is now widely accepted in Ottawa that the Expenditure Review Committee fell far short of the mark. Indeed, this became quite obvious within months of its establishment.[49] What went wrong? The answer is that Mulroney scarcely attended another meeting after the first and delegated the chairmanship to the deputy prime minister. His interest in cutting spending waned as he began to devote more and more of his energy to resolving the country's national unity and constitutional woes. With the prime minister essentially out of the picture, spending decisions, according to a senior central agency official, were 'taken all over the place, depending on the individuals and the circumstances involved.'[50] With Mulroney no longer attending, there were in fact 'very few meetings of the Expenditure Review Committee ever held.'[51]

Contrast this with Chrétien's program review exercise. Chrétien did not sit on the ministerial review committee, but he controlled its work by remote control and focused a great deal of his time and energy in ensuring its success. He carefully selected its members and 'signed off' on *all* spending cuts recommended by the committee. He rebuffed all ministers – in some instances in no uncertain terms – who appealed a proposed cut, and forcefully brought into line those trying to sidestep the program review. He had two senior advisers from his own office, Eddie Goldenberg and Chaviva Hosek, attend all committee meetings. Chrétien also made sure that no light would appear between him and his minister of Finance in reaching the targets. At a crucial moment in the program review, Chrétien and Martin were helped immensely by a bolt of electricity from outside of Canada – the Mexican currency crisis and an editorial in the *Wall Street Journal*.

Chrétien and Martin agreed on the expenditure reduction targets and Chrétien asked Marcel Massé to chair the ministerial committee. Massé, a former clerk of the Privy Council and long-serving deputy minister, as already noted, was ideal for the task, given his intimate knowledge of government operations.

Massé put forward a list of potential committee members to Chrétien. The list included ministers well known for their views on the need to cut government spending. Chrétien turned down Massé's suggestions. He instead appointed Brian Tobin, Sheila Copps, and Sergio Marchi to the committee, all well known for their support of a strong government presence in society. Chrétien knew exactly what he was doing. He did not need ministers of like mind to simply argue the obvious. He wanted significant spending cuts and a specific list of actual cuts to be implemented. He knew that if there were to be any resistance, it would be from ministers like Tobin, Copps, and Marchi and concluded it was best 'to have them in the tent at the outset.'[52]

As noted in chapter 6, the program review exercise did produce substantial spending cuts in every area of government activity. The great majority of the ministers and permanent officials I consulted and who participated directly in the program review singled out Chrétien's role as one of the most important reasons for the review's success. Another reason, in their opinion, was that there was an enemy in their sights and that the prime minister made it clear that he expected everyone to contribute to its defeat. Chrétien also made sure that those who sought to avoid fighting the enemy, like John Manley, ended up losing more than those who enlisted in the battle.[53]

If, as Tom Axworthy claims, 'it takes a herculean effort [for the prime minister] to coordinate the government machine,' what must it be like for a minister? If prime ministers, with all the levers of power at their fingertips, must still produce a Herculean effort to coordinate the government machine, then things must be downright impossible for individual ministers. For the most part, it is.

Managing the Rest

From a comparative perspective, the Canadian House of Commons has a particularly high turnover rate in its membership. Perhaps for this reason Canadian prime ministers have a limited talent pool from which to pick ministers.[54] As well, the need to have regional, linguistic, and gender balance in Cabinet also means that some strong members of Parliament will be overlooked in favour of weaker ones who can fill a political or regional need. Advisers to Prime Ministers Trudeau, Mulroney, and Chrétien all made the point that some ministers have to operate under a kind of receivership in that they can hardly be trusted to lead an important policy review or even an internal review of departmental programs. Since the 1970s prime ministers now have in their hands an important instrument to keep the policy ambitions of ministers in check – notably, the mandate letters from the centre as ministers assume their new responsibility, as well as those to their deputy ministers.

But what about the rest? What about strong ministers wishing to pursue policy initiatives? Other than the minister of Finance, can strong ministers produce bolts of lightning on their own? The answer is no, even in their own areas of responsibilities, unless, of course, they are requested to do so by the centre.

As preceding chapters make clear, the days of the 'departmental Cabinet,' when individual ministers 'were very much in charge of government decision making' as it applied to their departments are clearly over, and have been since the 1970s.[55] To be sure, line ministers to this day would prefer to revert back to the former model. Arthur Kroeger, for example, writes that 'my own assessment would be that Mr. Pearson's approach, which was characterized by strong relations between ministers and their departments, corresponded best to the ways in which ministers like to function.'[56]

Chrétien, in abolishing most Cabinet committees on coming to power, said that he wanted to return decision making to ministers and their departments. And, indeed, there are now fewer Cabinet committee meetings to attend (and they now, for the most part, end on schedule) and there are markedly fewer Cabinet documents presented to read. But very little else has actually changed. One minister who served under both Trudeau and Chrétien denies that line ministers have more decision-making authority under Chrétien than was the case under Trudeau. He acknowledges that there 'are less committee meetings and less paper,' but he argues 'that is not where power lies or does not lie. Issues are brought to Cabinet committee whether there are twelve or only three, and they are all resolved in the same way.'[57] I met with present and former ministers who have chaired Cabinet committees under Trudeau, Mulroney, and Chrétien. They all revealed that major or extremely controversial issues are often resolved by the prime minister, a few key advisers, and a few senior ministers outside the Cabinet committee system. Chrétien, for example, will often establish an ad hoc Cabinet committee to resolve a delicate matter. As for the rest, one former committee chair summed up the situation well when he said that by the time something comes to Cabinet committee, 'it is pretty clear which way the decision is going. PCO will have done its homework and the consensus will already have been set.'[58] Chrétien, he adds, has retained 'far more power in his office over appointments than Trudeau ever did.'[59] In any event, Chrétien, like Trudeau and Mulroney, does not like surprises and will take steps to avoid them. As Greenspon and Wilson-Smith argue, Chrétien 'wants the game under control,' and subscribes fully to the view that the 'secret of political success is not what you do right, but what you avoid doing wrong.'[60] After several years in office, Chrétien has left the machinery of government at the centre intact and as large and as powerful as it was under Trudeau and Mulroney. If anything, he has enlarged its scope by establishing a new agency at the centre, The Leadership Network, to support the collective management of the assistant deputy minister community.

Leaving aside the prime ministerial priorities, the centre of government has no stomach for bold tries and bold failures. As Colin Campbell writes, 'Larger staffs can increase the capacity of the chief executive to influence operational departments.' But this comes at a price. Campbell echoes Gordon Robertson when he argues that 'a law of diminishing returns sets in' when the staff becomes very large. A large staff at the centre of government can, he claims, 'cut down on the amount of diversity and criticism in the system. They make for a relatively harmonious, but unimaginative administration in which a chief executive accepts non-creativity in most policy actors.'[61] This is not unique to the Canadian government, as Campbell makes clear in his comparative study of central agencies.

Central agency officials have demonstrated deftness at diverting ministers from bold measures, unless of course this is what the prime minister has made clear that he wishes. Paul Thomas writes that the 'job of central agencies is to make a mush of things.'[62] At the risk of overgeneralizing, when it comes to policy issues outside the prime minister's immediate interest, central agencies perform two major functions. They play a *coordinator* role by ensuring that an initiative of a minister and his department does not conflict with the interest of another or other ministers and their departments. If it does, which is very often the case, they will outline a compromise, or solution. This speaks to their second role – their *arbitrator* role. They will not only sort out the cause of the dispute but will also make a recommendation to the chair of the Cabinet committee as to its resolution. Meanwhile, the prime minister and his office will always be kept informed of significant developments.

Central agency officials in Ottawa attach a great deal of importance to their coordinator and arbitrator roles and to their capacity to iron out the wrinkles in proposed initiatives. A student of government from Australia visiting Canada compared decision making in both countries and recorded his views. He wrote, 'Canadian bureaucratic and political culture places great emphasis on consultations to avoid conflict between ministers. In Australia, there is a greater tolerance for robust debate and perhaps a greater unwillingness to allow officials to decide the details of policy. A consequence is that the nature of bureaucratic consultation differs – in Canada, it is typically an attempt to secure agreement and in Australia it is more about defining the outstanding issues.'[63] It will also be recalled that Paul Martin expressed his impatience with the 'process-oriented' nature of government policy making, saying that 'everybody in the system is happy ... as long as the meeting breaks up with nobody throwing a punch.'

Still, as noted in earlier chapters, the majority of Cabinet proposals are quite straightforward and do not require much work on the part of the PCO officials. Earlier, for example, we reported on a Canadian Mortgage and Housing Corporation proposal to extend ongoing programs by finding the necessary funding from its own budget.

But what happens when a proposal is not straightforward, when it holds the potential to generate controversy, or when it can lead to regional tensions? In such cases, the Privy Council Office will again make sure that the prime minister is kept fully briefed as the proposal works its way through the Cabinet committee process. If the proposal is particularly controversial, the prime minister may establish an ad hoc committee to manage the issue. Ad hoc committees of Cabinet have the added advantage of reporting only to the prime minister, not to Cabinet or another Cabinet committee. Chrétien has often used ad hoc committees to sort out politically difficult issues ranging from the purchase of helicopters to revisions to the drug patent regulations.

The Mulroney government, it will be recalled, had secured parliamentary approval in 1993 to delay the introduction of cheaper generic versions of patented prescription drugs. The Chrétien government began a review of the drug patent law and regulations in late 1996. The proposal to change the regulations would pit brand name multinational drug companies against generic drug companies. The Department of Industry favoured the brand name firms because of their research and development activities, while the Department of Health favoured lower-cost drugs for consumers. Finally, Ontario, home to most of Canada's generic drug firms, was pitted against Quebec, home to most of the multinational brand name copies.

The dispute also pitted Alan Rock, a strong minister, and his Department of Health (which is not regarded in Ottawa circles as particularly strong, given that it has no presence in any debate on Canada's economic performance or plans), against John Manley, a relatively weak minister, at least to some Ottawa insiders (known for his willingness to embrace whatever his department officials put forward during the program review exercise), and a relatively strong Department of Industry, which is always present in economic issues. It also pitted Ontario Cabinet ministers and the large Ontario government caucus against a much smaller Quebec caucus. In addition, given the regional factor, ministers from Herb Gray to Marcel Massé began to voice their views in 'stronger than usual terms in Cabinet committee meetings.'[64]

The debate between the two camps was clear. Rock wanted sweeping changes favouring generic drug manufacture while Manley favoured only relatively minor adjustments. The prime minister agreed with Manley, but it became clear that Rock was winning the debate against Manley and also that he had the numbers in Cabinet and caucus needed for his views to prevail.[65] The prime minister decided to establish an ad hoc committee to review the case. He appointed ministers who had clear views on the issue, including Herb Gray (the senior minister from Ontario), Rock, Manley, and Marcel Massé (the senior minister from Quebec).

When the matter came to Cabinet, John Manley won the day. The outcome, as a Privy Council official explained, was a 'modified version' of the status quo. A decision was also struck on how the regulations would be adjusted. The final question was when to make the decision public. Some Ontario ministers argued that it should be put off until after the Liberal Party policy conference, scheduled for the weekend of 20 March 1998. They feared that making the decision public before then could give rise to regional tensions at the conference. The prime minister told Cabinet, as prime ministers very often do, that he was reserving the right to decide when to make the decision public. He finally decided it would be done before the party conference took place.

One minister said that 'the prime minister got his way on the substance, on how the regulations would be revised, and on timing in terms of the announcement.'[66] I asked if this did not confirm the point that one of his colleagues had made in an interview with me that Cabinet was not a decision-making body but rather a focus group for the prime minister. His response, 'No, the focus group argument is a bit too simplistic. We were more than a focus group in this case. We were advisers to the prime minister.'[67] In discussing the case with another minister, I mentioned that Cabinet decisions are supposed to be reached by consensus, and that, by all accounts, if there were a Cabinet consensus, it would have been with Rock. His answer, 'Consensus in Cabinet does not mean a majority. You must understand that consensus means any group of ministers that includes the prime minister.'[68] In light of this and other developments outlined in preceding chapters, the Privy Council Office should review its claim that 'power flows from ministers.'

Privy Council Office officials report that they did not have a strong view on the drug dispute and that in any event it is in their tradition not to have strong views on a particular issue. If they did, they insist, it would seriously inhibit their capacity to serve the system and to assist the prime minister. As always, however, they supported the prime minister. They were also anxious that the debate and the division in Cabinet not be played out in the media. They were encouraged to see a 'modified version of the status quo' emerge, so that Rock and his colleagues from Ontario could claim that they were able to secure at least some movement away from the status quo. Still, they were anxious that the 'protagonists did not come to believe that they were taking sides.' Health Canada officials, however, report that they 'never doubted where PCO stood on the issue.'[69]

The above describes very well what the Privy Council Office does in files that are not straightforward. It keeps a lid on things, it puts out fires, it defuses crises. Often it manages equivocally. The office will ask questions about proposals rather than developing them from scratch. PCO explains that its perspective is geared to the 'overview,' and its 'criteria are previous decisions, precedents, continuity, priorities and related activities.'[70] By its own admission, it is often 'sought by departments as a broker,' and it becomes 'involved in firefighting on important issues.'[71]

A long-serving Privy Council Office official observed that 'personalities change, and it does make a difference in how we operate, but some things do not change. The prime minister has his priorities, and some ministers think that they have a bright idea which the government should run with. Our job is to cope with all of this.'[72] The federal government task force of senior officials on strengthening policy capacity spoke to this observation when it reported that 'real policy making is characterized by complexity and often confusion. We do not live in a textbook world in which Ministers have fully articulated objectives and officials always prepare rigorous analyses of costs and benefits of alternatives. While this is an ideal to strive for, a great deal of policy making must be made on short notice, with limited information. Decisions are frequently incremental. The policy capacity in the public service should strive to be as professional as possible, but that requires flexibility and the ability to serve Ministers in different ways and in what are often less than ideal circumstances.'[73]

We saw in earlier chapters that comprehensive planning exercises, notably Trudeau's priorities exercise in the mid-1970s, which sought to involve all ministers and their departments, failed badly. Trudeau learned from that failure. Returned to office with a majority mandate in 1980, he determined that he, together with his key advisers, would establish the government's priorities and decide which major initiatives to pursue. The system would take care of the rest by taking the edge off things. Again, Mulroney and Chrétien have both adopted a similar approach.

To decide on the government's major initiatives offers a number of advantages for prime ministers. It is of course quicker and more decisive. However, it well may also be the only way to give the government a sense of direction and purpose. In the absence of political ideology, perhaps all that can be expected from Cabinet is that it will have some ministers with a bright idea. The regional factor, which always lurks close to the surface of any public policy issue, also inhibits the federal Cabinet's capacity to provide a sense of coherence and to point the way to a consensus on the priorities to be pursued. Meanwhile, public servants operating at the centre cannot fill a political vacuum.

In the absence of Cabinet being able to establish a coherent set of priorities, central agency officials spend a great deal of their time firefighting on behalf of the prime minister. Firefighting, however, can be an important source of influence for PCO officials, particularly the more junior officials. They will also assist the prime minister in launching his initiatives, his bolts of electricity, as he pursues his handful of priorities.

The prime minister will turn to his most trusted ministers to assist in developing and implementing his initiatives, leaving the other ministers to protest if they dare. As for the other policy issues, it appears things have simply been allowed to shift from analysis to process and from policy to positioning.[74] Meanwhile, the growth at the centre of government, the centre's unwillingness to shed large numbers of staff members as line departments have done, and the development of new processes of coordination (e.g., regularly weekly and monthly meetings of deputy ministers) have all provided new sources of intelligence and a capacity at the centre to enable the prime minister to control better the large bureaucratic machine.

Managing the Managers

Several officials I consulted referred to Paul Tellier's dictum at a deputy ministers' meeting that he wanted 'error-free administration.' This rattled deputy ministers, coming, as it did, on the heels of PS 2000 and all its accompanying talk about empowerment. A former deputy minister recalls that at their weekly meetings Tellier would 'give us a bolt of electricity about one thing or another. I remember one occasion when Tellier expressed his deep annoyance over a leak out of Veterans Affairs. What did he expect us to do, sit in the mailroom to make sure that no one would leak things?'[75] Close associates of Tellier insist, however, that he meant not that he expected the federal public service to go about its work with the overriding objective of making no mistakes but that he should be alerted if someone in a department had committed an error that could blow up in the media. 'Tellier did not like surprises,' one of his former associates explains, at least in part 'because Mulroney did not like surprises.' He adds the reason Tellier was 'so annoyed with the Al-Mashat thing was because no one had warned him that the file was about to blow up in the media. As a result, he could not alert the prime minister of what was coming.'[76]

The Privy Council Office believes that 'the possibility [of a blow-up] lurks behind every question put to a minister and the quality of the answers could weaken the minister's or the government's position.'[77] To be sure, neither the Privy Council Office nor the Prime Minister's Office can ensure that every question put to a minister in the House of Commons will be handled with dexterity. But the centre thinks that it can avoid surprises if deputy ministers call the clerk the moment they sense that a potential problem or embarrassment to the government lurks within their departments.

Central agencies sit at the centre of what C.E.S. Franks has labelled 'multiple accountability processes and instruments'[78] under which all government departments must operate. Accordingly, they actively seek out information and there is a constant flow of intelligence from departments to the centre. In fairness to central agencies, however, they are not always the ones responsible for requesting information from departments. Parliament must also share some of the responsibility. The president of the Treasury Board, for example, must still answer to Parliament and be responsive to the concerns of the auditor general and the commissioner of official languages.[79]

Members of Parliament also try to use central agencies to tame departments or demand that they employ their clout to push departments to act. Parliament's Public Accounts Committee, for example, took the secretary of the Treasury Board, Peter Harder, to task for taking too long to implement standards of service to the public. Members of the committee were reacting to a survey produced by the Office of the Auditor General reporting, among other things, that when citizens telephone a department, 'six of the federal government's busiest services have a worse than 50–50 chance of [their] getting an answer. At Revenue Canada, 19 out of 20 callers got a busy signal.' Michel Guimond, the then committee chair, urged Harder to 'put his foot down,' calling him 'the most important mandarin' with power to 'terrorize departments into compliance.'[80]

The media has also become much more aware of how government works. It has also learned to use Access to Information legislation to secure information. When it uncovers problems or controversial issues, it is often the centre of government that is left scrambling to prepare a communication strategy. An example will make this point clearer. The *Globe and Mail* reported on 29 June 1994 that documents disclosed under Access to Information show that the 'monthly charge [to the government] for cellular phones and services was $874,000 the previous December which translates to at least $10.4 million a year.' It added that the document also reveals that 'approximately 280 cell phones were assigned to the Privy Council Office.' The article remarked that this was the case 'despite a change of government and promises of cost-cutting.'[81] The Access to Information request was made after a minister had told an opposition member that it was 'too expensive to find out what cell phones were costing.'[82] In this instance the Access to Information request was intended to secure information about the government as a whole, not a single government department.

The *Globe and Mail*, the Ottawa *Citizen*, and Montreal's *La Presse*, among others, report regularly on administrative foul-ups in government departments. In a front page article, for example, the *Globe and Mail* reported that empowerment had been taken a bit too far. Officials in the Department of Health came up with a scheme to turn their $500,000 travel budget into $630,000 worth of travel. They had been granted the travel budget after they were asked to carry out an ambitious computer project to redesign income-security programs. They prepaid the entire travel budget to American Express to enable it to invest the fund to buy more air tickets. No one benefitted personally, and the only intention had been to stretch the department's travel budget. It meant, however, spending for services to be delivered at a later date, and it certainly did not square with standard federal government accounting practices. Auditors argued that the 'cheque issuing provided an opportunity for misuse and was not prudent.' For its part, the *Globe and Mail* reported that the incident served 'as a reminder that where public money is concerned, there is value in safeguards, watchdogs, and even red tape.'[83]

Alasdair Roberts writes about a 'control lobby' in his review of the PS 2000 reforms. Roberts points to controversies involving public servants purportedly 'running amok' which captured media attention. One such controversy was the Canada Communications group, which he describes as 'a child of the PS 2000 exercise.' The group had been granted Special Operating Agency status and given a mandate to 'be more businesslike' and 'entrepreneurial' in its operations. It soon became the target of complaints from businesses against which it was competing. Five industry associations presented a brief to the government on the matter, and David Dingwall, the minister responsible, responded by asking an outside group to undertake an audit. The media, including the *Citizen*, the *Globe and Mail*, and the *Financial Post* got into the act with 'abuse of governmental power' storylines.'[84] Even government members of Parliament started to voice their concerns, one suggesting that the group was 'scaring the hell out of private business.'[85]

Things took a turn for the worse when it was revealed that the group had accepted a payment of $2.5 million from the Department of Industry for work that had not been completed. The purpose, it appears, was to 'park' a part of the department's appropriations in the group's revolving fund. The media had a field day, with the *Citizen* running a front page story suggesting that the incident 'might have been predictable when a public institution was ordered to operate like a private business.'[86] David Dingwall was urged in question period to punish the public servants responsible. The head of the agency was removed from his position, and a few months later the government declared its intention to sell off the agency.[87]

Roberts insists that the 'control lobby did more than influence the character of talk about public service reform. It also constrained the path of reform itself.'[88] He even suggests that the lobby inhibited attempts by central agencies to achieve a cultural change in the federal public service. He defines members of the control lobby as the Office of the Auditor General, the media, legislators, in particular those on the opposition benches, and public service unions.

It is hardly possible to overstate the point that public servants operate in a highly politicized world. Government managers do not enjoy the same kind of privacy that their private sector counterparts do. Any decision a government manager makes can become the subject of a public debate, a question in Parliament, or give rise to a ten-second clip on the nightly news. The government managers who decided, for example, to replace windows at the Department of External Affairs never expected that their decision would become the subject of intense media coverage, give rise to questions in Parliament, and move the minister of Government Services to declare that the decision was 'stupid' and that he 'wanted a full explanation' since he had never been made aware of the file.[89]

Such developments matter a great deal to the centre of government. A considerable amount of time is spent on them at daily morning meetings in the Prime Minister's Office and the Privy Council Office. They also matter a great deal to the prime minister and senior ministers simply because they are convinced that there is a limit to how many times the media or the opposition can uncover administrative foul-ups before the media begins to accuse the government of no longer being in control.

As already noted, the clerk of the Privy Council, as head of the public service, meets with the prime minister most mornings when he is in Ottawa. Consultations for this book make it clear that discussions at these meetings do not always centre on major policy issues. Indeed, they invariably turn to the media. It may well be that what Paul Tellier meant by 'error-free administration' was that he wanted no surprises reaching the media before he got a proper briefing from the relevant deputy minister.[90] The point remains, however, that the centre attaches a lot of importance to how management issues are handled in departments.

Empowerment in government has important limits, not so much because the centre of government opposes the concept, but because a code of behaviour is expected of government managers that is not found anywhere else. Little wonder that there is a 'disbelief culture' in the federal public service whenever yet another attempt to 'empower managers' or to 'import' better business management practices is unveiled.[91] Big answers to management constraints in government departments will not be possible until Parliament and the control lobby first change their ways. Senior public servants intuitively know that their greatest risk is not whether their draft of a Cabinet document will be found lacking or if a program will perform poorly, but if a scandal or embarrassment erupts in full view of the media. They have, however, earned the right to tell members of the control lobby, notably Parliament, to 'heal thyself' before they embark on yet another attempt to empower front line managers, telling them to earn rather than spend. Until the control lobby changes its ways, line managers would be well advised to greet any reform measure by battening down the hatches and waiting out the passing storm. If history is a guide, it will come around again, sporting a new set of initials.

Is the Centre Malfunctioning?

The federal government, at least from the mid-1970s to today, has given up pursuing a systematic approach to coordination, not only across the whole gambit of government activities, but also within general policy fields.[92] There is no longer even any pretence. The elaborate decision-making process and the growth of the centre of government serve another purpose. This is to serve the centre of government, in particular the prime minister, by keeping a lid on things.

Policy coordination has had some success when the prime minister takes charge, identifies his three or four key priorities, and remains focused on them. When the prime minister's hand is not visible, policy becomes muddled. Regional economic development policy is an excellent case in point. When Trudeau first came to office, he declared that regional development was as important to Canadian unity as the language issue.[93] He established a new department, appointed his close friend and Quebec lieutenant Jean Marchand as its minister, and Tom Kent, a powerful presence in his own right in Ottawa, as the first deputy minister. Though the new Department of Regional Economic Expansion (DREE) was also given a large budget, the department decided to limit its programming to selected areas. It also established a clear policy (e.g., the growth pole concept) and successfully resisted powerful forces to change course. Trudeau, however, gradually lost interest in regional development policy. In time, its programming was pushed and pulled to cover every region of the country and virtually every conceivable form of economic activity. One is reminded of Arthur Schlesinger's observation that it was Roosevelt himself, not his newly implemented machinery of government at the centre, who promoted coordination. As we saw in chapter 2, Schlesinger wrote that 'proof of his control was the way, once the reins fell from his hands, the horses plunged wildly in all directions.'

Trudeau appointed Pierre De Bané as DREE minister in 1980 and, as already noted, De Bané asked for a fundamental review of federal regional development policy, including a review of his department's mandate. Trudeau agreed and asked the Privy Council Office to lead the review, but by all accounts he only took a passing interest in the exercise, deciding rather to focus his energy on the Constitution, energy policy, inflation, and an international peace initiative.

The Privy Council Office review led to the abolition of DREE and to the establishment of a new department and a new approach. That approach, however, was done away within a few years. In time Mulroney decided once again to overhaul federal regional development policy and, in the process, established new regional economic development agencies. Things went well in the early months, but then the agencies began to lose their focus. There are precious few people, outside of those who actually work in these agencies, who are happy with the current policy. Mulroney, like Trudeau, lost interest in the policy he had introduced when he turned his attention to national unity and his attempt to amend the Constitution. Chrétien has not made regional development policy one of his priorities. The field remains muddled.

Prime ministers since Trudeau have recognized that the overload problem in government is now such that effective coordination and policy success can only be achieved in a handful of policy fields and with their own active participation. In short, they and their advisers need to play on the field. As for the rest, departments operate in a kind of policy vacuum. The centre of government, notably the Privy Council Office, will man the lookouts to steer the ship of state away from icebergs. The purpose of coordination then becomes more one of protecting the government than of bringing coherence to policy fields. This, in turn, explains the findings of a recent federal government task force report on ways to strengthen the government's policy capacity. As we saw in chapter 3, the task force concluded that 'the most notable weaknesses at present relate to long term strategic and horizontal issues. Resources are disproportionally consumed by short term demands.'

Accordingly, policies still emerge from 'stovepipes' that link functional experts to other levels of government and to interest groups.[94] However, policy issues are increasingly difficult to contain with the boundaries of the conventional departmental structure. This explains in part the 1993 restructuring initiative and also various task forces established by the clerk of the Privy Council in recent years not only to strengthen the government's policy capacity, but also to promote more horizontal thinking in government. These efforts have thus far had limited impact.

One way to resolve horizontal policy issues is, of course, to press for their resolution at the centre of government. As earlier chapters make clear, there has been a tendency for line departments to lose some of their policy and analytic capacity while the centre has been able to retain its capacity. But the centre itself is coming under attack for its failure to provide strategic leadership. Peter Aucoin writes that 'strategic leadership constitutes the value-added by public service central agencies to the management of the state of government.' He also argues that the centre is failing on this front at least in part because it is failing to distance itself from the political leadership. He explains, 'There has recently developed a "politicization" of the central agencies of government (and thus the public service leadership generally) that has diminished the understanding of the need for the public service to be distanced from the political leadership.'[95] The problem is not just partisan; it also involves the growth of personal loyalty to the prime minister. Either way central agencies tend to become an extension of the political leadership. This can only serve to shift their focus away from strategic policy and corporate management functions towards the partisan and personal interests of the political leadership which happens to be in office. Yet it is expected that central agencies should be role models for line departments, given that the clerk of the Privy Council is also head of the public service.

The day after Solange Denis told Brian Mulroney 'Goodbye, Charlie Brown,' officials of the Privy Council Office were scrambling to manage the political fallout.[96] They looked at various options, including having the minister of Finance back down from his commitment to reduce spending on old age pensions. The measure of success was not how pension reform can be best implemented, but rather on how the head of the government could be protected. The objective was clear: get the issue out of the media and out of question period.

To sum up, for the centre of government, coordination now means operating an early warning system for the prime minister, anticipating and managing political crises, and pursuing prime ministerial priorities. The emphasis is less on policy coherence and more on keeping the lid on, so that the prime minister and the centre can get things done in areas that matter a great deal to the prime minister. Governing by bolts of electricity describes well how things actually work at the centre of government.

11

Incentives, Constraints, and Behaviour

In the summer of 1989, Doug Young, sitting in opposition as member of Parliament for Acadie–Bathurst, declared his firm intention to fight the Mulroney government's plan to reduce Via Rail services in Atlantic Canada and to introduce cuts to the Unemployment Insurance program. He urged New Brunswickers to help him stop the government dead in its tracks, on the grounds that both measures would have a very harmful impact on the provincial economy.[1] He even offered to organize public hearings to enable all New Brunswickers to demonstrate their opposition to the plans.

Now, fast forward to Chrétien's first mandate, where that same Mr Young turned all his energy to fiscal concerns. He took to the program review exercise with gusto and promoted a policy to sell the country's air navigation system, privatize CN Rail, reduce still further subsidies to Via Rail, and do away completely with freight rate subsidies for Atlantic manufacturers.[2] Moreover, he came out in favour of substantial cuts to the Unemployment Insurance program. What explains Young's remarkable about-face?

The answer lies in the incentives and constraints that motivate politicians when in opposition, as opposed to those that motivate them once their party is in power. But that is not all. Incentives and constraints within the government itself vary considerably, depending on where one sits, and the differences are substantial. Indeed, they are such that we now have several cultures warring in the bosom of the federal government's political and public service institutions. The differences are sharp, and they even exist within the centre of government itself. In brief, organizational culture within the federal government itself is plural, not singular. Expressed in its most basic form, culture consists of shared meanings and common understandings, which provide the basis for concerted action.[3]

This chapter explores the dynamics that make the federal government work and argues that *la culture des métiers* matters a great deal more than has been assumed. The various incentives and constraints shaping behaviour in government are so powerful that they have prohibited the development of comprehensive policy agenda. Trudeau believed that he could marshal or, failing that, control these and other forces by fundamentally restructuring the centre of government. A substantially expanded centre, he concluded, would provide the necessary countervailing forces to check the influence of strong ministers and their long-serving permanent officials in line departments. It would also provide the capacity he felt was lacking to formulate at the centre of government itself a comprehensive policy agenda.

To be sure, Trudeau did considerably strengthen the centre of government, and no prime minister since has been willing to do more than play at the margins of his reform at the centre. In 1993, when she was deputy minister of Transport, Jocelyne Bourgon wrote that 'the policy machinery in place is basically the same as it was twenty years ago.'[4] This observation remains valid today. The same cannot be said about line departments, as the massive 1993 government reorganization made clear.

It is important to stress that much of the centre of government belongs to the prime minister and not to ministers, either collectively or as individuals – with the exception, of course, of the minister of Finance and the president of the Treasury Board, who lead their own central agencies. The strengthening of the centre of government has not, as was initially envisaged, strengthened the collective decision-making capacity of Cabinet by acting as a counterweight to line ministers and powerful mandarins in line departments. Rather, it has weakened both Cabinet and line ministers and their departments. On the other hand, the power and influence of the prime minister and his advisers – both partisan and permanent officials in central agencies – has in turn been considerably strengthened.

When the modern centre was born, it will be recalled, central agency officials were careful not to favour a particular departmental position – or to be seen to favour a particular position – on the grounds that it would compromise their ability to run the Cabinet decision-making process. They considered their job to be to manage the process on behalf of Cabinet, as a collective decision-making process. This is no longer the case. The interviews revealed case after case where central agencies clearly took sides and favoured a position – positions that would eventually prevail.

However, the strengthening of the centre has not meant that the federal government is now better able to articulate a comprehensive policy agenda. Indeed, the only time it is able to do so is when a powerful outside element comes into play which forces it to act. When this occurs, the various organizational cultures and even outside forces are held in check by a consensus that something must be done. The other necessary ingredient is for the prime minister to remain focused, firm, and tenacious. These circumstances, when they are all in sync, enable the centre to pursue successfully a new policy agenda – again, the war effort and the program review are two rare examples. But at no other time is a concerted and comprehensive policy agenda possible. Having abandoned any hope of defining an overarching policy agenda, the centre of government now seeks simply to control the various forces, if only to keep a lid on things, to enable a handful of overriding priorities as defined by the prime minister to see the light of day and to protect the government's political interests in the media and before the country's political institutions.

Why does this state of affairs exist? Put differently, why is it that the centre of government, notably the prime minister, has come to dominate so thoroughly the policy and decision-making process? Put differently again, why have all prime ministers since Trudeau chosen to pursue only a handful of key objectives, managing the rest by bolts of electricity, and essentially give up on producing a comprehensive policy agenda?

The answer is that we are witnessing institutional change, if not failure, on a very large scale. The power, influence, and even relevance of Parliament are under threat. This is serious, because Parliament is increasingly failing to hold the government to account.

But that is not all. The role of the media has also changed substantially. For the most part, it is no longer just a narrator or an independent observer reporting and commenting on political events. It has become an important political actor in its own right. Television and its tendency to turn to a thirty-second clip on the evening news to sum up major policy issues or, much more often, to report on something gone awry in government, have had a profound impact on government operations. The centre, broadly defined, has become extremely sensitive to potential media-inspired developments it cannot control and to surprises which can give rise to political problems and embarrassments.

Few inside the federal government still believe that Cabinet is a collective decision-making body setting policy and deciding on the key issues of the day. I put this question to a senior minister towards the end of my research: 'Do you believe that the Cabinet has become a focus group for the prime minister, as it has been suggested by another minister?' As already noted, his response was: 'There is some truth to it, but it is not the whole truth. There are too many large egos at the Cabinet table to think that we are a kind of a collective focus group.'[5] The power and influence of Cabinet itself are now under threat. This is serious, because it concentrates political power in the hands of one individual, the prime minister, and in those of his immediate advisers.

Another institution, the federal public service, under accusations that it had become too powerful, has in some respects lost its way. In its desire to become politically responsive, it has looked to the prime minister for direction: one of its most important priorities now is to protect his political interests, though not necessarily his partisan political interests, against the media and others who decide to challenge the government. The result of this, combined with the overload problem, has led the Canadian prime minister to pick only a few priority initiatives to pursue and to employ the machinery of government at the centre as leverage to control the rest and to keep a lid on things.

Politicians in the Waiting Room

Doug Young, in 1989, acted much like any other opposition member of Parliament. His purpose was clear enough – to exploit any opportunity to make the government look bad. He also had the luxury of ignoring the constraints that knowledge places on viable policy options, and there was not much of a centre to keep a watchful eye on him to ensure that he caused no embarrassment. There is not much need for an opposition centre since everyone in the party intuitively knows to shoot in the same direction – and that is at the government. The media reported on Young's activities, not to hold him accountable for his actions, but rather simply to report on his activities. The reason – he had no power. In some ways, the media's purpose was also his purpose, and that was to expose the government's weaknesses. More importantly, only the local media reported on his activities so that he could tailor his message to correspond to local circumstances.

It is important to recognize that when sitting in opposition politicians have limited access to substantial policy advice. Opposition parties are largely off-limits for senior public servants, and they will avoid contact with them to the extent possible. Certainly, few senior public servants would want to provide information on the finer points of a public policy issue to an opposition party member, fearing that it could well come back to haunt them in question period, in parliamentary committees, or in the media. Opposition parties, and in particular the leader of the Opposition, have resources to hire staff. However, the staff, much like assistants in ministerial offices, are partisan, young, and only in exceptional cases do they have experience in government. Their grasp of policy issues is superficial, and their purpose is less one of understanding the details of policy than to promote the partisan interests and electoral chances of their party or the member of Parliament they work for. They know that Parliament is about partisan politics and not about the policy process. They also know that Parliament and the media will pay more attention to triviality and bombast than to a finely crafted speech on a public policy issue. A former senior Privy Council

Office official summed up the role of Parliament well, at least as viewed from the public service perspective, when he observed, 'Parliament is about assigning blame and not much else.'[6] If Parliament is about assigning blame, then government must be about avoiding blame. These, then, are the forces that shape the work of an opposition political party. The incentives for embarrassing the government of the day are many and the constraints are few. The rewards for embarrassing the government is a step closer to political power, and there is no penalty if you fail.

Leaders of opposition parties do not have the clout to keep their members in line on most policy issues anywhere near the extent the prime minister does. In fact, they have very little to offer them other than the hope that things might be different in future. Any power, including the power of appointment, is, of course, conditional on the party winning office. This also explains why the interests of an opposition leader and his members of Parliament are the same. Nobody is fighting for his departmental corner or his region, and in most instances no one has to worry much about the consequences of what they say. There are no hard policy choices to announce, no tough decisions to make, and no elaborate machinery of government to manage. The objective is straightforward – to embarrass the government and position your party as best you can to win the next general election. There is no need to concern yourself with negative political consequences if you should misstep on a policy issue.

Opposition members of Parliament, perhaps because they have such limited access to policy advice, are free to walk in the unconstrained world of make-believe. Hubert Humphrey, in running for political office, declared, 'We need a new, fresh, buoyant, forward-looking economics to replace the tired, old economics telling us we can't do the things we want to do – the things we have to do.'[7] Any opposition member of Parliament in Canada could easily make a similar statement, and some would even see merit in it. In the absence of both knowledge and the kind of discipline political power imposes, one can make virtually any kind of grandiose statement about a better tomorrow, if only the right party were elected to power.

Ned Franks, one of Canada's leading students of Parliament, recently argued that 'unquestionably Parliament has become a less prominent place for major political announcements and debates, and the decline is continuing.' In reporting on the reasons for this decline, he in particular points to the media. He reveals that parliamentary committees do not enjoy much media attention and that the 'problems with the reportage of Parliament comes from the pack journalism reaction reporting, and other unattractive attributes of journalism in Canada.'[8] He quotes approvingly former *Saturday Night* editor John Fraser, who wrote that the problem begins with journalism schools 'which don't just feed into the post-Watergate cynicism and distrust anything or anyone worthy of an investigative report or in-depth profile, they positively foster institutional rancour and disbelieving zealotry with a righteousness no longer to be found even in a fundamentist divinity school.'[9] It is not an exaggeration to suggest that media interest in Parliament is now largely limited to sleaze, potential splits in the government caucus, ministers on the defensive, and prime minister's questions.

Though one can debate whether the media today is serving Canadians better than it did thirty years ago, there is no denying that its role has changed greatly. We saw in earlier chapters that former Cabinet ministers in both Liberal and Progressive Conservative governments have commented, in some cases in the strongest of terms, on the changing role of the media.

The media is far more aggressive and less deferential to political power than it was thirty years ago. Some suggest that Watergate was a defining moment for the media, not just in the United States, but in Canada as well. In an earlier chapter we saw that journalists will make full use of access to information to get information from government departments. John Crosbie writes that access to information legislation has added to the 'woes of politicians ... on the government side. [It] gives the media and other mischief-makers the ability to ferret out snippets of information with which to embarrass political leaders and to titillate the public. In the vast majority of instances, embarrassment and titillation are the only objects of access to information requests.'[10]

The role of the media began to change (post-Watergate) at about the same time the centre of government was expanding in size and broadening its scope of activities. The centre, no doubt in response to the wishes of prime ministers, decided to hunker down to anticipate and manage political and bureaucratic gaffes. Departments which caught the centre off guard with surprises of one kind or another or could not manage politically sensitive files would lose points in the system. Ministers and deputy ministers began to receive mandate letters from the centre so that they knew what was expected from them. No longer could a minister, working in close cooperation with the deputy minister, set out to redefine departmental policies. Given the modern media, national unity concerns, and the prime minister's own priority issues, this would be much too risky. In a sense, the centre of government fears ministerial and line department independence more than they do line department paralysis.

The work of the media by all accounts dominates the agenda of morning meetings between the prime minister and the clerk of the Privy Council. What the evening news on national television reported the night before and what the headlines in morning newspaper say have a profound impact on question period, and by extension, on government operations.

Politicians in the Room

To sit in the Cabinet room for the first time is, in the words of one Cabinet minister, 'quite a charge.'[11] For the majority of ministers, this is what they have worked towards. They have finally achieved their greatest political ambition. Once there, however, the purpose is not to rock the boat, to survive in Cabinet, get re-elected and make the government look good, or at least not to create problems or embarrassments. The life of Cabinet ministers is now essentially one of surviving and staying in Cabinet. As we saw in this study, very few ministers have resigned on matters of policy or principle during the past thirty years. One survives in Cabinet by avoiding political embarrassments and thus ensuring the prime minister's continued support. With political ideology not much of a factor in the two parties which have held power in Ottawa, and party manifestos hardly a force in Canadian politics, there are probably few policy issues which would warrant a Cabinet resignation.

To be sure, some ministers are more ambitious than that. Indeed, some can easily see themselves sitting in the prime minister's chair. Others, notably the mission participants, for example, will want to have an impact on public policy and lead their departments into new areas, or even to a new beginning. They are the ones senior officials in the Privy Council Office would disparagingly classify as 'ministers' with 'bright ideas.'

Putting aside their ambitions, a member of Parliament's move from opposition benches to the Cabinet room is dramatic. The rules of the game and group dynamics are suddenly completely different. Overnight, a member of Parliament, in the words of Pierre Trudeau, goes from being a 'nobody' to being a somebody. Suddenly, they are surrounded by senior government officials explaining the finer points of public policy and presenting them with voluminous briefing books, not only outlining the country's economic circumstances and the important challenges in every policy area, but also a list of dos and don'ts, albeit mostly don'ts. No longer can one make bold statements about virtually anything. All, as we have seen, now receive mandate letters on the day of their appointment, suggesting what they should or should not try to reform in their department. The most ambitious may try to push the envelope and go beyond the mandate outlined in the letter. But this is not without risk. Indeed, there is no assurance that his deputy minister will espouse the minister's agenda with much enthusiasm if it differs from that outlined in the prime minister's letter. The deputy minister will, of course, be well aware of the content of the mandate letter, and more than likely he was consulted in its preparation. It is in this sense and in how they are appointed that one can now make the case that deputy ministers are as much a part of the centre as they are the administrative heads of their departments.

New Cabinets in Canada are for the most part ill-prepared to govern. The large turnover in the House of Commons means that very few newly appointed ministers will have had previous experience in government. Their work in opposition does not prepare them well for their role in Cabinet. They come to their first Cabinet meeting with a very limited sense of purpose and direction, in part because, as already noted on several occasions, political parties which have held power in Canada have no firm political ideology, but also because they are ill-prepared from a policy perspective to assume office.

Political parties in Canada are essentially election-day organizations, more geared to raising funds and to supplying party workers than to articulating a plan of action for the party, should it come to power. Lowell Murray, a senior minister in the Mulroney Cabinet and a long-time political strategist for the Progressive Conservative Party, explains, 'In the Leader's speeches, spokesman's speeches, policy documents ... what do we have? Most of them are nothing but campaign literature which is written by campaign people for campaign purposes. We need a far better policy structure. The party needs a policy development staff that can prepare position papers ... Only if we put more meat on the bones of our policy positions will they mean something to the Minister or Deputy Minister who has to implement them when we take office.'[12] The 'Red Book' enjoyed a high profile in Chrétien's first mandate, but as already noted, it still did not qualify as a party manifesto in the British tradition. With no deep ideological roots and no shared policy interests, ministers do not walk into an established culture as they meet for the first time to assume power. If a culture is to emerge, it will take shape over time.

What, then, guides a new Cabinet in Ottawa? About the only common understanding found in the Cabinet room will be the need to govern without getting into political trouble. The prime minister will, once again, go over a list of dos and don'ts. He will also outline the broad agenda he wants to pursue, and ministers will quickly understand that he, not Cabinet, will take over the most difficult issues, such as national unity. Ministers will also soon learn that the prime minister will be pursuing a handful of priority initiatives and that they and their departments are not to get in the way. They will also come to terms, if they have not already done so, with the fact that the prime minister can appoint, dismiss, promote, and demote not just them, but also their deputy ministers. He can make all these decisions with whatever advice he chooses to seek and accept. Moreover, ministers will also come to see that concerns over performance are channelled to the prime minister so that they and their deputy ministers will have a particularly strong accountability relationship to him. This, for obvious reasons, has a profound impact on Cabinet and how individual ministers go about their work.

The interviews made it clear that the great majority of ministers develop a strong capacity to sense what the prime minister wants or where he stands on a given issue: they then become advocates of that position. The interviews also revealed that Doug Young was better than most in this. There was probably no minister better or more effective than Young in delivering the goods once he was certain of the prime minister's wishes. Officials who worked with him in transport report that Young was always careful not to push the envelope beyond what the prime minister wanted. When it became clear that Chrétien was four squares beyond Martin in the program review exercise, Young would simply not be deterred from reinventing the department and cutting several of its programs and subsidies. In any event, as we saw earlier, the prime minister retained the right to sign off on all program review decisions, effectively giving him a right of veto.Young's behaviour in government was vastly different from what it had been in opposition. The incentives and constraints at play were markedly different and in government there was a centre telling him what was expected of him.

Government ministers are always on the alert to see who is gaining influence with the prime minister. Some will want to test the water to see if they are in the ascendency. There are a number of signs, including who is being asked to take on a special assignment, to sit on an ad hoc committee of Cabinet, or to attend special meetings to advise the prime minister on any number of issues.[13]

The centre of government, notably the Privy Council Office, certainly starting with Pitfield, sees its role more as one of supporting the prime minister than Cabinet. As we have seen, briefing notes and policy advice from the centre on all policy issues are channelled to the prime minister and, to some extent, to the chair of Cabinet committees. Ministers are left to fend for themselves or to draw from whatever expertise may be available in their own departments to marshall their arguments to participate in Cabinet and Cabinet committee deliberations.

Little wonder, then, that past and present Cabinet ministers I consulted do not rank their participation in Cabinet and Cabinet committee meetings very high in terms of their most effective or productive activities. They do welcome opportunities to engage in general policy discussion which, many insist, are precisely what Cabinet and – albeit to a lesser extent, Cabinet committee meetings – are mostly about. But it is the specific initiatives they may be able to secure for their ridings or their province or their departments that they consider their most productive and rewarding activities.

To be sure, the prime minister is to be obeyed and always gets his way on virtually any matter he cares deeply about or is willing to invest the time to secure its implementation. But he hardly has the time to police the wants of all ministers and decide on every single spending proposal, some of which are clearly modest in scope. In the fall of 1997, the minister of Finance and the prime minister informed Cabinet committees that they could spend up to $300 million of new money. The Privy Council Office established a process to manage the new spending proposals and asked departments for suggestions. Within weeks, 'billions of dollars of new spending plans had been identified.'[14]

There is no need to go into detail of either the process or the proposals which were finally accepted.[15] Suffice to note that, in the words of one line minister, 'No one was happy with that process.'[16] The Ottawa *Citizen* ran an article describing the process with the headline 'Liberals back-biting over extra cash,' and quoted ministers' deep disappointment with it.[17] Some ministers even felt that the centre had set up the process deliberately to fail so that it could control all new spending, 'even the crumbs.'[18]

Thus, little has changed over the years, despite Trudeau's major reform of the centre of government, the deficit and debt crisis, and a successful program review exercise. Spending decisions still emerge from a struggle between departmental push and Finance, Treasury Board, and Privy Council shove. Considerations for a coherent whole, a fundamental rethink of some policy fields, or a new strategic direction for the whole government barely enter the debate. Planning at the centre still means trying as best it can to marry uncoordinated proposals coming up from the bottom.

Indeed, there are now signs that the centre has completely thrown up its hands on this front. It now reserves the right not only to establish the government's fiscal framework, but also to make decisions on all new major spending proposals – again, examples here include the $2.5 billion Canada Millennium Scholarship Foundation and the $850 million Foundation for Innovation, both taken with no prior consultation in Cabinet.

The centre has become convinced that ministers are not very capable of establishing priorities, that they lack the ability to look at spending proposals from a perspective broader than their respective department or region. Accordingly, it has also taken to deciding, on its own, a number of less costly decisions. An example will make this clear. The 1998 budget contains a $400 million provision to enable the government to deal with the year 2000 computer problem. The decision to allocate this amount was taken in private by the president of the Treasury Board, the minister of Finance, and the prime minister. When asked why the proposal was not taken to a Cabinet committee and then Cabinet, a senior minister responded, 'Who knows what ministers might have done with it. They could well have said, "This is not our most important priority," and spent the money on something else. We had no choice. We have to provide for the year 2K problem.'[19]

It is also important to remember that the media and, by extension, constituents and party members, will not judge the success of a minister by his contribution to the centre of government. In any event, discussions and developments there are not readily accessible to anyone other than the prime minister and the people employed at the centre. The media will, however, assess the performance of ministers by how well they do in question period and by their ability to lead their departments and keep them out of trouble. Ministers understand this and govern themselves accordingly. When Art Eggleton was asked about his tenure at National Defence, he responded that 'other than the flurry about helicopters, we have turned the page on Somalia,' and as proof that he was doing well, he observed that he doesn't 'get many questions in the House of Commons.'[20]

Departments always have on their shelves a whole series of projects at the ready, waiting for funding. All ministers are expected to promote departmental projects in the government's decision-making process, or when it comes to securing funding for a departmental initiative, to participate, in the words of a former Cabinet minister, in the '6/49 lottery game.'[21] The objective, according to a veteran Cabinet minister, is 'to break from the pack and get a breakaway to score one for your department.'[22] Comprehensive planning, strategic direction, or a coherent policy package are unlikely to emerge from a lottery game or breakaways. However, since ministers are not able to participate fully in the shaping of the government's strategic direction either because they are blocked from doing so or because the regional or departmental factor invariably gets in the way, then all that is left for them is to promote departmental projects, whether they square with overall government priorities or not. It is certainly rare to see a minister in Ottawa actually want to reduce his department's budget. Winning a bigger slice of the pie becomes the only true sign of a minister's political virility.

Ministers also quickly learn the full significance of the overload problem in modern governance. The machinery of government itself has now become a complex field to master, even for long-serving ministers. In addition, the machinery has to cope with a high number of diverse issues, ranging from a tax treaty with a foreign country to approving a proposal to support a particular industrial sector, a firm, or community. Ministers, most with past experience quite irrelevant to understanding how the federal government operates, must learn to position themselves and their departments to pursue a proposed initiative or express a point of view opposing a proposal coming from another department.

What about the prime minister? What motivates him? Consultations with present and former senior PMO staff members and Cabinet ministers reveal that history books matter much more to prime ministers than is generally assumed. The phrase 'under the prime minister's watch' was on numerous occasions used to describe what motivates Canadian prime ministers. One former senior PMO adviser remarked that 'a prime minister has reached the top of the mountain and there are no more peaks to climb. The challenge becomes keeping power, not winning it, and that's a different ball game. In other words, the question becomes 'what do you do with the power?'[23]

Former and present prime ministerial advisers say that prime ministers lead very lonely lives. One explained, 'As the old saying goes, it is lonely at the top in that you do not have any peer to compare notes with.'[24] As chapter 3 points out, even relations prime ministers had with colleagues while in opposition are deeply affected. While it is true that first ministers do meet and do share common concerns, they do not meet as equals. Though the relationships between first ministers is much closer to the *primus inter pares* model than is the case with the federal Cabinet, it remains that when the premiers' club meets with the prime minister the premiers invariably take advantage of the opportunity to promote projects for their respective provinces.

Prime ministers, certainly since Trudeau, but even more so under Mulroney and Chrétien, have often brought delicate federal-provincial issues, even bilateral issues, into their own offices for resolution. Premiers, on issues that matter a great deal to them, will also insist on bypassing the relevant ministers and deal directly with the prime minister. It is also less risky for the prime minister to offend or rebuke one of his ministers than a premier. The prime minister can always count on the continued support of his ministers, but not on that of the premiers. In addition, a prime minister knows full well that he may need the support of a premier who comes calling at some point in a future federal-provincial conference or constitutional initiative. The same is not true of a minister, who is clearly a subordinate.

If prime ministers have peers in Canada, they are found among former prime ministers. Mulroney took great pride in winning back-to-back majority mandates, something that no modern Progressive Conservative leader had been able to do. Similarly, Chrétien could boast that Liberals had to go back to St Laurent to see one of their leaders accomplish a similar feat.

There is one issue, national unity, that has dominated the prime minister's agenda at least since Trudeau. Given that no prime minister would want to see the country break up under his watch, they give the issue all the time needed. Trudeau, Mulroney, and Chrétien have all brought the issue to the centre of government to be managed directly. The issue can expand to cover all policy issues or concerns, depending on the circumstances, on public opinion surveys, and on the timing of a future Quebec referendum.

The election of the separatist Parti Québécois to power in Quebec in 1976 was a seminal event in Canada's political life. It continues to reverberate within the machinery of government in Ottawa. Indeed, the 1976 Parti Québécois election has probably had as much impact on how policy is made in Ottawa as Trudeau's decision to overhaul the centre of government in the late 1960s and early 1970s. No other issue can ever be its equal. It has remained in the prime minister's pending basket ever since. Most policy issues and new proposals are now assessed against its backdrop. The prime minister and his most immediate advisers, including senior career public servants at the centre, believe that they alone can see the broad picture and square all new proposals and assess political and bureaucratic gaffes against the national unity file. This explains in part why prime ministers and the various clerks of the Privy Council do not tolerate surprises from ministers and departments.

This study also reveals that national unity concerns have often pushed aside other important initiatives. The efforts of Mulroney's Expenditure Review Committee produced very little in the way of concrete results, essentially because he turned his attention to national unity concerns. It will also be recalled that in his exchange with Paul Tellier, the former clerk of the Privy Council Office, Ian Clark, the former secretary to the Treasury Board, suggested that the government's focus on a proposed constitutional initiative may well explain the limited success New Public Management measures, in particular PS 2000, had in the federal government.

Prime ministers also belong to an international club of heads of government. It is clear that Trudeau, Mulroney, and Chrétien committed a great deal of their agenda to international relations. One can easily appreciate why they would want to leave difficult domestic issues behind from time to time to play on the world stage. In addition, it is clear that heads of government can relate to each other's problems and compare notes on how to handle particular challenges.[25] We know that strong and lasting bonds of friendships were established between Trudeau and Helmut Schmidt and Jimmy Carter; between Mulroney and George Bush and Margaret Thatcher; and between Chrétien and Bill Clinton.

Meanwhile, keeping rather than winning power requires, as previous chapters have made clear, a capacity to avoid or at least to manage political and administrative mistakes. If there is one theme that emerges from the political memoirs of former Canadian politicians, it is that 'small mistakes will do you in, not large policy issues.'[26] As Chrétien observed, 'The art of politics is learning to walk with your back to the wall, your elbows high, and a smile on your face. It's a survival game ...'[27]

Still, sidestepping and managing 'small mistakes' have become much more difficult in recent years. Intense media scrutiny and access to information legislation have had a crucial impact on the dynamics of governing. Prime ministers since Trudeau have turned to a safe pair of hands at the centre, in particular in the Privy Council Office, to manage political or administrative crises, both those visible to the media and the public and those visible only inside government. Safe pairs of hands have become highly valued in government, which explains why newly appointed deputy ministers are drawn mostly from PCO, Finance, and the Treasury Board secretariat. In March 1998 the deputy ministers of Transport, Fisheries and Oceans, Agriculture, Heritage Canada, Industry, Human Resources Development, National Defence, Finance, Environment, and Revenue were appointed directly from positions they were occupying at the centre of government. When combined, the resources of these departments account for the bulk of Ottawa's expenditure budget and government activities.

The centre of government is where one can best hone horizontal rather than vertical thinking skills, manage up, learn to sense a political crisis in the making, and develop a capacity to manage it if it should blow up. People at the centre do not manage programs and rarely deal directly with citizens. Their 'client' is the political process, and their measure of success is if the political leadership is happy with their performance. This, however, has had a profound impact on the federal public service and on policy making.

The Public Service

Among other things, the role of the public service traditionally has been to introduce a reality check to a newly elected government. One of its most important purposes is to tell Hubert Humphrey–like politicians that there are actually things that they ought not to attempt; that it is one thing to plea for a replacement of the 'tired old economics' with a 'new, fresh, buoyant, forward-looking economics,' but that to define the new economics is quite a different matter. In their seminal work on the relationship between politicians and public servants, Aberbach, Putnam, and Rockman wrote, 'In a well-ordered polity, politicians and bureaucrats each can do what they are best able to do: politicians articulate society's dreams and bureaucrats help them gingerly to earth.'[28] The public service is best able to do this as an institution with shared values and beliefs.

Hugh Heclo and Aaron Wildavsky used the phrase 'village life' to describe the world of the British civil service. They argued that the British civil service had its own distinct culture, its own peculiar way of arriving at decisions. Members of the village lived in relative harmony, mainly because they saw themselves as part of the same team, sharing the same values and basic goals. Heclo and Wildvasky concluded that village life tended to muffle 'sensible insiders' and keep 'helpful outside critics in the dark.'[29] Later, B. Guy Peters extended the metaphor of village life to explain the relationship between public servants and their political masters in government.[30] The Canadian public service also operated much like a village in the immediate aftermath of the Second World War, up to and including the Pearson years.[31]

But it is no longer the case. Indeed, there are now several distinct villages, all working from different perspectives with their inhabitants motivated by different forces. The differences are deep and became readily apparent after only a handful of interviews. Indeed, the centre itself no longer constitutes a village with shared meanings and common understandings.

Three major developments have given shape to a different public service – the Trudeau reform, a consensus that the public service had become too powerful, and a deeply felt desire on the part of outside observers, some politicians, and some senior public servants to see the public service emulate the private sector.

A few years after Trudeau overhauled the centre of government, ostensibly to give his ministers more policy-making power, ministers began to voice publicly their concerns over the growing influence of public servants. Allan MacEachen, a veteran politician who, better than most, knew his way around the Ottawa system, declared that if the Liberals had learned anything during their brief stay in opposition in 1979, it was that his party would no longer rely as much as it had on the advice of public servants. Other senior Liberals soon joined in.[32] No sooner had the Progressive Conservatives lost power after only a few months in office than former senior ministers such as Flora MacDonald went on the lecture circuit to denounce 'the bureaucrats.'[33] But that is not all. The British satire *Yes Minister*, as already noted, had a significant impact on how the public service was perceived in Canada, not just in Britain.

The Mulroney government left little doubt as to where it stood on the public service – its power over policy had to be cut down to size. It introduced specific measures to strengthen the hand of politicians in their dealings with public servants. Although, in fact, the measures had precious little impact, they did not take away from the key message: the public service could not be fully trusted on policy.

All the while, there were few voices speaking on behalf of the public service. Individual public servants could hardly do so. The media ran few positive stories about the work of the public service. In fact, it gave a great deal of coverage to Flora MacDonald and other politicians of like mind. The academic community, by and large, also became increasingly critical of bureaucracy. One scholar wrote that 'bureaucracy is a word with a bad reputation.' Herbert Kaufman concluded by the early 1980s that 'antibureaucratic sentiment had taken hold like an epidemic.'[34]

To be sure, this bureaucratic bashing had an impact in Ottawa, as elsewhere, and there is evidence to suggest that senior public servants began to lose confidence in their institutions, if not in themselves.[35] Well aware of the criticism in the media and in learned journals, particularly from the public choice school, they began to doubt their policy advisory role. In some cases, they simply looked up to politicians and said, 'Okay, now you drive.' Many decided, at least in the early years of the Mulroney government, to step aside and to let politicians and their partisan advisers define the policy agenda. Gordon Osbaldeston, clerk of the Privy Council Office, 'insisted' when preparing the briefing material for the 1984 transition on a 'strict separation of background briefing from advice or, stated differently, the separation of administration from politics.'[36] His central purpose was to protect the public service from significant cuts or from being buffeted about by the new government rather than to identify and promote certain policy options.

All this is to say that senior public servants were clearly on the defensive, at least when it came to policy. But the new approach of letting the politicians drive was also running into problems. The political leadership soon discovered that driving without the full support of the public service was problematic. It will be recalled that the Mulroney government stumbled badly in its first years in office, plagued by ministerial resignations and an apparent inability to control the political and even its own policy agenda.[37] The exempt staff, including chiefs of staff, were no more likely to have government experience than the ministers they were serving, and a series of gaffes were committed.[38] But the damage was done, and the political leadership was to discover that the confidence of the public service could not be turned on and off at will.

In any event, by the mid-1980s, the public service as an institution was once again being told that it did not measure up. The evidence was sketchy at best, but bureaucratic bashing had clearly taken its toll. The solution to the problem of the public service came under the NPM heading, but the prescriptions came in the form of evocative phrases such as 'steering rather than rowing' and 'moving from covering your back to covering your costs.' If only senior public servants could learn to manage like their private sector counterparts, then all would be well. The objective then was to introduce a managerial culture in the public service. Some public servants responded by embracing each NPM fashion of the month, from Total Quality Management to the empowerment theme, others by showing that they were in fact much more businesslike than was assumed, and still others by going along with the rhetoric but not taking it too seriously, certain that it too would past.

No matter how sceptical public servants may have been about the new management culture, the centre of government did not let up in promoting its merit.

Certainly, PS 2000 had as its fundamental objective the need to change the culture of the public service to one that would embrace business methods. We presented in an earlier chapter a table detailing the shift from the 'old culture' to the 'new,' which had as its key words 'empowering' and 'managerial.' The government did not stop with PS 2000. There have been other attempts to introduce business methods since Mulroney left office, such as Chrétien's desire to see the Treasury Board shift to a Management Board concept. In addition, the centre of government is now asking departments to prepare business plans rather than, say, departmental or public plans.

The initial push to promote a business or managerial culture in the public service may well have come from politicians like Margaret Thatcher and Brian Mulroney. But it appears that at least some senior public servants are now happy to be doing the pushing themselves. The idea to introduce the business plans came as much from senior public servants operating at the centre of government as from politicians. But business plans can only be successful and have any kind of lasting impact if they are tied to rewards and sanctions, which are in turn tied to resource allocation. It is not at all clear, however, if political institutions are willing to buy into this development.

All of the above measures, like earlier efforts before them, conveniently overlooked the simple fact that governing in a parliamentary democracy and running a business are vastly different enterprises. Example after example and case after case in this book show that working in government is 'fundamentally different in all important ways.'[39] For one thing, no major firm would be expected to survive a potential takeover every four years or so, especially a hostile one (*circa* 1984). Professionals in large private firms are not ruled by amateurs, with most of the levers of power concentrated in the hands of one person who is responsible for appointing both the top amateurs and the top professionals. One can sum up the differences simply by saying that in government you manage publicly and in the private sector you manage privately.

Al Johnson wrote thirty years ago that 'it must never be forgotten that departments of government are in a monopoly position. They have no competitors.'[40] The implications of this simple fact have been overlooked by those who believe that a business culture can take root in government. Canadian society, for example, can readily accept that business activities will be dropped if it makes business sense to do so, but the same yardstick does not apply if it is the government that wants to drop activities which no longer make business sense to continue delivering.

A classic example here concerns the Canadian National Railways (CNR) repair and maintenance shops in Moncton, New Brunswick. As a crown corporation, CNR sought to close the shops because they were no longer required.

Roméo LeBlanc, the New Brunswick representative in the Trudeau Cabinet, made it clear to CN that closing 'the Moncton shops would not be acceptable – period.' When the Mulroney government came to office, CNR sought once again to close its Moncton shops. The reaction in Moncton was swift and highly vocal. A 'Save our Shops' committee was struck and it organized several high-profile demonstrations. They made the argument that Moncton was being treated unfairly and the federal government subsequently announced a delay in implementing the shop closure. In time, the government did close the shops, but not before it unveiled a special fund to attract new jobs to Moncton.

Subsequently, the federal government privatized the CNR. Shortly after CNR became a private firm, it announced significant job losses to Moncton. The news made the front page of the local newspaper but no public demonstration was organized and no one demanded that the company introduce a special fund to create new jobs for Moncton. CNR was a private firm, and it was accepted that if it made business sense to shut down some of its activities in Moncton, then so be it. All this is to make the point once again that the public and private sectors operate under vastly different rules. To suggest that business methods can be successfully introduced to government is ignoring the lessons of history. This, perhaps more than anything else, explains why students of public administration compared to the economists have shown little theoretical interest in the NPM.[41]

The lessons of history have been ignored many times throughout the 1980s and 1990s. Paul Tellier no doubt startled public servants when, a few years after he left government, he subscribed fully to the notion that private sector management practices were superior to what he found in government. In the private sector, he had seen the light, and saw that it was much better at making decisions. Tellier, it will be recalled, in his exchange with Ian Clark, then secretary to the Treasury Board, said, 'I introduced and implemented more change in the last 12 months at CN than I was able to do in my seven years in the public service,' and added, 'Had I known what I know now, I would have introduced more radical change.'[42] If nothing else, such comments served still more to sap the confidence of senior public servants. Paul Tellier had become the first clerk of the Privy Council to be formally designated 'head of the public service under the PS 2000 legislation which he had promoted.' Long-serving federal public servants could hardly imagine Arnold Heeny, Bob Bryce, or Gordon Robertson making similar comments about their institution.

To be sure, the federal government was not alone in trying to introduce a managerial culture in the public service. As already noted, Britain had pursued a similar objective in a much more aggressive manner. British politicians, however, were much more committed than their Canadian counterparts and went further in introducing and implementing change. British politicians made reform their priority and stayed the course. Canadian politicians, meanwhile, have had an on-again, off-again interest in reforming the public service.

But a tentative approach to reform is not without important implications for the public service and government operations. When you combine this with the kind of bureaucratic bashing we have seen over the past twenty years, you run the risk of seeing an institution lose its way. Promoting cultural change in an organization as large and as complex as the federal public service is not for the faint of heart. In addition, some may be tempted to promote cultural change because it represents an easy solution and frees the political leadership to focus on more pressing and immediate political problems. B. Guy Peters, for example, writes that cultural change holds strong appeal because it represents 'a relatively easy way to correct malfunctions.' But, he adds, advocates of cultural change 'often trade on a simplistic understanding of both organizations and culture.' He concludes that 'culture can be changed, but it usually requires a very long time to produce any large-scale change.'[43] No one has bothered to answer the questions of whether you can promote cultural change in the federal public service in complete isolation of the country's political culture, the requirements of Parliament, and the work of members of the 'control lobby,' notably the Office of the Auditor General and the media.

Recent developments have not led to completely different organizational cultures in all government departments. Some, particularly the few left intact in the 1993 restructuring, have long had their own shared understandings and culture.

The restructuring, however, did mix and match activities and merge different cultures into one department. To appreciate this, one only has to look at the Department of Human Resources, which has under one roof the old Department of Labour, responsibilities for promoting job creation, for identifying new training measures, and for policing the Employment Insurance program, as well as federal-provincial income support programs. The restructuring did bring some major issues more clearly into a single portfolio. However, the new, larger departments may well be more inward looking than their predecessors, given that they can bring more issues into one department. But in the process, they may well have created thicker walls.[44] The result is that it has made it more difficult for the centre to establish clear government priorities or even to define an issue as priority and then to force adjustment in affected policy areas and in the policies and programs of relevant government departments.

In January 1998 Lawrence Strong tabled the findings of his committee on Senior Level Retention and Compensation in the federal public service. He concluded that 'good people are leaving at a time when government needs the best and the brightest. In short, the Public Service is no longer able to retain the people it needs and frustration among those who stay could eventually impact productivity negatively.' The solution: introduce new pay raises and create 'a new vision and Public Service culture.'[45] The Strong committee was quite specific about the level of pay raises, but had precious little to say about what kind of 'vision' and 'culture' the public service should pursue. No sooner had he tabled his report than present and former public servants began to voice their opinions in letters to the editor. One wrote, 'Its [i.e., public service] leadership is all too often noted for [its] partisan compliance rather than, as it was within memory, for competence and integrity ... Rebuilding the ethical and professional standards of the PS is the thing required, especially at the top.'[46]

All this is to say that there is every reason to doubt now whether the public service still consists of a 'village' of common interests. Indeed, there are now several villages, each with its own field of common interests and shared understanding. Jocelyne Bourgon suggested as much in her 1998 report on the public service to the prime minister when she called for it to become a 'borderless institution.' By this, she means an institution 'committed to reducing the barriers to the flow of ideas and information.' She explained that 'some of the barriers are physical, others are built into our information systems, but most are cultural. The cultural barriers are the most difficult to overcome.'[47] The important challenge, she added, was for the federal public service to focus 'on the big picture and [develop] a culture oriented to attaining collective goals, not just individual objectives.'[48]

In this study, we reported on a fault line dividing senior level officials in Ottawa from those actually delivering programs. The former tend to manage up, to attach a great deal of importance to their ability to deal with political issues and crises. Front line and regionally based officials, meanwhile, tend to manage down and out – that is, they look to their employees and client groups to establish priorities and to secure feedback. For officials at the centre, the most important challenge is one of 'horizontality,' or creating a borderless institution. For officials in line departments, the main challenge is vertical, on how to deliver better services to Canadians.[49]

Line department officials claim that they can easily detect more than one culture, more than one set of values and understanding at the centre of government itself.[50] Some senior officials in the Treasury Board secretariat speak the language of managerialism and business plans, while others clearly have strong reservations about such developments. Senior officials in the Public Service Commission will, from time to time, applaud such managerial themes as empowerment, but resist efforts to marry their delegation or transfer of authority to departments to match those from the Treasury Board secretariat. Moreover, the commission insists that it must have its hand in government operations most everywhere to protect the 'merit principle.' Empowerment, it appears, is one thing, but trusting departments to protect the merit principle is quite another.

What the above suggests is that the centre of government has, since the early 1980s, sought to both empower individuals in government and, willingly or not, disempower the public service as an institution.[51] If one looks at a specific reform initiative in isolation from other developments, including other reform measures, it does not reveal a complete and true picture of the changes that have actually occurred over the years. Put differently, it is important to look carefully at the ways in which one change interacts with the others and how they relate to pre-existing institutions of government.

The empowerment theme is a case in point. The idea was not the child of the New Public Management school born in the early 1980s. One can trace it back to the Glassco Commission and to Trudeau's decision to overhaul the centre of government. Glassco's objective was to empower government managers, while Trudeau's was to empower ministers as a collective group.

But by the mid-1980s, it became clear that the empowerment theme was taking on a life of its own and that virtually everyone, both inside and outside government, was to be empowered. To be sure, program managers and front line employees needed to be empowered. But they were not the only ones. It became conventional wisdom that politicians and their advisers also needed to be empowered if they were to regain control over policy and the policy levers.[52] And then there were the 'clients' of government programs. They too needed to be empowered, and numerous attempts were made to transfer the concept of citizen into that of client and customer.[53] Even the Office of the Auditor General was being empowered with the introduction of comprehensive audits. Similarly, Parliament and parliamentary committees were to be empowered, and some measures were introduced to do just that in the aftermath of the McGrath report.[54]

One is tempted to ask the question can everyone be empowered? Put differently, is it possible to empower managers, front line government employees, politicians, and their advisers, clients, and parliamentary committees without disempowering someone or some institutions?

Many senior civil servants still consider the providing of policy advice to be one of their most important tasks. However, they, at least those in line departments, are finding that they have become much less influential on policy issues which have any kind of profile outside or even inside government. It also appears that public servants are no longer able to tell politicians that their pet schemes are not terribly practical, that they have been tried in the past and that they have failed. The career stability of public servants is not as strong as it once was, and the restructuring of government departments has meant that the institutional memory is less comprehensive. In brief, the federal public service is now less capable of bringing politicians back 'gingerly to earth.'

The public service as an institution may well have assumed a great deal of influence in the 1950s and 1960s. Mitchel Sharp tells us that it was understood and accepted when he was a public servant that policy was made by deputy ministers, while the ministers decided what was politically saleable and what was not. Writing in the early 1970s, J.E. Hodgetts pointed out that 'bureaucracy abhors a power vacuum' and explained that 'the aggrandizement of the powers of the public service may well be viewed as a reflection of the superior ability of that institution to make the adaptations or develop the innovations which have led to the bypassing of other public institutions, like parties, parliaments, or courts.'[55] Rather than recognizing the failings of their own institutions, political leaders set out to disempower the public service.

Still, it is clear that the political leadership looked, and continues to look, to individual public servants to advise on specific policy issues and to carry out a number of tasks, some more political than administrative. The pervasive role of the media has made error prevention a more central role in the public sector, and individuals working in central agencies often have had a major role to play in protecting Cabinet ministers from themselves, and if that is not possible, then to protect the prime minister. Politicians, at least starting with Mulroney, may well have suspected the public service of enjoying too much power or influence, but they have come to rely on some senior officials to manage their political agenda and on senior public servants to operate the bureaucratic system to secure compliance and minimize error. As we repeatedly showed in this study, a major political crisis will just as often flow from administrative matters or government operations as from major policy issues. The capacity of senior officials at the centre to prevent the damaging thirty-second clip on the evening news has come to be highly appreciated. No one in government is better suited to defuse emerging problems. Thus, when the Mulroney government was plagued by one crisis after another and when his own office was in disarray, Mulroney reached out to Derek Burney, a career public servant, to be his chief of staff.

Prime ministers are trained to think short term. They have their own projects to promote and priorities to pursue and have little patience for due process. They will turn to individuals at the centre to give them a helping hand and to keep other matters under control.

But this requires special skills, political skills. These, rather than an intimate knowledge of a sector or a policy field, have become of prime importance. In the process, however, we may have lost sight of something that was crystal clear thirty years ago. Hodgetts insisted then that we had 'long grasped the theoretical answer to the question' of what belongs to the centre and what belongs to line departments. He wrote, 'Decisions affecting policy and coordination should be made at the centre; decisions relating to implementation or operations are best left to the organization manning the front line.'[56] In the rush to micromanage files or issues that can cause political problems and to focus on the prime minister's key priorities, we are losing sight of what properly belongs at the centre and what belongs in line departments. We also appear to have given up on promoting policy coordination at the centre of government. In addition, pursuing initiatives on behalf of the prime minister cannot be done in a vacuum, nor can the management of politically difficult situations. One needs to be able to 'stick handle' his or her way through the system to make sure that relevant ministers and departments are on side.[57] While it is true that institutions, notably the public service, are not particularly adroit as political fixers, individuals are. However, the empowerment of individuals will not give rise to a 'culture oriented to attaining collective goals.' Rather, it is much better suited to pursuing individual objectives for the centre of government, notably the prime minister.

The prime minister is the key player in selecting which people will be empowered. The clerk of the Privy Council and secretary to the Cabinet, key staff members in the Prime Minister's Office, the minister and deputy minister of Finance, two or three ministers, and some deputy ministers are extremely powerful in Ottawa circles because the prime minister prefers it that way. If one of these should lose the confidence of the prime minister, and word of this should get out, then he or she would be well advised to leave. Bob Bryce, Gordon Robertson, and Simon Riesman became powerful figures in the federal government because of their work, their accomplishments, and knowledge of a particular policy field. This situation is now less often the case. Prime ministers now provide the basis for an official's influence. Michael Pitfield, Derek Burney, Paul Tellier, and Eddie Goldenberg, for example, became powerful figures in Ottawa, not least because of their special ties to the prime minister.

Having the centre micromanage selected files, make certain that the prime minister's priorities are fully implemented, fix specific cases for the prime minister, and manage political crises for the government can, of course, be extremely valuable for prime ministers. In some ways, prime ministers could not ask for better. It enables them and the centre to govern by 'bolts of electricity.' If one wants quick action in a few key areas and to avoid bold decisions or actions elsewhere, then there is no better way to govern.

But the approach comes at a price. The public service's ability to 'speak truth to power' and to promote a culture oriented to collective goals is affected. Senior public servants will be much more willing to speak truth to power if they are part of an institution that will protect them rather than if they are individuals flying solo.

When the sense of collectivity is lost, then the capacity to deal with the increasingly cross-cutting nature of public policy issues is significantly diminished.[58] With the emphasis being on an individual's ability to fix things, there is no longer an unambiguous career ladder to motivate members of the public service as a collectivity. In addition, there is less likelihood that a village built on shared understanding will emerge. This ironically comes at a time when the government stresses the importance of a horizontal approach to public policy issues which can no longer be contained within the federal government, let alone in one department.

But more importantly, the loss of a sense of collectivity in the public service comes on the heels of a loss of a sense of collectivity in Cabinet. The prime minister can roam throughout the federal government, pick and choose what he wants, and get most senior public servants to pursue his priorities and to manage specific cases or problems on his behalf. He never has to hit any barriers, whether they are constitutional or, as now, institutional.

Indeed, prime ministers since Trudeau have used central agencies as leverage to pursue their agenda to master events, to keep things under control, to corral bouncing ministers, and to get done what they want. The bias of central agencies now clearly favours the power of the prime minister and others operating at the centre of government. The study reveals, for example, that central agency officials define their work as 'falling on hand grenades' to stop problems from leaking out. It also reveals, among other things, that the centre was left essentially untouched by the massive 1993 government reorganization, only because the centre itself decided that this would be so.

Meanwhile, the minister and the Department of Finance can only pursue their agenda if the prime minister supports them. The moment light appears between the prime minister and Finance on a major issue, they lose. Michael Wilson and the Department of Finance were not as successful as they had hoped in introducing fiscal restraint measures because Mulroney turned his interest to other issues. Paul Martin and the Department of Finance officials were much more successful, and they credit Chrétien's support and his uncompromising desire to stay the course as a key factor.

The Treasury Board secretariat has sought to pursue a NPM agenda, but with only modest success. For example, as we saw in an earlier chapter, the SOAs concept has never taken flight in Ottawa largely because of a lack of coordination and coherence among central agencies. Prime ministers Mulroney and Chrétien have never put NPM initiatives high on their priority list, often being contented with simply issuing a press release announcing yet another measure.

Contrast this with Britain, Australia, and New Zealand, where NPM has had a more significant impact. It is no coincidence that prime ministers in these countries took a strong interest in pursuing an NPM agenda.[59]

The intergovernmental affairs group under its various guises since it was formally introduced under Trudeau has always been closely identified with the prime minister. Trudeau, it will be recalled, showed little interest in the traditions of the public service when he appointed Michael Kirby as secretary to the Cabinet responsible for federal-provincial relations. Kirby had worked in Trudeau's office in the 1970s, so his talents were well known. Trudeau explained that though Kirby 'had no feel for the subject ... he would know what pieces to cover, which tactics to cover, which tactics were needed with the premiers, the other Cabinet ministers, and so on. He was a very good executive assistant on this subject.'[60] Kirby also knew that his success in securing a constitutional agreement was directly linked to Trudeau, not Cabinet. The same can be said about Norman Spector, who held the same job under Brian Mulroney. He later became his chief of staff. The difference was that Kirby left PMO to go to the public service, while Spector left the public service to go to PMO. For Trudeau or Mulroney, the institution of the public service was not the issue. The issue was getting who they considered to be the right individual to do the job.

The Privy Council Office oversees due process in the government's policy and decision making. This study makes clear that there are now two due processes, one for the centre, notably for the prime minister's priorities, and one for line departments. Prime ministers have come to accept that they can only successfully pursue their priorities if they keep their number small and if they can keep a lid on everything else. PCO has developed a well-honed capacity to do just this.

This study also shows that the role of the clerk of the Privy Council and secretary to the Cabinet has evolved a great deal since Mackenzie King and Arnold Heeney established it in 1940. Heeney, it will be recalled, subsequently wrote that he successfully resisted King's desire to turn the position into a 'kind of deputy to the Prime Minister.'[61] Those who have occupied the position since Michael Pitfield have been much less successful. Clerks of the Privy Council now speak and write about wearing three hats – deputy minister to the prime minister, head of the public service, and secretary to the Cabinet. This study makes clear the implications for Cabinet government.

The power of appointment in government, much like the expenditure budget, steals the stage. It clearly lays down who wins and who loses. It also helps the centre to keep a lid on things. In the federal government, the power of appointment is firmly in the hands of the prime minister and the clerk of the Privy

Council, notwithstanding COSO's advisory role. This gives the centre enormous power and influence. In most Western countries, this power is shared.

The Public Service Commission is both a central agency and a parliamentary agency. This study reveals that the Public Service Commission has inhibited the implementation of several NPM initiatives and that, given its independence from the executive, it is extremely difficult for the centre to bring it to heel. This study also reveals, however, that the centre of government has slowly but surely stripped some of the commission's responsibilities. The recent establishment of a new agency, the Leadership Network, reporting to the clerk of the Privy Council Office and COSO for the collective management of the assistant deputy ministers' community is a case in point. The network may well be better suited than the commission to 'meet the ongoing challenges of renewal' in the federal public service, as the clerk described its principal task when she established it.[62] It also, however, serves to strengthen the Privy Council Office and, consequently, the prime minister.

Cabinet has now joined Parliament as an institution being bypassed. Real political debate and decision making are increasingly elsewhere – in federal-provincial meetings of first ministers, on Team Canada flights, where first ministers can hold informal meetings, in the Prime Minister's Office, in the Privy Council Office, in the Department of Finance, and in international organizations and international summits. There is no indication that the one person who holds all the cards, the prime minister, and the central agencies which enable him to bring effective political authority to the centre, are about to change things. The Canadian prime minister has little in the way of institutional check, at least inside government, to inhibit his ability to have his way. Prime Ministers Margaret Thatcher of Britain and Bob Hawke of Australia were tossed out of their offices before their mandates were finished. Their own caucuses showed them the door. This would be unthinkable in Canada. Even in the depths of Mulroney's unpopularity, there was no indication that his caucus was about to boot him out of office. In any event, in Canada the caucus holds no such power. In Britain prime ministers must deal with powerful ministers who have deep roots in their party and well-established party policies and positions on many issues. In Australia the prime minister must contend with an elected and independently minded Senate. In Canada national unity concerns and the nature of federal-provincial relations tend, in a perverse fashion, to favour the centre of government in Ottawa. They dominate our policy agenda and permeate government decision making to such an extent that the centre of government is only willing to trust itself to oversee their overall management.

Notes

Introduction

1 Consultation with a senior government official, Ottawa, February 1998.
2 Arthur Kroeger, 'The Central Agencies and Program Review,' in Peter Aucoin and Donald J. Savoie, eds., *Managing Strategic Change: Learning From Program Review* (Ottawa: Canadian Centre for Management Development, 1998), 11.
3 Consultations with a senior official in the Treasury Board secretariat, Ottawa, February 1993.
4 See, for example, Donald J. Savoie, *Thatcher, Reagan, Mulroney: In Search of a New Bureaucracy* (Pittsburgh: University of Pittsburgh Press, 1994).
5 Colin Campbell and George J. Szablowski, *The Superbureaucrats: Structure and Behaviour in Central Agencies* (Toronto: Gage, 1979), chapters 4 and 5.
6 Ibid.
7 Consultation with an official with the Privy Council Office, Ottawa, March 1993.
8 Thomas T. Mackie and Brian W. Hogwood, eds., *Unlocking the Cabinet: Cabinet Structures in Comparative Perspective* (London: Sage Publications, 1985), 1.
9 Campbell and Szablowski, *The Superbureaucrats.*
10 Peter Hennessy, *Cabinet* (Oxford: Basil Blackwell, 1986), 163.
11 See, for example, Donald J. Savoie, *The Politics of Public Spending in Canada* (Toronto: University of Toronto Press, 1990).
12 See, for example, Campbell and Szablowski, *The Superbureaucrats,* 11, and Colin Campbell, 'The Search for Coordination and Control: When and How Are Central Agencies the Answer?' in Colin Campbell and B. Guy Peters, eds., *Organizing Governance, Governing Organizations* (Pittsburgh: University of Pittsburgh Press, 1988), 55.
13 See, among others, Savoie, *The Politics of Public Spending in Canada.*
14 Peter Aucoin, 'Introduction: Restructuring in the Canadian Government,' in a study

on the 1993 reorganization prepared for the Canadian Centre for Management Development, Ottawa, 1996.

15 Robert B. Denhardt, *Theories of Public Organization* (Monterey, Calif.: Brooks/Cole Publishing, 1984), 186.

16 See, among many others, Donald J. Savoie, 'What is Wrong with the New Public Management?' *Canadian Public Administration* 38, no. 1 (Spring 1995): 112–21.

17 See, for example, B. Guy Peters and Donald J. Savoie, eds., *Reforming the Public Sector: Taking Stock* (Montreal: McGill-Queen's University Press, 1998).

18 Consultation with a former senior central agency official, Ottawa, February 1998.

19 Colin Campbell, *Governments Under Stress: Political Executives and Key Bureaucrats in Washington, London, and Ottawa* (Toronto: University of Toronto Press, 1983), 22.

20 See, among many others, Savoie, *Thatcher, Reagan, Mulroney.*

21 Quoted in Hennessy, *Cabinet* (Oxford: Blackwell, 1986), 34.

22 Ibid., 180.

23 Sharon L. Sutherland, 'The Evolution of Program Budget Ideas in Canada: Does Parliament Benefit from Estimate Reform?' *Canadian Public Administration* 33, no. 2 (Summer 1990): 138.

24 Robert F. Adie and Paul G. Thomas, *Canadian Public Administration: Problematical Perspectives* (Scarborough, Ont.: Prentice-Hall, 1987), 141.

25 G. Bruce Doern, 'From Sectoral to Macro Green Governance: The Canadian Department of the Environment as an Aspiring Central Agency,' *Governance* 6, no. 2 (April 1993): 179.

26 Woodrow Wilson, *The State: Elements of Historical and Practical Politics* (London: Isbister & Co., 1899), xxxiv.

27 Consultation with a senior official with the Privy Council Office, Ottawa, October 1997.

28 In Canada, unfortunately, one must rely on interviews with government policy and decision makers to a greater extent than their counterparts in, say, Britain and France. There is a tradition in those two countries for retired politicians and senior public servants not only to provide a written account of their work, but also of their experience with the policy and decision-making processes. In Canada we have a handful of ghost-written and self-serving books from former government officials reporting on their accomplishments, but precious few substantial contributions from former government officials. There are some exceptions and, as the reader will see, I make full use of them. Still, we certainly do not have any equal in intellectual rigour to Richard Crossman's three volumes, *The Diaries of a Cabinet Minister.* Others in Britain and France have also written books that give us a better understanding of how government works. In the absence of such comparable work in Canada, one-on-one interviews are necessary if we are to gain an appreciation of

what goes on in government offices and an understanding of how government actually works.

2: The Centre Is Born

1 See, for example, J.E. Hodgetts, *The Canadian Public Service: A Physiology of Government, 1867–1970* (Toronto: University of Toronto Press, 1973).
2 Paul Van Riper, *History of the United States Civil Service* (White Plains, N.Y.: Row, Peterson and Company, 1958), 312.
3 Quoted in Stephen Hess, *Organizing the Presidency* (Washington, D.C.: The Brookings Institution, 1976), 1.
4 See, for example, Simon James, *British Cabinet Government* (London: Routledge, 1992), 2.
5 Robert B. Bryce, *Maturing in Hard Times: Canada's Department of Finance through the Great Depression* (Montreal: McGill-Queen's University Press, 1986), 4.
6 Canada, Order in Council P.C.3, 1867.
7 Bryce, *Maturing in Hard Times*, 5.
8 Ibid., 1.
9 Canada, Department of Finance and the Treasury Board secretariat, *1996–97 Estimates*, Part III, Expenditure Plan, 1997, and *1998–99 Estimates*, Part III, Report on Plans and Priorities, 1998.
10 Bryce, *Maturing in Hard Times*, 3.
11 Canada, Office of the Auditor General, *1996–97 Estimates*, Part III, Expenditure Plan, 1997.
12 Bryce, *Maturing in Hard Times*, 4.
13 Donald J. Savoie, *Thatcher, Reagan, Mulroney: In Search of a New Bureaucracy* (Pittsburgh: University of Pittsburgh Press, 1994), 45.
14 J.A. Corry and J.E. Hodgetts, *Democratic Government and Politics* (Toronto: University of Toronto Press, 1946), 501.
15 R. MacGregor Dawson, *The Government of Canada* (Toronto: University of Toronto Press, 1970), 251.
16 O.D. Skelton, *Life and Letters of Sir Wilfred Laurier* (Toronto: Oxford University Press, 1921), 270.
17 Dawson, *Government of Canada*, 252.
18 Hodgetts, *The Canadian Public Service*, 265.
19 Skelton, *Sir Wilfred Laurier*, 503.
20 Hodgetts, *The Canadian Public Service*, 268.
21 Peter Hennessy, *Whitehall* (London: Fontana Press, 1989), 56.
22 S.S. Wilson, *The Cabinet Office to 1945* (London: HMSO, 1975), 2.

23 Herbert Morrison, *Government and Parliament: A Survey From the Inside* (London: Oxford University Press, 1954), 12.
24 Wilson, *The Cabinet Office to 1945*, 3.
25 'A broad outline of Conservative and Unionist policy – dated 16 October 1922,' quoted in Wilson, *The Cabinet Office to 1945*, 46.
26 Ibid.
27 Ibid.
28 Ibid., 50.
29 James, *British Cabinet Government*, 3.
30 Morrison, *Government and Parliament*, 16.
31 Wilson, *The Cabinet Office to 1945*, 113.
32 See, for example, Hennessy, *Whitehall*, chapter 3.
33 Alex Cairncross, *Years of Recovery: British Economic Policy, 1945–51* (London: Methuen, 1985).
34 See, among others, Hennessy, *Whitehall*, 110.
35 Ibid., 88.
36 A.D.P. Heeney, 'Mackenzie King and the Cabinet Secretariat,' *Canadian Public Administration* 10 (September 1967): 367.
37 J.R. Mallory, *The Structure of Canadian Government* (Toronto: Macmillan of Canada, 1971): 98–9.
38 Lester B. Pearson, *Mike: The Memoirs of the Right Honourable Lester B. Pearson*, vol. 3, 1957–68, John A. Munro and Alex I. Inglis, eds. (Toronto: University of Toronto Press, 1975), 92–3.
39 See J.L. Granatstein, *The Ottawa Men: The Civil Service Mandarins, 1935–1957* (Toronto: Oxford University Press, 1982), 189.
40 Quoted in ibid., 195.
41 Ibid., 193.
42 Quoted in ibid., 197.
43 Ibid., 203–4.
44 Ibid., 206.
45 Ibid.
46 A.D.P. Heeney, 'Mackenzie King and the Cabinet Secretariat,' *Canadian Public Administration* 10 (September 1967), 367.
47 Ibid., 373
48 Ibid.
49 Lester B. Pearson, *Mike* 2, 1973, chapter 7.
50 C.G. Power, 'Career Politicians: The Changing Role of the M.P.,' *Queen's Quarterly* LXIII, no. 4 (Winter 1956): 488–9.
51 J.R. Mallory, 'Delegated Legislation in Canada,' in *Canadian Journal of Economics and Political Science* XIX, no. 4 (November 1953): 1681.

52 Ottawa, PC 1121 of 20 March 1940.
53 Power, 'Career Politicians,' 489.
54 Quoted in David C. Whitney, *The American Presidents* (New York: Doubleday & Co., 1969), 288.
55 Ibid., 289.
56 See William T. Gormley, *Taming the Bureaucracy: Muscles, Prayers and Other Strategies* (Princeton, N.J.: Princeton University Press, 1989), 9.
57 John Hart, *The Presidential Branch* (Oxford: Pergamon Press, 1987), 1.
58 Richard Nathan, 'The Administrative Presidency,' in Francis E. Rourke, ed., *Bureaucratic Power in National Policy Making*, 4th ed. (Boston: Little, Brown and Co., 1986), 209.
59 Gerald J. Garvey and John J. DiIulio, Jr., 'Sources of Public Service Overregulation,' in John J. DiIulio, Jr., ed., *Deregulating the Public Service: Can Government Be Improved?* (Washington, D.C.: The Brookings Institution, 1994), 17.
60 *Report of the President's Committee on Administrative Management* (Washington, D.C.: U.S. Government, January 1937), 53.
61 See, for example, Hess, *Organizing the Presidency*, 172.
62 *Report of the President's Committee on Administrative Management*, 3.
63 Ibid., 5.
64 Memorandum for the Director of the Bureau of the Budget, 20 July 1939.
65 Ed Flynn, quoted in Arthur M. Schlesinger, Jr., *The Coming of the New Deal: The Age of Roosevelt* (Boston: Houghton, Miflin Co., 1959), 532.
66 Quoted in ibid., 546.
67 See D. Owen Carrigan, *Canadian Party Platforms, 1867–1968* (Toronto: Copp Clark Publishing, 1968), 81–2.
68 Quoted in Robert M. Campbell, *Grand Illusions: The Politics of the Keynesian Experience in Canada* (Peterborough, Ont.: Broadview Press, 1987).
69 Canada, Department of Reconstruction and Supply, *Employment and Income* with special reference to the *Initial Period of Reconstruction* (Ottawa: King's Printer, 1945), 21.
70 A.W. Johnson, *Social Policy in Canada: The Past as It Conditions the Present* (Halifax: Institute for Research on Public Policy, 1987).
71 Quoted in Aaron Wildavsky, *How to Limit Government Spending, or How a constitutional amendment tying public spending to economic growth will decrease taxes and lessen inflation ...* (Berkeley: University of California Press, 1979), 169.
72 Ibid., 173.
73 Ibid.
74 Quoted in R.F. Harrod, *The Life of John Maynard Keynes* (New York: Harcourt, Brace, 1951), 447.
75 Ibid., 241.

76 Bryce, *Maturing in Hard Times*, 228.
77 Ibid., 121.
78 Ibid., 233.
79 Sir Ian Bancroft, quoted in Hennessy, *Whitehall*, 150.
80 Canada, The Royal Commission on Government Organization, vol. 1 (Ottawa: Queen's Printer, 1962).
81 United States, *The Budget of the United States Government – 1968* (Washington: Government Printing Office, 1968), 36.
82 Edgar Benson, 'The New Budget Process,' *Canadian Tax Journal* (May 1968): 161.
83 Al Johnson, 'PPBS and Decision Making in the Government of Canada,' *Cost and Management* (March–April 1971), 16.
84 Hugh Heclo and Aaron Wildavsky, *The Private Government of Public Money* (London: Macmillan Press, 1981), 268.
85 Robert F. Adie and Paul G. Thomas, *Canadian Public Administration: Problematical Perspectives* (Scarborough, Ont.: Prentice-Hall, 1987), 141.
86 Aaron Wildavsky, *The Politics of the Budgetary Process* (Boston: Little, Brown, 1984), 184.
87 Quoted in Savoie, *The Politics of Public Spending in Canada* (Toronto: University of Toronto Press, 1990), 60.
88 Ibid., 61.
89 Ibid.
90 Quoted in ibid., 62.
91 R. Van Loon, 'Stop the Music: The Current Policy and Expenditure Management System in Ottawa,' *Canadian Public Administration* 24, no. 2 (1981): 189.
92 See, among others, Savoie, *The Politics of Public Spending in Canada.*
93 Ian Clark, 'PEMS and the Central Agencies: Notes for a Presentation to a Seminar on Making Government Planning Work,' North American Society for Corporate Planning, 27 October 1983, 16.
94 See 'Trudeau-Pitfield Bureaucracy First Item on Turner's Overhaul,' *Globe and Mail*, 2 July 1984, A5; see also Canada, Office of the Prime Minister, 'Government Organization Measures,' News Release, 30 June 1984.
95 See Granatstein, *The Ottawa Men*, 183.
96 Schlesinger, *The Coming of the New Deal*, 544.
97 See Ian Clark, 'Ottawa's Principal Decision-Making and Advisory Committees' (Ottawa: Privy Council Office 1 December 1983), 12–13. Mr Clark adds that the requirement that a decision be made 'in Council' (i.e., with the queen's privy councillors) can be satisfied by a quorum of four ministers making a recommendation, which the governor general then signs separately. Orders-in-council requiring policy decisions are normally passed in Cabinet, and in those cases – as well as for orders passed in the Special Committee of Council – only the chairman's signature is

required, and the assistant clerk of the Privy Council attests to the fact that at least four ministers were present. Where the order-in-council involves a significant policy decision, the policy discussion and agreement will have been obtained in advance through the normal Cabinet committee process. On rare occasions when an order-in-council is required on an urgent basis between meetings, it can be secured by obtaining the individual signatures of four ministers (usually including the prime minister or a senior minister). The Special Committee of Council usually meets weekly. The supporting documentation consists of a list of orders and explanatory material which is circulated to all the members a day before the meeting.

98 Mulroney had Cabinet committees for the public service, communications, legislation and house planning, government operations, economic and regional development, social development, Priorities and Planning, Treasury Board, Special Committee of Council and Security and Intelligence. It should be noted that Chrétien has also retained Special Committee of Council (ratification of decisions) and the Security and Intelligence Committee, which now meet only once a year. See also Ian Clark, 'Recent Changes in the Cabinet Decision-Making System' (Ottawa: Privy Council Office, 3 December 1984), 8.

99 Peter Aucoin, 'Organizational Change in the Machinery of Canadian Government: From Rational Management to Brokerage Politics,' *Canadian Journal of Political Science* XIX, no. 1 (March 1986): 3.

3: Render Unto the Centre

1 Denis Smith, 'President and Parliament: The Transformation of Parliamentary Government in Canada,' Thomas A. Hockin, ed., *Apex of Power: The prime minister and political leadership in Canada*, 2d ed. (Scarborough, Ont.: Prentice-Hall, 1977), 114.

2 J. Aberbach et al., *Bureaucrats and Politicians in Western Democracies* (Cambridge: Harvard University Press, 1981), 16–17.

3 See *Responsibility in the Constitution* (Ottawa: Privy Council Office 1993), 23. See also Nevil Johnson, *In Search of the Constitution: Reflections on State and Society in Britain* (London: Methuen, 1977) and Geoffrey Marshall and Graeme C. Moodie, *Some Problems of the Constitution*, 5th ed. (London: Hutchinson University Library 1971).

4 *Responsibility in the Constitution*, 23–5.

5 Marshall and Moodie, *Some Problems of the Constitution*, 5.

6 R. MacGregor Dawson, *The Government of Canada*, 5th ed., revised by Norman Ward (Toronto: University of Toronto Press, 1970), 179.

7 R.G. Robertson, 'The Canadian Parliament and Cabinet in the Face of Modern Demands,' paper presented to the Institute of Public Administration of Canada, 1967, 18.

8 R.G. Robertson, 'The Changing Role of the Privy Council Office,' *Canadian Public Administration* 14, no. 4 (Winter 1971): 487.
9 John Mackintosh, *The British Cabinet* (London: Methuen, 1962; University Paperback, 1968), 51.
10 See, among many others, Peter Hennessy, *Cabinet* (Oxford: Basil Blackwell, 1986).
11 Consultation with a Cabinet minister, Ottawa, 1 November 1994.
12 See Hennessy, *Cabinet*. The author reproduces the British *Cabinet Procedure* in 8–13.
13 Ibid., 190.
14 W.A. Matheson, *The Prime Minister and the Cabinet* (Agincourt: Methuen, 1975), 31.
15 Peter Aucoin, 'Accountability: The Key to Restoring Public Confidence in Government,' *The Timlin Lecture*, University of Saskatchewan, undated, 10.
16 Johnson, *In Search of the Constitution*, 74.
17 This point was made by Sharon Sutherland at a seminar sponsored by the Canadian Centre for Management Development, Ottawa, May 1990.
18 Edward S. Corwin, *The President, Office and Powers, 1787–1957*, 4th ed. (New York: New York University Press, 1957), 82.
19 Ibid., 209.
20 John Hart, *The Presidential Branch* (Oxford: Pergamon Press, 1987), 126.
21 Quoted in Arthur M. Schlesinger Jr., *The Coming of the New Deal: The Age of Roosevelt* (Boston: Houghton, Miflin Co., 1959), 518.
22 Ibid., 520.
23 Quoted in Richard F. Fenno Jr., *The President's Cabinet: An Analysis in the Period from Wilson to Eisenhower* (New York: Vintage Books, 1959), 138.
24 A. Crossman quoted in Patrick Weller, *First Among Equals: Prime Ministers in Westminster Systems* (Sydney: George Allan & Unwin, 1985), 132.
25 Schlesinger, *The Coming of the New Deal*, 520.
26 Hart, *The Presidential Branch*, 121.
27 Thomas E. Cronin, *The State of the Presidency* (Boston: Little, Brown, 1975), 177.
28 See, for example, Joseph Califano, *Governing America* (New York: Simon and Schuster, 1981): 402–48.
29 Hart, *The Presidential Branch*, 120.
30 Ibid.
31 Ibid., 123.
32 Lou Canon, *President Reagan: The Role of a Lifetime* (New York: Simon and Schuster, 1991), 70.
33 See, among others, Charles O. Jones, *The Presidency in a Separated System* (Washington, D.C.: Brookings Institution, 1994), 100.
34 There are many excellent studies which compare the British Cabinet system and the

American presidential system. A classic is H.J. Laski, *The American Presidency: An Interpretation* (New York: Harper and Brothers, 1940).

35 Aberbach et al., *Bureaucrats and Politicians in Western Democracies*, 16–17.

36 The quotation is drawn from Marshall and Moodie, *Some Problems of the Constitution*, 55.

37 Herman Finer, *The British Civil Service* (London: Allen and Unwin, 1937), 196.

38 Ibid.

39 The Al-Mashat case in Canada jumps to mind. For an excellent account of the case, see Sharon Sutherland, 'The Al-Mashat Affair: Administrative Responsibility in Parliamentary Institutions,' *Canadian Public Administration* 34, no. 2 (Winter 1991): 573–604.

40 Robin Butler, 'Reinventing British Government,' *Public Administration* 72, no. 3 (Summer 1994): 270.

41 Schlesinger Jr., *The Coming of the New Deal*, 521–2.

42 Gerald Kaufman, *How To Be a Minister* (London: Sidgwide and Jackson, 1980), 30.

43 James Q. Wilson, *Bureaucracy: What Government Agencies Do and Why They Do It* (New York: Basic Books, 1989), 1, 11.

44 Paul H. Appleby, *Policy and Administration* (University, Ala.: University of Alabama Press, 1949), 13.

45 'Foggy windows become $3M for taxpayers,' *Citizen* (Ottawa), 11 January 1995, A1.

46 'Public Works issuing more window dressing,' *Citizen* (Ottawa), 13 January 1995, A2.

47 'Foreign Affairs window deal cancelled,' *Globe and Mail* (Toronto), 20 January 1995, A4.

48 Consultations with government officials, Ottawa, various dates between September 1997 and January 1998.

49 Alfred Diamant, 'The Bureaucratic Model: Max Weber Rejected, Rediscovered, Reformed,' in Ferrel Heady and Sybil L. Stokes, eds., *Papers in Comparative Public Administration* (Ann Arbor: University of Michigan, Institute of Public Administration, 1963), 85.

50 See, for example, Donald J. Savoie, *Regional Economic Development: Canada's Search for Solutions* (Toronto: University of Toronto Press, 1992).

51 William Rodgers, 'Westminster and Whitehall: Adapting to Change,' in *Policy and Practice: The Experience of Government* (London: Royal Institute of Public Administration, 1980), 13.

52 See Savoie, *Regional Economic Development*.

53 G. Bruce Doern, 'From Sectoral to Macro Green Governance: The Canadian Department of the Environment As An Aspiring Central Agency,' *Governance* 6, no. 2 (April 1993): 179.

54 See Savoie, 'Globalization and Governance' (Ottawa: Canadian Centre for Management Development, 1993).
55 See Aaron Wildavsky, 'A Budget for All Seasons? Why the Traditional Budget Lasts,' *Public Administration Review* 38 (November/December 1978): 501–9.
56 Canada, *Task Force on Managing Horizontal Policy Issues*, Ottawa, 15 October 1996, 21.
57 Ibid., 25.
58 Ibid.
59 Ibid., 29–37.
60 Canada, *Strengthening Our Policy Capacity*, Report of the task force to the Coordinating Committee of Deputy Ministers (Policy), Privy Council Office, 3 April 1995, 34.
61 Ibid.
62 Ibid., 35.
63 Ian Clark, 'Recent Changes in the Cabinet Decision-making System' (Ottawa: Privy Council Office, 3 December 1984), 5–8.
64 Consultations with a senior official with the Privy Council Office, Ottawa, November 1997. See also ibid.
65 Peter Aucoin, 'Prime Minister and Cabinet,' in James Bickerton and Alain G. Gagnon, eds., *Canadian Politics: An Introduction to the Discipline* (Toronto: Broadview Press, 1994), 275.
66 See, among many others, Savoie, *Thatcher, Reagan, Mulroney: In Search of a New Bureaucracy* (Pittsburgh: University of Pittsburgh Press, 1994).
67 Ibid.
68 Donald J. Savoie, 'What Is Wrong with the New Public Management?' *Canadian Public Administration* 38, no. 1 (Spring 1995).
69 Quoted in Pierre Gravelle, Deputy Minister of Revenue, Government of Canada, 'Management: A Central Agency and Line Department Perspective,' Ottawa, Notes for a Speech, 3 March 1989.

4: *Primus*: There Is No Longer Any *Inter* or *Pares*

1 G.W. Jones, 'The Prime Minister's Secretaries: Politicians or Administrators?' in J. Griffith, ed., *From Policy to Administration: Essays in Honour of William A. Robson* (London: George Allen & Unwin, 1976), 36.
2 Quoted in Arthur M. Schlesinger Jr., *The Coming of the New Deal: The Age of Roosevelt* (Boston: Houghton, Miflin Co., 1959), 518.
3 See John C. Crosbie, *No Holds Barred: My Life in Politics* (Toronto: McClelland and Stewart, 1997), 301.
4 Consultation with a former Cabinet minister in the Trudeau government, Ottawa,

February 1993.

5 Consultation with a former Cabinet minister in the Mulroney government, Ottawa, March 1993.

6 See, among others, 'Eastern fishermen to get help,' *Globe and Mail* (Toronto), 4 May 1998, A1, and 'Liberals keep up fish deal,' *Citizen* (Ottawa), 19 June 1998, A1, A2.

7 'Ottawa sweetens aid for fisheries,' *Globe and Mail* (Toronto), 19 June 1998, A1, A5.

8 Consultation with an official with Western Diversification Department, Ottawa, December 1997.

9 Based on information provided by Senator Lowell Murray, a former Mulroney Cabinet minister, Ottawa, July 1998.

10 Patrick Weller, 'Administering the Summit: Australia,' paper presented to the ESRC Conference, Nuffield College, Oxford, 20–1 June 1997, 1.

11 'A Burning Issue,' *The Economist* (London), 25 January 1997, 54.

12 Peter Aucoin, 'Prime Minister and Cabinet,' in James Bickerton and Alain G. Gagnon, eds., *Canadian Politics: An Introduction to the Discipline* (Toronto: Broadview Press, 1994), 268.

13 Quoted in Sharon L. Sutherland, 'Does Westminster Government Have a Future?' (Ottawa: Institute of Governance, Occasional Paper Series, 11 June 1996), 5.

14 Ibid., 11.

15 I was invited in August 1993 to review parts of the Red Book in the Office of the Leader of the Opposition and to provide any comments. It was obvious to me that, contrary to press reports, a number of people in the office had a hand in its preparation.

16 *Creating Opportunity: The Liberal Plan for Canada* (Ottawa: Liberal Party of Canada, 1993), preface.

17 Consultation with a former assistant to the Right Honourable Jean Chrétien, Ottawa, November 1997.

18 See, among many others, Edward Greenspon and Anthony Wilson-Smith, *Double Vision: The Inside Story of the Liberals in Power* (Toronto: Doubleday, 1996), chapter 2.

19 Ibid., 22.

20 Quoted in ibid., 133.

21 *Creating Opportunity*, 111.

22 Harold D. Clarke et al., *Absent Mandate: Interpreting Change in Canadian Elections*, 2d ed. (Toronto: Gage Educational Publishing Co., 1991), 8, 10.

23 See, for example, Richard Johnston et al., *Letting the People Decide: Dynamics of a Canadian Election* (Montreal: McGill-Queen's University Press, 1992), 244.

24 Nelson W. Polsby and Aaron Wildavsky, *Presidential Elections: Strategies of American Electoral Politics* (New York: Free Press, 1991), 246.

25 Johnston et al., *Letting the People Decide*, 244.
26 Ibid., 168.
27 Ibid., 225.
28 Consultation with a senior official in the Prime Minister's Office, Ottawa, December 1997.
29 Patrick Weller, *First among Equals: Prime Ministers in Westminster Systems* (London: George Allen & Unwin, 1985), 8.
30 Evert Lindquist and Graham White, 'Analysing Canadian Cabinets: Past, Present and Future,' in Mohamed Charih et al. eds., *New Public Management and Public Administration in Canada* (Toronto: IPAC, 1997), 120.
31 John L. Manion and Cynthia Williams, 'Transition Planning at the Federal Level in Canada,' in Donald J. Savoie, ed., *Taking Power: Managing Government Transitions* (Toronto: IPAC, 1993), 100.
32 Ibid., 108.
33 Ibid., 99.
34 Donald J. Savoie, 'Introduction,' in *Taking Power*, 8.
35 Ibid., 1.
36 See, among others, James R. Mallory, *The Structure of Canadian Government* (Toronto: Macmillan, 1971), 90–109.
37 For example, John Crosbie, a leadership candidate at the time Brian Mulroney was elected leader of the Progressive Conservative Party, was named minister of Justice when Mulroney came to power in 1984, rather than Allan Lawrence, former attorney general of Ontario, solicitor general in Joe Clark's government in 1979, and opposition Justice critic between 1980 and 1984. Lawrence, however, had supported Crosbie rather than Mulroney in the leadership race. There are many other examples. Doug Young supported Jean Chrétien in his party leadership race, and Chrétien appointed him to Cabinet in 1993 over George Rideout, a highly respected former mayor of Moncton, who had supported Paul Martin.
38 Consultation with a former Cabinet minister in the Mulroney government, Ottawa, March 1993.
39 Gerald Kaufman, *How To Be a Minister* (London: Sidgwide & Jackson, 1980), 19.
40 Richard D. French, 'The Privy Council Office: Support for Cabinet Decision-Making,' in R. Schultz et al., eds., *The Canadian Political Process* (Toronto: Holt, Rinehart and Winston, 1979), 2d ed., 365.
41 Peter Aucoin, 'Organizational Change in the Machinery of Canadian Government: From Rational Management to Brokerage Politics,' *Canadian Journal of Political Science* XIX, no. 1 (March 1986): 8.
42 Quotes in George Radwanski, *Trudeau* (Toronto: Macmillan, 1978), 172.
43 Ibid., 173.

44 Consultation with a senior official in the Privy Council Office, Ottawa, November 1997.
45 Consultation with a former senior PCO official, Ottawa, January 1998.
46 Consultation with a former federal Cabinet minister, Ottawa, December 1997.
47 Ibid.
48 Consultation with a former official with PCO, Ottawa, October 1997.
49 Marc Lalonde, 'The Changing Role of the Prime Minister's Office,' in *Canadian Public Administration* 14, no. 4 (Winter 1971): 513.
50 Consultation with the president of a crown corporation, Ottawa, September 1997.
51 See Radwanski, *Trudeau*, 114.
52 Elliott Jacques, *Requisite Organization: A Total System for Effective Managerial Organization and Managerial Leadership for the 21st Century* (Cason Hall: Arlington, VA, 1996), 97.
53 Ibid., 20–1.
54 Consultation with an official in the Prime Minister's Office, Ottawa, November 1997.
55 See, for example, 'Salesman Chrétien packs bags again,' *Citizen* (Ottawa), 30 December 1994, A3.
56 Simon James, *British Cabinet Government* (London: Routledge, 1992), 104.
57 Quoted in Radwanski, *Trudeau*, 14.
58 William Greiter, 'The Education of David Stockman,' *Atlantic Monthly*, 1 December 1981, 47.
59 Consultation with a former government caucus member, Ottawa, October 1997.
60 Ibid.
61 Ibid., November 1997. See also David C. Docherty, *Mr. Smith Goes to Ottawa: Life in the House of Commons* (Vancouver: University of British Columbia Press, 1997).
62 Warren Allmand, 'Policy Meets Politics,' in *Strengthening Policy Capacity* (Ottawa: Canadian Centre for Management Development, 1996), 1.
63 Ibid., 3.
64 James R. Mitchell and Sharon Sutherland, 'Relations Between Politicians and Public Servants' in Charih et al., eds., *New Public Management and Public Administration in Canada* (Toronto: IPAC, 1997), 185.
65 See, for example, Richard Rose, 'British Government,' in Richard Rose and Ezra N. Suleiman, eds., *Presidents and Prime Ministers* (Washington, D.C.: American Enterprise Institute, 1980), 12.
66 Mitchell and Sutherland, 'Relations Between Politicians and Public Servants,' 192.
67 Crosbie, *No Holds Barred*, 254.
68 Tom Rosenstiel, *The Beat Goes On: President Clinton's First Year with the Media* (Washington, D.C.: The Twentieth Century Fund Essay, 1994), 30.
69 Erik Nielsen, *The House Is Not a Home* (Toronto: Macmillan of Canada, 1989), 207.

70 David Taras, *The Newsmakers: The Media's Influence on Canadian Politics* (Scarborough: Nelson Canada, 1990), and Joshua Meyrowitz, *No Sense of Place* (New York: Oxford University Press, 1985).
71 See, among others, 'No Credibility Any More,' *Maclean's* (Toronto), 8 December 1997, 81.
72 Crosbie, *No Holds Barred*, 300.
73 Rosenstiel, *The Beat Goes On*, 31.
74 Ibid.
75 David A. Stockman, *The Triumph of Politics: How the Reagan Revolution Failed* (NY: Harper & Row, 1986), 300.
76 Consultations with present and former staff members in the Prime Minister's Office, Ottawa, October to December 1997.
77 'Simpson takes a swipe at the year's political books,' *Globe and Mail* (Toronto), 31 December 1994, C12.
78 George Bain, *Gotcha: How the Media Distorts the News* (Toronto: Key Porter Books, 1994).
79 'Disillusioned CBC bureau chief signs off,' *Citizen* (Ottawa), 3 August 1993, A2.
80 Consultation with a Cabinet minister, Ottawa, December 1994.
81 Greenspon & Wilson-Smith, *Double Vision*, 7.
82 See, for example, Margaret Thatcher, *The Downing Street Years* (New York: HarperCollins, 1993).
83 'Fraser resigns post,' *Globe and Mail* (Toronto), 24 September 1985, A1.
84 Ibid.
85 'Contradictions led to resignation,' *Globe and Mail* (Toronto), 10 May, 1986, A11.
86 Nielsen, *The House Is Not a Home*, 254.
87 A PMO official quoted in Colin Campbell and George J. Szablowski, *The Superbureaucrats: Structure and Behaviour in Central Agencies* (Toronto: Gage, 1979), 60.
88 Trudeau quoted in Radwanski, *Trudeau*, 146.
89 Tom Kent, *A Public Purpose: An experience of Liberal opposition and Canadian government* (Montreal: McGill-Queen's University Press, 1988), 225.
90 Peter Aucoin, 'Organizational Change in the Machinery of Canadian Government: From Rational Management to Brokerage Politics,' *Canadian Journal of Political Science* XIX, no. 1 (March 1986): 22.
91 Lalonde, 'The Changing Role of the Prime Minister's Office,' 519.
92 Thomas D'Aquino, 'The Prime Minister's Office: Catalyst or Cabal? Aspects of the development of the office in Canada and some thoughts about its future,' *Canadian Public Administration* 17, no. 1 (Spring 1974): 76–7.
93 See, among others, Richard French, *How Ottawa Decides: Planning and Industrial Policy-making 1968–1980* (Ottawa: Canadian Institute for Economic Policy, 1980), 77–84.

94 See Lalonde, 'The Changing Role of the Prime Minister's Office,' 526.
95 See 'Pelletier reorganizes PMO staffers,' *The Hill Times* (Ottawa), 24 November 1997, A1.
96 Consultation with a senior adviser to the prime minister, Ottawa, December 1997.
97 Consultation with a former assistant to Prime Minister Chrétien, Ottawa, October 1997.
98 Derek Burney, a senior permanent official, was seconded to the Prime Minister's Office under Brian Mulroney.
99 Lalonde, 'The Changing Role of the Prime Minister's Office,' 520.
100 Consultation with a senior official with the Privy Council Office, Ottawa, November 1997.
101 Hugh Winsor, 'Decision on Nova Scotia road hides flexing of strong PMO arm,' *Globe and Mail* (Toronto), 24 August, 1995, A1.
102 See Donald J. Savoie, *Regional Economic Development: Canada's Search for Solutions*, 2d ed. (Toronto: University of Toronto Press, 1992), chapter 4.
103 See Greenspon and Wilson-Smith, *Double Vision*, 37–42.
104 Quoted in ibid., 188.
105 John Crosbie, for example, writes that he was scolded by a senior PMO staff member for having told a colleague that he was being appointed minister of Justice. See Crosbie, *No Holds Barred*, 248.
106 Consultation with a Cabinet minister, Ottawa, October 1997.
107 Quoted in James, *British Cabinet Government*, 94.
108 Weller, *First Among Equals*, 1.
109 John Mackintosh, *The British Cabinet* (London: Methuen, 1962). Professor Mackintosh was also a Labour member of Parliament from 1966 to 1974.
110 See Richard Crossman, *The Diaries of a Cabinet Minister*, vols. 1–3 (London: Hamish Hamilton and Jonathan Cape, 1975, 1976, and 1977).
111 Weller, *First Among Equals*, 4.
112 John Mackintosh, *The British Cabinet*, 3d ed., 1977, 631.
113 Denis Smith, 'President and Parliament: The Transformation of Parliamentary Government in Canada,' Thomas A. Hockin, ed., *Apex of Power: The prime minister and political leadership in Canada*, 2d ed. (Scarborough, Ont.: Prentice-Hall, 1977).
114 Based on material including correspondence made available by the Prime Minister's Office, Ottawa, December 1997.
115 Crosbie, *No Holds Barred*, 476.
116 See, among others, 'PM not sounding valedictory note,' *Globe and Mail* (Toronto), 23 March 1998, A3.
117 See, among others, Donald J. Savoie, 'Globalization and Governance' (Ottawa: Canadian Centre for Management Development, 1993), 8 and Daniel Bell, 'The World and the United States in 2013,' *Daedalus*, 116, no. 3 (1984): 19–26.

118 Over a three-day period at the end of November 1997, Prime Minister Chrétien met with the Japanese prime minister, the Chinese president, and the president of the Philippines. See, for example, 'Chrétien plays host to leaders,' *Telegraph Journal* (Saint John), 27 November 1997, B3.

119 Harlan Cleveland, 'The Twilight of Hierarchy: Speculations on the Global Information Society,' *Public Administration Review* 45, no. 1 (January/February 1985): 195.

120 Quoted in Greenspon and Wilson-Smith, *Double Vision*, 48.

121 See, among others, Peter Hennessy, *The Hidden Wiring: Unearthing the British Constitution* (London: Victor Gollancz, 1995), 78.

5: The Privy Council Office: A Safe Pair of Hands

1 R.G. Robertson, 'The Changing Role of the Privy Council Office,' *Canadian Public Administration* XIV, no. 4 (1975): 488.

2 Consultation with a former senior official with the Privy Council Office, Ottawa, May 1997.

3 Ibid.

4 Quoted in Peter Hennessy, *Cabinet* (Oxford: Basil Blackwell, 1986), 15.

5 An official from the Prime Minister's Office provided me a copy of the document *Retreat on the Government-Citizen Relationship*, a background document on the joint PMO/PCO retreat on citizen engagement, 26 and 27 June 1997, Econiche-in-the-Gatineau.

6 Canada, *The Functioning of the Privy Council Office* (Ottawa: Privy Council Office, December 1978), 4–8 and 4–30.

7 See the mandate discussion in Canada, *Privy Council Office 1997–98 Estimates*, Part III, Expenditure Plan, 1997, 7.

8 Gordon Osbaldeston, *Organizing to Govern* vol. 1 (Toronto: McGraw-Hill Ryerson, 1992) 115.

9 A.D.P. Heeney, 'Mackenzie King and the Cabinet Secretariat,' *Canadian Public Administration* 10 (September 1967): 373.

10 Consultation with a senior PCO official, Ottawa, February 1998.

11 Heeney, 'Mackenzie King and the Cabinet Secretariat,' 367.

12 Colin Campbell, *Governments under Stress: Political Executives and Key Bureaucrats in Washington, London, and Ottawa* (Toronto: University of Toronto Press, 1983), 83.

13 Ibid.

14 Consultations with three former federal Cabinet ministers, Ottawa, March and October 1997.

15 Canada, *The Role and Structure of the Privy Council Office* (Ottawa: Privy Council Office, October 1997), 1.

16 See the mandate discussion in Canada, *Privy Council Office 1997–98 Estimates*.
17 Consultation with a former senior PCO official, Ottawa, November 1997.
18 Canada, *The Functioning of the Privy Council Office*, 4–8.
19 Mitchell Sharp, 'Relations Between Politicians and Public Administrators,' in *Bulletin* (Toronto: Institute of Public Administration, 1985), 1.
20 Consultation with a senior official with the Prime Minister's Office, Ottawa, December 1997.
21 Consultation with a senior PCO official, Ottawa, February 1998.
22 Canada, *The Functioning of the Privy Council Office*, 12.
23 Frank Swift, *Strategic Management in the Public Service: The Changing Role of the Deputy Minister* (Ottawa: Canadian Centre for Management Development, 1993), 43.
24 Jacques Bourgault and Stéphane Dion, *How Should the Performance of Senior Officials Be Appraised? The Response from Federal Deputy Ministers* (Ottawa: Canadian Centre for Management Development, 1997), 4.
25 Ibid., 8.
26 Consultation with a deputy minister in a line department, Ottawa, January 1993.
27 Bourgault and Dion, *How Should the Performance of Senior Officials Be Appraised?* 6.
28 Ibid., 61.
29 See also Donald J. Savoie, *The Politics of Public Spending in Canada* (Toronto: University of Toronto Press, 1990), chapter 9.
30 Joe Clark, 'Recent Changes in the Cabinet Decision-Making System' (Ottawa: Privy Council Office, 3 December 1984), 26.
31 Ian Clark, 'Ottawa's Principal Decision-Making and Advisory Committees' (Ottawa: Privy Council Office, 1 December 1993), 22.
32 Ibid., 21.
33 See, for example, ibid.
34 Ibid.
35 Colin Campbell and George J. Szablowski, *The Superbureaucrats: Structure and Behaviour in Central Agencies* (Toronto: Gage, 1979), 80.
36 Consultation with a deputy minister in a line department, Ottawa, January 1993.
37 Richard French, *How Ottawa Decides: Planning and Industrial Policy-making 1968–1980* (Ottawa: Canadian Institute for Economic Policy, 1980), 6.
38 Ibid.
39 Canada, *The Role and Structure of the Privy Council Office*, 5.
40 Ibid., 6.
41 Ibid., 8.
42 Ibid., 9.
43 Campbell, *Governments under Stress*, 87.

44 Ibid., 10.
45 Ibid., 12.
46 Ibid., 10.
47 Ibid. See also Canada, Privy Council Office, *Outlook*, report to the Standing Committee on Government Operations, April 1996, 5–9.
48 Based on written comments prepared by Senator Lowell Murray, Ottawa, July 1998. As already noted, Murray was a minister in the Mulroney government and executive assistant to the minister responsible for the RCMP in the early 1960s.
49 Consultation with a former senior official with the Privy Council Office, Ottawa, October 1997.
50 Ibid., December 1997.
51 Ibid.
52 Ibid.
53 Canada, *The Functioning of the Privy Council Office*, 4–21.
54 Ibid., 4–40.
55 Canada, *Release*, Office of the Prime Minister, 4 November 1993, 2.
56 Peter Aucoin, 'Prime Minister and Cabinet,' in James Bickerton and Alain G. Gagnon, eds., *Canadian Politics: An Introduction to the Discipline* (Toronto: Broadview Press, 1994), 279.
57 Thomas J. Mackie and Brian W. Hogwood, 'Decision Making in Cabinet Government,' in Thomas J. Mackie and Brian W. Hogwood, eds., *Unlocking the Cabinet: Cabinet Structures in Comparative Perspective* (London: Sage, 1985), 11.
58 Consultation with a former senior PCO official, Ottawa, February 1998.
59 Ibid., December 1997.
60 Consultation with a former PCO official, Ottawa, December 1997.
61 Ibid., November 1997.
62 Consultation with a senior PCO official, Ottawa, November 1997.
63 Ibid.
64 Consultation with a former senior deputy minister, Montreal, October 1997.
65 Consultation with a PCO official, Ottawa, November 1997.
66 Ibid.
67 Consultation with a senior adviser to the prime minister, Ottawa, November 1997.
68 Consultation with a former senior official in the Prime Minister's Office, Ottawa, January 1995.
69 This observation was made by a former senior PCO official, Ottawa, November 1997.
70 Consultation with a senior PCO official, Ottawa, November 1997.
71 Ibid.
72 Ibid., January 1998.
73 Consultations with a senior Department of Finance official, Ottawa, November 1997.

74 Consultation with a PCO official, Ottawa, November 1997.
75 Consultation with a former senior PCO official, Ottawa, December 1997.
76 Consultations with a senior PCO official, Ottawa, November 1997. See also, 'The Manitoba Flood,' *Globe and Mail* (Toronto), 2 May 1997, A1.
77 Consultation with a federal government official, Ottawa, December 1997.
78 Consultation with a former PCO official, Ottawa, October 1997.
79 Ibid.
80 The same applies in Britain. See, for example, Simon James, *British Cabinet Government* (London: Routledge, 1992), 140.
81 Colin Campbell, 'Political Leadership in Canada,' in Richard Rose and Ezra N. Suleiman, eds., *Presidents and Prime Ministers* (Washington, D.C.: American Enterprise Institute, 1980), 65.
82 Consultations with a Treasury Board secretariat official who attended the conference, Ottawa, December 1997.
83 Consultations with a senior PCO official, Ottawa, November 1997. See also, 'Envoys pour into Ottawa for land-mines summit,' *Citizen* (Ottawa), 29 November 1997, A1.
84 She made the comment on CBC Radio, *This Morning*, 5 December 1997.
85 James, *British Cabinet Government*, 137.
86 Edward Greenspon and Anthony Wilson-Smith, *Double Vision: The Inside Story of the Liberals in Power* (Toronto: Doubleday, 1996), 218.
87 Andrew F. Cooper, *In Between Countries: Australia, Canada and the Search for Order in Agricultural Trade* (Montreal: McGill-Queen's University Press, 1997), 217.
88 James, *British Cabinet Government*.
89 See Canada, Privy Council Office, *Improved Reporting to Parliament* – Pilot document, for the period ending 31 March 1997 (Ottawa: Minister of Public Works and Government Services, 1997), 7
90 Consultation with a former senior PCO official, Ottawa, November 1997.
91 Ibid., December 1997.
92 Consultation with a minister in the Chrétien Cabinet, Ottawa, October 1997.
93 Consultation with a former senior PCO official, Ottawa, December 1997.
94 See Donald J. Savoie, 'Restructuring the Government of Canada: Leading from the centre' (Ottawa: Canadian Centre for Management Development, 1996), 1.
95 Osbaldeston, *Organizing to Govern* 1, 115.
96 Ibid., 145.
97 Quoted in Savoie, 'Restructuring the Government of Canada,' 6.
98 See Donald J. Savoie, *Regional Economic Development: Canada's Search for Solutions*, 2d ed. (Toronto: University of Toronto Press, 1992), 77.
99 'De Bané's Future Appears Bright Despite New Post,' *The Gazette* (Montreal), 13 January 1982, 13.

100 At the time of Trudeau's announcement, I was senior policy adviser to Pierre De Bané, minister of the Department of Regional Economic Expansion.
101 Quoted in 'Bickering over car plant led to Cabinet shake-up,' *Sunday Star* (Toronto), 17 January 1982, 1.
102 Canada, *Press Release*, Office of the Prime Minister, 25 June 1993.
103 Ibid.
104 Ibid., 2.
105 'Power shift,' *Globe and Mail* (Toronto), 5 July 1993, A1.
106 See Savoie, 'Restructuring the Government of Canada,' 13.
107 Ibid., 14.
108 Ibid., 20.
109 See Patrick Weller, *Machinery of Government in Canada 1993: A Comparative Perspective*, Ottawa, Canadian Centre for Management Development, mimeo, 1995, 1.
110 Peter Aucoin, 'Introduction,' in a study on the 1993 reorganization prepared for the Canadian Centre for Management Development, Ottawa, 1996, 27.
111 Quoted in ibid., 23. See also 'Taking aim at bureaucracy's bloat,' *The Financial Post* (Toronto), 31 July 1995, 5.
112 See Marcel Massé, 'Getting Government Right,' an address to the Public Service Alliance of Canada, Regional Quebec Conference, Longueuil, 12 September 1993, 7.
113 Aucoin, 'Introduction,' 47.
114 Ibid., 42.
115 'Power Shift,' *Globe and Mail* (Toronto), 13 July 1993, A1.
116 'Taking aim at bureaucracy's bloat,' 5.
117 Savoie, 'Restructuring the Government of Canada,' 9.
118 Consultations with a former senior PCO official, Ottawa, December 1997.
119 Based on material provided to me by a former senior official with the Federal-Provincial Relations Office, Ottawa, January 1993.
120 Canada, Privy Council Office, *Improved Reporting to Parliament*, 3.
121 Canada, *The Role and Structure of the Privy Council Office*.
122 The director general for intergovernmental communications provides strategic advice on the intergovernmental aspects of government-wide communications activities and initiatives. The division is also responsible for preparing speeches, letters, and other written material related to intergovernmental relations. In addition, the division oversees parliamentary affairs related to intergovernmental issues when the House is in session. The director general, Policy and Research, is responsible for conducting policy analysis and providing advice on issues related to the medium- and long-term evolution of the Canadian federation; for conducting research on social, economic, fiscal and other issues, including public opinion, that

impact on intergovernmental relations, the operation of the federation and Canadian unity; and for monitoring relevant information and research in the academic and policy communities across Canada. The director general, Constitutional Affairs and Intergovernmental Policy, is responsible for the provision of advice on issues related to constitutional reform and the ongoing evolution of the Canadian federation; and for monitoring, screening, and processing information related to constitutional issues between the federal and provincial governments. The director general, Strategy and Plans, provides strategic planning, research, and policy advice on the conduct of intergovernmental relations in the context of the government's objectives for national unity. This includes development of scenarios and options to assist the prime minister, the minister, and the Cabinet in decision making on unity. All directors generals direct the work of several officials. Quoted in ibid.

123 Ibid.

124 Director general, Provincial Analysis, provides the prime minister and the minister of Intergovernmental Affairs with strategic and tactical advice on overall management of federal-provincial relations. This group monitors the changing situation in the provinces and territories, identifies issues and trends, and assesses the provincial government's approaches and positions on files concerning the federation. It plays a leading role in organizing and managing bilateral and multilateral First Ministers meetings, including First Ministers' Conferences. The director general, Coordination and Advisory Services, provides departments with strategic and tactical advice in the development of their intergovernmental negotiations on major issues, as well as an assessment of how the situation is evolving in the province concerned. On request, it provides departments with strategic advice for the development of policies and programs containing an intergovernmental component. The group monitors ongoing negotiations and offers its services to the departments concerned, identifies problematic questions and evaluates possible approaches with a view to concluding the negotiations to the parties' satisfaction. The director general, Strategic Analysis, undertakes strategic analyses of pan-Canadian federal-provincial issues and approaches that affect the federation. It also provides strategic advice on nonconstitutional means of modernizing the federation, and on the management of policy initiatives key to the government's national unity agenda. The assistant deputy minister, Aboriginal Affairs, provides advice and support on aboriginal policy and constitutional matters and is responsible for the strategic policy framework for federal-provincial-aboriginal relations. The division coordinates intergovernmental consultations on federal policy development, and provides advice on the domestic implications of Canadian government interventions in international fora dealing with aboriginal issues. The division also provides support to the minister designated as Federal Interlocutor for Métis and Non-Status Indians. In this capacity, the division represents the federal government in tripartite self-government negotiations

with provincial governments and representatives of Métis and off-reserve aboriginal people. It also engages in bilateral consultations with national aboriginal organizations. Finally, it provides policy and strategic advice on the management of issues related to Métis and off-reserve aboriginal people within the federal government. Quoted in Canada, *The Role and Structure of the Privy Council Office.*

125 Consultation with a former senior official with the Federal-Provincial Relations Office, Ottawa, October 1997. The official also made available written material to assist in my research.

126 Quoted in material provided by a former senior official from the Federal-Provincial Relations Office, Ottawa, May 1983.

127 Consultations with senior PCO officials, December 1997.

128 Ibid., January 1998.

129 Consultations with a deputy minister, Ottawa, February 1998.

130 Consultations with a senior PCO official, Ottawa, January 1998.

131 Canada, *The Functioning of the Privy Council Office*, 4–26.

132 '$3-billion for your thoughts,' *Globe and Mail* (Toronto), 5 December 1997, A1.

133 Consultations with officials in the Prime Minister's Office, Ottawa, November to December 1997.

134 Consultations with PCO, Finance, and Treasury Board officials, Ottawa, various dates between September 1997 and January 1998.

135 See, among others, Hugh Heclo and Aaron Wildavsky, *The Private Government of Public Money* 2d ed. (London: Macmillan Press, 1981) and in Canada, see Savoie, *The Politics of Public Spending in Canada.*

6: Finance: Let There Be No Light

1 Consultation with a senior official in the Prime Minister's Office, Ottawa, December 1997.

2 Donald J. Savoie, *The Politics of Public Spending in Canada* (Toronto: University of Toronto Press, 1990), 74.

3 Quoted from a document made available by a senior Department of Finance official in March 1993: *The Organization of Finance/Treasury Ministries in the G-7* (Department of Finance, Ottawa: International Economic Analysis, 13 February 1993), 10.

4 Irving Brecher, 'A Case for Receiving the Economic Council,' *Citizen* (Ottawa), 15 December 1997, A11.

5 See, among others, Richard French, *How Ottawa Decides: Planning and Industrial Policy Making 1968–1980* (Ottawa: Canadian Institute for Economic Policy, 1980), 27–31.

6 Consultation with a deputy minister, Ottawa, November 1997.

7 Quoted in Edward Greenspon and Anthony Wilson-Smith, *Double Vision: The Inside Story of the Liberals in Power* (Toronto: Doubleday, 1996), 43.
8 Arthur Kroeger, 'A Retrospective on Policy Development in Ottawa,' Ottawa, Canadian Centre for Management Development, mimeo, 1998, 2.
9 Canada, Department of Finance, *1996–97 Estimates*, Part III Expenditure Plan (Ottawa: Minister of Supply and Services, 1997).
10 Quoted from a document made available by a senior Department of Finance official in March 1993.
11 Canada, Department of Finance, *1996–97 Estimates*, 2–21.
12 Ibid., 2–21 and 2–22.
13 Ibid., 2–25.
14 Ibid., 4–9.
15 Ibid.
16 Ibid., 4–10. The department is also responsible for other smaller transfer payments, notably the Youth Allowances Recovery (with Quebec), alternative payments for standing programs (again with Quebec), and the preferred share dividend taxes.
17 Ibid., 4–9.
18 See, for example, Colin Campbell and George J. Szablowski, *The Superbureaucrats: Structure and Behaviour in Central Agencies* (Toronto: Macmillan, 1979), 90–1.
19 Consultation with a former official with the Department of Finance, Ottawa, October 1997.
20 For a list of former deputy ministers of Finance, see Robert B. Bryce, *Maturing in Hard Times* (Montreal: McGill-Queen's University Press, 1986), 236.
21 Quoted in ibid., 86.
22 Consultation with a senior official in the Department of Finance, Ottawa, January 1998.
23 Quoted in 'Paul Martin's right-hand man,' *Globe and Mail* (Toronto), 24 December 1997, B4.
24 Tom Kent, *A Public Purpose: An experience of Liberal opposition and Canadian government* (Montreal: McGill-Queen's University Press, 1988), 224.
25 David A. Good, *The Politics of Anticipation: Making Canadian Federal Tax Policy* (Ottawa: Carleton University, School of Public Administration, 1980), 65.
26 Quoted in Richard W. Phidd and G. Bruce Doern, *The Politics and Management of Canadian Economic Policy* (Toronto: Macmillan, 1978), 210.
27 Quoted in Savoie, *The Politics of Public Spending in Canada*, 80.
28 Ibid., 94.
29 Walter L. Gordon, *A Political Memoir* (Toronto: McClelland and Stewart, 1977), 139.
30 Ibid., 140.
31 *Mike: Memoirs of The Right Honourable Lester B. Pearson*, vol. 3, 1957–68, John A. Munro and Alex Inglis, eds. (Toronto: University of Toronto Press, 1975), 103–9.

32 Sir John G. Diefenbaker, *One Canada: The Years of Achievement 1957–1962* (Toronto: Macmillan, 1976), 266–8.
33 Peter Aucoin, 'Organizational Change in the Machinery of Canadian Government: From Rational Management to Brokerage Politics,' *Canadian Journal of Political Science* XIX, no. 1 (March 1986): 7.
34 Bryce, *Maturing in Hard Times*, 236.
35 They are Simon Reisman, Thomas K. Shoyama, William Hood, Grant Reuber, Ian Stewart, Marshall A. Cohen, Stanley Hartt, Bob Gorbet, David Dodge, and Scott Clark.
36 Quoted in Christina Newman, 'Michael Pitfield and the Politics of Mismanagement,' *Saturday Night*, October 1982, 35.
37 See, among others, French, *How Ottawa Decides*.
38 Quoted in Campbell and Szablowski, *The Superbureaucrats*, 94.
39 French, *How Ottawa Decides*, 78.
40 Ibid., 79.
41 Ibid., 83.
42 George Radwanski, *Trudeau* (Toronto: Macmillan, 1978), 304.
43 Canada, *The Way Ahead: A Framework for Discussion* (Ottawa: Privy Council Office, October 1976), 5.
44 Ibid., 34.
45 Savoie, *The Politics of Public Spending in Canada*, 34.
46 Ibid., 152.
47 'Mr. Trudeau Tries Again,' *Globe and Mail* (Toronto), 3 August 1978, A6.
48 Jean Chrétien, *Straight from the Heart* (Toronto: Key Porter Books, 1985), 117.
49 Consultation with a former senior Department of Finance official, Ottawa, April 1993. See also ibid., 105.
50 Consultation with a former Cabinet minister, Ottawa, January 1998.
51 Consultation with a former senior PCO official, Ottawa, December 1997.
52 See, among others, Savoie, *The Politics of Public Spending in Canada*, 75.
53 Ibid.
54 Canada, Office of the Prime Minister, *News Release*, 21 October 1982.
55 Donald Johnston, *Up the Hill* (Montreal: Optimum Publisher International, 1986), 67.
56 Consultation with a former senior PCO official, Ottawa, December 1997.
57 Savoie, *The Politics of Public Spending in Canada*.
58 Consultation with a former PCO official, Ottawa, December 1997. See also Jeffrey Simpson, *Discipline of Power* (Toronto: Personal Library, 1980).
59 Consultation with present and former Cabinet ministers in the Chrétien government, Ottawa, September to December 1997.
60 Richard Van Loon, 'Stop the Music: The Current Policy and Expenditure Management System in Ottawa,' *Canadian Public Administration* 24, no. 2 (1981), 189.

61 Consultation with a former deputy minister, Ottawa, October 1997.

62 There were, however, some exceptions. See Savoie, *The Politics of Public Spending in Canada*, chapters 4 and 8.

63 Consultations with a former senior official in the Prime Minister's Office, Ottawa, January 1998.

64 See, among others, Savoie, *The Politics of Public Spending in Canada*, 84.

65 Greenspon and Wilson-Smith, *Double Vision*, 161.

66 See Savoie, *The Politics of Public Spending in Canada*, 82.

67 Ibid., 81.

68 Quoted in ibid., 82.

69 Greenspon and Wilson-Smith, *Double Vision*, 159.

70 Canada, *The Budget Plan*, Department of Finance, 22 February 1994.

71 Canada, *Budget Speech*, Department of Finance, 22 February 1994, 14.

72 'Getting Government Right,' address by Marcel Massé at the Public Service Alliance of Canada, Regional Quebec Conference, Longueuil, 12 September 1993, National Campaign Committee, 4.

73 'Getting Government Right: The Challenge of Implementation,' notes for an address by Marcel Massé, president of the Queen's Privy Council of Canada, minister of Intergovernmental Affairs and minister responsible for Public Service Renewal to the National Conference on Government Relations, 1 December 1993, 1.

74 Ibid., 2.

75 Canada, *The Budget Plan*, 29.

76 Savoie, *The Politics of Public Spending in Canada*.

77 Consultation with a senior government official, Ottawa, March 1993.

78 Greenspon and Wilson-Smith, *Double Vision*, 156.

79 See Arthur Kroeger, 'The Central Agencies and Program Review,' a paper prepared for the Canadian Centre for Management Development, Ottawa, undated, 11.

80 Consultation with a senior official, Ottawa, October 1997.

81 Greenspon and Wilson-Smith, *Double Vision*, 38.

82 Consultation with a senior Department of Finance official, Ottawa, December 1997.

83 Kroeger, 'The Central Agencies and Program Review,' 1.

84 Consultations with federal government officials, Ottawa, October to December 1997.

85 Kroeger, 'The Central Agencies and Program Review,' 4–5.

86 Ibid., 5.

87 Consultation with a senior Department of Finance official, Ottawa, January 1998.

88 See Peter Aucoin and Donald J. Savoie, 'Launching and Organizing a Program Review Exercise,' a paper prepared for the Canadian Centre for Management Development, Ottawa, 1988, 2.

89 Ibid.

90 Consultations with government officials, Ottawa, September to December 1997.

91 Kroeger, 'The Central Agencies and Program Review,' 6.
92 Ibid.
93 Consultations with present and former government officials, Ottawa, September to December 1997.
94 Consultations with government officials, Ottawa, September to December 1997.
95 Consultation with a former Cabinet minister, Ottawa, November 1997.
96 Consultations with various government officials, Ottawa, October 1997 to January 1998.
97 Consultations with PCO officials, Ottawa, November 1997.
98 Greenspon and Wilson-Smith, *Double Vision*, 225.
99 Consultation with a senior Department of Finance official, Ottawa, January 1998.
100 Quoted in Greenspon and Wilson-Smith, *Double Vision*, 211.
101 Consultations with senior government officials, Ottawa, September to December 1997.
102 Consultations with senior PCO and Finance officials, Ottawa, September to December 1997.
103 Canada, *The Budget Speech*, 12.
104 See, for example, Armelita Armit and Jacques Bourgault, eds., *Hard Choices or No Choices: Assessing Program Review* (Toronto: Institute of Public Administration, 1996).
105 Kroeger, 'The Central Agencies and Program Review,' 15.
106 Ibid.
107 Canada, *Getting Government Right* (Ottawa: Treasury Board, 20 February 1997), 7.
108 Canada, *Third Annual Report to the Prime Minister on the Public Service of Canada* (Ottawa: Privy Council Office, 1995), 20.
109 Ibid., 19.
110 Canada, *Fourth Annual Report to the Prime Minister on the Public Service of Canada* (Ottawa: Privy Council Office, 3 February 1997), 3.
111 Ibid., 20.
112 Janice Charette, 'Program Review: Lessons Learned and Challenges Ahead,' a report for the Canadian Centre for Management Development, Ottawa, 1997, 20.
113 Ibid., 12.
114 Ibid.
115 Peter Aucoin and Donald J. Savoie, eds., 'Program Review' (Ottawa: Canadian Centre for Management Development, 1997).
116 Armit and Bourgault, eds., *Hard Choices or No Choices.*
117 Consultation with a senior Department of Finance official, Ottawa, November 1997.
118 Gilles Paquet, 'The Fruit that Tastes of Ignorance,' in Armit and Bourgault, eds., *Hard Choices or No Choices*, 185.

119 See, among others, 'As interest rises, so do chances of tax increases,' *Citizen* (Ottawa), 4 January 1995, A4.
120 Consultation with a senior government official, Ottawa, October 1997.
121 Paul Wells, 'Marcel Massé,' *Citizen* (Ottawa), 4 January 1995, A1.
122 Consultations with senior Department of Finance officials, Ottawa, November 1997 to January 1998.
123 Consultations with senior central agency government officials, Ottawa, November to December 1997.
124 Ibid.
125 Consultation with a senior government official, Ottawa, December 1997.
126 Ibid., October 1997.
127 Glen Toner, 'Environment Canada's Continuing Roller Coaster Ride,' in Gene Swimmer, ed., *How Ottawa Spends 1996–97: Life Under the Knife* (Ottawa: Carleton University Press, 1996), 100.
128 Consultations with Environment and central agency officials, Ottawa, September 1996.
129 Peter Aucoin and Donald J. Savoie, 'Lessons for Strategic Change in Government,' a paper prepared for the Canadian Centre for Management Development, Ottawa, 1998, 7.
130 Consultation with a senior line department government official, Ottawa, October 1997.
131 Consultations with central agency government officials, Ottawa, October to December 1997.
132 Canada, *Privy Council Office – Outlook*, report to the Standing Committee on Government Operations (Ottawa: Privy Council Office, April 1996), 3.
133 Greenspon and Wilson-Smith, *Double Vision*, chapter 16.
134 Canada, *The Budget Speech* (Ottawa: Department of Finance, 15 February 1984).
135 Canada, *The Budget Speech* (Ottawa: Department of Finance, April 1983).
136 Canada, *The Budget Speech* (Ottawa: Department of Finance, 25 February 1992), 3.
137 Consultations with former Cabinet ministers, Ottawa, February 1993.
138 See Canada, *Budget Speeches* (Ottawa: Department of Finance, 6 March 1996 and 18 February 1997).
139 Savoie, *The Politics of Public Spending in Canada.*
140 Consultation with a former Cabinet minister, Ottawa, October 1997.
141 'Spending limits irk cabinet,' *Globe and Mail* (Toronto), 3 December 1997, A1.
142 Ibid. See also A28.

7: Treasury Board and the Public Service Commission: Pulling against Gravity

1 Consultation with a former secretary to the Treasury Board, Ottawa, March 1993.

2 Consultation with a senior Treasury Board secretariat official, Ottawa, November 1997.
3 Ian Clark, 'Ottawa's Principal Decision-Making and Advisory Committees' (Ottawa: Privy Council Office, December 1993), 11.
4 Ibid., 6.
5 Consultation with a senior government official, Ottawa, April 1993.
6 Evert Lindquist, 'On the Cutting Edge: Program Review, Government Restructuring, and the Treasury Board of Canada,' a paper prepared for the Canadian Centre for Management Development, Ottawa, January 1996, 8.
7 A.W. Johnson, 'The Treasury Board of Canada and the Machinery of Government of the 1970s,' *Canadian Journal of Political Science* 4, no. 3 (September 1971): 346.
8 Gérard Veilleux and Donald J. Savoie, 'Kafka's Castle: The Treasury Board of Canada Revisited,' *Canadian Public Administration* 31, no. 4 (Winter 1986): 519.
9 R.D. MacLean, 'An Examination of the Role of the Comptroller of the Treasury,' *Canadian Public Administration*, no. 7 (March 1964): 26.
10 Robert B. Bryce, *Maturing in Hard Times* (Montreal and Kingston: McGill-Queen's University Press, 1986), 76–7.
11 Ibid.
12 Ibid., 153.
13 J.E. Hodgetts et al., *The Biography of an Institution* (Montreal and Kingston: McGill-Queen's University Press, 1977), 152.
14 Bryce, *Maturing in Hard Times*, 157.
15 Ibid., 155.
16 Canada, Royal Commission on Government Organization, *Management of the Public Service* 1, abridged version (Ottawa: Queen's Printer, 1962), 91.
17 Ibid.
18 'Prime Minister Announces New Ministry,' *Release*, Office of the Prime Minister, 11 June 1997, 4.
19 See, among others, Donald J. Savoie, *The Politics of Public Spending in Canada* (Toronto: University of Toronto Press, 1990), chapter 5.
20 Progressive Conservative Party of Canada, 'Towards Production Management,' background notes, undated, 1.
21 Peter Aucoin and Herman Bakvis, *The Centralization-Decentralization Conundrum: Organization and Management in the Canadian Government* (Halifax: Institute for Research on Public Policy, 1988), 22.
22 Canada, *The Fiscal Plan* (Ottawa: Department of Finance, February 1986), 26.
23 Hon. Robert R. De Cotret, 'Notes for an address to the Financial Management Institute,' Treasury Board secretariat, November 1986.
24 'Realigning and Revitalizing the Treasury Board secretariat,' *Canadian Government Executive* (Ottawa), 1997, 19.

25 Johnson, 'The Treasury Board of Canada and the Machinery of Government of the 1970s,' 346.
26 Canada, Treasury Board of Canada, *Improved Reporting to Parliament,* pilot document for the period ending 31 March 1997 (Ottawa: Minister of Public Works and Government Services, 1997), 14.
27 Consultations with government officials, Ottawa, September to November 1997. See also Lindquist, 'On the Cutting Edge.'
28 Johnson, 'The Treasury Board of Canada and the Machinery of Government of the 1970s,' 346.
29 Canada, Position of CIO Created to Help Streamline Operations, *News Release*, Treasury Board of Canada, 22 July 1993, 1–2.
30 Ibid.
31 Lindquist, 'On the Cutting Edge.'
32 See, for example, Canada, Treasury Board of Canada Secretariat, *1996–97 Estimates*, Part III Expenditure Plan (Ottawa: Minister of Supply and Services, 1996), 2–17.
33 For a review of the secretariat's five lines of business, see Canada, *Improved Reporting to Parliament*, 1–37.
34 Ibid., 20.
35 Canada, Treasury Board secretariat, *Performance Report* for the period ending 31 March 1997 (Ottawa: Minister of Public Works and Government Services, 1997).
36 Ibid., 32.
37 Ibid., 27.
38 'Report of the Independent Review Panel on Modernization of Comptrollership in the Government of Canada,' Ottawa, Treasury Board Secretariat, 1997, 1.
39 Ibid., 2.
40 Ibid., 3.
41 J.R. Mallory, 'The Lambert Report: Central Roles and Responsibilities,' *Canadian Public Administration* 22, no. 4 (1979): 517.
42 Veilleux and Savoie, 'Kafka's Castle,' 22.
43 See Canada, *Role of the Treasury Board secretariat and the Office of the Comptroller General* (Ottawa: Treasury Board, March 1985).
44 Quoted in Sonja Sinclair, *Cordial But Not Cosy* (Toronto: McClelland and Stewart, 1979), 139.
45 Canada, Office of the Auditor General, *Annual Report, Year Ended 1976* (Ottawa: Minister of Supply and Services, 1976), 9.
46 Quoted in Sinclair, *Cordial But Not Cosy*, 144.
47 Quoted in Savoie, *The Politics of Public Spending in Canada*, 114.
48 H.L. Laframboise, 'Government Spending: Grappling with the Evaluation Octopus,' *Optimum* 9, no. 4 (1978): 30.

49 See Canada, Royal Commission on Financial Management and Accountability, *Final Report* (Ottawa: Minister of Supply and Services, 1979), 7.

50 Ibid., 21.

51 Ibid., chapter 9.

52 Ibid., 68.

53 Ibid., chapter 7.

54 Ibid., 117.

55 Ibid.

56 See Savoie, *The Politics of Public Spending in Canada*, 131.

57 Ibid.

58 Ibid.

59 Several former senior government officials expressed this view in my consultations, Ottawa, September to December 1997.

60 De Cotret, 'Notes for an address to the Financial Management Institute,' Ottawa, Treasury Board Secretariat, June 1987, 7.

61 See, among others, Savoie, *The Politics of Public Spending in Canada*, chapter 5.

62 Ibid., 118–20.

63 Donald J. Savoie, *Thatcher, Reagan, Mulroney: In Search of a New Bureaucracy* (Pittsburgh: University of Pittsburgh Press, 1994), 269.

64 Canada, *Public Service 2000* (Ottawa: Privy Council Office, 1990), 1.

65 John Edwards, 'Notes for a Presentation on Public Service 2000,' Ottawa, PS 2000 Secretariat, 1991, 2.

66 David Osborn and Ted Gaebler, *Reinventing Government: How the Entrepreneurial Spirit Is Transforming the Public Sector* (Reading, Mass.: Addison-Wesley, 1992). See also Michael Barzelay and Babak J. Armajani, *Breaking Through Bureaucracy* (Los Angeles: University of California Press, 1992).

67 John Edwards, Chair of the PS 2000 secretariat, 'Revitalization of the Canadian Public Service,' notes for a speaking engagement to the Association of Professional Executives, 11 March 1991, Ottawa, 131.

68 Paul M. Tellier, 'Public Service 2000: The Renewal of the Public Service,' *Canadian Public Administration* 33, no. 2 (Summer 1990): 131.

69 See Canada, Treasury Board, 'Loiselle Introduces Bill to Support the Overhaul of the Federal Public Service,' *News Release*, Ottawa, 18 June 1991; *Highlights of the White Paper on Public Service 2000: The Renewal of the Public Service of Canada* (Ottawa: Government of Canada, 1990), 4–3.

70 Ibid.

71 See, for example, Savoie, *Thatcher, Reagan, Mulroney*, 231.

72 Some observers outside government were also asking the same question. See, for example, Gene Swimmer et al., 'Public Service 2000: Dead or Alive?' in Susan Phillips, ed., *How Ottawa Spends 1994–95* (Ottawa: Carleton University Press, 1994), 122.

73 Canada, *Public Service 2000: The Renewal of the Public Service of Canada* (Ottawa: Minister of Supply and Services, 1990), 95–6.

74 See Gene Swimmer et al., 'Public Service 2000,' 172.

75 Sharon L. Sutherland, 'The Al-Mashat Affair: Administrative Accountability in Parliamentary Institutions,' *Canadian Public Administration* 34, no. 4 (Winter 1991): 601.

76 Canada, Minister responsible for Public Service Renewal, Speech by the Hon. Marcel Massé presented to the National Conference on Government Relations, Ottawa, 1 December 1993, 2.

77 Canada, *Report of the Auditor General of Canada to the House of Commons, 1993* (Ottawa: Supply and Services, 1994), 173–4.

78 Quoted in Savoie, *Thatcher, Reagan, Mulroney*, 241.

79 Ibid.

80 John L. Manion, 'Leadership – Notes for an Address by J.L. Manion to the Advanced Management Program,' Ottawa, 25 June 1993, 6.

81 Paul Tellier's speech was reproduced as 'It's time to re-engineer the public service,' in *Public Sector Management* 4, no. 4 (1992): 22–3.

82 Ian Clark, 'On Re-engineering the Public Service of Canada: A Comment on Paul Tellier's Call for Bold Action,' *Public Sector Management* 4, no. 4 (1992): 20–2.

83 Canada, *A Manager's Guide to Operating Budgets* (Ottawa: Treasury Board, 1992).

84 Canada, *Public Service 2000*, status report by the Honourable Robert De Cotret, president of the Treasury Board, 30 April 1990, 6–18.

85 Canada, *Treasury Board, Towards a Shared Management Agenda* (Ottawa: Treasury Board, 25 July 1991).

86 Quoted in Savoie, *Thatcher, Reagan, Mulroney*, 242.

87 I.D. Clark, 'Special Operating Agencies: The Challenges of Innovation,' *Optimum* 22, no. 2 (1992), 13.

88 *The Special Operating Agency* (Ottawa: Treasury Board, undated), 1.

89 Ibid.

90 Nick Mulder, 'Managing Special Operating Agencies: A Practitioner's Perspective,' *Optimum* 22, no. 2 (1989): 13.

91 Clark, 'Special Operating Agencies,' 13.

92 Quoted in Savoie, *Thatcher, Reagan, Mulroney*, 241.

93 Canada, 'Central Agency Intervention/Withdrawal,' Critical Management Issues Network (Ottawa: Canadian Centre for Management Development, 13 March 1997), 1.

94 Ibid.

95 Consultation with a senior government official, Ottawa, January 1998.

96 Alti Rodal, 'Special Operating Agencies: Issues for Parent Departments and Central Agencies' (Ottawa: Canadian Centre for Management Development, 1996), 7.

97 See, among others, Savoie, *Thatcher, Reagan, Mulroney.*
98 Ibid., 5.
99 Ibid., 17.
100 Consultations with two senior officials with the Treasury Board secretariat, Ottawa, January 1998.
101 Lindquist, 'On the Cutting Edge,' 234.
102 Evert Lindquist, 'Critical Issues in Departmental Business Planning,' a paper prepared for the Canadian Centre for Management Development, Ottawa, 1997, 15.
103 Quoted in ibid., 3.
104 Consultations with various government officials, Ottawa, October 1997 to January 1998.
105 Ibid. See also, Lindquist, 'Critical Issues in Departmental Business Planning,' 10.
106 See, among others, Johnson, 'The Treasury Board of Canada and the Machinery of Government of the 1970s,' 350–8.
107 Quoted in Arthur Kroeger, 'A Retrospective on Policy Development in Ottawa,' Ottawa, Canadian Centre for Management Development, January 1998, mimeo, 8.
108 'Government Revamps Expenditure Management System,' *News Release* (Ottawa: Treasury Board of Canada, 15 February 1995) 1.
109 Ibid.
110 A Strengthened Expenditure Management System for the New Mandate – A Presentation by the Treasury Board, Ottawa, 2 September 1997, 14.
111 Canada, *The Expenditure Management System of the Government of Canada* (Ottawa: Minister of Supply and Services, 1995), 9.
112 Ibid., 9.
113 Ibid.
114 Canada, *Getting Government Right: Improving Results Measurement and Accountability*, Annual Report to Parliament by the president of the Treasury Board, 1996 (Ottawa: Minister of Public Works and Government Services, 1996).
115 Ibid., 1.
116 Ibid., 3.
117 See, among others, Osborne and Gaebler, *Reinventing Government.*
118 Canada, *The Public Service Commission: Its Role and Responsibilities*, http/www.psc, 1.
119 Canada, Public Service Commission of Canada, *1996–97 Estimates,* Part III Expenditure Plan (Ottawa: Minister of Supply and Services, 1997), 11–17.
120 Ibid.
121 J.E. Hodgetts, *The Canadian Public Service: A Physiology of Government, 1867–1970* (Toronto: University of Toronto Press, 1973), 263.
122 Ibid.
123 See, for example, ibid., 255.

124 See ibid., and Canada, Royal Commission on Administrative Classifications in the Public Service, *Report* (Ottawa, 1945).

125 See Savoie, *Thatcher, Reagan, Mulroney*, 63.

126 Canada, *Final Report*, 223.

127 Ibid., 125.

128 Consultations with senior federal government officials, Ottawa, September and December 1997 and January 1998.

129 Consultation with a former senior federal government official, Ottawa, November 1997.

130 Consultation with a Treasury Board secretariat official, Ottawa, January 1998.

131 Ibid.

132 Ibid.

133 See, among many others, Public Service Commission: Executive Programs – *La Relève* – a new way of thinking (Ottawa: Public Service Commission, undated), 2.

134 Canada, *Fourth Annual Report to the Prime Minister on the Public Service of Canada* (Ottawa: Privy Council Office, 1997), 39, 44.

135 Ibid., 48.

136 Ibid., 49.

137 Consultations with senior officials with PCO, TBS, and PSC,(Ottawa, November 1997 to February 1998.

138 Supporters of *La Relève* report that 'significant experience' in a central agency was one of several conditions for promotion.

139 Consultation with a senior official from the Public Service Commission, Ottawa, February 1998.

140 Consultations with senior PCO and Treasury Board officials, Ottawa, September 1997 to January 1998.

141 Consultation with a senior PCO official, Ottawa, December 1997.

142 Consultation with a senior Public Service Commission official, Ottawa, January 1998.

143 Copy of the letter signed by the secretary of the Treasury Board on 10 April 1990 was made available to me by secretariat officials.

144 *Staffing Reform*, Public Service Commission, Ottawa, 4 December 1997, 5.

145 Ibid., 8.

146 *Staffing Reform: Questions and Answers*, Ottawa, Public Service Commission, 7 January 1998, 4.

147 Ottawa, *Release*, 'Prime Minister Announces Creation of the Leadership Network,' Office of the Prime Minister, Ottawa, 4 June 1998, 1.

148 *Supporting Excellence in the ADM Community: An Overview of the New Collective Management System* (Ottawa: Privy Council Office, May 1998), 1.

149 Ibid., 4.

150 Max Weber, *The Theory of Social and Economic Organization* (New York: Oxford University Press, 1947).
151 *Supporting Excellence in the ADM Community*, 3.
152 Consultation with a senior government official, Ottawa, November 1997.
153 Kroeger, 'A Retrospective of Policy Development in Ottawa,' 6–7.
154 See Clark, 'Ottawa's Principal Decision-Making and Advisory Committees,' 15.
155 Savoie, *The Politics of Public Spending in Canada*, 118.
156 Information provided by the Treasury Board secretariat, Ottawa, December 1997.
157 Consultation with a senior Treasury Board official, Ottawa, January 1998.
158 Consultation with a senior departmental official, Ottawa, January 1998.
159 Consultation with a senior official with the Atlantic Canada Opportunities Agency, Moncton, February 1990.
160 Consultations with senior Treasury Board secretariat officials, Ottawa, December 1997 to January 1998.
161 Consultation with a senior Treasury Board secretariat official, Ottawa, January 1998.
162 Consultation with a Treasury Board secretariat official, Ottawa, January 1998.
163 Consultation with a former official with CCMD, Ottawa, February 1993.
164 Auditor General of Canada, 'Payments to Employees Under the Work Force Adjustment Policy,' in *Report of the Auditor General of Canada to the House of Commons 1992* (Ottawa: Supply and Services, 1992), 187–208.
165 Consultation with a deputy minister who was present at the Deputy Ministers' Breakfast meeting, Ottawa, January 1998.
166 Ibid.
167 Lindquist, 'On the Cutting Edge,' 13.

8: Ministers: Knowing When to Land

1 Edward Greenspon and Anthony Wilson-Smith, *Double Vision: The Inside Story of the Liberals in Power* (Toronto: Doubleday, 1996), 253.
2 Gordon Robertson, 'The Changing Role of the Privy Council Office,' *Canadian Public Administration* 14, no. 4 (Winter 1971): 497.
3 Ibid.
4 Ibid., 501.
5 Consultation with a federal Cabinet minister, Ottawa, October 1997.
6 Ibid., January 1998.
7 John M. Reid, 'A Limited Resource,' notes for an address to the Institute of Public Administration, Ottawa, 7 May 1980, 7.
8 One former Cabinet minister observed that 'in Canada, we have elections and commitments, but no politics. By politics he meant policy debate.' Quoted in Donald J.

Savoie, *The Politics of Public Spending in Canada* (Toronto: University of Toronto Press, 1990), 182.

9 Consultation with a senior government official, Ottawa, December 1997.

10 James L. Payne and Oliver H. Woshinsky, 'Incentives for Political Participation,' *World Politics*, 24 (1972), 519.

11 See 'Dear Minister. A Letter to an Old Friend on Being a Successful Minister,' notes for remarks by Gordon Osbaldeston to the Association of Professional Executives of the Public Service of Canada, Ottawa, 22 January 1988, 2.

12 Ibid., 4.

13 Consultations with present and former Cabinet ministers and members of Parliament, Ottawa, September 1997 to February 1998.

14 Consultation with a senior government official, Ottawa, January 1998.

15 Jean Chrétien, *Straight From the Heart* (Toronto: Key Porter Books, 1985), 125.

16 I consulted Kathryn O'Handly and Caroline Sutherland, eds., *Canadian Parliamentary Guide* (Scarborough: Gale Canada, 1997).

17 See also Oliver H. Woskinsky, *The French Deputy* (London: Lexington Books, 1973) and James L. Payne, *Patterns of Conflict in Columbia* (New Haven: Yale University Press, 1968).

18 See Savoie, *The Politics of Public Spending in Canada.*

19 Quoted in Timothy W. Plumptre, *Beyond the Bottom Line: Management in Government* (Halifax: Institute for Research on Public Policy, 1988), 130. See also ibid., 192.

20 See, among others, Donald Johnston, *Up the Hill* (Montreal: Optimum Publisher International, 1986).

21 'Cuts for farmers agonizing to long-time Liberal pols,' *Globe and Mail* (Toronto), 16 January 1995, A1.

22 Ibid., A6.

23 Ibid.

24 Consultation with a former federal deputy minister, Ottawa, February 1998.

25 Ibid.

26 Quoted in Greenspon and Wilson-Smith, *Double Vision*, 209.

27 Quoted in 'Now for the tough part,' *Maclean's* (Toronto), 23 February 1998, 17.

28 Consultation with a senior PCO official, Ottawa, February 1998.

29 Consultation with a Cabinet minister, Ottawa, January 1998.

30 Ibid., February 1998.

31 See 'Manley wants piece of Ottawa's fiscal dividend,' *Globe and Mail* (Toronto), 6 October 1997, B3.

32 Consultation with a senior PCO official, Ottawa, February 1998.

33 J.W. Pickersgill, The W. Clifford Clark Memorial Lecture, 1972, 'Bureaucrats and Politicians,' *Canadian Public Administration* 15, no. 3 (Fall 1972): 420.

34 Ibid.
35 Quoted in Donald J. Savoie, 'The Minister's Staff: The Need for Reform,' *Canadian Public Administration* 26, no. 4 (1983): 523.
36 Ministers have three separate budgets, including the House of Commons budget, which is available 'to all Members of Parliament and covers the cost of the member's constituency work ... the exempt budget (for his ministerial staff) ... and the departmental budget, which covers the expenses of the minister and his exempt staff for travel, hospitality ... In addition, regional ministers are supplemented by funds for salaries or operations related to their added responsibilities.' See Jeanne M. Flemming, 'The roles of executive assistant to a federal minister,' *Optimum* 27, no. 2: 66.
37 Quoted in Savoie, *Thatcher, Reagan, Mulroney: In Search of a New Bureaucracy* (Pittsburgh: University of Pittsburgh Press, 1994), 224.
38 Ibid., 225. See also Sharon Sutherland, 'The Al-Marshat Affair: Administrative Responsibilities in Parliamentary Institutions, *Canadian Public Administration* 34, no. 2 (Winter 1991): 592.
39 Consultations with a former senior official with the Prime Minister's Office, Ottawa, December 1997.
40 Flemming, 'The roles of executive assistant to a federal minister,' 63.
41 Ibid., 64–5.
42 Ibid., 66.
43 Ibid., 67.
44 Ibid.
45 Ibid., 68.
46 Consultations with a senior PCO official, Ottawa, February 1998.
47 See Savoie, 'The Minister's Staff,' 516–19. See also, 'The Axworthy empire,' *Globe and Mail* (Toronto), December 1984, A1.
48 Consultation with a former federal Cabinet minister, Ottawa, December 1997.
49 Canada, *Discussion Paper on Values and Ethics in the Federal Service* (Ottawa: Privy Council Office, December 1996), 32.
50 Consultation with a senior official in the Privy Council Office, Ottawa, February 1998.
51 Consultations with various ministers and senior government officials, Ottawa, September 1997 to February 1998.
52 Jean Chrétien, *Straight From the Heart*, 71–2.
53 Consultations with senior government officials, Ottawa, various dates in the fall of 1992.
54 See, among others, Canada, *Discussion Paper on Values and Ethics in the Federal Service.*
55 Consultation with a senior government official, Ottawa, January 1998.
56 Consultation with a former deputy minister, Ottawa, February 1998.

57 See, among others, Jack Granatstein, *The Ottawa Men: The Civil Service Mandarins, 1935–1957* (Toronto: Oxford University Press, 1982), 189.
58 P.M. Pitfield, 'Politics and Policy Making,' Address to the Alma Mater Society, Queen's University, Kingston, Ontario, 10 February 1983, mimeo, 6.
59 See, among others, Robert Presthus, *Elite Accomodation in Canadian Politics* (Toronto: University of Toronto Press, 1973).
60 Mitchell Sharp, 'The Role of the Mandarins,' *Policy Options* 11 (May–June, 1981): 43–4.
61 Consultation with a former senior public servant, Ottawa, October 1997.
62 Consultation with a former senior official, Ottawa, November 1997.
63 Canada, *Responsibility in the Constitution* (Ottawa: Minister of Supply and Services, 1993), 58, 62.
64 Consultation with a senior PCO official, Ottawa, December 1997.
65 Arthur Kroeger, 'A Retrospective on Policy Development in Ottawa,' Ottawa, Canadian Centre for Management Development, January 1998, mimeo, 4.
66 Consultation with a former Cabinet minister, Ottawa, February 1998.
67 Ibid.
68 See, for example, Walter L. Gordon, *A Political Memoir* (Toronto: McClelland and Stewart, 1997).
69 See, among others, Chrétien, *Straight From the Heart.*
70 Sandford F. Borins, 'Public Choice: "Yes Minister" Made It Popular, But Does Winning the Nobel Prize Make It True?' *Canadian Public Administration* 32, no. 1 (Spring 1988): 22.
71 See, for example, John Sawateky, *The Insiders: Government, Business, and the Lobbyists* (Toronto: McClelland and Stewart, 1987).
72 Consultation with a deputy minister, Ottawa, February 1998.
73 Quoted in Greenspon and Wilson-Smith, *Double Vision*, 212.
74 Canada, *Responsibility in the Constitution* (Ottawa: Minister of Supply and Services, 1993), preface.
75 Ibid., 44.
76 Ibid.
77 Ibid., 51.
78 Ibid., 62.
79 Consultation with a federal Cabinet minister, Ottawa, September 1997.
80 Consultation with a former Cabinet minister, Ottawa, October 1997.
81 Consultations with a federal Cabinet minister, Ottawa, March 1998.
82 Consultation with a former Cabinet minister, Ottawa, February 1998.
83 Consultation with a Cabinet minister, Ottawa, December 1997.
84 Consultations with a former PCO official, Ottawa, January 1998.
85 Consultation with a senior PCO official, Ottawa, February 1998.

86 Ibid.
87 Ibid.
88 Consultation with a former Cabinet minister, Ottawa, February 1998.
89 Consultation with a former PCO official, Ottawa, November 1997.
90 Consultation with a former minister, Ottawa, February 1998.
91 Consultation with a former Cabinet minister, Ottawa, October 1997.
92 Ibid., February 1998.
93 'Chrétien set to remake top court,' *Citizen* (Ottawa), 14 December 1997, A7.
94 Ibid.
95 Quoted in Kroeger, 'A Retrospective on Policy Development in Ottawa,' 10.
96 Ibid.
97 Ibid.
98 Consultation with a former Cabinet minister, Ottawa, February 1998.
99 Consultation with a senior PCO official, Ottawa, February 1998.
100 Ibid.
101 Ibid.
102 Quoted in John C. Tait and Mel Cappe, *Perspectives on Public Policy* (Ottawa: Canadian Centre for Management Development, October 1995), 34.
103 Consultation with a senior PCO official, Ottawa, November 1997.
104 Consultations with CMHC officials, Ottawa, December 1997. See also, *Release*, 'Minister Gagliano Announces Extension of Three Popular Programs' (Ottawa: Central Mortgage and Housing, 30 January 1998), 1–2.
105 Consultations with present and former PCO officials, Ottawa, September 1997 to February 1998.
106 Consultation with a former Cabinet minister, Ottawa, February 1998.
107 Ibid.
108 Consultations with PCO officials, Ottawa, November 1997 to February 1998.
109 Consultation with a Cabinet minister, Ottawa, January 1998. See also 'Copters could be career breaker,' *Globe and Mail* (Toronto), 22 December 1997, A6.
110 'PM justifies reversal on helicopter deal,' *Globe and Mail* (Toronto), 19 December 1997, A4.
111 Quoted in Greenspon and Wilson-Smith, *Double Vision*, 128.
112 Chrétien, *Straight from the Heart*, 86.
113 Ibid., 87.
114 Consultations with present and former PCO officials, Ottawa, October 1997 to February 1998.
115 Consultation with a former Cabinet minister, Ottawa, February 1998.
116 Ibid.
117 Consultation with a former senior PCO official, Ottawa, November 1997.
118 Consultation with a former Cabinet minister, Ottawa, January 1998.

119 Robertson, 'The Changing Role of the Privy Council Office,' 500.
120 Chrétien, *Straight from the Heart*, 85.
121 Sharon Sutherland, 'Responsible Government and Ministerial Responsibility: Every Reform is Its Own Problem,' *Canadian Journal of Political Science* XXIV, no. 1 (March 1991): 101.
122 Ibid., 103.

9: Departments: Running on the Track

1 Jocelyne Bourgon, 'Management in the New Public Sector Cultures,' a paper presented to Public Policy Forum, Ottawa, 28 October 1993, mimeo, 11.
2 See Guidance to the Principal on Research Priorities for 1998–99 (Ottawa: Canadian Centre for Management Development, 1998), 7. The survey instrument is called SYMLOG, which was developed by Robert Bale and Bok Koenigs from Harvard.
3 Ibid., 10.
4 See, among others, Donald J. Savoie, *The Politics of Public Spending in Canada* (Toronto: University of Toronto Press, 1990).
5 Canada, Discussion Paper on Values and Ethics in the Public Service (Ottawa: Privy Council Office, December 1996), 57.
6 See, for example, Donald J. Savoie, *Thatcher, Reagan, Mulroney: In Search of a New Bureaucracy* (Pittsburgh: Pittsburgh Press, 1994).
7 Canada, Discussion Paper on Values and Ethics in the Public Service, 37.
8 See, for example, presentation made by Nevil Johnson to the Treasury and Civil Service subcommittee, 29 January 1986 (London: Her Majesty's Stationery Office), 170–1.
9 Quoted in Savoie, *Thatcher, Reagan, Mulroney*, 317–18.
10 The study was prepared by the Public Management Research Centre for the Treasury Board secretariat and made public in early 1998. See 'PS leaders put politics before public interest, report says,' *Citizen* (Ottawa) 11 November 1997, A3.
11 Ibid.
12 Consultation with a former senior PCO official, Ottawa, December 1997.
13 Ibid., March 1998.
14 Consultation with a former deputy minister, Ottawa, March 1998.
15 Consultation with a deputy minister, Ottawa, November 1997.
16 Robert Normand, 'Les relations entre les hauts fonctionnaires et le ministre,' *Canadian Public Administration* 27, no. 4 (Winter 1984): 528.
17 See, among others, Timothy Plumptre, *Beyond the Bottom Line: Management in Government* (Halifax: Institute for Research on Public Policy, 1988), 151–2.
18 Canada, *Responsibility in the Constitution* (Ottawa: Privy Council Office, 1993), 86.
19 Ibid.

20 Plumptre, *Beyond the Bottom Line*, 151–2.
21 Canada, *Office of the Deputy Minister* (Ottawa: Privy Council Office, undated), 13.
22 See, for example, H.V. Kroeker, *Accountability and Control: The Government Expenditure Process* (Montreal: C.D. Howe Institute, 1978), 18.
23 Jacques Bourgault, 'De Kafka au Net: la lutte incessante du sous-ministre pour contrôler son agenda,' *Gestion* 22, no. 2 (Summer 1997): 21–2.
24 Ibid.
25 Jacques Bourgault, 'La satisfaction des ministres du gouvernement Mulroney face à leur sous-ministre, 1984–1993' (Ottawa: Centre canadien de gestion, 1998), 41.
26 Consultation with a Cabinet minister, Ottawa, November 1997.
27 'Lewis Mackenzie: On choosing a chief of defence staff,' *Globe and Mail* (Toronto), 27 May 1996, A17.
28 Consultations with a deputy minister, Ottawa, October 1997.
29 Consultations with a federal deputy minister, Ottawa, October 1997.
30 Canada, *Office of the Deputy Minister*, 1.
31 Ibid.
32 See, among others, Herbert R. Balls, 'Decision-Making: The Role of the Deputy Minister,' *Canadian Public Administration* 19, no. 4 (1976): 417–31.
33 Audrey D. Doerr, *The Machinery of Government in Canada* (Toronto: Methuen, 1981), 78.
34 See Savoie, *The Politics of Public Spending in Canada*, 253.
35 Gordon Osbaldeston, *Organizing to Govern* 1 (Toronto: McGraw-Hill Ryerson, 1992), 120.
36 J.E. Hodgetts, *The Canadian Public Service: A Physiology of Government, 1867–1970* (Toronto: University of Toronto Press, 1973), 89.
37 G. Bruce Doern, 'Horizontal and Vertical Portfolios in Government,' in G. Bruce Doern and V. Seymour Wilson, eds., *Issues in Canadian Public Policy* (Toronto: Macmillan of Canada, 1974), 310–19.
38 J.R. Mallory, *The Structure of Canadian Government* (Toronto: Macmillan of Canada, 1971), 121.
39 Ibid., 122.
40 Quoted from a background document circulated by Janice Cochrane to her colleagues on the departmental reorganization of the Department of Citizenship and Immigration, Ottawa, 31 October 1997, 1.
41 Richard J. Van Loon and Michael S. Whittington, *The Canadian Political System: Environment, Structure and Process* (Toronto: McGraw-Hill Ryerson, 1981), 567.
42 See, among others, Les Metcalfe and Sue Richards, *Improving Public Management* (London: Sage, 1987), 187.
43 Consultation with a Treasury Board secretariat official, Ottawa, December 1997.
44 See Savoie, *The Politics of Public Spending in Canada*, 213.

45 Consultation with a Treasury Board secretariat official, Ottawa, December 1997.
46 Mallory, *The Structure of the Canadian Government*, 122.
47 Consultation with a government official, Montreal, November 1997.
48 Ian D. Clark, 'Special Operating Agencies: The Challenge of Innovation,' *Optimum* 22, no. 2 (1992): 17.
49 Quoted in Bourgault, 'De Kafta au Net,' 24. The translation is mine.
50 Consultation with a senior government official, Ottawa, December 1997.
51 Ibid., January 1998.
52 Consultation with a government official, Ottawa, December 1997.
53 Consultation with a senior official, Ottawa, November 1997.
54 Ibid., January 1998.
55 Ibid.
56 Consultation with a government official, Ottawa, November 1997.
57 'Ottawa flunks own quiz in history,' *Globe and Mail* (Toronto), 11 February 1998, A1, A11.
58 'Bar foreign boat, MPs urge,' *Globe and Mail* (Toronto), 5 March 1998, A1.
59 'Risk low, but troops in gulf to get shots,' *Globe and Mail* (Toronto), 17 February 1998, A1.
60 See, among others, 'Public scrutiny pushed Liberals to fire Weatherill,' *Globe and Mail* (Toronto), 4 December 1997, A4.
61 Public Opinion, *This Morning*, 3 December 1997.
62 Ibid.
63 Ibid.
64 Herman Finer, *The British Civil Service* (London: Allen and Unwin, 1937), 196.
65 Consultation with a senior government official, Ottawa, December 1997.
66 Consultation with a deputy minister, Ottawa, December 1997.
67 Based on consultations with various line department officials, Ottawa, October 1997 to February 1998.
68 Consultation with a deputy minister, Ottawa, December 1997.
69 Ibid., January 1998.
70 Consultation with a senior government official, Ottawa, November 1997.
71 Ibid.
72 Consultations with various government officials, Ottawa, Montreal, Moncton, and Amherst, September 1997 to March 1998.
73 Pierre Gravelle, 'Management: A Central Agency and Line Department Perspective,' Revenue Canada, 3 February 1989, mimeo, 3.
74 See, among others, Savoie, *Thatcher, Reagan, Mulroney*.
75 Consultation with a senior line department official, Ottawa, December 1997.
76 Based on information made available to me by the Privy Council Office, March 1998.

77 Canada, *Second Annual Report to the Prime Minister on the Public Service of Canada* (Ottawa: Privy Council Office, 1994), 9.

78 Consultation with a line department official, Ottawa, January 1998.

79 See *Annual Report*, Office of the Auditor General, Ottawa, 1986.

80 Ibid.

81 Letter to deputy ministers and heads of agencies from the secretary of the Treasury Board and comptroller general of Canada, Ottawa, 26 February 1998, 1–2.

82 Consultation with a line department official, Ottawa, February 1998.

83 See Savoie, *Thatcher, Reagan, Mulroney*, 271.

84 Consultation with a former PCO official, Ottawa, January 1998.

85 Consultation with a senior government official, Ottawa, November 1997.

86 Consultation with a deputy minister, Ottawa, December 1997.

87 Consultation with a former deputy minister, Ottawa, February 1998.

88 Based on information prepared by the Privy Council Office for the 1993 Government Restructuring Initiative (Ottawa: Privy Council Office, 1993).

89 Ibid. See also Canada, *Budget des dépenses pour l'année financière se terminant le 31 mars 1969* (Ottawa: Imprimerie de la Reine, 1969), 106, 109, 349, 365, 436, 438; and *Part III Estimates, 1996–97*.

90 Consultation with a government official, Ottawa, March 1998.

91 Jacques Bourgault and Stephane Dion, 'The Changing Profile of Federal Deputy Minister, 1867 to 1988,' Research Paper no. 2. (Ottawa: Canadian Centre for Management Development, March 1991), 28.

92 Ibid., 39.

93 Frank Swift, 'Strategic Management in the Public Service: The Changing Role of the Deputy Minister' (Ottawa: Canadian Centre for Management Development, November 1993), 59.

94 Gordon F. Osbaldeston, *Keeping Deputy Ministers Accountable* (Toronto: McGraw-Hill Ryerson, 1989), 177–8.

95 Swift, 'Strategic Management in the Public Service,' 63.

96 Canada, Discussion Paper on Values and Ethics in the Public Service, 45.

97 Swift, 'Strategic Management in the Public Service,' 23.

98 Ibid. Frank Swift calls it bringing 'the issue under control.'

99 Consultations with former government officials, Ottawa, November to December 1997.

100 Jake Warren, quoted in George Post, *Conversations with Past Public Service Leaders*, 3d draft (Ottawa: Canadian Centre for Management Development, March 1996), viii–ix.

101 Roméo LeBlanc, 'The Public Service: Connecting with People,' *Management* 8, no. 3 (1997): 8.

102 Consultation with the Honourable Mitchell Sharp, Ottawa, March 1998.

103 Ibid.
104 Consultation with a former deputy minister, Ottawa, March 1998.
105 The term was coined by Hugh Heclo and Aaron Wildavsky in *The Private Government of Public Money: Community and Policy Inside British Politics*, 2d ed. (London: Macmillan, 1981).
106 Bernard Ostry, 'Making Deals: The Public Official as Politician,' in *Fear and Ferment: Public Sector Management Today*, John W. Langford, ed. (Toronto: The Institute of Public Administration of Canada, 1987), 166–72.
107 See B. Guy Peters and Donald J. Savoie, 'Empowering Individuals and Disempowering a Class: The Politics of Administrative Reform,' Ottawa, Canadian Centre for Management Development, February 1998, mimeo, 9.
108 James Q. Wilson, 'The 1994 John Gaus lecture – Reinventing Public Administration,' *Political Science and Politics* (December 1994): 671.
109 Consultation with a government official, Ottawa, December 1997.
110 Quoted in 'PS leaders put politics before public.'
111 Sharon Sutherland, 'The Al-Mashat Affair: Administrative Responsibility in Parliamentary Institutions,' *Canadian Public Administration* 34, no. 2 (Winter 1971): 595.

10: Governing by Bolts of Electricity

1 Jean Chrétien, *Straight from the Heart* (Toronto: Key Porter Books, 1985), 18.
2 Edward Greenspon and Anthony Wilson-Smith, *Double Vision: The Inside Story of the Liberals in Power* (Toronto: Doubleday, 1996), 259.
3 Consultation with a former federal Cabinet minister, Ottawa, 1993.
4 Greenspon and Wilson-Smith, *Double Vision*, 261.
5 The Honourable John Crosbie made the comment on CBC's 'Prime Time,' 29 November 1997.
6 Donald Johnston, *Up the Hill* (Toronto: Optimum Publisher International, 1986), 241–2.
7 Ibid., 70.
8 Consultation with a former deputy minister, Ottawa, October 1997.
9 Quoted in Alasdair Roberts, 'Worrying About Misconduct: The central lobby and the PS 2000 reforms,' *Canadian Public Administration* 39, no. 4 (Winter 1996): 504.
10 Thomas S. Axworthy, 'Of Secretaries to Princes,' *Canadian Public Administration* 31, no. 2 (Summer 1998): 247.
11 Ibid., 260.
12 Ibid., 251.
13 Ibid., 259.
14 Ibid., 53.

15 See, among others, Donald J. Savoie, *Thatcher, Reagan, Mulroney: In Search of a New Bureaucracy* (Pittsburgh: University of Pittsburgh Press, 1994).
16 Ibid., chapter 7.
17 Consultation with a Cabinet minister, Ottawa, November 1997.
18 Consultation with a former government official, Ottawa, January 1998.
19 Ibid.
20 Johnston, *Up the Hill*, 54.
21 Quoted in Stephen Clarkson and Christina McCall, *Trudeau and Our Time*, vol. 1 (Toronto: McClelland and Stewart, 1990), 282.
22 Ibid.
23 Ibid., 69.
24 Ibid., 72.
25 Ibid.
26 See, among many others, the two regional development agencies under Mulroney and the Canadian Millennium Scholarship Foundation under Chrétien and major constitutional proposals or statements under both Mulroney and Chrétien.
27 James Douglas, 'Review Article: The Overloaded Crown,' *British Journal of Political Science* 6, no. 3 (1976): 492.
28 R.M. Punnett, *The Prime Minister in Canadian Government and Politics* (Toronto: Macmillan of Canada, 1997), 75.
29 Axworthy, 'Of Secretaries to Princes,' 250.
30 See, among others, Samuel Beer, 'Political Overload and Federalism,' *Polity* X (1977): 8.
31 Gordon Robertson, 'The Changing Role of the Privy Council Office,' *Canadian Public Administration* 14, no. 4 (Winter 1971): 500.
32 Ibid., 505.
33 John L. Manion, 'Leadership,' Notes for an address to the Advanced Management Program, Ottawa, Canadian Centre for Management Development, 25 June 1953, mimeo, 12.
34 Ibid.
35 See, among others, John C. Crosbie, *No Holds Barred: My Life in Politics* (Toronto: McClelland & Stewart, 1997); Chrétien, *Straight from the Heart*; and John Roberts, *Agenda for Canada: Towards a New Liberalism* (Toronto: Lester and Orpen Dennys, 1985).
36 Axworthy, 'Of Secretaries to Princes,' 260.
37 Christina McCall and Stephen Clarkson, *Trudeau and Our Times, The Heroic Delusion*, vol. 2 (Toronto: McClelland & Stewart, 1994).
38 Axworthy, 'Of Secretaries to Princes,' 262.
39 Greenspon and Wilson-Smith, *Double Vision*, 72.
40 See, among many others, 'Our crushing deficit,' *Citizen* (Ottawa), A Special Report-Section H., 8 April 1989, H1–12; 'The debt: where does all the money go?' *Globe*

and Mail (Toronto), 8 April 1989, D1; 'Are we sinking or just swimming in debt?' *Gazette* (Montreal), 18 February 1989, B1; 'Mathematics of federal debt add up to necessity for drastic measures,' *Globe and Mail* (Toronto), 24 April 1989, B1.

41 Quoted in 'The budget: that deficit was just hiding,' *Citizen* (Ottawa), 7 May 1989, A10.

42 'Mulroney to crack down on government spending,' *Gazette* (Montreal), 31 January 1989, D1.

43 'Inner cabinet will centralize control over government spending,' *Globe and Mail* (Toronto), 31 January 1989, A3.

44 'Mulroney to crack down on government spending,' D1.

45 Quoted in Donald J. Savoie, *The Politics of Public Spending* (Toronto: University of Toronto Press, 1990), 351.

46 Canada, Department of Finance, *The Fiscal Plan: Contracting the Debt* (Ottawa: Department of Finance, 27 April 1989), 30.

47 Canada, Department of Finance, *Budget Papers* (Ottawa: Department of Finance, 27 April 1989), 21.

48 See Savoie, *The Politics of Public Spending*, 355–6.

49 Ibid., 358.

50 Quoted in Savoie, *Thatcher, Reagan, Mulroney*, 228.

51 Ibid.

52 Consultation with a senior government official, Ottawa, October 1997.

53 See, among others, Peter Aucoin and Donald J. Savoie, ed., *Managing Strategic Change: Program Review and Beyond* (Ottawa: Canadian Centre for Management Development, 1998).

54 Peter Aucoin, for example, argues that there was 'a lack of ministerial competence in many portfolios during the Mulroney regime,' in 'Restructuring the Canadian Government: The Management of Organizational Change,' in Peter Aucoin, ed., *Restructuring of Government* (Ottawa: Canadian Centre for Management Development, forthcoming).

55 The term 'departmental Cabinet' was coined by Stefan Dupré, 'The Workability of Executive Federalism in Canada,' in Herman Bakvis and William Chandler, eds., *Federalism and the Role of the State* (Toronto: University of Toronto Press, 1987), 236–58. See also Peter Aucoin, 'Prime Minister and Cabinet,' in James Bickerton and Alain G. Gagnon, eds., *Canadian Politics: An Introduction to the Discipline* (Toronto: Broadview Press, 1994), 28.

56 Arthur Kroeger, 'A Retrospective on Policy Development in Ottawa,' Ottawa, Canadian Centre for Management Development, January 1998, mimeo, 13.

57 Consultation with a former Cabinet minister, Ottawa, February 1998.

58 Ibid.

59 Consultation with a federal Cabinet minister, Ottawa, February 1998.

60 Greenspon and Wilson-Smith, *Double Vision*, 26.

61 Colin Campbell, *Governments under Stress: Political Executives and Key Bureaucrats in Washington, London and Ottawa* (Toronto: University of Toronto Press, 1983), 17.
62 Paul Thomas, 'Central Agencies: Making a Mush of Things,' in Bickerton and Gagnon, eds., *Canadian Politics*, 288.
63 Patrick Weller, 'A comparison of the budget decision-making processes used in Canada and Australia,' a paper published in mimeo form by the Canadian Centre for Management Development, Ottawa, August 1995, 6.
64 Consultation with a PCO official, Ottawa, December 1997.
65 Consultation with various officials, Ottawa, December 1997 to March 1998. See also 'Drug-patent plan to delay generic,' *Globe and Mail* (Toronto), 22 January 1998, A1, A5.
66 Consultation with a Cabinet minister, Ottawa, March 1998.
67 Ibid.
68 Ibid.
69 Consultation with a senior Department of Health official, Ottawa, March 1998.
70 Canada, *The Functioning of the Privy Council Office* (Ottawa: Privy Council Office, December 1978) 4–39.
71 Ibid., 4–40.
72 Consultation with a senior PCO official, Ottawa, December 1997.
73 Canada, *Strengthening Our Policy Capacity*, report of the Task Force on Strengthening the Policy Capacity as the federal government submitted to the Coordinating Committee of Deputy Ministers (Policy), Ottawa, 3 April 1995, 2.
74 See, for example, Richard French, 'Postmodern Government,' The John L. Manion Lecture – 1992, Ottawa, Canadian Centre for Management Development, 1.
75 Consultations with a former deputy minister, Ottawa, March 1998.
76 Consultation with a former PCO official Ottawa, November 1997.
77 Canada, *Responsibility in the Constitution* (Ottawa: Privy Council Office, 1993), 72.
78 See document prepared for C.E.S. Franks, *Accountability and Canada's Federal Public Service* (Ottawa: Canadian Centre for Management Development, June 1997), 25.
79 See, for example, R.J. Giroux, 'Institutional Opportunities Central Agencics,' a paper prepared for R.J. Giroux, secretary to the Treasury Board for the 1994 IPAC Conference in Charlottetown, PEI, 30 August 1994, mimeo, 6.
80 'Panel blasts slow pace of PS reform,' *Citizen* (Ottawa) 6 November 1996, A3.
81 'Cuts won't disconnect government cell phones,' *Globe and Mail* (Toronto), 29 June 1994, A5.
82 Ibid.
83 'Have zeal, will travel,' *Globe and Mail* (Toronto), 15 February 1997, A1.

84 Alasdair Roberts, 'Worrying about misconduct: the control lobby and the PS 2000 reforms,' *Canadian Public Administration* 39, no. 4 (Winter 1996), 511.
85 Quoted in ibid., 510.
86 'Minister blows gasket over agency,' *Citizen* (Ottawa), 11 September 1994, A1. See also 'Agency restructuring over conflict,' *Globe and Mail* (Toronto), 26 May 1994, A4.
87 Roberts, 'Worrying about misconduct,' 511.
88 Ibid., 515.
89 'Public works issuing more window dressing,' *Citizen* (Ottawa), 13 January 1995, A2.
90 In the course of the research for this book, I wrote a letter to Paul Tellier asking for an interpretation of what he meant by 'error-free administration.' He did not respond.
91 See, among others, Savoie, *Thatcher, Reagan, Mulroney*, chapter 7.
92 See, for example, Peter Aucoin, 'Administrative Reform in Public Management: Paradigms, Principles, Paradoxes and Pendulums,' *Governance* 3, no. 2 (April 1990): 132.
93 See Donald J. Savoie, *Regional Economic Development: Canada's Search for Solutions* (Toronto: University of Toronto Press, 1992), chapter 6.
94 See, for example, M.M. Atkinson and W.D. Coleman, 'Policy Networks, Policy Communities and the Problem of Governance,' *Governance* 5, no. 7, (1992): 154–80.
95 Peter Aucoin, 'Re-engineering the Centre,' *Management* 6, no. 1 (1995): 16.
96 Consultation with former officials with the Privy Council Office, Ottawa, September 1997 to February 1998.

11: Incentives, Constraints, and Behaviour

1 'Young participera aux audiences publiques sur Via Rail et la loi sur l'assurance-chômage,' *L'Acadie Nouvelle* (Caraquet), 31 July 1989, A3.
2 See, for example, Herman Bakvis, 'Transport Canada and Program Review,' in Peter Aucoin and Donald J. Savoie, eds., *Managing Strategic Change: Program Review and Beyond* (Ottawa: Canadian Centre for Management Development, 1998).
3 There is a rich literature on organizational culture. See, among many others, Michael Thompson, Richard Ellis, Aaron Wildavsky, *Cultural Theory* (Boulder: Westview Press, 1970), and Mary Douglas, *In the Active Voice* (London: Routledge and Regan Paul, 1982).
4 Jocelyne Bourgon, 'Management in the New Public Sector Culture,' a paper presented to the Public Policy Forum, Ottawa, 28 October 1993, 4.
5 Consultation with a Cabinet minister, Ottawa, March 1998.
6 Consultation with a former senior government official, Ottawa, November 1997.

7 Quoted in Richard Lipsey, 'Macdonald Commission tells a vital tale,' *Financial Post* (Toronto), 26 October 1985, 25.
8 C.E.S. Franks, 'The decline of the Canadian Parliament,' *The Hill Times*, Ottawa, 25 May 1998, 15.
9 Quoted in ibid.
10 John Crosbie, *No Holds Barred: My Life in Politics* (Toronto: McClelland and Stewart, 1997), 300.
11 Consultation with a federal Cabinet minister, Ottawa, October 1997.
12 Quoted in Ralph L. Sykes, 'Government Transitions: Theory, Experience and Recommendation,' Toronto, Government of Ontario, Management Board, April 1987, mimeo, 20.
13 See, for example, Erik Nielsen, *The House Is Not a Home* (Toronto: Macmillan of Canada, 1989), 275.
14 Consultations with senior government officials, Ottawa, November 1997 to January 1998.
15 For a list of new spending initiatives contained in the 1998 budget, see Canada, *Briefing Book Budget 1998* (Ottawa: Department of Finance, 24 February 1998).
16 Consultation with a federal Cabinet minister, Ottawa, March 1998.
17 'Liberals back-biting over extra cash,' *Citizen* (Ottawa), 1 December 1997, A3.
18 Consultation with a Cabinet minister, Ottawa, March 1998.
19 Ibid.
20 'Copters could be career breaker,' *Globe and Mail* (Toronto), 20 December 1997, A6.
21 Consultation with a former Cabinet minister, Ottawa, October 1997.
22 Ibid., February 1998.
23 Ibid., November 1997.
24 Ibid.
25 See, for example, Margaret Thatcher, *The Downing Street Years* (New York: Harper/Collins, 1993), chapters 16, 17.
26 See, among many others, Crosbie, *No Holds Barred*; Nielsen, *The House is Not a Home*, and Donald Johnston, *Up the Hill* (Montreal: Optimum Publishers International, 1986).
27 Jean Chrétien, *Straight from the Heart* (Toronto: Key Porter Books, 1985), 18.
28 J.D. Aberbach, R.D. Putnam, and B.A. Rockman, *Bureaucrats and Politicians in Western Democracies* (Cambridge, MA: Harvard University Press, 1981), 187.
29 Hugh Heclo and Aaron Wildavsky, *The Private Government of Public Money*, 2d ed. (London: Macmillan Press, 1981), iv.
30 B. Guy Peters, 'Burning the Village: The Civil Service Under Reagan and Thatcher,' *Parliamentary Affairs* 39 (1986): 79–97.
31 See, among others, J.L. Granatstein, *The Ottawa Men: The Civil Service Mandarins, 1935–1957* (Toronto: Oxford University Press, 1982).

32 See, for example, Donald J. Savoie, *Thatcher, Reagan, Mulroney: In Search of a New Bureaucracy* (Pittsburgh: University of Pittsburgh Press, 1994), 82.

33 See, for example, Flora MacDonald, 'The Minister and the Mandarins,' *Policy Options* 1, no. 3 (September–October 1980): 29–31 and Jeffrey Simpson, *Discipline of Power* (Toronto: Personal Library, 1980), 119–20.

34 Carol H. Weiss, 'Efforts at Bureaucratic Reform,' 10; Stephen Michelson, 'The Working Bureaucrat and the Working Bureaucracy,' in Carol H. Weiss and Allan H. Barton, eds., *Making Bureaucracies Work* (Beverley Hills, Calif.: Sage Publications, 1980), 175; Herbert Kaufman, 'Fear of Bureaucracy: A Raging Pandemic,' *Public Administration Review* 59, no. 3 (1981): 1.

35 See, among others, Savoie, *Thatcher, Reagan, Mulroney*, chapters 10, 11.

36 John L. Manion and Cynthia Williams, 'Transition Planning at the Federal Level in Canada,' in Donald J. Savoie, ed., *Taking Power: Managing Government Transitions* (Toronto: Institute of Public Administration of Canada, 1993), 109.

37 The controversy over reforms of the old age pension plan is a case in point, as were the resignations of Ministers Sinclair Stevens, John Fraser, and André Bissonnette.

38 See Micheline Plasse, 'Les chefs de cabinet de ministres du gouvernement fédéral en 1990: profils, recrutement, fonctions et relations avec la haute fonction publique' (Ottawa: Canadian Centre for Management, 1991), 16–27.

39 Graham T. Allison, 'Public and Private Management: Are They Fundamentally Alike in All Unimportant Respects?' in J.M. Shafritz and A.C. Hyde, eds., *Classics of Public Administration* (Chicago: Dorsey Press, 1987), 525.

40 Al Johnson, 'Management Theory and Cabinet Government,' a paper presented to the Management Improvement Symposium, Winnipeg, 19–21 October 1970, 10.

41 See also Andrew Dunsire, 'Administrative Theory in the 1980s,' 19.

42 Ian Clark, 'On Re-engineering the Public Service of Canada: A Comment on Paul Tellier's Call for Bold Action,' *Public Sector Management* 4, no. 4 (1992): 22–3.

43 B. Guy Peters, 'Administrative Culture and Analysis of Public Organizations,' *Indiana Journal of Public Administration* 36, no. 3 (1980): 426, 428.

44 See, for example, Canada, *Strengthening Policy Capacity: Conference proceedings* (Ottawa: Canadian Centre for Management Development, 1996), 16.

45 Advisory Committee on Senior Level Retention and Compensation, *First Report* (Ottawa: Treasury Board 1998), 5, 34.

46 'Rebuilding ethical, professional standards needed to save PS,' *Citizen* (Ottawa), 1 April 1998, A.14.

47 Jocelyne Bourgon, *Fifth Annual Report to the Prime Minister on the Public Service of Canada* (Ottawa: Privy Council Office, 1998), 20.

48 Ibid., 21.

49 See, for example, *Report of the Deputy Ministers' Task Force on Service Delivery Models* (Ottawa: Canadian Centre for Management Development, 1996).

50 For a discussion on culture and shared values see, among others, Thompson, Ellis, Wildavsky, *Cultural Theory.*

51 See B. Guy Peters and Donald J. Savoie, 'Empowering Individuals and Disempowering A Class: The Politics of Administrative Reform' (forthcoming).

52 J.H. Knott and G.J. Miller, *Reforming Bureaucracy: The Politics of Institutional Choice* (Englewood Cliffs, N.J.: Prentice-Hall, 1987).

53 J. Pierre, 'The Marketization of the State: Citizens, Consumers and the Emergence of the Public Market,' in B. Guy Peters and Donald J. Savoie, eds. *Governance in a Changing Environment* (Montreal: McGill-Queens University Press, 1995).

54 Donald J. Savoie, *The Politics of Public Spending in Canada* (Toronto: University of Toronto Press, 1990), 32.

55 J.E. Hodgetts, *The Canadian Public Service: A Physiology of Government, 1867–1970* (Toronto: University of Toronto Press, 1973), 344.

56 Ibid., 348.

57 See Norma M. Riccucci, 'Execucrats, Politics and Public Policy: What Are the Ingredients for Successful Performance in the Federal Government?' in *Public Administration Review*, 55, no. 3 (May/June 1995): 220.

58 B. Guy Peters, *The Future of Governing* (Lawrence, KS: University of Kansas Press, 1996).

59 See, for example, Peter Aucoin, *The New Public Management: Canada in a Comparative Perspective* (Montreal: IRPP, 1995).

60 Donald Johnston, *Up the Hill* (Toronto: Optimum Publisher International, 1986), 54.

61 Canada, Department of Finance, *The Fiscal Plan Contracting the Debt* (Ottawa: Department of Finance, 27 April 1989), 35.

62 Release, 'Prime Minister Announces Creation of the Leadership Network,' Office of the Prime Minister, 4 June 1998.

Index